W9-BXX-355

fun with the family
Southern California

hundreds of ideas for day trips with the kids

Eighth Edition

Laura Kath & Pamela Price

travel

Guilford, Connecticut

All the information in this guidebook is subject to change. We recommend that you call ahead to obtain current information before traveling.

Editor: Amy Lyons
Project Editor: Heather Santiago
Layout: Joanna Beyer
Text Design: Nancy Freeborn and Linda R. Loiewski
Maps: Rusty Nelson © Morris Book Publishing, LLC
Spot photography throughout © Photodisc and © RubberBall Productions

ISSN 1541-8952
ISBN 978-0-7627-5723-7

Printed in the United States of America
10 9 8 7 6 5 4 3 2 1

Contents

SOUTHERN CALIFORNIA

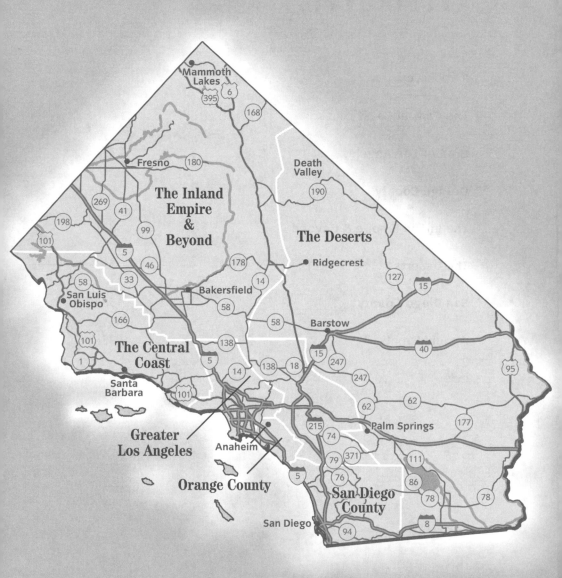

To Anna Hubble Kath, my inspirational mom, the matriarch
—Laura Kath

To Harris Jacob Lechtman, my darling travel-minded grandson
—Pamela Price

About the Authors

Coauthors **Laura Kath** and **Pamela Price** have more than 60 years combined travel and life experience in sunny Southern California; and in addition to this volume, are proud co-authors of *Day Trips from Los Angeles* (Globe Pequot Press, 2010). Pamela resides in Palm Springs when she is not globe-trotting and writing/broadcasting about her adventures. She is the author of *100 Best Spas of the World* (Globe Pequot Press) and consults with her children and grandson for the hottest trends in family travel. Laura is the author of eighteen nonfiction books and president of Mariah Marketing, her Santa Barbara County–based consulting business. She is a member of the International Food, Wine & Travel Writers Association and the Society of Incentive Travel Executives. She credits her active nieces and nephews for keeping her in the latest know. This dynamic duo blend the best of real-life family travel experience with the most up-to-the-minute tourism and visitor information—making this book a must-read.

Acknowledgments

Researching the best family fun throughout Southern California could not have been accomplished without the invaluable assistance of so many generous individuals, organizations, and attractions. From the tips of our achy fingers to our swollen feet, we gratefully acknowledge just a few of the many (and hereby apologize if we've neglected to mention anyone).

Anaheim/Orange County Visitor and Convention Bureau; Big Bear Lake Resort Association (Dan McKernan); California Travel & Tourism Commission; Casa Cody (Frank Tyson & Marilyn Will); Catalina Island Chamber of Commerce; Disneyland Resort; Janet Newcomb Public Relations; Grand Amore (Philip Alvidriz); Janis Flippen Public Relations; Joshua Tree National Park; Jackie Olden of *The Jackie Olden Show* on KNEWS–AM Palm Springs; Los Angeles, Inc., The Convention and Visitors Bureau; Long Beach Area Visitors and Convention Bureau; Oxnard Convention and Visitors Bureau; Palm Springs Art Museum (Bob Bogard); Palm Springs Bureau of Tourism (Hillary Angel); Palm Springs Desert Resorts Convention and Visitors Bureau (Mark Graves); Palm Springs Follies (Greg Purdy); Riverside Convention and Visitors Bureau; San Diego Convention and Visitors Bureau; San Luis Obispo Conference and Visitors Bureau; Santa Barbara Conference and Visitors Bureau; SeaWorld; Smoke Tree Ranch (Tracy Conrad); Solvang Conference & Visitors Bureau (Tracy Farhad); Sunnylands Rancho Mirage (Mary Perry); Universal Studios; Ventura Visitors and Convention Bureau; West Hollywood Marketing & Visitors Bureau.

Pamela thanks her son Tony for his continued outspoken opinions on what families will find festive in Southern California and her son Artie, his wife Pam, and grandson Harris for their unflagging enthusiasm in exploring dozens of attractions on and off the road maps. Laura especially appreciates her supportive family members and friends who are always eager to explore the wonders of SoCal attractions with her. "Ant Laura" thanks nieces and nephews John, Lisa, Emi, Eli, Jen, Bill, Alexandra, Amanda, and Cameron for their special insights. Laura gratefully acknowledges the caring "author encouragement" provided by Jane Baxter, Rev. Dr. Sandra Cook, Thomas Keough, Fred Klein, Mr. Bill Morton, Peggy Wentz, and Lee Wilkerson. Ultimately, Laura will always treasure "the Kath Party" for providing her very first "fun with the family" car trips!

Last but never least, we acknowledge the supportive staff at Globe Pequot Press for giving us the opportunity to write about all this Southern California fun starting back in 1994!

Introduction

Southern California is a kaleidoscope—no matter which way you turn, something amazing appears! There is just no way we can include every fun-worthy thing and place for your family in a volume this size. However, we do believe that this guide will give you and your family a very practical, yet comprehensive way to experience the Golden State, starting from the Central Coast and heading south all the way to the Mexican border.

Both of us, along with our families, have traveled thousands of miles by trains, planes, automobiles, horses, mules, and aching feet to discover the best in Southern California family fun. We are very proud of our adopted home state—Pamela originally hails from Minnesota and Laura from Michigan—and have spent more than 60 combined years as journalists researching and describing life on the "left coast" of the United States. We are thrilled to share the adventure with you!

We believe the most important element to family fun in Southern California is . . . time. Be sure you allow yourself and the kids plenty of it. Concentrated in this golden nugget of real estate are enough activities, sights, sounds, and sensations to fill a dozen or more visits. Be sure to carefully select the elements that satisfy your family's unique tastes. Don't kid yourself; Southern California is not as laid-back as you might think. Just ask any parent who has been done in by a day at an amusement park or managed to hit one of our famous freeway rush hours near dinnertime. Distance between activities can be deceptive. Five miles does not necessarily mean five minutes away. Be sure you plan "kick back" time—to relax on a beach or bench and to soak up some of Southern California's 300-plus days of sunshine. Don't worry, we will be sure to save more for your next visit—promise!

If you and your family seek natural beauty, Southern California offers you the Pacific Ocean and its awesome beaches—some favorites include Moonstone Beach near Cambria, Butterfly Beach in Santa Barbara, Venice Beach near Santa Monica, and the pristine sands of Coronado Island. The mountain ranges, inland valleys, rivers, and freshwater lakes such as Nacimiento, Cachuma, Big Bear, and Arrowhead are wonderful total recreation zones. Deserts such as Anza-Borrego, Palm Springs, Mojave, and Death Valley provide amazing contrasts to the palm-lined shores.

How about recreation? Participant or spectator, you can experience it all here. Teams such as basketball's Los Angeles Lakers, hockey's Mighty Ducks of Anaheim, baseball's L.A. Dodgers and Los Angeles Angels of Anaheim, and football's San Diego Chargers offer the thrill of professional action. Needless to say, waterfront activity should rate high on your list when visiting Southern California—boating, fishing, sailing, sunbathing, surfing, and swimming are what "California dreams" are made of. If you visit between December and April, whale watching along the Pacific is an absolute must-see thrill. You and the kids can get into the swing of golf and tennis at hundreds of public facilities. Of course, biking and hiking trails abound to explore, yet they preserve all the area's natural beauty. Don't forget to pack a picnic basket and take time to smell the perennially blooming flowers.

You can visit natural parks full of wildlife and sea life or human-made amusement parks stocked with thrills. Southern California museums are filled with hands-on displays of fun things from archives to outer space. Be certain to include the magnificent J. Paul Getty Museum and the Getty Villas as well as the California Science Center in Los Angeles. California's history, rich with Native American, Spanish, and Mexican influences, provides your family with plenty of cultural diversity education, not to mention the thrill of deciphering foreign names—such as San Luis Obispo, Port Hueneme, Ojai, and Temecula.

We have also included just a few of our preferred accommodations, family-friendly dining, and shopping places to make your stay more enjoyable. We hope you will take the time to try some one-of-a-kind places to eat and stay that are not part of national chains. But let's be honest here—your kids would never forgive you if you didn't make a stop at a Carl's Jr., Hard Rock Café, or In-N-Out Burger, all headquartered here.

Southern California is blessed with hundreds of annual special events—starting with January's immensely popular Rose Parade in Pasadena, right through holiday lighted boat parades all along the coast. There is always Carpinteria's Avocado Festival, Solvang's Danish Days, or the numerous film festivals held in many towns. Since special events have varying dates from year to year, we have included phone numbers and websites you can use for specifics.

Southern California is like an endless summer vacation. Where else can you travel from the desert to a futuristic metropolis to some mountain snow skiing and, finally, take in the sunset at the beach—all in one day, all year-round? Would you expect anything less from the birthplace of Hollywood and Disneyland?

In this edition we have provided special sections under many area listings entitled "Where to Stay" and "Where to Eat"—describing just a few of the many outstanding establishments available for your family's enjoyment. Dollar signs provide a very general sense of the price range for each property. For meals, the prices are per individual dinner entree, without tax or gratuity. For lodging, the rates are for a double-occupancy room, European plan (no meals unless indicated), exclusive of hotel "bed tax" or service charges.

Please keep in mind that meal prices generally stay the same throughout the year, but lodging rates fluctuate seasonally and by day of the week. Higher rates generally prevail in the summer season and holidays (when more families are on the go). Always be sure to inquire about special packages and promotional discounts.

RATES FOR LODGING

$	Less than $50
$$	$50 to $75
$$$	$75 to $100
$$$$	More than $100

RATES FOR ATTRACTIONS

(for adults and children; price per person)

$	Less than $5
$$	$5 to $10
$$$	$10 to $20
$$$$	More than $20

RATES FOR RESTAURANTS

$	Most entrees less than $10
$$	$10 to $15
$$$	$15 to $20
$$$$	More than $20

Please let us know what you like about our *Fun with the Family Southern California* guidebook. What other activities or attractions do we need to include in future editions? We really value your impressions. Write us today care of Globe Pequot Press, P.O. Box 480, Guilford, CT 06437.

Imagination, recreation, relaxation, nature, geography, cultural diversity, and history—complemented by a warm, sunny year-round climate—are waiting here for you. We know this guidebook will map out memorable family fun you will treasure and want to repeat, because Southern California makes every visitor feel young at heart. Enjoy!

Attractions Key

The following is a key to the icons found throughout the text.

SWIMMING		**FOOD**	
BOATING/BOAT TOUR		**LODGING**	
HISTORIC SITE		**CAMPING**	
HIKING/WALKING		**MUSEUM**	
FISHING		**PERFORMING ARTS**	
BIKING		**SPORTS/ATHLETICS**	
AMUSEMENT PARK		**PICNICKING**	
HORSEBACK RIDING		**PLAYGROUND**	
SKIING/WINTER SPORTS		**SHOPPING**	
PARK		**PLANTS/GARDENS/NATURE TRAILS**	
ANIMAL VIEWING		**FARM**	

The Central Coast

The Central Coast has always been considered the northern edge of Southern California. However, there is really a Midwestern-like feeling of friendliness and hospitality in the three geographically close yet quite diverse counties of San Luis Obispo, Santa Barbara, and Ventura, locally known as the "tri-counties." You have all the quintessential Southern California trademarks here—great year-round weather, fun-filled recreation, attractions, and, of course, sandy beaches woven between wide-open fields planted with veggies and fruit (including grapes), soaring foothills, mountains, streams, and the glittering Pacific—all presented by locals with warm graciousness. With fewer people than the megalopolises to the south, the Central Coast is much more laid-back and casual.

So much about the Central Coast says "welcome" to your family. Hearst Castle in San Simeon, spring hikes through the wildflowers of Montana de Oro State Park, the trendy beaches and shopping of Santa Barbara, kids' hands-on museums and zoos, boat cruises out to the Channel Islands, and surfing on the Rincon—or how about the simple pleasures of just hanging out in the 300-plus days of annual sunshine and basking in the waves and smiles from fellow Golden State dwellers and visitors? The Central Coast's two main arteries, the magnificent Pacific Coast Highway 1 and the inland Highway 101, can be your twin pathways to some of the best, and surprisingly most affordable, tastes of your Southern California dream vacation.

San Luis Obispo County

San Luis Obispo County's 3,304 square miles contain the Central Coast's most varied terrain—from windswept beaches to interior lakes, from grass-covered rolling hills to meticulously tended farmlands, plus recurring topographical evidence of seismic shifts along California's main earthquake zone, the San Andreas Fault. There are more than 80 miles of coastline for exploring.

THE CENTRAL COAST

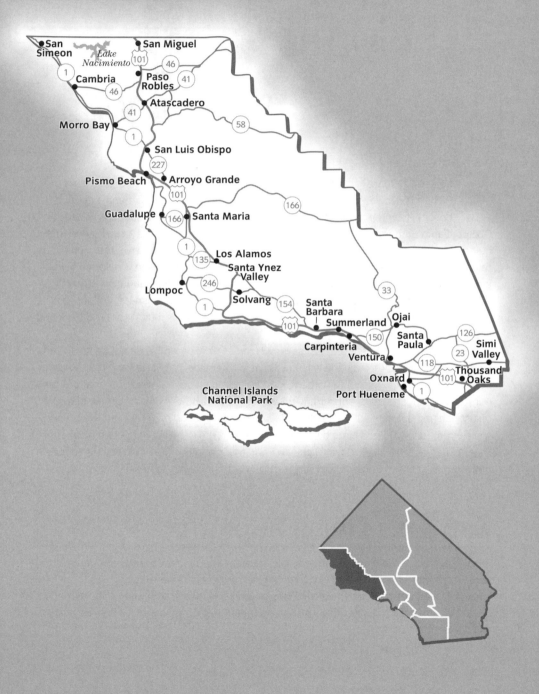

The climate of San Luis Obispo (San Lewis Oh-bis-poe) features mild summers and winters, with patches of dense seasonal fog along the coast. Temperatures range from coastal lows in the 30s in the winter to inland valley highs in the 90s-plus in the summer. Year-round temperatures average 60 to 70 degrees, with around 22 inches of rain, mostly in the winter.

Native Americans occupied the land for thousands of years before its discovery by Spanish explorers in the 16th century. Two of California's famous chain of 21 missions are here in San Luis Obispo County, preserving the area's Spanish and Mexican heritage. The railroad arrived in the late 1890s, bringing more families and increasing the dominance of agriculture and tourism in the area. Outdoor recreation and historic attractions top the must-see list of county adventures.

For More Information

San Luis Obispo Chamber of Commerce. 1039 Chorro St., 93401; (805) 781-2777; www.visitslo.com.

San Luis Obispo County Visitors and Conference Bureau. 811 El Capitan Way, Suite 200, 93401; (805) 541-8000 or (800) 634-1414; www.sanluisobispocounty.com.

San Simeon

Founded in the 1850s by fishermen and whalers, the little seaside village of San Simeon really came into its own in the late 1800s, when most of the area's land was purchased and developed by senator George Hearst. His son, William Randolph Hearst, began construction on his fantasy "ranch" in 1919. This incredible estate, and the opportunity to visit it, has put San Simeon on the map. Most of the original village has faded, but Sebastian's General Store and Post Office is fun for kids to explore (and for adults to fuel up with coffee at the new espresso bar; 805-927-4217). The tourist town of San Simeon Acres is 4 miles south of Hearst Castle on Pacific Coast Highway 1 and plays host to various motels and restaurants—facilities to snap you back into modern-day realities.

Hearst San Simeon State Historical Monument (ages 6 and up)

Forty-one miles north of San Luis Obispo on Pacific Coast Highway 1; (805) 927-2020 or (800) 444-4445 (have your credit card ready to purchase tour tickets in advance); www .hearstcastle.org. Open daily, except New Year's Day, Thanksgiving, and Christmas. $$$$.

Don't miss a chance to go on a fascinating tour of publishing baron William Randolph Hearst's real-life fantasy home built between 1928 and 1951, officially called Hearst San Simeon State Historical Monument and unofficially called Hearst Castle. See for yourself the lifestyle of someone rich and famous. Advance ticket reservations are strongly recommended.

Piedras Blancas **Elephant Seal Rookery**

Have you ever seen a 5,000-pound animal sunbathing on the beach? Here's your chance! There are only a few places in the world where elephant seals live and even fewer places where elephant seals are accessible to the public—and about 6 miles north of San Simeon on the ocean side of Highway 1 is an amazing vista point. Watch for signs, then park and learn all about these magnificent creatures through educational and interpretive guideposts, by viewing the animals at close quarters, and through volunteer guides who, after graduating from Elephant Seal School, are able to help visitors understand these magnificent marine mammals. Check out these stats: Males weigh between 3,000 and 5,000 pounds and are 14 to 16 feet long; females weigh from 900 to 1,800 pounds and are 9 to 12 feet long. Remember to view the elephant seals from a safe and respectful distance. Never get between an elephant seal and the ocean. Federal law protects elephant seals and it is illegal to harass any marine animal. For complete information and best viewing times, visit the **Friends of the Elephant Seals** office at 250 San Simeon Ave., Ste. 3B, San Simeon; (805) 924-1628; www.elephantseal.org.

This is the most popular attraction on the Central Coast, and there are a limited number of tickets and tour times available. If you arrive without reservations, you most likely will have to wait and might find a sold-out/standby situation (especially in the busy summer, weekend, and holiday times).

There are 5 different guided tours to choose from plus a new self-guided tour. Each guided tour is 75 minutes long, plus a 30-minute bus ride to and from the castle. For first-timers, **Tour Number 1,** also called the Experience Tour, is the best bet. It includes the National Geographic movie *Hearst Castle: Building the Dream*. When you arrive at the "castle," park **free** at the modern visitor center just off the highway. This family-friendly center has a snack bar, gift shop, restrooms, lockers, and a fascinating **free** exhibition on Hearst himself, which you can visit as you wait for your tour number to be called. You'll then board school buses for the 5-mile, 15-minute drive up the hill to see highlights of the 165-room "La Casa Grande"—the main house—plus 3 separate guest houses on the 127-acre grounds overlooking the Pacific and the surrounding Santa Lucia Mountains.

There is something for every member of your family to ogle in Hearst Castle, including enormous swimming pools; the lavish dining room (complete with Hearst's favorite Heinz ketchup bottle among the silver and china); the playroom with billiards and trophy animal heads; incredible art, antiques, tapestries, and collectibles from around the world; plus Hearst's private movie theater with his vintage home movies for your viewing pleasure.

If you want more of a Hearst fantasy fix, take **Tour Number 2** for upper levels of the main house, the libraries, and the kitchen or **Tour Number 3** for the North Wing, gardens, and a special video on the construction of the castle. **Tour Number 4,** for more gardens, the wine cellar, and another private guesthouse, is offered April through October. **Tour Number 5,** also known as "The Evening Tour," is a very special lighted night-time tour on Friday and Saturday October through December (call for specific times). Docents in period dress from the Living History Program and a newsreel shown in the theater add life to the magnificent surroundings and take visitors back to the castle's 1930s heyday. The tour lasts 100 minutes, plus a 30-minute bus ride. Tour 5 combines the best elements of Tours 1, 2, and 4 at a higher fee, but it really is appropriate only for older children, teens, and adults.

Instituted in 2010, the Self-Guided Gardens and Vistas Tour from late afternoon to sunset allows you and your family the unique opportunity to spend time on your own enjoying the gardens and magnificent views of the Pacific from the hilltop estate, but it does not enter the historic buildings. Be sure to call for special pricing and tour dates.

For More Information

San Simeon Chamber of Commerce. 250 San Simeon Ave; (805) 927-3500; www.san simeonchamber.org.

Cambria

Nine miles south of San Simeon and 33 miles northwest of San Luis Obispo on Highway 1 is the quaint, small-town artist's haven of Cambria. This village is a welcome respite from the excesses of Hearst Castle and is a family-friendly place to stay for this part of your coastal explorations. The West Village is adjacent to Highway 1; the East Village, or Old

Moonstone **Beach**

Just north of Cambria, Moonstone Beach is the place to find smooth, milky-white stones and gnarled pieces of driftwood. Don't think about swimming here, because the water is really too cold, but beachcombing is the best! You can often see migrating whales passing by in January and February and hear the cries of sea otters and sea lions year-round. There are several bed-and-breakfast inns, motels, and restaurants along Moonstone Beach Drive if you want to savor the crashing surf.

Town, is about a mile inland. Moonstone Beach Drive is right on the Pacific and has many inns and beachcombing spots. Both parts of town are connected by Main Street. Cruise down Main Street and check out the art galleries, antiques emporiums, children's bookstores, and toy shops. There is a farmers' market every Friday afternoon at the Vet's Hall on Main Street (805-924-1260).

Where to Eat

Linn's Easy as Pie Café and Linn's Gourmet Goods. 4241 Bridge St.; (805) 924-3050; Linn's Main Bin Restaurant, 2277 Main St.; (805) 927-0371; www.linnsfruitbin .com. Famous for Olallieberry Pie, preserves, and bakery delights. Serving breakfast, lunch, and dinner classics since 1989. Not to be missed. $

Robin's Restaurant. 4095 Burton Dr., (805) 927-5007; www.robinsrestaurant.com. In the East Village since 1985, Robin's signature dish, salmon bisque, is a smooth, delicious delight along with many other wholesome and authentic international dishes as well as homemade curries, grilled seafood, salads, and desserts. Open daily for lunch and dinner, plus Sunday brunch. Voted best Cambria restaurant for many years. $$

Where to Stay

Best Western Fireside Inn on Moonstone Beach. 6700 Moonstone Beach Dr.; (805) 927-8661 or (888) 910-7100; www

.bestwesternfiresideinn.com. You'll find spacious rooms, many with fireplaces and ocean view patios. Other highlights include refrigerators, coffeemakers, complimentary continental breakfast, a heated pool, and a whirlpool. Excellent value along the beach. $$$

Cambria Pines Lodge. 2905 Burton Dr.; (805) 927-4200 or (800) 445-6868; www .cambriapineslodge.com. A wonderful place for families to stay. Located on a hilltop overlooking the village, the lodge has 125 units, including nice 2-room family suites with connecting baths, fireplaces, microwaves, fridges, and coffeemakers. You'll also enjoy an indoor heated pool, whirlpool, game room, lawn sports, and a restaurant serving California cuisine for breakfast, lunch, and dinner. $$

For More Information

Cambria Chamber of Commerce. 767 Main St.; (805) 927-3624; www.cambria chamber.org.

Lake Nacimiento

Just over the mountains from Hearst Castle lies Nacimiento, arguably the Central Coast's most beautiful human-made lake. Damming the Nacimiento River created 165 miles of gorgeous shoreline. Fishing, boating, water sports galore, and outstanding hiking make this one of the most popular family recreation destinations in San Luis Obispo County.

Lake Nacimiento Resort

From Highway 101 take County Road G-14 out of Paso Robles, drive 16 miles northwest; 10625 Nacimiento Lake Dr., Paso Robles, 93466; (805) 238-3256 or (800) 323-3839; www .nacimientoresort.com. $$$.

Facilities include a boat launch, picnic grounds, playground, volleyball and basketball courts, swimming pool, and hiking trails around the meandering 165-mile shoreline. There is a full-service marina and dock where you can rent Jet Skis, Wave Runners, canoes, boats (power, paddle, and pontoon), sport fishing tackle, and equipment for diving and wind-surfing.

The lake is famous for its plentiful white bass, waterskiing, and salt-free swimming. The fully stocked general store has everything, including provisions for a barbecue or picnic; plus a restaurant called the Dragon Grill serves breakfast, lunch, and dinner daily from mid-May to mid-September.

Overnight accommodations include 19 lodge units; 1-, 2-, and 3-bedroom town houses (complete with mini-kitchens and decks) right on the lakeshore; plus 40 RV hookups and 270 campsites and some rental mobile homes as well. Extremely popular April to October, but winter season has mild weather, fewer crowds, and, of course, the same gorgeous scenery.

Paso Robles & Atascadero

Paso Robles (Spanish for "pass of the oaks") is located at the junction of Highway 101 and Highway 46. Atascadero (Spanish for "place of much water") is just south of Paso Robles at the crossroads of Highway 101 and Highway 41. To enjoy the local waters, consider boating, fishing, picnicking, and camping at nearby Lake San Antonio Recreation Area (info: 805-472-2313) or Santa Margarita Lake Regional Park (info: 805-788-2357). This area is famous for its stately trees, agriculture, and award-winning 180-plus wineries and 26,000 vineyard acres. Perhaps a taste of the grape for Mom and Dad before hitting the dusty trail again? (Phone the Paso Robles Wine Country Alliance at 805-239-8463 for current maps and tasting rooms or visit www.pasowine.com.) Meanwhile, be sure to explore these area attractions with the entire family.

Paso Robles Event Center/California Mid-State Fair

Riverside Avenue between 21st and 24th Streets, just off Highway 101, Paso Robles; (805) 239-0655; www.midstatefair.com.

Top draws at the center include the Central Coast Roller Derby, Mid-State Fall Home Show, Central Coast Boat Show, and the Great Western Bike Rally. Call for annual lineup of musical and rodeo events. For two weeks in late July/early August, the annual fair turns Paso Robles into a rockin' and thumpin' western town. Kids will enjoy the 4-H animal exhibits, crafts, art, food booths, carnival rides, plus world-class live entertainment (in years past, Justin Bieber, Aerosmith, Kenny Rogers, Julio Iglesias, and the Beach Boys have appeared).

Pioneer Museum

2010 Riverside Ave. between 19th and 20th Streets, Paso Robles; (805) 239-4556; www .prpioneermuseum.org. Open year-round Thurs through Sun from 1 to 4 p.m. Free admission; donations welcome.

Young cowpokes can amble over to see the farm equipment from the turn of the last century, while their folks check out home furnishings.

Lake Atascadero Park and Charles Paddock Zoo

South of Paso Robles, Morro Bay/Highway 41, exit off Highway 101, west 1.5 miles, Atascadero; (805) 461-5080; www.charlespaddockzoo.org. Open 10 a.m. to 4 p.m.; hours extended in summer and vary by season. $.

Thirty-five acres of water and wonder. This very intimate site allows close proximity to some one hundred rare and wonderful species. Among the selection: gleaming black brother-and-sister jaguars from Brazil, a pair of Bengal tigers, furry lemurs, sinewy pythons and boas, stately pink flamingos, and crested porcupines (can you make them strut their stuff?). Lake Atascadero is next to the zoo. Walk around the 2-mile perimeter of the lake and picnic on benches or dockside at the Lakeside Pavilion's snack bar. Strollers, a gift shop, refreshments, and restrooms all make a visit easier for families.

The Ravine Waterpark

2301 Airport Rd. (off Highway 46 East), Paso Robles; (805) 237-8500; www.ravinewaterpark .com. $$$.

Open seasonally May through September. Call for hours, special events. Opened in 2007, this wet and wild water adventure has slippery slides and interactive fun for all ages. Hop on a tube and race down the 325-foot-long flume slides; drift along Kickback Kreek; surf the 175,000-gallon wave pool, or head to 9,000-square-foot Kiddie Cove for little ones.

Ag Adventures

The **Central Coast Agritourism Council** is a nonprofit organization dedicated to supporting small farmers and ranchers by promoting their homes and farms as visitor destinations. Members love showing you and the kids where food starts on its journey to your table and answering questions about their livelihood. You can experience life on a family farm, explore the open trail on horseback, ride in a stagecoach, learn about fiber and wine grape production, sample olive oil, or pick your own lavender and olallieberries out in the field. For events, classes, open houses, and more, call (805) 238-3799 or visit www .agadventures.org.

Children's Museum at the Paso Robles Volunteer Firehouse

623 13th St., Paso Robles; (805) 238-7432; www.pasokids.org. Ages 2 to 13. Open Thurs through Mon. Call for times and special events. $.

This historic former volunteer firehouse was transformed in 2007 into an interactive, educational, play-filled environment. Exhibits include a fire truck and gear, naturally, plus an oak tree for exploration, a toddler farm and goofy grape stomp, Newton's playhouse, a physical science corner, pizza kitchen, El Mercado, puppet theater, and arts and crafts stations.

Where to Eat & Stay

Big Bubba's Bad to the Bone BBQ. 8050 El Camino Real, Atascadero, 93422; (805) 466-9866; 1125 24th St., Paso Robles; www.bigbubbasbadbbq.com. Since opening the first restaurant in Paso in 2002, Bubba's has become a fave family place for its generous portions of smokey ribs, chicken, pulled pork, turkey legs, and yummy sides. Ride the mechanical bull, enjoy the country-western music, and have some fun at lunch and dinner daily. The "10 Under $10" lunch value menu is a great deal Mon through Fri 11 a.m. to 4 p.m. $$$

Holiday Inn Express Hotel & Suites. 2455 Riverside Ave., Paso Robles; (866) 224-6196 or (805) 238-6500, www.hixpaso.com.

Right across from Events Center/Mid-State Fair. Family suites, **free** Smart breakfast daily. Smart Collection beds, Smart Bathroom amenities, high-speed Internet, fridge, microwave, 27-inch TV with HBO, coffee/tea maker. Heated indoor pool. Special family packages available year-round. $$$

For More Information

Atascadero Chamber of Commerce. 6550 El Camino Real; (805) 466-2044; (888) 55-VISIT; www.visitatascadero.com.

Paso Robles Chamber of Commerce and Visitors and Conference Bureau. 1225 Park St.; (805) 238-0506 or (800) 406-4040; www.pasorobleschamber.com.

Morro Bay

Noted for two landmarks—nature's awesome Morro Rock and the human-made trio of smokestacks at the waterfront power plant—bustling Morro Bay has a busy commercial fishing fleet and is a prized recreational and tourist town. You can't miss the magnificent 578-foot, dome-shaped Morro Rock, a long-extinct volcano, which marks the oceanfront end of the Embarcadero—several miles of waterfront filled with shops, restaurants, motels, and dozens of companies with boats, barges, kayaks, canoes, and sailing vessels for charter or guided excursions. Plus, don't miss the farmers' market every Saturday from 3 p.m. to 6 p.m. downtown at Main and Harbor Streets (info: 805-602-1009).

Sub/Sea Tours and Kayaks

699 Embarcadero #9; (805) 772-9463; www.subseatours.com. Call for reservations and current rates. $$$.

The company offers 45-minute trips in a semi-submersible vessel daily, generally on the hour depending on the tides. Got to love "diving" and seeing kelp forests and marine life. All trips narrated by a naturalist. Canoe and sit-on-top kayak rentals are available daily as well; seasonal whale watch trips are offered aboard the 24-passenger power catamaran *Dos Osos*.

Morro Bay State Park

At the south end of town, off State Park Rd.; (805) 772-2560 or (800) 444-7275; www.parks .ca.gov. Open daily year-round.

Nearly 2,000 acres along the Pacific shore contain many picnic and camping areas, an 18-hole golf course, a marina, a cafe, a primitive natural area, an estuary (great for bird-watching), and boat rentals.

Museum of Natural History

Perched on White Point, overlooking the bay and Morro Rock inside the Morro Bay State Park; (805) 772-2694; www.morrobaymuseum.org. Open daily 10 a.m. to 5 p.m. except New Year's Day, Thanksgiving, and Christmas. $.

Traditional and educational interpretive displays of local marine life, geology, and the history and culture of Native peoples predominate. Video presentations in the auditorium. This is the last remaining blue heron rookery reserve between San Francisco and Mexico. These rare birds can be observed from hiking trails on the museum grounds.

Montaña de Oro State Park

Highway 101 at Los Osos Valley Rd., just south of Morro Bay in the tiny town of Los Osos; (805) 528-0513; www.parks.ca.gov. Open year-round. Free day use; camping fees vary.

It is considered the Central Coast's premier park for hiking, nature walks, tide-pooling, horseback riding, camping, and shore fishing. The Spanish name means "mountain of gold," referring to the golden fields of poppies, mustard grass, and wildflowers enveloping the hillsides every spring. You can easily spend a day at this incredibly beautiful, 8,000-acre paradise.

Where to Eat & Stay

Harbor Hut Restaurant and Lil Hut (take-away). 1205 Embarcadero; (805) 772-2255. It's right in the heart of the waterfront action. The seafood is fresh from the trawlers docked in front, making the Hut popular with locals and visitors alike. Meals served daily from 11 a.m. $$

The Inn at Morro Bay. One mile south on Main Street, right before the entrance to Morro Bay State Park, 60 State Park Rd.; (805) 772-5651 or (800) 321-9566; www.innatmorro bay.com. Located on the bay, this comfortable 98-room, full-service hotel has both water- and garden-view rooms. Be sure to ask for a bay view with a balcony or patio; some now have hot tubs. Enjoy the Wellness Center & Spa as well as complimentary beach cruiser bikes. Two dining rooms offer unobstructed views of the estuary and bay frontage while you are enjoying California cuisine for breakfast, lunch (The Bay Club), and dinner (The Orchid). $$$

For More Information

Morro Bay Visitors Center and Chamber of Commerce. 845 Embarcadero Rd., Suite D; (805) 772-4467 or (800) 231-0592; www.morrobay.org.

City of San Luis Obispo

This county seat sits in an inland valley ringed by pretty hills. A remarkably friendly municipality of 45,000 that is also home to California Polytechnic State University (known as Cal Poly), San Luis Obispo has a vibrant downtown area filled with historic sites, shopping, and restaurants. On Thursday afternoons, the 25-cent downtown trolley runs a circuit that will give you and the kids a chance to take in the sights and sounds during the famous Farmers' Market event.

Mission San Luis Obispo de Tolosa

Chorro and Monterey Streets, in the heart of Mission Plaza; (805) 543-6850; www.mission sanluisobispo.org. Open daily 9 a.m. to 5 p.m. except major holidays. Free admission; donations welcome.

Founded in 1772 and still in operation, the mission is the 5th in the 21-mission chain of parishes founded by Father Junípero Serra. Take a self-guided tour through the Life at the Mission history exhibits and pause in the adobe-brick chapel constructed by the native Chumash people. The mission is named for a 13th-century saint, the bishop of Toulouse, often called "Prince of the Missions."

San Luis Obispo Children's Museum

1010 Nipomo St., corner of Monterey Street, downtown (same side of the creek as the mission); (805) 545-5874; www.slocm.org. Generally open Tues through Sun. Call for hours since they vary seasonally. $$.

Since 1990, the museum has provided a safe, educational environment for ages 2 through 12; the original building closed in September 2004 and reopened in Fall 2008 with a brand-new 8,400-square-foot facility and 21 amazing indoor and outdoor activities. Some faves include *Magic Portal,* a cool communication device; the *Claymation Volcano*; the *Shake Table*; and back by popular demand, the *Giant Bubble*, which surrounds your entire body with a giant soap bubble.

Gum Alley
Higuera Street, between Garden and Broad Streets.

Before leaving downtown, you must seek out a relic you'll probably hate and your kids will undoubtedly love. Since the late 1950s, locals (mostly collegians) and visitors alike have been depositing their used gum on the narrow alley walls. Folk art or disgusting nuisance, who's to say, for this representation (it's the one and only) has been featured in *Smithsonian* magazine and on the *Ripley's Believe It or Not* TV show. Care to leave your sticky imprint? Let your taste decide.

Thursday Night Farmers' Market
Downtown, all along Higuera Street. Every Thurs from 6:10 to 9 p.m. year-round.

Since 1983, not to be missed is this world-famous farmers' market (a 6-block-long street fair). Kids will love the excitement of musicians, puppeteers, face painters, skate dancers, fire eaters, and, obviously, loads of fresh fruit, veggies, and mouthwatering barbecue and food-stuffs. Don't be shy—join thousands of curbside dining families downing tasty ribs, chicken, or beef tri-tip sandwiches. Fantastic people-watching, too!

California Polytechnic State University (Cal Poly)
About 2 miles north of downtown via Santa Rosa Street and Highland Drive; (805) 756-1111 or (805) 756-5734; www.calpoly.edu. Call for general information and to ask about guided inner-campus tours.

Located on more than 6,000 acres at the base of the Santa Lucia Mountain range, Cal Poly is renowned for its agribusiness department and the West's largest schools of engineering and architecture. Visitors and families are always welcome. Hike into Poly Canyon to see experimental architecture and construction or visit the Leaning Pine Arboretum. Kids of all ages will want to check out the Dairy Creamery, where you can buy fresh-made cheese and ice cream from Cal Poly's own cows. Info: (805) 756-6644 or www.calpolycheese.com.

Where to Eat & Stay

Apple Farm Mill House, Restaurant and Inn. 2015 Monterey St. at Highway 101, just outside downtown San Luis Obispo; (805) 544-2040 or (800) 255-2040 for reservations and **free** video tour; www.applefarm.com. An authentic working gristmill is set among gardens and waterfalls. The kids will love watching, and then drinking, the results of an intricate series of pulleys, shafts, gears, and water producing fresh apple cider; and even ice cream is available for purchase at the Market at the Mill, which also features gourmet sandwiches, salads, candies, and gifts. The family restaurant here serves American favorites for breakfast, lunch, and dinner daily. The inn has 65 deluxe accommodations and 35 Trellis Court motel rooms, plus 2 deluxe Millhouse suites and 2 Family suites; all 104 units have gas fireplaces and Country-Victorian decor. Prices here will not "grind" you! $$$

Madonna Inn. Roadside just south of downtown at Highway 101 and Madonna Road; (805) 543-3000 or (800) 543-9666; www.madonnainn.com. Not named after the provocative entertainer, this nonetheless hard-to-miss pink-and-white inn was built

Carizzo Plain National Monument
& San Andreas Fault

If your kids want to see evidence of earthquakes, this is the place, remote though it is, to accomplish that wish. North of San Luis Obispo off the Santa Margarita exit of Highway 101, head almost 50 miles east on SR 58 to discover the Carizzo Plains. This nearly 250,000-acre expanse of land is bordered on the west by the Caliente Range and the northeast by the Temblor Range and the famous San Andreas Fault. Naturalists on staff at the Guy L. Goodwin Education Center (805-475-2131, located ½ mile west of the junction of Painted Rock Road and Soda Lake Road; generally open Thurs to Sun 9 a.m. to 4 p.m. from Dec to May) can point out recent earthquake scarps, sag ponds, and stream channels, all earthquake-related. This area is the largest single native grassland remaining in California, and in the spring, wildflowers smother the area with colorful beauty. For complete, detailed information on safely experiencing this amazing, remote area of geological and biological diversity, be sure to visit the website at www.blm.gov.

in 1958 by Alex and Phyllis Madonna. Each of the 109 guest rooms is wackily different. The Caveman Room was carved out of solid rock, for heaven's sake. The men's restroom is world famous for its imaginative waterfalls. The kids will definitely want to check this out! Enjoy freshly baked treats from the Pastry Shop adjoining the Copper Café. The Gold Rush Steak House is over the top in its pink decor (and its prices, too) for basic American fare. Stay if you dare (the cast of the reality TV show *The Bachelor* did in 2009), but eat elsewhere if you are value-conscious. $$$

Pismo Beach Area

The Pismo Beach coastal resort area actually comprises the neighboring communities of Oceano, Grover Beach, Pismo Beach, Shell Beach, Avila Beach, and Port San Luis. The area stretches along Highway 101 and is only 10 minutes south of the city of San Luis Obispo. Don't miss the Pismo Monarch Butterfly Grove, where these beautiful creatures congregate each winter (www.monarchbutterfly.org). Tide-pooling is a great family activity at low tide; you never know what marine life or artifact you may find. Outdoor recreation is prime here, including such exciting activities as kite surfing, horseback riding, paragliding, airplane and helicopter rides, and Hummer and ATV dune tours. The 1,200-foot Pismo Pier downtown is prime for fishing and strolling.

Oceano Dunes State Vehicular Recreation Area

Call (805) 473-7223 (recorded), (805) 473-7220 or (800) 444-7275; or visit www.ohv.parks.ca
.gov for complete details and entrance fees. Open daily.

This is a geologically unique sand-dune complex that is an impressive off-highway vehicular (OHV) playground that also offers activities such as swimming, surfing, fishing, camping, and hiking. Children younger than 18 must be accompanied by an adult over 21 years old and take a 2-hour state certification safety test to pilot their own dune buggy here.

B.J.'s ATV Rentals

197 Grand Ave., Grover Beach; (805) 481-5411 or (888) 418-5411; www.bjsatvrentals.com.
Cost per ATV starting at $45 for two hours. Children's machines also available.

Since 1982, this has been the best place to rent your dream ATV machine, with more than 200 to choose from. The staff is really helpful and concerned with your safety.

Port San Luis Harbor

At the very end of Avila Beach Road, Avila Beach; (805) 595-5400; www.portsanluis.com.

This is a bustling fishing pier and commercial marina. Don't miss the chance to stroll down Harford Pier to find the **free** marine touch tank and look into a fish-processing plant. You'll be amazed how fast sea creatures are transformed into seafood. Tons of salmon, crab, albacore, halibut, cod, shark, and swordfish are brought in here every year by approximately 70 commercial fishing vessels. There are plenty of places to eat the catch of the day. One fave is Fat Cat's Café, open 24/7 (www.fatcatscafe.com).

Great American Melodrama and Vaudeville Theatre

1863 Front St. (Highway 1), Oceano; (805) 489-2499 for schedule and ticket prices; www
.americanmelodrama.com.

Enjoy side-splitting comedy and family entertainment. Don't be put off by the industrial surroundings. Once inside this more-than-200-seat old-fashioned cabaret-style hall, complete with sawdust on the floor, you'll feel completely at home. The theater has been owned and operated by Lynne Schlenker and her family since 1975. The actors and actresses do triple duty—they serve you food and drinks before they perform, and then act onstage, and finally they fraternize with you and other audience members after the show. The best time to attend is definitely during December for the Holiday Extravaganza.

Where to Eat

F. McLintock's Saloon & Dining House.
750 Mattie Rd., off Highway 101 between Spyglass Drive and Price Street exits, Pismo Beach; (805) 773-1892; www.mclintocks.com. No visit to this area would be complete without enjoying dinner at this joint. It's easy to avoid the saloon and slip right into the dining rooms (voted as having the best kids' menu in SLO County), where servers will amaze you with their fun attitudes and ability to pour water. (Don't ask, just go and experience this!) The onion rings are a personal favorite,

especially dipped in homemade salsa. Open for dinner daily. $$$

Splash Café. 197 Pomeroy, Pismo Beach; (805) 773-4653; www.splashcafe.com (also a sister cafe/bakery in downtown San Luis Obispo at 1491 Monterey St.). Since 1989, famous for award-winning clam chowder in fresh-baked sourdough bread bowls (more than 15,000 gallons served annually), plus other fish dishes, burgers, and salads in a totally casual, friendly, beachy plastic-chair joint. Open daily at 10 a.m. with most menu items under $5. $

Where to Stay

Spyglass Inn & Restaurant. 2705 Spyglass Dr., Pismo Beach, adjacent to Highway 101–Pacific Coast Highway 1, between Spyglass and Price Street exits; (805) 773-4855; www.spyglassinn.com. Located on the cliffs overlooking the Pacific Ocean, this nautical-themed 82-room property is a super family value. Be sure to inquire about seasonal packages and specials. Guest rooms are spacious, and many have ocean views. The heated pool and whirlpool make a relaxing destination after a day of "doing the coast." The Spyglass Restaurant, with its outdoor terraced decks, provides stunning ocean views and serves traditional American breakfast, lunch, and dinner daily—at prices that won't shock your wallet. Highly recommended. $$

Sycamore Mineral Springs Resort. 1215 Avila Beach Dr., Avila Beach; (805) 595-7302 or (800) 234-5831; www.smsr.com. Built around a natural spring in 1897 on one hundred wooded acres only 1 mile from the beach, this facility has magically evolved to become a luxurious, 74-unit full-service resort featuring standard rooms, 2-room suites, and an ideal family 3-bedroom/3-bath guest house (all with private spas, and many fed by the natural mineral springs). Amenities include the Treatment Center, with massage and skin care; the Healing Arts Institute; pools, gardens, labyrinth walk, and hiking trails; a gift shop; and Gardens of Avila Restaurant (which serves healthy California cuisine for breakfast, lunch, dinner, and Sunday brunch). Ask about special packages that are extra values. A definite favorite with our family. $$$$

For More Information

Pismo Beach Chamber of Commerce and Conference & Visitors Bureau. 581 Dolliver St.; (805) 773-4382 or (800) 443-7778; www.pismochamber.com and www.classiccalifornia.com.

California Welcome Center–Pismo Beach. 333 Five Cities Dr. at Highway 101 exit, in the Prime Outlets Mall, Pismo Beach; (805) 773-7924; www.visitcwc.com. **Free** statewide information and local area specifics.

Arroyo Grande

"Wide gulch or streambed" is an English translation of this village's Spanish moniker. Founded in 1862, "A-roy-oh Grahn-day" was settled in a wide, fertile valley on either side of a creek that flows from the Santa Lucia Mountains to the Pacific Ocean. Branch Street is the main thoroughfare, a quarter mile east of Highway 101. Many of the 19th-century buildings, like the Methodist church, have been restored, and several have been turned into bed-and-breakfast inns, shops, and restaurants. Access www.arroyograndecc.com for information on the annual Strawberry Festival (Memorial Day weekend) and events at the Clark Center for Performing Arts.

Doc Burnstein's Ice Cream Lab

114 West Branch St., downtown; (805) 474-4068; www.docburnsteins.com. Open daily 11 a.m. to 9:30 p.m., Fri and Sat until 10:30 p.m. $.

Features hand-crafted, super-premium (16 percent butterfat) ice cream presented in glass dishware in the only nostalgic ice cream parlor on the Central Coast. You can also watch through the Lab viewing window as the Doc (proprietor Greg Steinberger) and his Lab Assistants turn fresh hormone-free dairy cream into 140-plus flavors of award-winning treats including malts, floats, sundaes, mud pies, and banana splits. Delish, not to be missed!

Mustang Water Slides and Lopez Lake Recreational Area

Outside Arroyo Grande, only 15 minutes off Highway 101 via Branch Street; 6800 Lopez Dr., Arroyo Grande. (805) 489-8898 or (805) 788-2381 for specific operating hours; www.mustangwaterslides.com and www.slocountyparks.org/activities/lopez.htm.

There is camping (354 sites), fishing, picnicking, waterskiing, and windsurfing year-round at Lopez Lake, with 22 miles of man-made shoreline The water slide is open from Apr through Sept and features two 600-foot curving waterslides, a "Stampede" inner tube ride down a 38-foot drop, tot pool with mini-slides, waterfall trees, and relaxing picnic areas. A refreshing good time!

Santa Barbara County

What do wine, olives, lemons, avocados, strawberries, Danish pastries, and tri-tip barbecue have in common? They all are produced in the richly varied domain known as Santa Barbara County, named after the patron saint of mariners and travelers. With such a blessing, no wonder people from around the world are drawn here to visit and experience the joys of life. Santa Barbara County's Pacific sea breezes mean warm days and cooler nights both along the coast and in the interior valleys. The average annual temperature in Santa Barbara County is a mild 62 degrees. Very seldom do temperatures drop below 40 in the winter or climb above 90 in the summer. Such great weather makes visitors as well as plants happy.

The region's colonial history began when Portuguese explorer Juan Rodriguez Cabrillo sailed along the California coast in 1542 and claimed everything he saw for the Spanish crown. Sixty years later, another Portuguese seafarer, Sebastian Viscaino, dropped anchor in the bay. The day was December 4, the feast day of Saint Barbara, which explains the name given to the area. Both explorers were greeted warmly by the native Chumash Indians, who for 10,000 years or so had thrived in the area's gorgeous climate and year-round growing season. Viscaino's diary records the first evidence of the vaunted and legendary

Santa Barbara hospitality. Today you can still experience the same warm welcome here with your family. Start at the northern boundary of the county's Santa Maria River. Here's what you will discover.

Santa Maria

Heading south from San Luis Obispo County on Highway 101, you will cross into the Santa Maria Valley and find gentle foothills that descend toward the city of Santa Maria. It is surrounded by well-tended commercial and family farms, where yummy you-can-pick-them strawberries and lots of produce are cultivated. Many award-winning vineyards and wineries are also located here; growers have discovered a microclimate very similar to that in France. The town's roots are very deep in agriculture and ranching. The 21st century has seen dramatic growth in housing and retail shopping.

Santa Maria Valley Discovery Museum

705 South McClelland St.; (805) 928-8414; www.smvdiscoverymuseum.org. Open Mon through Sat. Call for seasonal times and fees. $.

More than 35 activities with 11 permanent exhibits and many rotating displays means you'll always find something fun for kids of all ages. Favorites include Shark Tank, Shipwreck, Fish Market, First 5 Garden Infant Playground, Creation Station, and plush "cowches" to rest and relax upon.

Santa Maria Museum of Flight

3015 Airpark Dr.; (805) 922-8758; www.smmof.org. Open Fri through Sun 10 a.m. to 4 p.m. $.

Aviators and wannabe pilots need to gear up for a visit to this exhibit, located next to the (SMX) city airport within two historic hangars. You can see the Fleet Model 2 and Stinson

The History of **Santa Maria–Style Barbecue**

The region's ranching heritage is most evident in the continuing tradition of **Santa Maria–style barbecue.** This cooking style dates from the Spanish vaquero (cowboy) days, when a special cut of beef was butchered, marinated, and slow-cooked over red-hot oak wood. This triangular cut of sirloin, the "tri-tip," is served with special Santa Maria Valley–grown pinquito beans, garden fresh tossed salad, toasted French bread, and spicy salsa. You can find tri-tips sizzling most every weekend in barbecue pits on downtown street corners or marketplaces, presided over by cooks who are generally raising money for local service clubs.

Guadalupe **Dunes**

Head 9 miles west out of Santa Maria to the end of State Route 166, and your kids will think you've landed in the Sahara Desert by the Sea—officially known as the Guadalupe-Nipomo Dunes Preserve. Sand dunes up to 500 feet tall stretch for 18 miles along the Pacific Ocean here. More than 1,400 species of animals, including 200 kinds of birds, and 244 species of plants migrate through or live in this undisturbed, windswept landscape. To fully appreciate this magnificent work of nature, make your first stop at the Dunes Visitor Center, located in a restored Victorian house in downtown Guadalupe at 1055 Guadalupe St. (805-343-2455; www.dunescenter.org). This wonderful, family-oriented facility provides entertaining interactive exhibits on dune mammals, birds, plants, and history. (Did you know that Cecile B. DeMille's 1923 film set of *The Ten Commandments* is buried underneath these dunes?) **Free** maps and tour programs are provided. If hunger strikes, mosey into the Far Western Tavern, the Minetti family-owned and -operated dining hall serving lunch and dinner daily since 1958 at 899 Guadalupe St. (805-343-2211; www.farwesterntavern.com). Your kids will get a kick out of the rawhide booths and ranching artifacts while you savor the excellent steaks (as featured on Food Network's *BBQ with Bobby Flay* TV show).

V77-Reliant airplanes, an extensive collection of model planes, and the once-secret Norden bombsight and its accessories.

Santa Maria Speedway

One-third mile north of Highway 101/Highway 166, Bakersfield exit to Hutton Road; Infoline (805) 922-2233 or office (805) 202-1492; www.racesantamariaspeedway.com. $$.

Take your family to the stock-car races in a natural amphitheater surrounded by eucalyptus trees. Every Sat night mid-Apr through Oct. The dedicated family section with no smoking or alcohol allowed is our best suggestion for a good time.

Waller County Park

300 Goodwin Rd., Orcutt Expressway and Waller Lane; (805) 934-6123; www.countyofsb .org. Open daily 8 a.m. to sunset. Free admission for day use; group fees apply.

A 153-acre park with lake, fountains, a waterfall, fishing, playgrounds, baseball diamonds, and a Frisbee golf course.

YMCA Skateboard Park

3400 Skyway Dr.; (805) 937-8521; www.smvymca.org/skate.html. Call for fees and operating hours. $.

Located adjacent to the YMCA facility, this 15,000-square-foot park contains numerous ramps, including quarter pipes, half pipes, boxes, rails, jumps, hills, and a vertical ramp. A special area for beginners is available.

Where to Eat & Stay

Klondike Pizza. 2059 South Broadway; (805) 348-3667. Open daily from 11 a.m. Total family-fun food—pizza, burgers, salads—and **free** roasted peanuts in shells that you're encouraged to throw on the floor. We sure do! $

Historic Santa Maria Inn. 801 South Broadway, exit Main Street west off Highway 101, then south on Broadway; (805) 928-7777; www.santamariainn.com. Near Santa Maria Town Center Mall shopping and area attractions, this English-style country inn was built in 1917 and has expanded over the years to include a restaurant serving lunch and dinner, a wine cellar, a gift shop, and newer tower suites for a total of 164 units. Be sure to inquire for current family package plans and special deals. A good choice for value in the area. $$$

For More Information

Santa Maria Valley Chamber of Commerce and Visitor & Convention Bureau. 614 South Broadway; (805) 925-2403 or (800) 331-3779; www.santamaria .com.

Lompoc Valley

Say Lompoc (Lahm-poke) with me now, and then your entire family can start saying "oooh" and "aahhh" if you visit during the late spring and summer, when awesome fields of flowers bloom practically everywhere you gaze. Lompoc is a Chumash Indian word meaning "little lake" or "lagoon." More than 67,000 people call this beautiful valley home now, including the military personnel at Vandenberg Air Force Base. Don't miss the more than 60 murals throughout the city. (Contact the Chamber of Commerce for a map.)

Lompoc Flower Fields

Historically, this valley has produced much of the world's flower seeds; however, this has dwindled in recent years to only several growers of marigolds, asters, larkspur, calendula, lavender, and cornflowers. To help "blooming idiots" identify the current locations of these gems, contact the Chamber of Commerce for their weekly map and directions during flowering season (usually mid-May to Aug) The Lompoc Flower Festival is held every June to celebrate this still incredible presentation of nature (www.flowerfestival.org).

La Purisima Mission State Historic Park

Three miles northeast of Highway 246 at 2295 Purisima Rd.; (805) 773-3713; www.lapurisima mission.org. $.

See the Americanos' complete and authentic restoration of this important mission back to the way it was in the 1800s. La Purisima Mission was the 11th of the 21 Spanish missions established on December 8, 1787. There are gardens, hiking trails, and picnic facilities. Living History Days are not to be missed—call for scheduled activities and reenactments.

Vandenberg Air Force Base (ages 10 and up)

Public Affairs Office, 747 Nebraska Ave., Room #A103, VAFB; (805) 606-3595; www.vanden berg.af.mil.

This base, begun in 1941, is located on the outskirts of Lompoc on 99,000 acres of incredibly beautiful Pacific oceanfront property that also includes an ecological preserve. Vandenberg Air Force Base is headquarters for the 30th Space Wing—which manages Department of Defense space and missile testing, and places satellites into polar orbit from the West Coast. Two-hour public base tours are offered through the Public Affairs office the second Wednesday of each month. Reservations are required at least two weeks in advance. No walk-ons are accepted the day of the tour. Tours may be cancelled when mission requirements dictate. Call for current policy and schedules.

Lassoed into **Los Alamos**

As you travel Highway 101, midway between San Luis Obispo and Santa Barbara, you'll discover a genuine old-western-style town worth a quick visit back in time. Now inhabited by about 1,600 friendly folks, Los Alamos (Spanish for "the cottonwoods") was founded by ranchers in 1876 and became a popular stagecoach and railroad stop—its appearance hasn't changed much since. For accommodations, check into the hillside Skyview Motel, with stunning 360-degree valley views at value rates (805-344-3770). The historic 1880 Union Hotel & Saloon is undergoing restoration; call for current availability and hours of operation (805-344-2744). For foodstuffs all on the main drag (Bell Street/Highway 135), check out the Café Quakenbush and Art Brut Gallery, Full of Life Flatbread (for delicious weekend dinners), or Charlie's Diner (you can't miss the stuffed buffalo outside). Don't miss the Depot Mall Antique Mall & Pub with 60-some dealers in the old railroad station and several other galleries and antiques stores as well. The town honors its heritage during the last weekend of September with an annual Old Days Celebration. See www.losalamosvalley.org.

For More Information

Lompoc Valley Chamber of Commerce and Visitors Bureau. 111 South I ("Eye") St.; (805) 736-4567 or (800) 240-0999; www .lompoc.com.

The Santa Ynez Valley

South of Santa Maria on Highway 101, bordered by the Santa Ynez and San Rafael Mountains, lies the Santa Ynez Valley. Some families bypass this magnificent triangle bisected by Highways 154 and 246, home of more than 75 award-winning wineries and vineyards—some of which were seen in the 2005 Academy Award–winning movie *Sideways*. Don't you dare miss these five towns that are only 45 minutes inland from the coastal city of Santa Barbara yet feel like a world away: Buellton—home of the original Pea Soup Andersen's Restaurant, and the commercial gateway to the valley; Ballard—with its continuously operating one-room school; Los Olivos—where the movie *Return to Mayberry* was filmed and more than two-dozen wine tasting rooms and art galleries reside; Santa Ynez itself—a thoroughly western burg; and the largest city, Solvang—truly another world, it is Southern California's little bit of Denmark, founded by Danish-Americans in 1911. It is celebrating its centennial year in 2011 with myriad festivities (check out www.solvang100.com). Solvang means "sunny fields" in Danish. You and your family will find plenty of sunny hospitality in this beautiful village, where the spirit of the founding Danes lives on. Visualize windmills, thatched-roof cottages with dormers and gables, fresh Danish pastries, groaning smorgasbords, 150 unique shops (no chain stores), friendly folks, comfortable lodging choices from full-service hotels to inns, and lots of sunshine. You may become laden with goodies, including porcelain figurines, handmade lace, music boxes, jewelry, sweaters, candies, and western wear.

Hans Christian Andersen Museum

1680 Mission Dr. in the Book Loft building; (805) 688-2052; www.bookloftsolvang.com/ museum.htm. Open daily; generally 9 a.m. to 5 p.m. Free.

Andersen was the Danish father of the modern fairy tale. See his books, sketches, paper cutouts, and collages. Celebrate his April 2 birthday every year at the party here.

Elverhoj Museum of History and Art

1624 Elverhoj Way; (805) 686-1211; www.elverhoj.org. Open Wed through Sun afternoons. Call for hours and special event times. Free admission, suggested donation is $3.

Located on a residential street, this former home of artist Viggo Brandt-Erichsen and his wife, Martha Mott, lets you discover the origins of Solvang's fascinating heritage and Danish legacy with rotating exhibits of Danish and modern art, free events, workshops, and craft classes.

Old Mission Santa Ines

1760 Mission Dr., right near the village center; (805) 688-4815; www.missionsantaines
.org. $.

Number 19 in the chain of 21 missions along the California coast. Dedicated in 1804, Mission Santa Ines continues to hold services as well as to provide a fascinating museum for original Chumash Indian paintings, 17th-century European artworks, and religious vestments (self-guided audio tours available). The mission also houses a serene meditation garden in a quadrangle inside the walls. A perfect escape if your family is overdoing Danish.

Pacific Conservatory of the Performing Arts (PCPA)

In Solvang's outdoor Festival Theater at 420 Second St.; (805) 922-8313 or (800) 549-7272
for tickets and schedules; www.pcpa.org. Open June through Sept. $$$.

Stages world-class professional theater under the stars, a Santa Barbara County family tradition. Don't miss out on the experience during your visit! The 2011 season will feature the American premiere of *My Fairytale* (a musical honoring author/artist Hans Christian Andersen, first staged in Denmark); Alfred Hitchcock's *The 39 Steps, Hairspray,* and more.

Windhaven Glider Rides

Santa Ynez Valley Airport, off Highway 246, near intersection of Highway 154; (805) 688-
2517; www.gliderrides.com. Scenic flights are available weekends from 10 a.m. until 5 p.m.,
weather permitting. Reservations highly recommended. Call for fares.

Two-seater planes flown by FAA-certified commercial pilots at approximately 2,500 feet and, pardon the pun, up from there! There are no age restrictions; however people over

Danish **Culinary Delights**

No visit to Solvang would be complete without tasting *aebleskiver*—the raspberry-jam-draped, powdered-sugar-coated Danish pancake balls sold throughout the village—which are made with a special flour mix in a unique round cast-iron pan and are definitely delicious. Be on the lookout for *frikadeller* (meatballs), *medisterpolse* (sausages), and *rodkaal* (red cabbage), as well as decadent pastries, tarts, butter cookies (grab a tub to take along, bet they won't last) and breads at four Danish-owned bakeries as well as numerous family-friendly restaurants, such as the Bit O'Denmark Restaurant & Lounge (located in Solvang's first building constructed in 1911), Red Viking (plentiful smorgasbord), and Solvang Restaurant (where you can purchase *aebleskiver* through a take-out window, too) Don't miss the annual Taste of Solvang festival the third weekend of March each year. See www.solvangusa .com for a complete list and hours of operation.

Horsing around **the Valley**

The valley is well known throughout the equestrian world for its thoroughbred, Arabian, and Icelandic horse ranches and training and breeding facilities. For periodic shows and events, contact the Santa Ynez Valley Equestrian Association (www.syvea.org) or the Santa Ynez Valley Arabian Horse Association (www.syvaha.com).

If your family is hankering to ride, check out Rancho Oso Guest Ranch & Stables, off Highway 154 and Paradise Road; (805) 683-5110; www.rancho-oso .com. Offering guided trail rides to children ages 8 and older, camping in covered wagons, cabins, and backcountry grub. The ranch was featured on the TV show *Best of America by Horseback*.

about 6-foot-4-inches or 250 pounds (dependent on pilot's weight) may not be able to fit in the glider. We recommend this experience for children at least 10 years old, but let your judgment decide.

Nojoqui Falls County Park

Seven miles southwest of Solvang on Alisal Road; (805) 934-6123; www.countyofsb.org. Open daily 8 a.m. to sunset. **Free.**

This 182-acre site is worth a visit to see the 164-foot waterfall (after a rainy season, of course; in the summer it can be a vigorous trickle). Head for the waterfall on the well-marked, easy-to-walk trail. Plenty of picnic spots, barbecue grills, a playground, and places to savor your Danish treats from nearby Solvang.

Quicksilver Miniature Horse Ranch

1555 Alamo Pintado Rd., just east of Solvang; (805) 686-4002. www.qsminis.com. Open daily except Thanksgiving and Christmas from 10 a.m. to 3 p.m. **Free.**

Has everything from 18-inch-high newborns to 34-inch-"tall" mature horses that will be sure to amaze and delight everyone. Breeding and caring for minis since 1983.

Ostrich Land

610 East Highway 246 between Buellton and Solvang; (805) 686-9696; www.ostrichlandusa .com. Generally open every day at 10 a.m. Tours and feeding opportunities for all ages. $.

This ranch is home to hundreds of the biggest birds in the world, reaching 8.5 feet in height and weighing up to 350 pounds when mature. Impress your children with the fun fact that ostriches run faster than any two-legged animal. How fast? Up to 45 miles per hour! There's a gift shop and farm stand as well where you can buy ostrich eggs in season.

10,000 Acres of Family **Resort Fun** **Since 1946**

This is a truly one-of-a-kind family-owned and family-focused haven. The Alisal Guest Ranch and Resort is two minutes south of the village of Solvang at 1054 Alisal Rd.; (805) 688-6411 or (800) 4-ALISAL; www.alisal .com. Rates include dinner and full American breakfast daily served in the comfortable Ranch Room. The resort boasts 73 family bungalows with wood-burning fireplaces and no television or telephones in your room. (There is Wi-Fi in the business center if you must stay connected.) The peace of this 10,000-acre working ranch envelops you immediately upon driving up the tree-lined lane.

Organized family activities and supervised play are featured all summer long. Year-round, you and yours can swim, spa, take in a movie, read in the library, play on one of the Alisal's two championship golf courses, try your hand at tennis, go horseback riding, or spend a day at Alisal's private 90-acre spring-fed lake for fishing, swimming, canoeing, and sailing. A two-night minimum stay is required—and worth every moment! Be sure to call for special seasonal packages. The Alisal has been welcoming generations of families with its western hospitality and charm. We recommend you consider starting a family tradition of your own here. $$$$

Santa Ynez Valley Historical Museum and Parks-Janeway Carriage House

3596 Sagunto St., downtown Santa Ynez; (805) 688-7889; www.santaynezmuseum.org. Open Wed through Sun, noon to 4 p.m.; closed most major holidays. Tours by Appointment Tues to Fri. Admission: adults $4; children (16 and under) free.

You can relive the valley's Old West origins with vehicles, including a full-size, outfitted covered wagon, phaetons, donkey carts, and stagecoaches (the largest collection west of the Mississippi). Learn about local cultural history from native Chumash to Spanish, Mexican, and American times. The annual Vaquero Show & Sale every November honors the cowboy lifestyle.

Cachuma Lake Recreation Area

Twenty minutes southeast of Solvang (18 miles northwest along Highway 154 over the San Marcos Pass from Santa Barbara); (805) 686-5054; www.cachumalake.com. $$.

This human-made lake (pronounced Ka-choo-ma) takes its name from a nearby ancient native Chumash village. The reservoir has a dual purpose as Santa Barbara's water supply, but it is more famous as the winter home of hundreds of bald eagles. The eagle cruises, aboard comfortable pontoon (patio) boats, bring you and your "eagle-eyed" children within 200 yards of the birds' roosting sites. More than 275 other species of birds have been identified on the lake, plus plenty of fish, other wildlife, trees, and plants. Call for schedule and fees. The nature center offers **free** hikes, docent-led programs, and family activities year-round.

Forty-two miles of shoreline offer 550 regular campsites, rental cabins, and 90 EWS hookups on a first-come, first-served basis. There are hiking, fishing, boating, and other facilities galore, including a general store, laundromat, snack bar, marina, picnic areas, and barbecues for daytime use year-round. Check out the yurt camping option. A cross between a tepee and a tent, yurts are on platforms, sleep five to six people, and have gorgeous lake views.

Where to Eat & Stay

See also Danish Culinary Delights (page 22).

Hadsten House Inn, Restaurant & Spa. 1450 Mission Dr., Solvang; (800) 457-5373 or (805) 688-3210; www.hadstenhouse.com. In the village, within easy walking distance of shops and attractions, this completely revitalized 2-story motor inn (no elevator, so ask for a unit on the ground floor) has 71 rooms and suites outfitted with luxurious beds, flat-screen TVs, and **free** Wi-Fi; many with fireplaces and whirlpools. Rates include **free** full breakfast and evening wine and cheese tasting. The Haven Day Spa provides daily pampering options. The kids will love splashing in the only indoor hotel pool in Solvang and you'll love the huge outdoor whirlpool spa in a private walled courtyard. Best of all, children dine **free** in the popular restaurant serving dinner nightly from 6 p.m. $$–$$$

Pea Soup Andersen's Restaurant and Inn. Restaurant: 376 Avenue of the Flags, Buellton; (805) 688-5581; www.peasoup andersens.net. Inn: 51 E. Hwy. 246, Buellton; (800) PEA-SOUP or (805) 688-3216; www .peasoupandersens.com. One block west of junction of Highway 101 and Highway 246 in Buellton. Restaurant open from 6:30 a.m. to 10:30 p.m. every day. Home of the original (1924) restaurant serving hearty, bottomless bowls of split pea soup and other American favorites. This is one of our family's traditional

stopovers, no matter what the occasion. The inn has 97 tasteful rooms around an attractive central courtyard with a pool, spa, and putting green. Good value for a roadside respite. $$

Cold Spring Tavern. 5995 Stagecoach Rd., 0.5 mile off Highway 154, approximately 30 minutes from Solvang and 20 minutes from Santa Barbara; (805) 967-0066; www .coldspringtavern.com. Make a detour as you go over the San Marcos Pass upon leaving the Santa Ynez Valley and wet your whistle like horse-drawn passengers on the stagecoaches of yesteryear did. Since the 1880s, this historic spot has been serving lunch and dinner and libations daily. Hearty country breakfast on Sat and Sun. Kids will love the rustic walls, stone floors, and chance to eat buffalo burgers and venison stew. $$$

For More Information

Buellton Visitors Bureau & Chamber of Commerce. 376 Avenue of Flags; (805) 688-STAY or (800) 324-3800; www.buellton.org.

Los Olivos Business Organization. Box 280, Los Olivos 93441; (805) 688-1222; www.losolivosca.com.

Santa Ynez Valley Visitors Association. Box 1918, Santa Ynez 93460; (800) 742-2843; www.syvva.com.

Solvang Conference & Visitors Bureau. 1511 Mission Dr.; (805) 688-6144 or (800) 468-6765; www.solvangusa.com.

Santa Barbara

If you and the kids want outdoor recreation, nature, scenery, stars, shopping, history lessons, museums, art, culture, great restaurants, and trendy places to hang out, just make your plans for the destination resort of Santa Barbara, the "American Riviera." The city of Santa Barbara was first hailed as a prime tourist stop in 1872 by East Coast travel writer Charles Nordhoff, who said, "Santa Barbara certainly is the most pleasant place throughout the state." The blend of Chumash, Spanish, Mexican, and American cultures has given Santa Barbara an extremely rich heritage—which is visible in the city's lovely buildings with red-tiled roofs and whitewashed adobe walls. Devastated by an earthquake in 1925, downtown Santa Barbara was rebuilt in a Spanish-Moorish colonial motif that is strictly regulated by law.

Along with architecture, locals are proud of their area's well-preserved natural beauty, bounded by the Santa Ynez Mountains to the north and Pacific Ocean to the south. Yes, that's right. All the beaches face south along the Pacific (the only place in the United States where this happens), so when you want to check out the magnificent sunsets, you face the beach and look to the right over your shoulder!

Mission Santa Barbara

2201 Laguna St., at the corner of Laguna and East Los Olivos Streets, approximately 5 minutes from downtown; (805) 682-4149; www.sbmission.org. Open daily from 9 a.m. to 5 p.m. except Easter, Thanksgiving, and Christmas. $.

You will definitely want to tour "the Queen of the Missions" and still the longest continuously operating parish among California's renowned chain of 21 missions. Founded on December 4, 1786, the feast day of Saint Barbara, and finally completed in 1820, it is one of the best-preserved missions in California. A fascinating self-guided walking tour that includes artworks, fountains, a courtyard, and a cemetery is recommended.

Santa Barbara Museum of Natural History and Planetarium

2559 Puesta del Sol Rd. (just around the corner from the Mission Santa Barbara); (805) 682-4711; www.sbnature.org. Open daily (except major holidays). $$, free to all on the third Sunday of every month.

Special **Santa Barbara Festivals**

Festivals and celebrations abound in the city of Santa Barbara year-round. Oak Park, on the city's north side, hosts ethnic and cultural festivals (including Greek, French, and Jewish) in the spring and summer. However, the following two events are worth a special visit for your entire family, from toddler to grandparent.

Summer Solstice Celebration. This is a fantasy fun romp celebrating the arrival of summer on the Friday and Saturday closest to the first day of summer. The festival opens on Friday afternoon and the Saturday parade features no motorized floats or amplified music, but almost a hundred "nonfloats," including bands, clowns, dancers, perhaps a rubber sea of sharks, rolling bubble machines, or even a briefcase brigade of lawyers. A different theme is carried out each year. The theme for 2010 was Carnival. After the parade up State Street from the waterfront, the participants and spectators all congregate at Alameda Park at the corner of Sola and Anacapa Streets. You will love the energy, color, food booths, and vendors at this post-parade party until early evening. The **free** Children's Area features a stage with storytellers, musicians, drama, mimes, and more. For more information and a detailed schedule of events, call (805) 965-3396 or visit www.solstice parade.com.

Old Spanish Days (Fiesta). If you visit during the first weekend of August, experience the sights, sounds, and foods of California's early settlers during Old Spanish Days. Commonly known as Fiesta, the celebrations begin with the padre's blessing on the steps of the historic mission on Wednesday evening, followed by performances by the junior (younger than age 12) and senior (younger than age 18) Spirit of Fiesta Dancers. Your family will shout "Viva la Fiesta!" along with the natives during Friday's Annual El Desfile Historico—one of the world's most colorful parades, attracting the most horses and riders in America, along with 100,000 enthusiastic spectators.

Your kids can participate in El Desfile de Los Niños (The Children's Parade) on Saturday morning. During the five-day festival, the entire family can enjoy the *mercados* (marketplaces with traditional foods); carnival rides at the beach; and the family entertainment spectacular, Noches de Ronda, each evening under the stars in the gardens of the courthouse. Call (805) 962-8101 year-round for **free** brochures and schedules or visit www.oldspanish days-fiesta.org.

The museum has exhibits on early Native American tribes as well as animals, birds, insects, plants, minerals, marine science, and geology. The planetarium hosts impressive star shows. Call (805) 682-3224 for a "sky" schedule.

Santa Barbara Botanic Garden

1212 Mission Canyon Rd., just above the natural history museum, about 2 miles into Mission Canyon; (805) 682-4726; www.sbbg.org. Open daily at 9 a.m. except for major holidays; call for seasonal hours and special exhibits. $.

Kids will love exploring the miles of trails through forests and plant life on 78 exquisite acres devoted only to California species. Self-guided and guided tours available. There is also a gift shop, library, and retail nursery to purchase native plants.

Santa Barbara Historical Museum and Covarrubias Adobe

136 East de la Guerra St., downtown; (805) 966-1601; www.santabarbaramuseum.com. Open Tues through Sat 10 a.m. to 5 p.m., Sun noon to 5 p.m., closed Mon. Guided tours are offered on Sat at 2 p.m. Free. Donations appreciated.

The museum's permanent exhibits include documents, furniture, decorative and fine arts, and costumes that tell the region's story from the age of the Chumash Indians to the Space Age. Casa Covarrubias Adobe, circa 1817, may have served briefly as the headquarters of Pio Pico, the last Mexican governor of California, and represents an easier, slower lifestyle.

El Presidio de Santa Barbara State Historic Park

100–200 blocks of East Canon Perdido Street, downtown; (805) 965-0093; www.sbthp.org/presidio.htm. Open daily 10:30 a.m. to 4:30 p.m. except for major holidays. $.

This was the last military outpost built by Spain in the New World, dedicated in 1782. A continuous project restores the actual structures, including El Cuartel, the padre's quarters; the chapel; and the commandant's office. A slide show and guided tours are offered upon request. This is a piece of living history you just can't ignore. Our kids really liked the story of the lost cannon. Ask a docent for the details.

Santa Barbara Museum of Art

1130 State St.; (805) 963-4364; www.sbmuseart.org. Tues to Sun 11 a.m. to 5 pm. Closed Mon. $.

The museum has important works by American and European artists, including Monet and other impressionists. Displays include American, Asian, and 19th-century French art, plus Greek and Roman antiquities and major photographic works. Special exhibits rotate throughout the year. The Children's Gallery is outstanding. And don't miss the lovely Museum Store and Museum Café, open museum hours.

Karpeles Manuscript Library Museum

21 West Anapamu St. (0.5 block off State); (805) 962-5322; www.rain.org/~karpeles. Open daily 10 a.m. to 4 p.m. Closed Christmas and New Year's Day. Free.

Book **Zone**

Located along Anapamu Street on opposite sides of State Street, this area is affectionately called "book row." It is anchored by the impressive 250,000-volume Santa Barbara Public Library at 40 East Anapamu St. (805-962-7653). You and your family will discover the joy of finding every type of literature imaginable in the following unique, independent Santa Barbara bookstores. Special events with authors and storytellers abound, so be sure to contact each shop for schedules and hours of operation.

The Travel Store of Santa Barbara. 12 West Anapamu; (805) 963-4438; www.sbtravelstore.com. Guidebooks, maps, and luggage.

Metro Comics & Entertainment. 6 West Anapamu; (805) 963-2168; www.metro-entertainment.com.

The Book Den. 15 East Anapamu; (805) 962-3321; www.bookden.com. Used, rare, and out-of-print books.

Paradise Found. 17 East Anapamu; (805) 564-3573; www.paradise-found.net. Metaphysical books.

Houses original manuscripts of great authors, scientists, and leaders from all periods of history, including an original copy of the Declaration of Independence. Rotating exhibits show fascinating glimpses into antiquity.

Kids World

In Alameda Park, at the corner of Micheltorena and Garden Streets, downtown. **Free.**

Designed by city children and built by them, as well as adult community volunteers, this 2-story wooden playland is truly a kid's dream come to life. A tot lot and sandbox are available for the very young, while older sibs can cruise through tunnels and stride over bridges or clamber up the tree house. Highly recommended!

Santa Barbara County Courthouse

1100 Anacapa St., downtown; (805) 962-6464; www.sbcourts.org. Open Mon through Fri 8 a.m. to 5 p.m., Sat and Sun 10 a.m. to 5 p.m. **Free.**

Most kids would not want to tour a courthouse, except in Santa Barbara, where you can climb the 80-foot clock tower stairs (or take the elevator, for us fogeys) for a stunning panoramic view over the city, all the way to the ocean. The courthouse was built in 1929. You cannot miss the award-winning Spanish-Moorish design from anywhere in the city. Its sunken gardens are perfect for picnicking and are the site of many events during the year, such as the **Free** Movies in the Summer Series and Fiesta.

Take a Vacation **from Your Car!**

It's easy to do by accessing www.santabarbaracarfree.org, calling (805) 696-1100, or writing Santa Barbara Car Free Project, Box 60436, Santa Barbara 93160. Discover free walking tours, bike maps, bus routes, AMTRAK schedules, maps, and vacation packages/hotel discounts. Santa Barbara is extremely pedestrian- and family-friendly, especially the downtown State Street corridor that leads to the beach—with benches, outdoor dining, and plenty of greenery. When you get tired of walking, hop aboard the nifty 25-cent electric shuttle buses (operated by the Metropolitan Transit District [MTD]; www.sbmtd.gov). Recipient of the EPA's National Clean Air Award of Excellence in 2009, Santa Barbara Car Free Project is a multiple award-winning ecotourism partnership sponsored by the County Air Pollution Control District, committed to alternative transportation for cleaner air and a healthier planet.

Santa Barbara Zoological Gardens

500 Ninos Dr., 2 blocks from East Beach off Cabrillo Boulevard; (805) 962-5339; www.santa barbarazoo.org. Open daily 10 a.m. to 5 p.m. except Thanksgiving and Christmas. $$.

This is as wild as Santa Barbara gets! The 30-acre zoo is renowned for its easy accessibility and more than 80 exhibits with 500 child-friendly animals, including big cats, roaring elephants, and gangly giraffes. The huge aviary is a favorite. The zoo, on a former estate overlooking the glittering Pacific, is a must-see. Take a picnic lunch to eat after your morning visit or savor a tasty snack in the Ridley-Tree House Cafe. The miniature train that circumnavigates the zoo's beautiful garden setting is a big plus, and so are the dedicated playground and all the services (easy-access bathrooms, strollers, guided tours, and zoo-camp programs for children, just to name a few).

Chase Palm Park & Carousel

Stretching east from Stearns Wharf along the waterfront on both sides of beachfront Cabrillo Boulevard. Free.

The 10-acre north side of the park has a totally festive antique carousel (enclosed in its own pavilion, nominal fee, and open daily); a kids-only (toddler through age 12) Shipwreck Playground with a rubberized deck; grassy knolls and picnic tables; restrooms; a snack bar; and an entertainment zone. Adjacent is Skaters Point, a popular beachfront 12,000-square-foot concrete mecca for skateboarders open dawn to dusk.

The University of California at Santa Barbara (UCSB)

In the neighboring town of Isla Vista, 8 miles north of downtown Santa Barbara via Highway 101 and the Ward Memorial Boulevard (Highway 217) exit; (805) 893-2485; www.ucsb.edu.

Free campus tours can be arranged through the visitor center located on the first floor of the Student Affairs Administrative Services Building (SAASB) at Ocean and Mesa Roads.

The gorgeous 989-acre, oceanfront campus features the landmark Storke Tower, University Center, and renowned Marine Sciences Institute, home of 18,000 students and 900 faculty, including five Nobel Prize winners. During July and August, the UCSB Alumni Association offers the Family Vacation Center, with 8 weeklong sessions, providing a fully programmed family resort. Rates include 3 meals daily, residential-hall living, recreational and social activities, all-day child care, and themed programs. This incredible Santa Barbara family vacation bargain sells out each summer. Visit www.familyvacationcenter.com or call (805) 893-3123.

South Coast Railroad Museum

300 North Los Carneros Rd. in adjacent town of Goleta; (805) 964-3540 for track times for the miniature train; www.goletadepot.org. Generally open Wed through Sun. $.

Budding conductors and engineers will want to explore the wooden Goleta depot. Built in 1901, the depot was in use until 1973, when it was dismantled and moved to its current site. Restoration began in 1981, and the collection of railroad memorabilia continues to grow.

Where to Eat

Beachside Cafe. 5905 Sandspit Rd., on the sand at Goleta Beach County Park, Goleta; (805) 964-7881. Open daily 10:30 a.m. to 11:30 p.m. Seafood is queen here, as well as popular American dishes and killer desserts matched by the oceanfront location. Try to snag a table on the outdoor heated patio with fireplace to fully enjoy the view and crashing surf. Families of all ages return again and again (we do!). Close to UCSB and Santa Barbara Airport as well. $$

Sambo's on the Beach. 216 West Cabrillo Blvd., 2 blocks from Stearns Wharf; (805)

Whale-**Watching**

The Santa Barbara Channel is becoming well known not only for the traditional California gray whale migration that occurs annually here between late January and mid-April but also as a year-round whale-viewing and research destination. More than 27 different types of whales inhabit the waters offshore. Blue whales, the largest animals ever to live on earth, have been seen here for the past few summers, apparently feeding on the abundant krill. Humpback whales, minke whales, and orcas, or killer whales, are also often sighted on channel excursions, not to mention porpoises, dolphins, sea lions, and harbor seals. Contact any of the charter boat operators at the harbor or marina for current whale-watching schedules and fees.

On the **Waterfront**

Stearns Wharf. At the foot of State Street on the waterfront; (805) 564-5518; www.stearnswharf.org. Parking is $2 per hour or reduced rate with a wharf merchant purchase validation. Built in 1872 to serve cargo and passenger ships, this Santa Barbara historic landmark is now the site of specialty shops, family-friendly restaurants, the Ty Warner Sea Center, a boat charter dock, and fishing spots. You can actually drive as well as walk onto the wharf. The kids think it sounds like rumbling thunder when you drive across the wooden planks. Don't worry, it really is quite safe.

Ty Warner Sea Center. 211 Stearns Wharf; (805) 962-2526; www.sbnature .org/seacenter. Open daily 10 a.m. to 5 p.m.; closed major holidays. $$; children under 2 free. Owned and operated by the Santa Barbara Museum of Natural History. Enter the 2-story glass foyer and be greeted by a 39-foot, life-size model of a California gray whale and her calf. Crawl through a tunnel inside a 1,500-gallon surge tank to see ocean life such as sea stars, urchins, limpets, and more up close and personal. Many interactive exhibits are perfect for kids of all ages to experience the wonders of oceanography, including live tide pool animal encounters.

Santa Barbara Maritime Museum. In the marina, 113 Harbor Way; (805) 962-8404; www.sbmm.org. Open daily except Wed, 10 a.m. to 4 p.m. Call for hours and admission fees. Free on the third Thursday of the month. Located in the former Naval Reserve Building in the heart of the harbor, the museum illustrates the evolution of nautical technology, starting with local origins in the Chumash culture up to modern-day boats and submarines. Highly interactive exhibits are kid friendly and approved!

Santa Barbara Yacht Harbor, Marina, and Breakwater. West of Stearns Wharf, motor entrance along Cabrillo Boulevard just past Castillo Street

965-3269. This is the original and only remaining Sambo's restaurant, founded here in 1957 by two Santa Barbara friends (Sam Battistone and Newall "Bo" Bohnett). Owned and operated by Sam's grandson Chad Stevens, Sambo's dishes up hearty breakfasts, featuring its famous pancakes and syrup, and all-American lunches, served seven days a week. $$

McConnell's Ice Cream & Yogurt Shop. 201 West Mission; (805) 569-2323; www .mcconnells.com. Open daily at 11 a.m. Since 1949, serving super premium (17 percent butterfat) ice cream with no artificial ingredients or stabilizers, ever. Incredibly delicious if not nutritious, don't leave Santa Barbara without having some (also available in pints in grocery intersection. Harbor Master's office phone, (805) 564-5520. More than 1,000 work and pleasure craft rest here, home to the city's commercial fishing fleet. Where else can you get so close to a spiny sea urchin heading off to market or purchase shrimp, rock cod, and crab fresh from the fisherfolk themselves?

Sea Landing. 301 West Cabrillo Blvd.; (805) 963-3564; www.sealanding.net. Hook your own seafood on a fishing expedition charter boat that docks here, or sign up for a dive trip or whale-watching excursion. A full-service tackle shop, dive shop, and rental department are also available.

Condor Cruises. (805) 882-0088; www.condorcruises.com. Call (888) 77-WHALE for current schedules and fares. Sea Landing is the home dock of the award-winning *Condor Express*, a 75-foot, 149-passenger high-speed jet-powered catamaran, custom designed specifically for naturalist-led whale-watching trips, sunset cruises, and group charters.

Truth Aquatics. In the marina; (805) 962-1127; www.truthaquatics.com. Call for seasonal times, schedules, and fares. Arranges popular sea kayaking, scuba, and diving charters and also acts as official concessionaire for boat trips to the Channel Islands National Park, some 20 miles offshore. (See listing in Ventura County section for more details on the park.)

Santa Barbara Sailing Center. In the marina; (805) 962-2826 or (800) 350-9090; www.sbsail.com. Rent a sailboat—there are more than forty to choose from (with or without a skipper). This is the home dock of the Double Dolphin catamaran, a 49-passenger sailboat that runs whale-watching trips, sunset cruises, and private charters. The ASA-certified sailing school here offers beginning through advanced instruction.

stores as well as served in area restaurants). Chocolate Burnt Almond and Island Coconut (our faves) even attract celebs like Barbra Streisand and Kelsey Grammer. $

Santa Barbara County Certified Farmers Market. (805) 962-5354 for seasonal times; www.sbfarmersmarket.org. The freshest fruits and veggies available for a super-fresh family picnic. The most popular site is in downtown Santa Barbara every Saturday at the corner of Cota and Santa Barbara Streets (2 blocks off State St.) from 8:30 a.m. to 12:30 p.m. Kids will love the musicians, jugglers, and clowns, plus the **free** samples available from generous vendors. Also in Goleta, Carpinteria, and Montecito.

Summerland

About 5 miles southeast of Santa Barbara is this historic antiques and artists' haven just off Highway 101. Exit and head toward the oceanfront Lookout Park, with restrooms, volleyball courts, playground, and easy access to an uncrowded 2-mile stretch of beach. Pick up picnic ingredients at **Cantwell's Gourmet Market & Deli** (2580 Lillie Ave., Summerland, 805-969-5893, www.cantwells.com; also in downtown Santa Barbara). We always enjoy stopping at the **Summerland Beach Cafe,** 2294 Lillie Ave.; (805) 969-1019; www.summerlandbeachcafe.com. Located in a rambling white clapboard house with a big veranda, this is the place for the best omelets and breakfast fare, as well as lunch, served daily from 7 a.m. to 3 p.m. The decor is eclectic and sure to hold the family's interest, including some old booths with their own phones.

Where to Stay

El Capitan Canyon. 11560 Calle Real, Goleta; (805) 685-3887 or (866) 352-2729; www.elcapitancanyon.com. An oceanside retreat only 17 miles from downtown Santa Barbara, this property on 300 acres features cozy cabins and safari-canvas tents. A kids' camp, botanical hikes, massages, swimming pool, campfires, and outdoor summer concerts are highlights, along with bicycling. It's only a half-mile from the State Beach for water sports. A grocery store, gift shop, and deli are here, too. Absolutely ideal for families. $$$

Fess Parker's Doubletree Resort. 633 East Cabrillo Blvd.; (805) 564-4333 or (800) 879-2929; www.fpdtr.com. Owned in part by the family of the late Fess Parker (famous for his Davy Crockett acting role), this Spanish Mission–style property has all the requirements of a headquarters for your family oceanfront vacation. Located on 23 acres across from East Beach, this 360-room resort (Santa Barbara County's largest) has a heated outdoor swimming pool, whirlpool, fitness center, spa, beauty salon, gift shop, putting green, tennis courts, bicycle and skate rental shop, game room, and full concierge services. Try the California cuisine of Cafe Los Arcos for breakfast, lunch, and dinner (best for kids); Rodney's Steakhouse for dinner; and Barra Los Arcos, hosting happy hours and live entertainment. Roomy accommodations feature ocean, mountain, or courtyard views—many with patios or decks—great for enjoying the fresh sea breezes. Call for seasonal specials and package plans. $$$$

Upham Hotel & Garden Cottages. 1404 De La Vina St., just 2 blocks off State Street, downtown; (805) 962-0058 or (800) 727-0876; www.uphamhotel.com. Built in 1871, the Upham is Santa Barbara County's oldest continuously operating hotel. It is located on an acre of eye-catching gardens. You can choose from 50 different Victorian-style rooms or cottages, filled with comfortable, not stuffy, antiques. Kids like to play in the garden courtyard, while the older folks enjoy complimentary afternoon wine and cheese. All rates include a deluxe continental all-you-can-eat breakfast buffet, plus Oreo cookies and milk in the evening. The hotel has always been independently owned and operated and feels like a family home. Call and inquire for special rates and packages. Louie's Restaurant on premises serves delicious California-cuisine lunch weekdays and dinner every night on the historic veranda. $$$

For More Information

Santa Barbara Region Chamber of Commerce Visitor Center. 1 Garden St. at Cabrillo Boulevard; (805) 965-3021; www .sbchamber.org. Walk-up info on the beachfront. Open 364 days a year.

Santa Barbara Conference & Visitors Bureau and Film Commission. 1601 Anacapa St.; (805) 966-9222, (800) 927-4688, or (800) 676-1266; www.santabarbaraca.com.

Outdoor Santa Barbara Visitor Center. 113 Harbor Way, fourth floor; (805) 884-1475; http://outdoorsb.noaa.gov.

Carpinteria

The small seaside community of Carpinteria, about 12 miles southeast of Santa Barbara, down the coast along Highway 101, was originally a Chumash fishing village and canoe-building spot. It boasts the Carpinteria State Beach, aka the "world's safest beach"—a claim justified, perhaps, by a natural reef breakwater that prevents most nasty riptides. There are outstanding recreational opportunities and a variety of camping facilities around and inland from the beach. Many flower firms are based here, growing roses, orchids, and mums. Another of Carpinteria's blossoms, a hardy perennial fruit if you will, is celebrated with the popular California Avocado Festival, held the first weekend of October downtown on Linden Avenue (www.avofest.com). From April through October, thrill to the sport of kings at the Santa Barbara Polo Club (www.sbpolo.com), located in the Carpinteria foothills.

Carpinteria Valley Historical Society and Museum

956 Maple Ave.; (805) 684-3112; www.carpinteriahistoricalmuseum.org. Open Tues through Sat from 1 to 4 p.m.; closed holidays. Free. Donations welcome.

Check out the valley's heritage from Chumash Indian settlement to today with charming exhibits and knowledgeable docents.

Where to Stay

Holiday Inn Express Hotel & Suites. 5606 Carpinteria Ave.; (805) 566-9499. This 108-unit property has easy access to Highway 101, beaches, and local attractions. A nice outdoor pool, a spa, and complimentary continental breakfast buffet are other highlights. Ask about special package rates. $$$

For More Information

Carpinteria Valley Chamber of Commerce. 1056-B Eugenia Place, Box 956; (805) 684-5479 or (800) 563-6900; www.carp chamber.org.

Ventura County

The mighty Highway 101, known hereabouts as the Ventura Highway (and popularized in the 70s hit song by America), winds south from Santa Barbara County. It is the major artery through such rapidly growing communities as San Buenaventura (Ventura for short), Oxnard, Port Hueneme, Camarillo, Westlake Village, and Thousand Oaks. Exiting this concrete thoroughfare into the interior of Ventura County will reveal such treasures as the artistic and spiritual town of Ojai, rugged Santa Paula, and burgeoning Simi Valley. Embracing its cultural and geographic diversity is a key to enjoying Ventura County. With its mild climate and proximity to Los Angeles, the county offers an affordable getaway less than an hour from the big city. If you have limited time to show your family some California beach living, you can quickly and easily do it in the place Los Angelinos call "up the coast."

Ventura

Wrapped around the east-west ribbons of Highway 101, the city of Ventura has a historic downtown area that includes the restored Mission San Buenaventura; the Ventura Pier and State Beach (approximately 6 blocks from downtown); and the Ventura Harbor Village (some 2 miles away). Ventura is one of the few remaining classic California districts along the coast with its eclectic Art Deco, Craftsman, Neoclassical, and Victorian architecture all lovingly preserved in storefronts, offices, and residences. The city is home to more than 125 antiques dealers. Ventura has a population of about 100,000 and is a major agricultural center for citrus and other fruits. Its warm, sunny climate and value-priced accommodations and restaurants make this a very affordable family vacation spot as well as a jumping-off point for visiting the Channel Islands National Park.

Ventura Harbor Village

1583 Spinnaker Dr., about 1 mile west of the Harbor Boulevard/Seaward exit from Highway 101; (877) 89-HARBOR or (805) 642-8538; www.venturaharborvillage.com.

Sailing, fishing, scuba diving, and sightseeing trips can all be arranged at this 33-acre destination "village." Dozens of shops and restaurants too are along the scenic Promenade, home of the Channel Islands National Park Visitor Center. (See sidebar in this chapter for more information.)

Island Packers Company

1691 Spinnaker Dr., Suite 105 B, adjacent to Channel Islands National Park Visitor Center; (805) 642-1393; www.islandpackers.com. $–$$$$.

Island Packers is a tour operator based here since 1968 and offering scheduled charters to all the islands, as well as whale-watching trips and cruises. This location is

Our Fortieth **National Park**

The Channel Islands National Park Robert J. Lagomarsino Visitor Center is located at 1901 Spinnaker Dr. in Ventura Harbor Village (805-658-5730; www .nps.gov/chis). It is open daily, except Thanksgiving and Christmas. Less than 20 miles off the coast of Ventura and Santa Barbara Counties, the Channel Islands National Park comprises five of the eight offshore Channel Islands: Santa Barbara, Anacapa, Santa Cruz, Santa Rosa, and San Miguel. These islands provide an unparalleled introduction for your family to the flora and fauna of the local marine environment. Nature, unspoiled and unsullied by humans, is the main attraction here; quite frankly, it's the only attraction! Because the balance of nature on these islands and their surrounding waters is so fragile, visitors' activities are strictly regulated. For instance, there are no snack bars or RV campgrounds, and when you tour the area, you must bring (and take back what remains of) your own food, water, and other supplies. Rangers conduct guided hikes on San Miguel and Santa Rosa. Private concessionaires' boats or charter craft provide transportation across the channel to specific embarkation points.

The waterfront visitor center houses quality exhibits that graphically describe the entire park, including its ecosystem, mammals, and birds. Plus, the center has an indoor tide pool, great for learning about the sea creatures your kids will see en route. There is also a movie and video about the islands shown here. A stairway and elevator lead up to the observation tower that will give you a 360-degree view of the harbor and, on most clear days, all the way to the islands themselves. Taking a day to visit our fortieth national park is well worth the effort and will be a sea journey to another dimension your family won't forget.

home dock for the *Islander* and the *Island Adventure*. Call for special packages and itineraries.

Where to Eat & Stay

Pierpont Inn & Austen's Restaurant. 550 Sanjon Rd., adjacent to Highway 101, northbound exit Sanjon Road, southbound exit Seaward Avenue; (805) 643-6144 or (800) 285-4667; www.pierpontinn.com. Children ages 12 and younger stay **free** at this attractive, 77-unit property, established in 1928. Check out the two cottages! Some rooms have fireplaces, and most rooms have ocean views with balconies. Even though you are across the highway from the beach, this property has two heated pools (one indoor). It also has 12 lighted tennis courts and a very friendly, helpful staff. The

Digging into **History**

These three nearby attractions all make for refreshing steps back into early California history. Each is located in downtown Ventura, within easy walking distance, and can be accomplished in a long morning. While you're in the downtown shopping and dining zone, catch some of the dozens of vintage stores and antiques emporiums.

The Museum of Ventura County. 100 East Main St.; (805) 653-0323; www .venturamuseum.org. Open 11 a.m. to 5 p.m. Tues through Sun. Closed most holidays. It features attractive displays blending local chronicles and illustrations along with the popular George Stuart historical figures, changing exhibits, and a good research library detailing the city's origins—after a brief period of Mexican rule, following California statehood in 1850, Ventura became a bustling frontier town.

Albinger Archaeological Museum. 113 East Main St.; (805) 648-5823; www.albingermuseum.org. Open Wed through Sun 10 a.m. to 4 p.m. Free. Museum contains artifacts spanning 3,500 years, all excavated from a single dig site next to the Mission San Buenaventura. Available on request: audiovisual programs describing the labor-intensive process of excavation.

Mission San Buenaventura. 211 East Main St.; (805) 648-4496; www.san buenaventuramission.org. Open Mon through Fri 10 a.m. to 5 p.m., Sat 9 a.m. to 5 p.m., and Sun 10 a.m. to 4 p.m. $. Founded in 1782 and completed in 1809, 9th in the chain of 21 California missions. The current mission includes a small museum and a restored church that continues to be an active parish. It's the only mission in the United States with bells made of wood. The reason is still a mystery.

ocean-view restaurant serves breakfast, lunch, and dinner daily as well as Sunday brunch. $$$$

Andria's Seafood Restaurant & Market. 1449 Spinnaker Dr., Suite A, in Ventura Harbor Village; (805) 654-8228; www.andrias seafood.com. Open seven days a week from 11 a.m. For a relaxed, casual, family-friendly atmosphere, this is your seafood place.

Since 1982, the food's always fresh off the nearby boats, cooked to order—grilled, fried, baked, or broiled—and served with a smile. $–$$

Rocket Fizz. 105 South Oak St.; (805) 641-1222; www.rocketfizzstore.com. Call for hours. Check out this crazy candy shop! To fit in with Ventura's classic California vibe, your kids (and you, of course) need the sweets to match! Discover more than 500 different bottled soda pops manufactured from all corners of the United States, plus an enormously awesome candy cornucopia. $

For More Information

Ventura Convention and Visitors Bureau. 101 South California St.; (805) 648-2075 or (800) 333-2989; www.ventura-usa .com.

Ojai

From Ventura, you can take either Highway 150 or Highway 33 inland to reach Ojai, a warm, dry, spiritually inclined artists' colony nestled in a peaceful valley. Say "Oh-high," and you will have mastered the most difficult part of the area. That's how you pronounce the city's moniker used by original Chumash Indian inhabitants, believed to mean "Valley of the Moon." The region features a Mediterranean climate with hot, dry summers and mild winters with unique topography. Ojai is surrounded by an east-west mountain range, one of few places in the world to have a "pink moment" occur as the sun is setting: Look to the east over the Topa Topa Mountains and you'll see a brilliant shade of pink reflected at that end of the valley. Try to time your visit here for this phenomenon; it never fails to astonish. Conversely, the rising moon over Ojai's mountain ranges creates a gorgeous lunar glow.

The drive here alone is worth the trip because of the scenic mountains and lakes. The quaint downtown features Libbey Park—home of the annual Bowl Full of Blues concert series and the Ojai Music Festival. The Ojai Center for the Arts has displays by California artists and a changing calendar of events. Call (805) 646-1107 or visit www.ojaiartcenter .org for current happenings.

Ojai Theatre

145 East Ojai Ave.; (805) 646-1011; www.ojaitheatre.com.

Beautifully restored in 2008, this circa-1910 building now features the best viewing technologies with classic Hollywood charm, including Art Deco–style chandeliers, movie posters, and heavy curtains. First-run features, matinees, weekly independent film series, special events, and concerts are featured—and the theater is home to the Ojai Film Festival each autumn. No matter what's playing, you and the kids can have a blast from the past with all of today's comforts.

Lake Casitas Recreation Area

Off Highway 150, approximately 3 miles west of junction of Highway 33, about 15 minutes from downtown Ojai; 11311 Santa Ana Rd., Ventura; reservations: (805) 649-1122 or info: (805) 649-2233; www.lakecasitas.info. Open year-round for day use during daylight hours. 400 overnight campsites subject to availability; fees vary.

Set in a valley of its own, this 35-mile-long, irregularly shaped lake is actually a human-made reservoir that provides drinking water for Ventura County. Consequently, there is no swimming in the lake, but the fishing for trout, bass, crappie, and catfish is excellent. Powerboats, canoeing, and sailing are fun here, too, year-round. There is a basic snack bar, small grocery store, boat rental, bait shop, and a large kids' playground. The Water Adventure Area offers two distinctly wet playgrounds—an 18-inch-deep pool or the Lazy River tube float pool, both open only in summer. Our advice is to pack a picnic lunch and come kick back here for the day.

Where to Eat

Boccali's. 3277 Ojai-Santa Paula Rd., at the corner of Reeves Road; (805) 646-6116; www .boccalis.com. Casual, fun dining inside or outside on the patio. Great pizzas and loads of pastas. Family owned and operated since 1986; friendly atmosphere; takeout available. Serving dinner seven nights a week and lunch Wed through Sun. $

Where to Stay

Ojai Valley Inn & Spa. 905 Country Club Rd., just west of town off Highway 150; (805) 646-5511 or (800) 422-6524; www.ojairesort .com. This magnificent AAA five-diamond rated resort nestled in the foothills has been a one-stop family fun destination since 1923. If you and yours can't find something to keep you happy here, go home! Situated on 220 landscaped acres, the resort offers 308 first-class rooms and suites overlooking gardens, pools, a golf course, and woods. The 18-hole golf course is very challenging, yet forgiving. Warm up on the putting green, or perhaps try tennis (4 courts), horseback riding, a jogging course, hiking, and biking (rentals available). Better yet, let the kids enjoy the petting zoo and incredible supervised Camp Ojai children's programs (ages 5 to 12) that change with the season and feature a small-animal farm tour and pony rides available 365 days a year. Meanwhile, you can experience the 31,000-square-foot spa facility—featuring a full complement of deluxe services such as hydrotherapy, massage, facials, manicures, beauty, toning, aromatherapies, and more. Maravilla Dining Room (dinner guests over age 13 only) and Oak Café (all ages, breakfast, lunch, and dinner) and Spa Café (lunch) are open daily, but feasting poolside is our favorite. Be sure to call for special family packages and rates. A destination resort not to be missed! $$$$

For More Information

Ojai Valley Chamber of Commerce. 201 South Signal St.; (805) 646-8126; www.ojai chamber.org.

Santa Paula & Fillmore

Exiting Highway 101 onto Highway 126 leads you through the region known as the Heritage Valley—filled with citrus groves and ranches—to the pretty villages of Santa Paula and Fillmore. Santa Paula celebrates its heritage and culture with special events throughout the year, including the Citrus Festival and the Citrus Classic Balloon Festival in July, Moonlight at the Ranch in the fall, the Pumpkin Patch at Faulkner Farm throughout October, and the year-end downtown Christmas Parade. At any time of year, there is a fun family event for everyone. The Santa Paula Airport at Santa Maria and 8th Streets has an extensive collection of privately owned antique, classic, and homebuilt aircraft. Call the Chamber of Commerce for a current schedule of tours and air shows or visit www .discoversantapaula.com.

California Oil Museum of Santa Paula

1001 East Main St., Santa Paula; (805) 933-0076; www.oilmuseum.net. Open Wed through Sun; closed holidays. $.

Operated by the City of Santa Paula Community Services Department, the museum highlights the inner workings of the state's "black gold" industry through interactive displays, videos, working models, games, photographs, restored gas station memorabilia, and an authentic turn-of-the-century cable-tool drilling rig. The collection of gas station memorabilia is one of the largest displays of vintage gas pumps in California.

Fillmore & Western Railway

Central Park Plaza, downtown Fillmore. Will call/ticket office is the Red Ticket Caboose, located next to Fillmore City Hall, 250 Central Ave.; (805) 524-2546 or (800) 773-TRAIN; www .fwry.com. Runs Sat and Sun, but not all major holidays. Times change seasonally. $$$.

This antique train offers one-hour scenic sightseeing trips between Fillmore and Santa Paula. Vintage cars include a 1920s Pullman and restored dining, sleeper, and parlor carriages. Train workers dress in period costume. Theme parties and dinners are popular, especially the Pumpkinliner and Christmas tree trains. Call for a current schedule and fares.

For More Information

Santa Paula Chamber of Commerce. Santa Barbara at 10th Street; (805) 525-5561; www.santapaulachamber.com.

Fillmore Chamber of Commerce. 275 Central Ave.; (805) 524-0351; www.fillmore chamber.com.

Heritage Valley Tourism Bureau. 270 Central Ave., Fillmore; (805) 524-7500; www .heritagevalley.net.

Oxnard

What could you possibly find to do, see, or enjoy in a place with the funny name of Oxnard? Plenty of affordable family fun! The town got its name from entrepreneur Henry T. Oxnard, a visionary who foresaw that the fertile plains just north of the Conejo Hills would be an excellent place to raise sugar beets. When the day came in 1903 to register the town's name with the clerk in the state capital of Sacramento, Henry had a bad phone connection and settled for his surname. Sweet history aside, Oxnard has grown into a culturally and economically diverse community, with business parks, 7 miles of sandy beaches, and a fine marina, just 60 miles north of Los Angeles. Hailed as "California's Strawberry Coast," Oxnard boasts fields of fresh fruit, roadside farm stands you should not avoid, and the nationally recognized California Strawberry Festival held the third weekend in May. In late July, strawberries make way for spicy foods and sizzling entertainment at the Oxnard Salsa Festival celebrating the area's Latino culture.

Heritage Square

Downtown at 715 South A St.; (805) 483-7960. Open daily; guided tours Sat 10 a.m. to 2 p.m. Free.

The square reflects the area's past centuries, with its faithful restorations of a late-1800s church, water tower, pump house, and 11 vintage homes. The buildings were moved from various parts of Oxnard to this single block combined with fresh 21st century energy. Summer Friday Night Concerts delight audiences of all ages. It's also home to the Petit Playhouse and Oxnard's award-winning Elite Theatre Company as well as the nearby historic Woolworth Building, recently restored with a small museum, cafes, retail shops, and offices.

Gull Wings Children's Museum (ages 2 to 12)

418 West 4th St., downtown, a bit off the beaten path in the old USO Hall; (805) 483-3005; www.gullwings.org. Open Tues through Sat from 10 a.m. to 5 p.m. $.

Indoor sports abound at this innovative museum, from a variety of hands-on exhibits to a medical room with cutaway models to a simulated campground and farmers' market.

Carnegie Cultural Arts Center

424 South C St.; (805) 385-8157; www.carnegieam.org. Open Thurs through Sat 10 a.m. to 5 p.m. and Sun 1 to 5 p.m. $.

A dozen art galleries are scattered about like candy waiting to be unwrapped for the arty family unit. Carnegie Art Museum is housed in an imposing, 2-story structure built in 1906 as a library. The museum's permanent collection focuses on 20th-century California painters. Ever-changing exhibits highlight photography, sculpture, oils, watercolors, and some humorous displays. Across the street is Centennial Plaza, with a 14-screen first-run movie theater, specialty restaurants, and shops, plus, nearby for the adults, Herzog Wine Cellars (the nation's largest kosher winery/restaurant/gift shop; 3201 Camino Del Sol; 805-983-1560; www.herzogwinecellars.com).

Channel Islands Harbor & Visitor Center

2741 South Victoria Ave., Suite F; (805) 985-4852; www.channelislandsharbor.org.

Fisherman's Wharf, Harbor Landing, and the Marine Emporium Landing (www.marine emporiumlanding.com) have shopping, fine dining, and plenty of sailing and fishing options as well. Twenty-six hundred working and pleasure craft call this bustling port home. There are plenty of parks, a swimming beach, and the Maritime Museum.

Throughout the year various events are held including the Celebration of the Whales, visits by the Tall Ships, Fireworks by the Sea on July Fourth, the Ventura County Boat Show, Ventura Vintage Rods Harbor Run Classic Car Show, and the annual Holiday Parade of Lights. Fresh fruits and vegetables plus arts and crafts are at the harbor's Farmer's Market held at the Marine Emporium Landing from 10 a.m. to 2 p.m. every Sunday to create your perfect harborside picnic. The Channel Islands Water Taxi, with its painted-on smiling face, is the best way to see the seafront. Call (805) 985-4677 for current schedule and fares.

Ventura County Maritime Museum

2731 South Victoria Ave., just past Channel Islands Boulevard; (805) 984-6260. Open daily 11 a.m. to 5 p.m. Closed major holidays. **Free.**

You and your mates will find a collection of ship models, made with materials ranging from bone to wood to metals, which reflect maritime history from ancient to modern times. Changing exhibits deal with maritime commerce, art, Channel Islands history, whaling, and shipwrecks.

Murphy Classic Auto Museum

2230 Statham Blvd.; (805) 487-4333; www.murphyautomuseum.org. Open Sat and Sun 10 a.m. to 4 p.m. $$.

This museum's 16,000 square feet contain a wide variety of vintage, milestone, and special interest vehicles, including a large collection of Packards from 1927 to 1958. Have fun, fun, fun until daddy takes your T-bird away!

Where to Eat & Stay

Embassy Suites Mandalay Beach Resort & Capistrano's Restaurant. 2101 Mandalay Beach Rd. on the beach, just off Channel Islands Boulevard; (805) 984-2500; www.mandalaybeach.embsuites.com. All 250 units here are 2-room, 2-bath suites, just perfect for family accommodations. You will love the deluxe amenities in every suite—fridge, microwave, coffeemaker, two TVs, plus a **free** cooked-to-order hot breakfast every morning and **free** beverages and refreshments every evening in the garden courtyard. This resort is right on the sand, with its own beach, and you can rent boogie boards, bicycles, beach chairs, or snorkeling gear, or just kick back in the spacious serpentine pool. Dine at ocean-view

Capistrano's on fresh seafood and pasta for lunch and dinner or stop by for the award-winning Sunday brunch. $$$$

For More Information

Oxnard Convention & Visitors Bureau. 1000 Town Center Dr., Suite 130; (805) 385-7545 or (800) 2-OXNARD; www.visitoxnard .com.

California Welcome Center–Oxnard. 1000 Town Center Dr., Suite 120; (805) 385-7545; www.visitcwc.com/oxnard. This statewide **free** information center makes a great Central Coast concierge. (Shares space in an office park with the Oxnard CVB.)

Port Hueneme

In 1941 the US Navy took advantage of the only natural deepwater harbor between Los Angeles and San Francisco to build its Construction Battalion (known as CB or Seabee) in Port Hueneme (pronounced Why-nee-me). Named after a Chumash settlement, Weneme, that occupied the site, this town of 22,000 actually was plotted in 1869, but its prominence today is its military importance as the home base of the US Navy Civil Engineer Corps (CEC). These skilled construction experts have actively fought in military engagements around the world. Plus, it is also the only commercial port for international shipping between Los Angeles and San Francisco, employing more than 4,000 and boasting niche markets of cars and fruit cargoes. Public educational port tours are offered. For schedules, call (805) 488-3677 or visit www.portofhueneme.org.

CEC/Seabee Museum

US Naval Construction Battalion at Ventura Road and Sunkist Avenue, within the gates of the Naval Base Ventura County; www.seabeehf.org. Call ahead to confirm hours and current accessibility to civilians at (805) 982-5165. Children younger than age 16 must be accompanied by an adult. Free.

You can see models of equipment, actual weapons, and uniforms of the Civil Engineer Corps (CEC) and US Navy Seabees.

Simi Valley

The Simi Valley lies on a plateau at around 800 feet above sea level, about 20 minutes inland from Oxnard. Highway 118 (also known as the Ronald Reagan Freeway) bisects the valley, connecting it to Highway 23 with access to Highway 101 along the coast. With a population of more than 100,000, this area is a popular bedroom community for adjacent Los Angeles County. For more information call the Simi Valley Chamber of Commerce & Visitors Center at (805) 526-3900 or visit www.simichamber.org.

Ronald Reagan Presidential Library & Museum
and Air Force One Pavilion

40 Presidential Dr., 5 miles inland from Highway 101 at Simi Valley off Highway 118 (follow the signs); (805) 522-2977 or (800) 410-8354; www.reaganfoundation.org. Open daily 10 a.m. to 5 p.m.; closed New Year's Day, Thanksgiving, and Christmas. $$$.

Located in a Spanish Mission–style building constructed around a courtyard and set on a hilltop, this site provides you with an incredible view of the rolling hills leading down to the Pacific Ocean, including the late president's memorial site and final resting place. Within the library's museum are photographs and memorabilia of President Reagan's entire life (1911–2004), gifts of state he received during his administration, and a replica of the Oval Office. Perhaps most impressive to the younger generation is a piece of the crumbled Berlin Wall. This facility provides all generations with a compelling look at "The

Great Communicator" and his legacy as the 40th US president. The Air Force One Pavilion houses the former president's Boeing 707 airplane, available for boarding and tours, along with exhibits about presidential travel.

Where to Eat & Stay

Grand Vista Hotel. 999 Enchanted Way, exit First Street off Highway 118, only 2 miles from Reagan Library, Simi Valley; (805) 583-2000 or (800) 455-7464; www.grandvistasimi .com. Very spacious 195-room, full-service hotel with 2 swimming pools (one heated) and the Vistas Restaurant ($$$). Complimentary full breakfast buffet (Mon through Sat) will get your family off to a good start. $$$$

Thousand Oaks & Westlake Village

The adjoining cities of Thousand Oaks and Westlake Village (joint population estimated 125,000) are located just off Highway 101 in the southernmost section of Ventura County; halfway between Santa Barbara and Los Angeles and 12 miles inland from the Pacific Ocean. Originally part of a Spanish land grant called Rancho El Conejo (co-nay-ho), today this lovely residential area still has plenty of open rangeland, parks, and things for your family to savor. The **Santa Monica Mountains National Recreation Area Visitors Center** at 401 West Hillcrest provides guided walks, trail maps, and special events calendars (805-370-2301). For more information contact Greater Conejo Valley Chamber of Commerce at (805) 370-0035 or visit www.conejochamber.org. Conejo Valley Days (http://conejovalley.com) is an annual spring festival with parades, a rodeo, and a carnival.

Stagecoach Inn Museum

51 South Ventu Park Rd., off Highway 101, Newberry Park; (805) 498-9441; www.stagecoach museum.org. Open Wed through Sun 1 to 4 p.m.; closed holidays. $.

First opened in 1876, this Monterey-style structure, now faithfully restored, was a major stopover on the stage route between Los Angeles and Santa Barbara. The Tri-Village includes dwellings that represent the three historic eras in the Conejo Valley—the Newbury Pioneer House, the Spanish Adobe, and a Chumash Village—as well as changing exhibits will give the kids a great taste of western life here.

Thousand Oaks Civic Arts Plaza

2100 East Thousand Oaks Blvd., Thousand Oaks; (805) 449-2787; www.toaks.org. Admission fee may apply for special events.

Performance art in every shape and form takes place here year-round. This complex has beautiful sculpture, fountains, an 1,800-seat auditorium, a 400-seat theater, and a 7-acre park. Be sure to call for a current schedule of events and pricing. There is always something happening here for families.

Where to Eat & Stay

Westlake Village Inn. 31943 Agoura Rd., Westlake Village, exit Westlake Boulevard South off Highway 101; (818) 889-0230 or (800) 535-9978; www.westlakevillageinn.com. This beautifully landscaped, 17-acre full-service property has 140 rooms and 18 suites to house your family in luxury. Relax from your travels in the pool/whirlpool spa area or play golf (18 holes), practice on the putting green, play tennis (10 courts), or merely stroll around the pretty lake. Package plans and special rates for families abound at this deluxe oasis in the tony community of Westlake. **Mediterraneo** (818-889-9105; $$$$), overlooking the lake and gardens, serves Sunday brunch, and lunch and dinner daily, in an elegant atmosphere, best suited for older children and teens. $$$$

Greater Los Angeles

S ay it like a native—"El Ay"—and you're already on the road (or freeway, as it were) to unlocking the mystique of one of the most fascinating places on earth. For L.A. is many different things to many millions of ethnically diverse people. For some, the city is synonymous with Hollywood and the legends of glamour that go along with it. For others, it is the leading metropolis of the Pacific Rim, a cutting-edge capital of culture and industry where culture happens to be a thriving industry unto itself.

For just about everyone L.A. means paradise. Palm trees, beaches, and the best darned weather in the world. L.A. is the birthplace of the Internet, Barbie, DC-3 planes, the Mazda Miata, and BMX (bicycle motocross). The vaunted laid-back mind-set of Los Angelinos belies their determination to make L.A. as livable as it can possibly be. Creativity, hard work, and frequent trips to the beach help make civic aspirations come alive.

The size of the city provokes inspiration or consternation, depending on your point of view. On a clear day—of which, contrary to popular belief, there are many—one gets a sense of its general proportions. The core of Los Angeles, city and county, is a vast, level basin studded with palm trees and laced with freeways. (By the way, always remember the name *and* the number of the freeway you are on or looking for, as both locals and road signs use them interchangeably. Thus "the 5" is also the Golden State, "the 101" is also the Hollywood, which turns into the Ventura, etc. Radio traffic reports generally refer to freeways by their names.) Driving times in Greater Los Angeles are completely dependent upon time of day. Rush hours are generally weekdays 6 to 9 a.m. and 3 to 7 p.m. and are to be avoided.

The L.A. basin is flanked on all sides by foothills and the San Gabriel Mountains, many of which are snowcapped in winter. In the city itself, the higher up in the hills you go, the bigger the mansions get. These are actually the Santa Monica Mountains, an enchanting urban oasis with miles of hiking trails, scenic drives, and, after a good rain, even a waterfall or two. Of course, L.A. is prime beach country: In the land where Beach Blanket Bingo was born, there are 81 miles of county coastline, from Malibu in the north to Long Beach in the south. Oldies radio stations have an unabashed bias for Beach Boys hits. But despite

GREATER LOS ANGELES

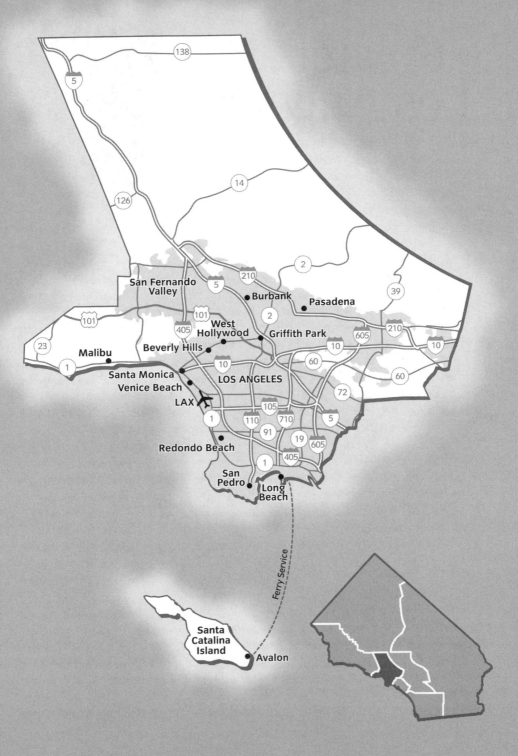

its reputation for sunshine and stars, L.A. County also boasts a vast array of stellar cultural attractions.

Over the years, a patchwork of quite separate cities and towns in the L.A. basin was incorporated into the City of Los Angeles, creating a sprawling urban tapestry of contrasting colors and textures. Even if you're super-parents, you won't be able to explore all 4,083 square miles of Los Angeles County, or even the City of Los Angeles's 467 square miles. No matter, because the most interesting things to see and do are relatively concentrated in five major areas: downtown; Hollywood; Westside and Beverly Hills; the valleys—San Fernando (including Burbank), San Gabriel (including Pasadena), and Santa Clarita; and coastal Los Angeles County—from northernmost Malibu heading south through Santa Monica, Venice Beach, Marina del Rey, LAX, Redondo Beach, the port of L.A./San Pedro, and Long Beach. By East Coast standards, things are still very spread out, but that merely adds to the adventure, even for natives. Equipped with a reliable car—an absolute necessity—a full tank of gas, and the stamina to tackle the world's most extensive network of freeways, you and your family are prepared for experiencing a great deal of the excitement this pocket of the world has to offer.

Downtown Los Angeles

Start at the historic "center" of El Pueblo de la Reyna de los Angeles (The Town of the Queen of the Angels). That's as good a rule as any for those unfamiliar with the greater L.A. area. Downtown Los Angeles has been the commercial and cultural core of this sprawling city since it was merely a pueblo. Downtown gives the city a focus, and many central district attractions are perennial favorites. You will instantly recognize downtown by its cluster of skyscrapers. There are seven major districts in downtown L.A.: the **Fashion District,** between Broadway and Wall Street, 7th Street and Pico Boulevard, designer wear at a discount anchored by the historic California Mart and Cooper Building at 9th and Los Angeles Streets; the **Jewelry District,** on Hill Street between 6th and 7th Streets, where you'll find discount diamonds, gold, and bangles galore; the **Toy District,** bordered by 3rd, 5th, Los Angeles, and San Pedro Streets, and a mecca for wholesale toys and children's clothing; **Little Tokyo,** between Central Avenue, 1st, 4th, and San Pedro Streets; **Chinatown,** between North Broadway and North Hill Streets, for Chinese shopping, dining, galleries, and cultural festivals; the **Theatre District,** on Broadway between 3rd and 9th Streets, where you'll find architecturally amazing theaters such as the Orpheum; and **Bunker Hill,** bordered by 1st, 5th, Flower, and Olive Streets, and featuring the Music Center, Disney Hall, and performing-arts venues.

The *Los Angeles Times* (ages 10 and older for tours mandated)
202 West 1st St., right across the street from City Hall; (213) 237-5757 (tour info); www.latimes.com.

The *Los Angeles Times* is the nation's biggest metro daily newspaper. Kids love to see the newsroom and printing facility, with its mesmerizing, rapid-fire machinery that churns out more than a million newspapers each day. **Free** tours are offered Tues and Thurs on the last day of each month by advance reservation only. The first option is the "editorial" tour of the newsroom, and the second is of the printing plant on Olympic Boulevard. Tour hours vary.

Music Center

135 North Grand Ave.; (213) 972-7211; www.musiccenter.org. Call for event pricing. Tours: free.

Tours are **free** at this world-class performing-arts complex that includes the Dorothy Chandler Pavilion (L.A. Opera; www.losangelesopera.com), the Mark Taper Forum (Center Theatre Group, www.taperahmanson.com), the Ahmanson Theatre, and the Walt Disney Concert Hall. The striking, stainless-steel $247 million Disney Hall (www.disneyhall.com), designed by Frank O. Gehry, premiered in October 2003 as the new home of the L.A. Philharmonic (www.laphil.com) and LA Master Chorale (www.lamc.org). Get your kids interested in arts and architecture with a self-guided audio tour, available daily for **free,** as well as guided tours of the Walt Disney Concert Hall plus a new Symphonian Four Theatre Tour encompassing architectural highlights and a historical overview of all four Music Center venues—the Ahmanson Theatre, Dorothy Chandler Pavilion, Mark Taper Forum and Walt Disney Concert Hall, as available.

Call (213) 972-4399 for schedule and times. The hall also features REDCAT (Roy & Edna Disney CalArts Theatre—www.redcatweb.org) for an eclectic performance, as well as gardens; a dedicated children's outdoor amphitheater; 5 restaurants of the Patina Group, under the direction of uber chef/founder Joachim Splichal; Library of Congress/Ira Gershwin Gallery; and an underground parking garage.

Grand Central Market

317 South Broadway; (213) 624-2378; www.grandcentralsquare.com. Open Mon through Sun 9 a.m. to 6 p.m. Free.

Opened in 1917, Grand Central Market is L.A.'s oldest and largest food market. Here you can sample not just a cross section of L.A.'s ethnic diversity but also some of the country's best Mexican and Asian food. Locals come here to bargain for bananas, try authentic burritos, or indulge in raspberry guava smoothies at the all-natural exotic juice bar. You may hear more Spanish than English, but that's half the fun, and *gracias* (thank you) is really all the Spanish you need to know anywhere in Los Angeles.

Museum of Contemporary Art (MOCA)

250 South Grand Ave., in California Plaza; (213) 626-6222; www.moca.org. Open Thurs through Mon 11 a.m. to 5 p.m.; may vary seasonally. Children under 12 free. $$.

Kids will find the often outrageous and totally unexplainable artwork here to be, well, mysterious. Many people do! The eclectic, always changing, never boring collections range from the cute to the controversial. Kids can roam at will through the museum to see an artistic show, including enormous multimedia sculptures, unpredictable creations

L.A. LIVE **Shines**

A 27-acre, one-of-a-kind sports, entertainment, hotel, restaurant, and residential complex has emerged adjacent to the Staples Center and the Los Angeles Convention Center downtown at the corner of Olympic Boulevard and Figueroa Street (actual address is 800 W. Olympic Blvd.). The 7,100-seat Nokia Theatre Los Angeles and Nokia Plaza opened in October 2007 as the first phase of this new district. The Nokia is now the home of the Primetime Emmy Awards, as well as live music concerts, comedy shows, family programs, short-run Broadway, and community theater productions. For current schedules, visit www.nokiatheatrelalive.com. Savor restaurants including Fleming's Prime Steakhouse, Katsuya, the Yard House, Rosa Mexicano, ESPN Zone Sports Bar, plus a Starbucks and a New Zealand Natural Ice Cream shop as well as Club NOKIA, the legendary Conga Room nightclub, and the Lucky Strike Bowling Center. You've got two choices to stay right in L.A. LIVE. The 124-room boutique Ritz-Carlton Hotel, home to WP24, the latest restaurant concept by celebrity chef Wolfgang Puck. You'll have some of the best views in Los Angeles from virtually any part of the hotel, including the 3,400-square-foot signature Ritz-Carlton Club Lounge and the exclusive, private rooftop pool and bar on the 26th floor where you probably won't be bringing the kids! The Ritz-Carlton Los Angeles shares the distinctive 54-story gleaming glass tower with its sister hotel—the JW Marriott Hotel Los Angeles (www.lalive-marriott.com), with 878 well-appointed guest rooms, all located between floors 4 and 21 of the tower. The Marriott is a more family-friendly property worth your consideration. For complete details on all the latest facilities and services, go to www.lalive.com.

of various shapes and sizes, and monochromatic paintings of nothing much at all. **Free** on-site children's workshops are offered. And stop by the museum's cafe, Patinette, for an imaginative California-style salad or pasta. After placing your order, you can sit inside or on the patio. First Sundays are **free** for families—drop in, create art together, and share Sunday with your family at an artist-led workshop for families with children 7 to 18. No reservations required for this activity.

Cathedral of Our Lady of the Angels

555 West Temple St.; (213) 680-5200; www.olacathedral.org. Call for current schedule of events, tours, and service times.

Whether you're Catholic or not, you can't miss this 21st-century architectural wonder that opened in 2002. Its concrete angularity and lighting is awe-inspiring inside and out. Open daily to the public for self-guided tours. Gardens, artwork, sculpture, fountains, a cafe, and a gift shop on the plaza surround this home of the Roman Catholic Archdiocese of Los Angeles. Daily masses in English and Spanish as well as other liturgies, special events, concerts, and exhibitions.

The Museum of Neon Art

136 West 4th St.; (213) 489-9918; www.neonmona.org. Open Wed through Sat noon to 6 p.m., Sun noon to 5 p.m. $$, children age 5 and younger free.

Here's the place to gaze upon a glowing collection of electronic-media neon signs. Nostalgia lovers will enjoy the exhibits of the neon signs their grandparents grew up with as well as hundreds of contemporary forms and uses. Check out the seasonal LA Neon Lights bus tour sponsored by MONA—it's radiant!

Wells Fargo History Center

333 South Grand Ave., 2 blocks south of the Music Center; (213) 253-7166; www.wellsfargo history.com. Open Mon through Fri 9 a.m. to 5 p.m. Closed on bank holidays. Free.

This center chronicles more than a century of western history. Step into an original Concord stagecoach; view a gold nugget, and see a re-created ticket agent's office.

Exposition Park Area

Just south of downtown Los Angeles, bounded by Figueroa Street, Vermont Avenue, Exposition Boulevard, and Martin Luther King Jr. Boulevard; www.nhm.org. Open daily until sunset. Free.

This has been a civic, cultural, and recreation area since the turn of the 20th century. Here you'll find the L.A. Memorial Coliseum, L.A. Memorial Sports Arena, Natural History Museum, the California Science Center and IMAX Theater, Expo Center Swim Stadium, and the California African American Museum, as well as a 7-acre Rose Garden containing 16,000-plus specimens of 190-plus varieties. Adjacent to the park is the world-famous urban campus of the University of Southern California (USC); www.usc.edu. Across the Harbor Freeway (Highway 110) is the ethnic restaurant, retail, and entertainment complex **Mercado La Paloma** (The Dove Marketplace), 3655 South Grand Ave.; (213) 748-1963; www.mercadolapaloma.com.

Natural History Museum of L.A. County

900 Exposition Blvd., Exposition Park; (213) 763-DINO (3466); www.nhm.org. Open Mon through Fri 9:30 a.m. to 5 p.m., Sat and Sun 10 a.m. to 5 p.m. Closed major holidays. $$, children younger than 5 free.

Kids love the museum because of its lifelike dinosaur replicas, animal habitat dioramas, insect zoo, and Native American Cultures exhibit, plus the Halls of Birds, Gems & Minerals, and Marine Life. The Discovery Center is awesomely interactive. Grab a bite at the cafe. Well worth your time!

The California Science Center & IMAX Theater

700 State Dr., west of the 110 freeway; (213) 744-2019; www.californiasciencecenter.org. Open 10 a.m. to 5 p.m. daily. Closed Thanksgiving, New Year's Day, and Christmas. **Free.**

Popular for its fun, innovative, and interactive exhibits, including the Air and Space Gallery with NASA capsules and a real jet fighter plane. The Explore Store is enlightening shopping. For current IMAX production schedule and admission fees, call (213) 744-2019. Attractions include Creative World, World of Life, and Science Court, or take a ride on the high-wire bicycle. Visit often to explore changing exhibits.

California African American Museum

600 State Dr; (213) 744-7432; www.caamuseum.org. Open Tues through Sat from 10 a.m. to 5 p.m. and Sun from 11 a.m. to 5 p.m. **Free.**

This 44,000-square-foot facility includes 3 full-size exhibition galleries, a theater gallery, Sculpture Court, a conference center/special events room, and an archive and research library. History, culture, and art are featured in ongoing and special exhibits.

Los Angeles Memorial Coliseum and Sports Arena

3911 South Figueroa St.; (213) 748-6136 or (213) 747-7111; www.lacoliseumlive .com/joomla. The Coliseum and Sports Arena Business Office, as well as the ticket office, is located at the South Sports Arena Entrance, 3939 South Figueroa St. Regular box office hours are Mon through Fri, 10 a.m. to 6 p.m.

First opened in 1923 and refurbished extensively in the 1990s, this 92,516-seat stadium hosted the 1932 and 1984 Olympics, two Super Bowls, NFL football teams, and it is currently home to the USC Trojan football team. On March 29, 2008, the Los Angeles Dodgers drew 115,300 people here for an historic exhibition game versus the Boston Red Sox (Dodgers lost 7–4). The total eclipsed the long-standing Guinness World Record for the largest crowd ever to attend a baseball game. The adjacent indoor Sports Arena opened in 1959 and hosts an incredible variety of events and concerts. Call for schedules.

Little Tokyo

Between Central Avenue, 1st, 4th, and San Pedro Streets.

This is the social, cultural, and economic center of Southern California's Japanese-American community. It was declared a National Historic Landmark District in 1995. The Kyoto Grand Hotel and Gardens (www.kyotograndhotel.com), the Japanese American Cultural and Community Center, and the Japanese American National Museum (www.janm.org) are here, along with great ethnic restaurants and shops for your family to explore—Village Plaza, Little Tokyo Plaza, and Weller Court Shopping Center—with no passport required.

Spectator **Sports**

There is a sport for all seasons in greater L.A., so if your family likes to watch professional sports action, here's where to go.

Auto Racing. NHRA drag racing takes place at Pomona Raceway (www .pomonaraceway.com) at the L.A. County Fairplex (800-884-6472). NASCAR, CART, Grand American Road Racing Association, IRL, and US Superbike races run at Auto Club Speedway in Fontana (800-944-7223; www.autoclubspeedway .com). Stock cars, midgets' legends, and trucks hit the track at Toyota Speedway at Irwindale (626-358-1100; www.toyotaspeedwayatirwindale.com).

Baseball. Head downtown for Chavez Ravine and Dodger Stadium, 1000 Elysian Park Ave. (866-DODGERS; www.dodgers.com), home of the MLB National League Los Angeles Dodgers. For an amazing VIP experience behind home plate, ask about the Dugout Club!

Basketball. The NBA champion Los Angeles Lakers (www.lakers.com), the NBA Los Angeles Clippers (213-742-7555; www.clippers.com), and the WNBA Los Angeles Sparks (www.wnba.com/sparks) all play round ball at the sparkling Staples Center, 1111 South Figueroa St. (www.staplescenter.com). For ticket information call (213) 742-7340.

Hockey. The Staples Center ices down and plays host to the NHL's Los Angeles Kings (888-KINGS-LA; www.lakings.com).

Soccer. The MLS Los Angeles Galaxy and Club Deportivo Chivas USA (877-244-8271) take to the field at the Home Depot Center, 18400 Avalon Blvd., Carson (www.homedepotcenter.com). For tickets call (877) 342-5299. The center has a 27,000-seat soccer stadium, 8,000-seat tennis stadium, 10,000-seat track-and-field facility, and a 2,450-seat indoor velodrome. The center is also home to Major League Lacrosse's (MLL) Los Angeles Riptide, the US Soccer Federation (USSF), and the United States Tennis Association (USTA), and is an official training site for USA Cycling and USA Track & Field.

Chinatown

Generally bordered by North Broadway and North Hill Streets and Cesar Chavez Avenue (near Union Station).

Chinese shops and restaurants line the "Street of the Golden Treasures" or Gin Ling Way. The Chinese Chamber of Commerce coordinates parades, festivals, and other events. Call (213) 617-0396 for information or visit www.lachinesechamber.org and www.chinatownla.com. The Chinese Heritage and Visitors Center at 415 Bernard St. is open on Sun from noon to 4 p.m. The Chinese Historical Society of Southern California has exhibits documenting the proud history of the Chinese-American community and its many contributions to Southern California and America.

El Pueblo de Los Angeles Historic Monument/Olvera Street
At the heart of El Pueblo de Los Angeles Historic Park, 125 Paseo de la Plaza; (213) 628-1274; www.olvera-street.com. Open Mon through Sat 10 a.m. to 3 p.m. (generally to 8 p.m. in the summer). Shops open 10 a.m. to 7 p.m.

This is an authentic L.A. experience that is ideal for the family. Kids will love the wide variety of brightly colored piñatas—splendid, reasonably priced souvenirs. Don't ask us how you'll get one on the plane or in your trunk. This 44-acre cluster of shops and landmark buildings is the birthplace of Los Angeles. Every day seems to be Cinco de Mayo at El Pueblo, located at the site of a Spanish farming village founded in 1781. Kids and adults alike may be surprised to learn Los Angeles was actually a Mexican city from 1835 (when Spain ceded it to Mexico) until 1847, when it became American. Nowhere in the city is the proud Spanish heritage kept alive to the extent it is here.

The effect is like making a detour to Mexico without a passport. More than 20 historic buildings line the colorful streets of El Pueblo. One is the Avila Adobe, built in 1818, today the oldest house still standing in Los Angeles. At the center of El Pueblo is La Placita (the Plaza), where the rich Spanish influence is visible in art and architecture. Kids love the old-fashioned candy shops and the sound of mariachi music in the Mexican marketplace. Everyone loves the aroma of Mexican food and the unparalleled sombrero-buying opportunities. Not even Disneyland has atmosphere like this.

Flyaway **Bus Service**

So you're flying into LAX (Los Angeles International Airport)—and don't want to rent a car (now or ever)—or just need to get into downtown, the Westside, or the San Fernando Valley cheaply and without a hassle? Check out the Flyaway Bus—comfortable, large motor coaches running 24/7 (usually every 30 minutes) to and from LAX to downtown's Union Station, Van Nuys in the San Fernando Valley, and Westwood/UCLA. In 2010 adult fares one-way were $7, children 5 to 14 were $5, children under age 5 were free. It's a super value, especially coming into Union Station—where you can connect to so many other alternative transportation options. Plus, new in 2010, the service expanded to Irvine Station, 15215 Barranca Pkwy. in Orange County (fares higher; call for times). For LAX Flyaway locations, schedules, service hours, parking, passenger drop-off/pick-up, and driving directions, dial (866) 435-9529 or visit www.lawa.org.

Experience L.A. **without a Car!**

Start at historic Union Station, 800 North Alameda St. (213-683-6875). First opened in 1939, it's an architectural gumbo of Spanish Mission, Art Deco, and Streamline Moderne styles that somehow fit together. The waiting room has marble floors, wood-beamed ceilings more than 50 feet high, and stunning Art Deco chandeliers. Huge archways lead to patio areas laced with flowering trees—and have been featured in many films, including *The Way We Were*, *Bugsy*, and *Blade Runner*. Union Station welcomes long-distance Amtrak trains (*Coast Starlight, Southwest Chief, Sunset Limited, Texas Eagle*; 800-USA-RAIL or www.amtrak.com); Amtrak children's discounts offer great savings for families. Kids ages 2 to 15 are entitled to a 50 percent discount every day, any day, when traveling with an adult paying full fare. Amtrak has excellent routes in the West, and it's the best way to circumvent the traffic. The train that does it best in Southern California is called the *Pacific Surfliner*, with daily service between San Diego, Los Angeles, Santa Barbara, and San Luis Obispo. Among the attractions along the route are Disneyland, the missions at San Juan Capistrano, Sea World in San Diego, the beaches of Santa Barbara, and bustling Los Angeles, with connections to the Metrolink buses and light rail and DASH shuttles. Metrolink trains run to Ventura, San Bernardino, Orange County, Riverside, and other destinations (www.metrolinktrains.com); plus Los Angeles' Metro subway and light-rail systems (Metro Rail Red, Gold, Blue, Orange, and Green lines; 800-COMMUTE or www.metro.net). The Metro Day Pass makes it easier than ever—you can ride any Metro bus or rail line all day long for just $5. Buy your Day Pass onboard any Metro bus or at any Metro Rail station. You'll get all of L.A. for 5 bucks a day. And here's an added incentive: **Metro Destinations Discounts** is a program for Metro riders to save money at popular destinations, sporting events, concerts, museums, theme parks, shops, and more around Los Angeles County simply by using Metro public transit. For example, at press time, you could save $3 on adult admission and $2 on child admission to the Los Angeles Zoo in Griffith Park by showing your Metro Rail Ticket/Day Pass or Metro Weekly/Monthly Pass. Discounts change month to month; visit www.metro.net/around/destination-discounts for current savings.

DASH shuttle buses (35 cents; children age 4 and younger ride for free and seniors 65-plus are 10 cents) are ideal for navigating all the great sites and scenes car-free. DASH Customer Service: (213) 808-2273; www.ladot transit.com/dash. Leave the driving to someone else—it's the "green" alternative to driving on your trip through Southern California.

Where to Eat

Ciudad. 445 South Figueroa St., Suite 100; (213) 486-5171; www.ciudad-la.com. As long as you are downtown, make it a point to visit this colorful (yellow!), noisy, and always busy restaurant. It has an exciting Latin-inspired menu for adults and a good one for the kids created by Mary Sue Milliken and Susan Feniger, known around these parts as the Two Hot Tamales (and seen on the Food Network). Featuring adventurous cocktails, tapas-style appetizers, homemade desserts, and authentic and new dishes from South America, Central America, Cuba, Spain, and Portugal. Among the choices *para los ninos* are El Cubanao Wedges with roasted pork, ham, Swiss cheese, and pickles, served with fries. $$$

The Original Pantry Cafe. 877 South Figueroa St., downtown Los Angeles; (213) 972-9279; www.pantrycafe.com. This historic downtown L.A. institution (since 1924) is owned by a former mayor of Los Angeles, Richard Riordan. His slogan is "Never closed. Never without a customer!" The restaurant has an incredibly diverse menu of traditional American favorites at exceptional values for L.A.—for example: 2 hotcakes, 1 egg, and potatoes with fresh orange juice for $4.75. Yes, still! Cash only—no credit cards. $–$$

Philippe The Original. 1001 North Alameda St.; (213) 628-3781; www.philippes.com. If the kids' taste buds don't blossom over the prospect of a platter of sushi or sopapillas, you might stroll over to Philippe's, the city's best-known place for classic sandwiches since 1908. Arrive early (before noon) to secure one of the roomy booths and dig into a classic Philippe's French Dip sandwich (beef, pork, ham, lamb, or turkey), a heaping portion of coleslaw or potato salad, and a fresh slice of pie or dish of tapioca pudding

(personal fave) all for under $10. Remember that there are no hamburgers served here, but beer and wine are available for us adults. An added perk: there's **free** parking adjacent to the restaurant, and it's only 2 blocks (easy walk) from Union Station. Open every day from 6 a.m. to 10 p.m. Closed Thanksgiving and Christmas. $–$$

Where to Stay

Millennium Biltmore Hotel. 506 South Grand Ave.; (213) 624-1011 or (800) 245-8673; www.thebiltmore.com. Host to presidents, kings, and Hollywood celebrities since it opened in 1923, the Biltmore's central location puts you and the kids in easy walking/shuttle distance of all the great downtown attractions. This landmark property has 683 luxurious rooms and suites, a full array of concierge services (super babysitting), health club facilities (love the gilded indoor pool), and 5 restaurants and lounges (including fresh sushi at Sai Sai; La Bistecca Italian-style steakhouse, open for dinner daily; and Smeraldi's, which serves breakfast, lunch, and dinner daily and has an excellent children's menu). For a real treat, check out the traditional afternoon tea served daily from 2 to 5 p.m. in the famed Rendezvous Court. $$$$

For More Information

City of Los Angeles. For civic information and assistance, dial 3-1-1 inside city limits or (866) 4-LACITY in Southern California, and visit this special city website for kids' activities: http://lacity.org/SubMenu/KIDS.LAcity .org.

L.A. Inc.—The Los Angeles Convention and Visitors Bureau/Visitor Center. 685 Figueroa St.; (213) 689-8822; www.discover losangeles.com.

Hollywood

Movie stars, glamour, palm tree–lined streets, and excitement in the air—hooray for Hollywood! If downtown is the city's historic center, Hollywood is its heart. For millions around the world, Hollywood *is* Los Angeles, an illusion promoted by movie studios that remains very much alive in these quarters. Although the "Golden Age" of Hollywood is long gone, the 50-foot-high HOLLYWOOD sign still proclaims it to be the entertainment capital of the world. With the exception of the beaches, Hollywood is probably where your kids will have the most fun in greater Los Angeles. For that reason we suggest you spend at least two full days here.

Hollywood & Highland

6801 Hollywood Blvd., corner of Hollywood Boulevard and Highland Avenue; (323) 817-8220 or visitor's center: (323) 467-6412; www.hollywoodandhighland.com. Admission is free. Small fee for parking: $.

Located in the thumping heart of Hollywood, this enormous complex is a must-see that's sure to please everyone in your family somehow! Opened in 2001 and hosting more than 15 million visitors annually, the center features over 60 top retailers, 9 of L.A.'s finest restaurants, 2 popular nightclubs, and Lucky Strike Lanes—and the world-famous Kodak Theatre, home of the Academy Awards ceremonies as well as other notable awards shows, concerts, and events. The on-site Renaissance Hollywood Hotel features 640 sumptuously appointed rooms, including 33 luxury suites and an elegant, mid-century modern decor.

Kodak Theatre

6801 Hollywood Blvd., anchor of the Hollywood & Highland Entertainment Complex; (323) 308-6300 or (323) 308-6363 (box office and guided-tour information); www.kodaktheatre .com. Daily 30-minute guided tours from 10:30 a.m. to 2:30 p.m. (subject to change depending on events scheduled). Be sure to call for tickets in advance since tours fill quickly, with only 20 people allowed per group. Children under 12 must be accompanied by an adult guardian. $$$.

Since opening in November 2001, the theater has hosted a range of prestigious artists and events, including the Academy Awards Ceremonies, Celine Dion, Prince, Elvis Costello, Barry Manilow, American Ballet Theatre, ESPY Awards, and even the *American Idol* finals. Be sure you don't miss this chance to step behind the velvet rope and personally experience the glamour of the permanent home of the Oscar ceremonies. During your tour, you'll see an Oscar statuette, visit the exclusive George Eastman VIP Room (where stars party), view 26 Academy Awards images, learn where this year's Oscar nominees sat (and maybe sit there, too), and gain an insider's view of behind-the-scenes production from friendly, knowledgeable actor/tour guides.

Save Big Bucks with **Hollywood CityPass**

CityPass is the best way to enjoy Hollywood at one low price (up to 50 percent savings off tickets purchased separately). With CityPass, you get to choose four admission tickets to famous attractions, including Hollywood Wax Museum, Starline Tours of Hollywood, Red Line tours, and your choice of Kodak Theatre Guided Tour or the Hollywood Museum in the Historic Max Factor Building. CityPass is good for nine days from first day of use. Visit www.citypass.com or call (888) 330-5008.

Walk of Fame

Hollywood Boulevard from Gower Street to La Brea Avenue and along Vine Street from Yucca to Sunset Boulevard; www.hollywoodchamber.net. Free.

In Hollywood even the sidewalks have stories to tell. This is most visibly apparent on the Walk of Fame. There is no admission charge to stroll along sidewalks with more than 2,000 terrazzo-and-brass stars etched into them. Some stars' famous sidewalk addresses are: 1644 Hollywood Blvd. (Marilyn Monroe), 1719 Vine St. (James Dean), 1750 Vine St. (John Lennon), and 6777 Hollywood Blvd. (Elvis Presley).

El Capitan Theatre

6838 Hollywood Blvd.; (323) 468-8262; www.elcapitantickets.com. Ticket prices vary by seating section. $–$$$$.

Disney and Pacific Theaters restored this historic theater in 1989, now on the National Register of Historic Places. Originally opened in 1926, it is now an exclusive first-run theater for Walt Disney Pictures and hosts live stage shows, world premieres, and other special events that have helped restore showmanship to Hollywood Boulevard. The restored 4/37 Wurlitzer pipe organ—known as the "Mightiest of the Mighty Wurlitzers"—is just one of the jewels of this architectural masterpiece. It is across the street from Mann's Chinese Theatre.

Mann's Chinese Theatre

6925 Hollywood Blvd.; (323) 461-3331; www.manntheatres.com/chinese. $$.

Hollywood doesn't get any more Hollywood than at the unofficial emperor's palace of Hollywood Boulevard. Both the young and young-at-heart revel at the sight of what looks like the entrance to a Chinese imperial fortress. But the main attractions here are in the theater's forecourt, where the handprints, footprints, and signatures of Hollywood celebrities dating from 1927 are quite literally cast in stone. "Gee, Mom, did Rita Hayworth really have such tiny feet?" The proof is in the pavement. VIP Backstage Tours are offered by reservation only seven days a week (323-463-9576).

On busy street corners along Hollywood Boulevard and particularly in front of Mann's Chinese Theatre, you might spot tanned young men and women wearing sun visors and holding clipboards. If they don't approach you, make a point of approaching them: They have passes for movie previews at area studios, and sometimes you are paid to see them. It's a way the studios get audience feedback before films are released and a way for you to learn about an important, if little known, aspect of the entertainment industry.

Madame Tussauds Hollywood

6933 Hollywood Blvd.; (323) 798-1670; www.madametussauds.com. Right next door to Grauman's Chinese Theatre. Open daily at 10 a.m., 364 days of the year, only closed the day of the Academy Awards.

Here you are guaranteed to "meet" almost a hundred celebrities at Hollywood's newest wax-figure attraction. Check them out on blockbuster-movie sets spread over three floors, and take plenty of photos to impress your friends, since these folks are really lifelike—really!

Hollywood Museum in the Historic Max Factor Building

1660 North Highland Ave. at Hollywood Boulevard; (323) 464-7776; www.thehollywood museum.com. Open Wed through Sun, 10 a.m. to 5 p.m.; closed Mon, Tues, and most holidays. $$$.

Housed in the edifice where the wizard of movie makeup worked his magic on motion-picture stars, here is where today you'll find more than 10,000 pieces of show business memorabilia from one hundred years of Tinseltown. The museum features displays of Elvis, Marilyn Monroe, and Johnny Depp, and you know your kids will love the *High School Musical*, *Twilight: New Moon*, *Hannah Montana*, and *Star Trek* exhibits.

Hollywood **Celeb Homes**

If you want a guided tour past Hollywood celeb homes, here are some choices:

Hollywood Tours. 7095 Hollywood Blvd. #705; (800) 789-9575; www.holly woodtours.us. Air-conditioned minivans, open-air trolley, or double-decker buses. Dozens of itineraries including options to see the Hollywood sign up close.

Starline Tours. (323) 463-3333 or (800) 959-3131; www.starlinetours.com. Has 2-hour tours in Beverly Hills and Bel Air. The company promises 40 celebrity homes and offers excellent value on more than 20 other Hollywood/ L.A. itineraries—in business with their infamous double-decker red buses since 1935 (other buses and vans and limos, too!).

Hollywood Guinness World Records Museum

6764 Hollywood Blvd.; (323) 463-6433; www.guinnessattractions.com. Open daily 10 a.m. to midnight. $$.

The museum showcases offbeat testimonials to a wide variety of facts, feats, and incredible achievements. It is located in Hollywood's first movie house, the Hollywood, which is now a National Historic Landmark. Hands-on exhibits include technology, space adventures, and natural phenomena.

Hollywood Wax Museum

6767 Hollywood Blvd.; (323) 462-8860; www.hollywoodwax.com. Open daily from 10 a.m. to midnight. $$.

The wax museum has 220 life-size renditions of celebrated film stars, political leaders, and sports greats. Park at the rear of the building and visit all the museums at one stop. For a discount, purchase one ticket for both the wax museum and the Guinness museum.

Ripley's Believe It or Not! Odditorium (ages 5 and up)

6780 Hollywood Blvd.; (323) 466-6335; www.ripleys.com. Open 10 a.m. to 10 p.m. daily, later on weekends and in summer. $$.

No problem finding the place; there's a giant Tyrannosaurus rex poking his mighty head and substantial torso out of the rooftop. The Odditorium claims to have the world's most outstanding collection of the bizarre and unusual, and it probably does. Kids love the innovative special effects, which actually help them learn some quirky facts of history they'd really have to dig for in schoolbooks.

Capitol Records

1750 North Vine St.; http://capitolrecords.com. **Free.**

This circular "stack of 45 RPMs" style landmark building is one of Hollywood's most recognized icons. The light on its rooftop spire flashes "Hollywood" in Morse code. In the lobby, gold albums of many Capitol recording artists, such as John Lennon and Garth Brooks, are displayed.

Hollywood Toys and Costumes

6600 Hollywood Blvd.; (323) 464-4444; www.hollywoodtoys.com. Open daily. **Free.**

Here's where kids can find that monster mask they won't find back home or that conversation-starter costume perfect for next Halloween. There are tiaras in all shapes and sizes and novelties too numerous to describe. In town since 1950, this has to be the biggest supermarket of Hollywood-inspired memorabilia and trinkets.

Hollywood Bowl and Hollywood Bowl Museum

2301 North Highland; (323) 850-2000; www.hollywoodbowl.org. Visit the museum Oct through June, Tues through Sat 10 a.m. to 4:30 p.m. and July through Sept, Tues through Sat 10:30 a.m. to 8:30 p.m. **Free.**

The summer home of the Los Angeles Philharmonic Orchestra, the bowl is a terrific place to take in a concert. *Pollstar* magazine's Best Major Outdoor Venue (2004–2009), the Hollywood Bowl is the largest natural outdoor amphitheater in the United States. Pack a picnic to get the most out of an outdoor performance at this gleaming Los Angeles landmark.

Hollywood's Rock Walk of Fame

7425 West Sunset Blvd., in the outer lobby of Hollywood's Guitar Center; (323) 874-1060; www.rockwalk.com. Open Mon through Fri 10 a.m. to 9 p.m., Sat 10 a.m. to 6 p.m., and Sun 11 a.m. to 6 p.m. Free.

Inductees include Black Sabbath, Elvis Presley, Johnny Cash, Bo Diddley, the Doobie Brothers, Jimi Hendrix, and Eddie Van Halen, just to name a few.

Where to Eat & Stay

Renaissance Hollywood Hotel & Spa. 1755 North Highland Ave.; (323) 856-1200; www.renaissancehollywood.com. This hospitality cornerstone of the stunning Hollywood & Highland complex features 632 sumptuously appointed rooms and suites with elegant, mid-century modern decor and green, ecoconscious amenities. We love the view from the rooftop outdoor pool (and the views from most of the guest rooms are pretty righteous as well—especially of the Hollywood Hills). You'll love the luxurious amenities and being able to walk with the progeny to all the local attractions (and to come back and take a nap in between adventures!). $$$$

Musso & Frank Grill. 6667 Hollywood Blvd.; (323) 467-5123. Open 11 a.m. to 11 p.m.; closed Sun and Mon. A Hollywood institution where movers and shakers have "done deals" over classic flannel cakes, steaks, and Thursday-only chicken potpies since 1919. Whether you go for the atmosphere or the food, you simply must go to say you've been! For kicks, request table number 1 in the west room; this was Charlie Chaplin's regular place. $$

Pink's. 709 North La Brea Ave. (corner of Melrose and La Brea); (323) 931-4223; www .pinkshollywood.com. Open daily 9:30 a.m. to 2 a.m. (sometimes later).You can't miss the line that has wrapped around this pink building since it opened in 1939, where they serve probably the best chili dog in L.A. Chili dogs, chili fries, chili burgers, turkey dogs, burrito dogs—every imaginable presentation of the wiener can be found here. No matter what time of day or night, you will find yourself standing in line with tourists, corporate climbers, and celebrities. Cash only. $

For More Information

Hollywood Chamber of Commerce. 7018 Hollywood Blvd.; (213) 469-8311; www.holly woodchamber.net.

The Hollywood Visitor Information Center. 6801 Hollywood Blvd.; (323) 467-6412; www.discoverlosangeles.com. Open Mon through Fri 8:30 a.m. to 5 p.m. Pick up the **free** handy pocket guides on dining, shopping, and entertainment in Los Angeles County.

Griffith Park

Located just west of the Golden State Freeway (I-5), roughly between Los Feliz Boulevard to the south and the Ventura Freeway (Highway 134) to the north; www.lacity.org. Open to the public from 6 a.m. to 10 p.m. daily. Bridle trails, hiking paths, and mountain roads are closed at sunset. Attractions and activities include Autry National Center, bicycle rentals, Greek Theatre, a merry-go-round, Griffith Observatory, L.A. Equestrian Center, L.A. Live Steamers Railroad Museum, L.A. Zoo, pony rides, and Travel Town.

Los Angeles Zoo

Griffith Park, Golden State Freeway at Ventura Freeway, downtown; (323) 644-6400; www .lazoo.org. Open daily from 10 a.m. to 5 p.m. $$.

Let your kids run wild in this 120-acre parklike setting where 1,200-plus mammals, birds, and reptiles from around the world now reside. Don't miss the Children's Discovery Center and Winnick Family Children's Zoo, Chimpanzees of Mahale Mountain, and World of Birds, all accessible via a tram around the perimeter. Campo Gorilla Reserve provides the gorillas with an environment that closely resembles their native West African homeland. There are seven cafes located throughout the zoo that feature a wide variety of meals suitable for almost everyone, so nobody can get too hungry when you see the animals being fed!

Griffith Observatory

2800 East Observatory Rd.; (213) 473-0800; www.griffithobservatory.org. Admission to the observatory building and grounds is free. There is a nominal charge to see shows in the Samuel Oschin Planetarium.

Colonel Griffith J. Griffith certainly had a clear vision for the public observatory that bears his name—specifying in his will that it be located in a prominent hilltop location on Mount Wilson and offer **free** public telescopes, a science theater, and exhibits featuring the best of new and classic astronomical wonders. Check out the **Samuel Oschin Planetarium,** now with a new dome, star projector, digital laser projectors, seats, sound system, and lighting, especially the show *Centered in the Universe*, which is scheduled every hour. Public telescopes, both optical and solar, are offered for **free** public viewing each day and evening when skies are clear and the building is open. Roughly 7 million people have looked through the observatory's 12-inch Zeiss telescope, more than have gazed through any other telescope on Earth. The triple-beam solar telescope is one of the largest such public instruments in the world. Your kids (and probably you, too) will be amazed at the new Robert J. and Suzanne Gottlieb Transit Corridor. This humongous 150-foot-long, 10-foot-wide glass-walled passageway depicts the motions of the sun, moon, and stars across the sky, and demonstrates how these motions are linked with time and the calendar. You can refresh yourself at the Café at the End of the Universe during your visit.

Autry National Center

4700 Western Heritage Way; (323) 667-2000; www.autry-museum.org. Open Tues through Sun 10 a.m. to 5 p.m. $$.

The Autry National Center celebrates the American West through three important institutions: the Museum of the American West, the Southwest Museum of the American Indian, and the Institute for the Study of the American West. The Autry was established in 2003 following the merger of the Southwest Museum, the Women of the West Museum, and the Museum of the American West (formerly the Autry Museum of Western Heritage that opened in 1988). Thousands of Old West artifacts and hands-on exhibits are here, including many designed with children in mind. Special exhibits explore America's western heritage, including Native American culture, early tourism, and weaving. Check out the Golden Spur Café for great grub.

Travel Town

Griffith Park, 5200 Zoo Dr.; (323) 662-5874. Open weekdays 10 a.m. to 4 p.m., weekends 10 a.m. to 5 p.m. Free admission. Rides $; donations appreciated.

Since 1952, kids have loved this outdoor transportation museum with steam locomotives to scramble over and Live Steamers, a large collection of miniature trains.

Universal City/North Hollywood

North of downtown Los Angeles, and known as "Gateway to the San Fernando Valley," this dynamic area has a population of more than 210,000 and is headquarters to entertainment industry giants such as NBC Universal Studios Hollywood, The Walt Disney Company, Warner Brothers, DreamWorks SKG, Academy of Television Arts & Sciences, Nickelodeon Animation Studios, and CBS Studio Center. For more info, contact the Universal City/North Hollywood Chamber of Commerce at (818) 508-5155 or www.noho.org. For our families, it's home to a not-to-be-missed movie-based theme park and incredible entertainment.

Universal Studios Hollywood

100 Universal City Plaza (Universal Center Drive or Lankershim Boulevard from the 101 Hollywood Freeway); (818) 622-3801 or (800) UNIVERSAL; www.universalstudioshollywood .com. Open daily 9 a.m. to 6 p.m.; expanded hours for summer and holidays. $$$$.

Ask about special values and packages including the "All You Can Eat Pass." Universal Studios is an integral part of L.A.'s history. And while another version is now in Florida, for Southern Californians there is but one Universal Studios. They are always adding mega-attractions—some of the latest are King Kong 360/3D; blockbuster TV series–based The Simpsons Ride; Universal's World of Entertainment (never-before-seen props, costumes, wardrobe, and artifacts, with special-effects displays from the latest to the earliest films amassed from the Universal Pictures film library); the Adventures of Curious George, a 30,000-square-foot interactive play zone featuring Curious George Flies to Space (where you can get drenched as you wait in the blast-off zone, but thankfully, there is a dry zone),

Universal Studios Hollywood
VIP Experience Tour

For the ultimate insider's perspective on the world's largest movie and television studio as well as genuine hospitality and personal special treatment, treat yourself and your family to the VIP Experience tour. You will have your own private tour escort (with encyclopedic knowledge) for the entire day (only 15 people per group) and enjoy front-of-the-line admission and the best views and seating at all attractions and rides. Plus your tour escort will take you deep into the backlot, where you'll have special access to soundstages—many in use by your favorite stars. Best of all, instead of the huge tram, you'll have a private trolley bus that can stop and let you out to take pictures. Feel like a movie star yourself. It's expensive but worth the truly VIP experience! For more information call (800) UNIVERSAL, option 3.

Curious George Goes to the Jungle, and Curious George Visits the Zoo. Also be sure to check out the cutting-edge roller coaster Revenge of the Mummy—the Ride, Shrek 4-D, House of Horrors, Backdraft, and Jurassic Park—The Ride (you will get soaked!).

But it's the classics that make Universal a genuine blast for both kids and adults. The staple is the 45-minute tram ride (catch one every 5 to 10 minutes), during which Hollywood history and special effects cast their magical spell. You're whisked past the set from Steven Spielberg's *War of the Worlds*, *Jurassic Park*, and the Norman Bates House (from the movie *Psycho*), over a collapsing bridge, into a Mexican village that falls prey to a flash flood, and through a Red Sea that parts just for you. Then there's a landslide and a simulated fishing village where the naughty shark from the movie *Jaws* surfaces with a vengeance. The tram ride also takes visitors past enormous studio backlots, reminding you that this is the world's biggest film and television studio. Something is almost always in production, and chances are you'll catch a bit of the action—scenes from shows such as *CSI* and *Desperate Housewives* are being filmed here regularly.

Universal CityWalk Hollywood

1000 Universal Center Dr., Universal City; (818) 622-4455; www.citywalkhollywood .com. Open Sun through Thurs 11 a.m. to 9 p.m., Fri and Sat 11 a.m. to midnight. Free **admission.**

An eclectic, electric outdoor pedestrian promenade with an atmosphere made to resemble a studio backlot. There are actually two streets lined with palms and joined by a central courtyard area with fountains. But all is not so sedate: A mammoth King Kong clings to the facade of one building. Get the picture? There are more than 30 retail shops and dozens of restaurants here, including B. B. King's Blues Club and a Hard Rock Cafe. Plus, CityWalk Hollywood boasts 19 movie theaters all with surround-sound, plush stadium-style seating,

Filmed before a **Live Studio Audience**

Hollywood is the place to see the television industry in action. Live studio audiences are always needed. Don't ever pay for TV taping tickets. They are given out free, always by production companies and studio representatives. Remember: Little taping is done during the summer months because shows are on hiatus. There are age requirements for attending most TV show tapings. Most sitcom tapings require audience members to be at least age 18, but game shows and children's variety shows sometimes set the age requirement at age 12. This rule is strictly enforced, so be sure to check in advance. Not all shows use audiences (e.g., most soaps). The more popular the show, the harder it is to get tickets. Comedies shoot a few times a month, usually from September to March. Besides having to show up early to get through security, most tapings last 3 to 6 hours, so allow yourself plenty of extra time. Soundstages generally have bleacher-type seating, and it's sometimes hard to see the action even though you're right in front of the stage, so most stages have video monitors that show what's going on. Most scenes are shot several times, and this can get boring for kids (and adults, too). To help pass the down times between shooting, a comic often entertains the audience. Soundstages are notoriously cold, so bring a sweater—the lights only heat up the actors. Here are some of the best sources for tickets.

Audiences Unlimited, Inc. (www.tvtickets.com). More than 40 sitcom, pilot, and talk-show tickets available. Tickets are offered online starting approximately 30 days prior to show date. This is an excellent website and a good source of information about what to expect, along with maps on how to reach the studios.

TV Tix (www.tvtix.com). This easy-to-navigate website offers tickets to a wide variety of game shows, talk shows, specials, and sitcoms. You can search by date and/or the show you want to see—and print out your ticket selection right away.

Paramount Pictures (5555 Melrose Ave., Hollywood; 323-956-1777; www.paramountstudios.com). This is the only remaining "big name" studio lot still located and operating in Hollywood. If you're up for a non–theme park and want an inside, historic look at a real working studio, Paramount is *the* place for a very special experience. Two-hour guided backlot tours are given Mon through Fri for ages 12 and up by advance reservations only. $$$$. To arrange tickets for TV shows taping at Paramount, contact Audiences Unlimited (see above listing).

and IMAX. For show times, visit www.citywalkhollywood.com/cinemas or call (818) 508-0711. CityWalk also connects to the Gibson Amphitheatre, an outstanding concert and performance venue with no seat more than 150 feet from the stage. Visit www.citywalk-hollywood.com/concerts or call (818) 622-4440 for event schedules.

Where to Stay

Sheraton Universal. 333 Universal Hollywood Dr., Universal City; (818) 980-1212 or reservations (800) 325-3535; www.sheraton.com/universal. A high-rise landmark since 1969 (with a $30 million renovation in 2008). Enjoy 436 rooms and suites with tremendous views. Excellent packages for families. You'll appreciate the **free** shuttle service to Universal Studios. $$$$

Hilton Los Angeles/Universal City Hotel. 555 Universal Hollywood Dr., Universal City; (818) 506-2500; www.hiltonuniversal.com. Rated AAA four-diamonds, this 24-story hotel high on the hilltop is located right at the main entrance to Universal Studios, central to all the action in greater L.A. Full-service property has all the amenities you expect in 482 rooms and suites with stunning views. Check out the award-winning **Café Sierra,** voted California's Number One Seafood & Prime Rib Buffet. $$$$

Sportsmen's Lodge Hotel. 12825 Ventura Blvd., Studio City; (818) 769-4700 or (800) 821-8511; www.slhotel.com. A valley classic since 1962, the lodge has 200 recently renovated country-style rooms, Olympic-size heated outdoor pool with large lounge deck, and the Patio Café for reasonably priced breakfast, lunch, and dinner daily; plus **free** Universal Studios shuttle and discount tickets for guests. $$$

West Hollywood

Pop-culture types regard West Hollywood (incorporated in 1984), while small by Los Angeles standards (just 1.9 square miles), as the creative center of L.A. This enclave, bordered by Beverly Hills on the west, is a trendy one that will appeal to older, more "cool-conscious" kids. Unpredictable and irreverent, West Hollywood-ites work and play by their own rules (of which there aren't many). Situated at the base of the Hollywood Hills, "WeHo" is known as the place where the stars come out to play. Few drives in Los Angeles are as exhilarating as Sunset Boulevard. Originating downtown, Sunset winds through WeHo and ends up at the Pacific Ocean. Zipping along its famous curves in Beverly Hills, you'll see stunning mansions and gorgeous gardens at every turn. But the most famous stretch, hands down, is the Sunset Strip, directly after Beverly Hills in West Hollywood. The heart of the action, the 1.2-mile portion between numbers 8221 and 9255 is the mecca of L.A. nightlife. Celebrities are sighted so often here that they hardly raise eyebrows. After cruising Sunset (preferably in a convertible), park your car **free** at 8600 Sunset Plaza, an open-air mall. From here you can see the entire city of L.A. teeming and (if it's night time) twinkling below.

Where to Eat

House of Blues. 8430 Sunset Blvd.; (323) 848-5100; www.hob.com. Open Wed to Sat 6 p.m. until close; Sun to Tues closed unless there is a concert. Take the kids to dinner at this Sunset Strip hot spot. Great Southern cooking, wild decor, and live blues performances will make for an unforgettable evening. The House of Blues Restaurant is the best compromise if you wish to steer the kids clear of the area's irresponsibly loud and obscenely crowded evening concerts. To enjoy the decor (recycled bottle caps, auto license tags, etc.), take your time. Don't leave without pigging out on a warm apple tart with vanilla ice cream and caramel sauce. Afterwards, work off those calories by simply strolling along the boulevard's trendy boutiques, sidewalk cafes, and record stores—all aglow under a sea of neon lights. $$

Mel's Drive-In. 8585 Sunset Blvd.; (310) 854-7201; www.melsdrive-in.com. Formerly Ben Frank's diner (that opened in 1952), this Mel's location opened in 1997 but still looks like the classic 1950s kitsch-and-neon joint made famous by the movie *American Graffiti*. Open 24 hours, it cannot be beat for burgers, fries, and shakes. A bonus is the 50-seat outdoor patio, perfect for people-watching and soaking up the sunshine. $

Where to Stay

Le Parc Suite Hotel. 733 North West Knoll Dr., (310) 855-8888 or (800) 5-SUITES; www.leparcsuites.com. Nestled in a charming, residential area on a tree-lined street, yet only blocks from all the action of WeHo. This 154-all-suite property is a perfect respite from L.A.'s hustle/bustle/go-go-go, attracting both a leisure and entertainment-industry clientele. The suites range from 650 to 1,000 square feet and all have a fireplace, kitchenette with microwave, refrigerator, coffeemaker, and 2 flat-screen TVs with DVD/CD players. You'll really catch the Hollywood vibe from the Rooftop Skydeck featuring a heated pool, whirlpool, and those cute cabanas for privacy. There's **free** Wi-Fi throughout LeParc, plus a gym, spa, tennis court, and Knoll—an intimate 42-seat restaurant serving breakfast, lunch, and dinner daily, best for us adults. Kids and your pets are all welcome at this upscale, yet very family-friendly enclave. $$$$

For More Information

West Hollywood Marketing and Visitors Bureau. 8687 Melrose Ave., Suite M-38; (310) 289-2525 or (800) 368-6020; www.visitwesthollywood.com.

Westside

In this immense, loosely defined swath of the city, punctuated by estates and eateries, museums and boutiques, trendiness reigns supreme. Here you may quite acceptably judge your neighbors according to where they "do lunch." You're probably more apt to bump into a celebrity in the Westside than in Hollywood, and if you spend only 5 minutes driving around tony Beverly Hills, you'll find out why. There is one (perhaps only one) rule in these parts: If you've got it, flaunt it—and preferably in style. And the sheer amount of wealth people have here simply must be seen to be believed, even in these economically challenging times. No tour of the Westside would be complete without visiting Westwood

Getty **Center**

Located at 1200 Getty Center Dr.; (310) 440-7300; www.getty.edu. Open Tues through Thurs and Sun 10 a.m. to 6 p.m. and Fri and Sat 10 a.m. to 9 p.m. Closed Mon and major holidays. Admission is **free.** Parking is $8. This landmark complex on a dramatic hilltop location commands breathtaking views of Los Angeles, the Santa Monica Mountains, and the Pacific. Its vast collection of art defies imagination. The 110-acre complex, designed by Richard Meier, is designed as a nexus for families and neighbors, as well as scholars and students. It all begins with a tram ride to the summit, where your family will be awed by panoramic views of the L.A. area. The center will fascinate every family member, even the two-year-olds in strollers with microscopic attention spans. At the central plaza, you'll find gardens, terraces, and dramatic architecture and a wonderful cafe.

Start your exploration by viewing the orientation film so you can best decide how to spend the next few hours. There are five 2-story pavilions around an open courtyard. Each gallery pavilion has an information room: Stop here to watch an artist carve a block of marble or have your kids handle a piece of wood. These hands-on experiences are accentuated by ongoing films, concerts, and demonstrations. Try to visit on the weekends when family festivals give you and your kids "new ideas about the cultures and people behind the art."

Just to give you a hint of the magnitude of the collection, there are 14 galleries of French furniture and decorative arts, including four 18th-century paneled rooms.

For more Getty art, check out the Getty Villa in Malibu, approximately 25 miles west of downtown L.A. (See the Malibu section for more information.)

Village, a vibrant neighborhood just west of Beverly Hills bounded by Wilshire Boulevard, the 405 (San Diego Freeway), and the UCLA (University of California, Los Angeles; www.ucla.edu) campus, where you can enjoy visiting the Botanical Garden, the Sculpture Garden, the Hammer Museum—a cutting-edge arts institution—and the Fowler Museum of Cultural History. UCLA's presence imbues Westwood with a youthful air. It is an ideal area for walking around, browsing in record stores, or simply "hanging out" at a cafe or ice-cream parlor. You may even run into a movie premiere or opening night at one of its many live theaters. For example, **The Hammer Museum** (10899 Wilshire Blvd.; 310-443-7000; www.hammer.ucla.edu) is known for impressionist, historic, and current art. The museum's also home to the **Billy Wilder Theater,** which along with the nearby **Geffen Playhouse** (10886 Le Conte Ave.; 310-208-5454; www.geffenplayhouse.com) presents wide-ranging original and familiar productions.

Museum Row

Stretching along the "Miracle Mile" of busy Wilshire Boulevard, Museum Row is the home of a singularly fun and educational selection of family-worthy museums.

Page Museum at the La Brea Tar Pits

5801 Wilshire Blvd.; (323) 934-7243; www.tarpits.org. Open Mon through Fri 9:30 a.m. to 5 p.m. and Sat, Sun, and holidays 10 a.m. to 5 p.m. $$; free admission on the first Tuesday of the month.

The La Brea Tar Pits are a black and slightly malodorous lake of ancient goo that trapped thousands of Ice Age creatures. More than a hundred tons worth of their fossilized remains have been extracted from the pits, and new discoveries are always being made. Dozens of saber-toothed tiger and wolf skulls, woolly mammoth skeletons, and other specimens are on display in the 57,000-square-foot museum. This is educational, unadulterated magic for adults and the under-12 crowd. You might recall the pits erupting in the film *Volcano*. Don't worry, the site is perfectly benign.

Los Angeles County Museum of Art

5905 Wilshire Blvd.; (323) 857-6000; www.lacma.org. Open Mon, Tues, and Thurs noon to 8 p.m., Fri noon to 9 p.m., Sat and Sun 11 a.m. to 8 p.m.; closed Wed. $$.

Explore a collection with more than 100,000 works of art at LACMA, the anchor museum for Museum Row and the largest encyclopedic museum west of Chicago. Experience European masterpieces, cutting-edge contemporary art, an extensive collection of American art from the United States and Latin America, a major Islamic art collection, one of the most comprehensive Korean art collections outside of Korea, and the stunning Pavilion for Japanese art. In February 2008, the Broad Contemporary Art Museum (BCAM) opened here, a $56-million, 3-story museum that you start visiting from the top down. Music, film, and educational events happen year-round, and there's a good chance something is happening during your stay. LACMA's "transformation" project is just that, and you don't want to miss it.

Petersen Automotive Museum

6060 Wilshire Blvd.; (323) 930-2277; www.petersen.org. Open Tues through Sun 10 a.m. to 6 p.m. $$, children 5 and younger free.

This museum, opened in 1997 and already a landmark by virtue of its striking, futuristic design, celebrates L.A.'s icon, the automobile—and its history and role in the development of Southern California. In its 300,000 square feet of exhibition space, you'll find more than 200 cars and motorcycles, plus loads of fascinating automotive memorabilia.

Farmers Market

6333 West Third St., a few footsteps north of Museum Row; (323) 933-9211; www.farmers marketla.com. Open Mon through Fri 9 a.m. to 9 p.m., Sat 9 a.m. to 8 p.m., and Sun 10 a.m. to 7 p.m. Some merchant hours may vary. **Free** entrance.

This is the Westside's answer to downtown's Grand Central Market, with 70 leased stalls of grocers, restaurants, produce stands, and retail stores thriving since 1934 (still owned and operated by the Gilmore family). Be sure to check out Kip's Toyland, Bennett's Ice Cream (where you can watch them make it), Thee's Continental Pastries (decorates cakes in the window), and more.

The Grove

189 The Grove Dr., adjacent to the Farmers Market at Third and Fairfax, 90036; (888) 315-8883 or (323) 900-8080; www.thegrovela.com. Open Mon through Thurs 10 a.m. to 9 p.m., Fri and Sat 10 a.m. to 10 p.m., and Sun 11 a.m. to 8 p.m.

Featuring more than a hundred of the finest retail emporiums, cafes, and 14 luxury movie theaters, and anchored by Nordstrom, The Grove is one of L.A.'s most "happening" places to see and be seen (you'll probably trip over a TMZ.com crew here most days). Don't miss the Dancing Fountain that shoots 32 pulsing water jets to heights of 60 feet every 30 minutes accompanied by hip music in the center courtyard.

Museum of Tolerance

At the Simon Wiesenthal Center, Simon Wiesenthal Plaza, 9786 West Pico Blvd., between Century City and Beverly Hills; (310) 553-8403; www.wiesenthal.com or www.museumof tolerance.com. Open Mon through Fri 10 a.m. to 5 p.m., and Sun 11 a.m. to 5 p.m. Closed every Sat, Jewish holidays, January 1, July 4, Thanksgiving, and December 25. Some exhibits recommended for kids ages 12 and older. Tickets are available for specific times and for specific exhibits. Pre-paid advance reservations are recommended to ensure admittance to the museum. $$

Founded in 1993, MOT is a one-of-a-kind facility that offers a series of high-tech exhibits dedicated to the promotion of understanding among people from all backgrounds and walks of life. Both children and adults will leave the museum enlightened and moved by history and the dangers of forgetting it.

The Skirball Cultural Center and Museum

2701 North Sepulveda Blvd.; (310) 440-4500; www.skirball.org. Open Tues through Fri noon to 5 p.m. and Sat and Sun 10 a.m. to 5 p.m. Closed Mon. $$, children younger than 2 admitted **free.**

This museum highlights the experiences of American Jews as they transitioned from the Old World to the New World. Do not miss the Noah's Ark experience—inspired by the ancient flood story, which has parallels in diverse cultures around the world. While visiting the galleries, meet a puppet, create a take-home art project, or hear a story. For lunch, Zeidlers, at the museum entrance, can't be beat, and the gift shop here has an impressive range of books covering the Jewish experience, with an excellent selection of books for children.

Where to Stay

Hilgard House Hotel & Suites. 927 Hilgard Ave.; (310) 208-3945; www.hilgardhouse.com. This small hotel located at the edge of the UCLA campus and within walking distance of Westwood Village has traditional European decor plus **free** parking, **free** continental breakfast, and **free** wireless in every guest room. And, perfect for families or for extended stays, one- and two-bedroom suites with full kitchens are available. $$

Where to Eat

Apple Pan. 10801 West Pico Blvd.; (310) 475-3585. Closed Mon. Here's a diner of sorts that has been feeding hungry Angelinos since the 1940s. The layout is simple: a long, three-sided countertop with a kitchen in the center. Wait for a vacant stool (there are no tables), then move in for the kill: The burgers served here are so divine they have been known to reconvert vegetarians. Many visit for the apple pie (it's the Apple Pan, after all), but the banana cream is also really luscious. $

Factor's Famous Deli. 9420 West Pico Blvd.; (310) 278-9175; www.factorsdeli.com. Open 7 a.m. to midnight daily. A favorite gathering place for Westsiders since 1948; take a seat in a booth or in the garden patio and enjoy all the traditional deli fare, including homemade soups and salads, and people watch to your heart's content. **Free** wireless Internet. $$

Eiger Ice Cream. 124 East Barrington Place, off Sunset Boulevard and North Barrington Avenue; (310) 471-6955. Hours vary daily. The decor is minimalist; the ice cream is not. With an 18 percent butterfat content, we're talking ice crème de la crème here. Most flavors, including the ever-popular dark chocolate and raspberry combo, taste surprisingly light because of the purity of the ingredients. No wonder Eiger is a favorite snack spot for quality-conscious Westside families. Cash only. $

Beverly Hills

If you continue west on Wilshire Boulevard, you will enter the heart of Beverly Hills. The chief appeal of this city (population 34,000) for many families will be strolling up and down Rodeo (row-DAY-oh) Drive, a scaled-down version of New York's Fifth Avenue, albeit with palm trees. It's fun to do a little window shopping at the most exclusive boutiques in Los Angeles. This is the center of the Golden Triangle district, framed by Crescent Drive and Wilshire and Little Santa Monica Boulevards, which represents the crème de la crème of Beverly Hills shopping. Two Rodeo (www.2rodeo.com), adjacent to Rodeo Drive, is a cobblestoned cache of shops and eateries at the Wilshire Boulevard end that resembles a charming European village.

After the price tags make you wonder who in the world can afford all of this stuff, hop in your car and find out. The gracefully curving palm- and jacaranda-lined streets between Santa Monica and Sunset Boulevards are home to affluent Mediterranean-style villas and many an elegant English Tudor–style mansion. North of Sunset, however, especially in the exclusive Bel Air neighborhood farther west on the boulevard, is where the real estate truly boggles the mind.

Beverly Hills Trolley Tours

Catch these trolleys on the southeast corner of Rodeo Drive and Dayton Way; (310) 285-2442; www.beverlyhills.org. Sat and Sun, 11 a.m. to 4 p.m. year-round; Tues to Sun from July 7 through Aug 31. $$.

These 40-minute narrated tours are a great way to get your bearing of the downtown center while learning about the city's architecture, history, and renowned areas.

Paley Center for Media

465 North Beverly Dr.; (310) 786-1000; www.paleycenter.org. Open Wed through Sun noon to 5 p.m.; closed on January 1, July 4, Thanksgiving, and Christmas. **Free** admission. Donations are welcome and suggested.

Previously known as the Museum of Television & Radio, the Paley Center was founded in 1975 by William S. Paley, a pioneering innovator in the industry. More than 140,000 archived broadcasts (duplicating the first museum founded in New York City) reside in this museum, which opened in 1996. Everything you and your family want to know about 80-plus years of broadcasting is here. Special exhibits and screenings year-round. Call for schedules and times.

Where to Eat & Stay

Nate 'n Al Delicatessen Restaurant. 414 North Beverly Dr.; (310) 274-0101; www.natenal.com. Open daily 7 a.m. to 9 p.m. Since 1945, serving top-notch smoked fish, cured meats, and matzo ball soup to hungry locals, visitors, celebrities, and families in a bustling, joyous atmosphere. Don't miss the matzo brei, potato latkes, corned beef brisket, and anything made with pastrami. $$

Sprinkles Cupcakes. 9635 South Santa Monica Blvd.; (310) 274-8765; www.sprinkles.com. Open 9 a.m. to 7 p.m. Mon to Sat, and 10 a.m. to 6 p.m. Sun. This is the store that started the cupcake phenomenon, when maven Candace Nelson opened her first cupcake-only bakery here in 2005. Pull up a chair at the cupcake bar and enjoy any of the myriad hand-crafted, freshly iced flavors, from banana to lemon coconut—and, of course, chocolate! Indulge yourself (and the kids!). $$

Beverly Wilshire, A Four Seasons Hotel. 9500 Wilshire Blvd.; (310) 275-5200, www.fourseasons.com/beverlywilshire. This 386-room and -suite world-class hotel is an oasis of elegance and impeccable service located at one of the world's most famous intersections—Wilshire Boulevard and Rodeo Drive (this place was featured in the movie *Pretty Woman*, starring Julia Roberts, remember?). When making your reservation, tell the agent the ages of your kids and they will receive complimentary welcome gifts like toys and cute robes. Family packages are also available. Enjoy a meal in The Blvd restaurant that looks out onto Rodeo Drive, or experience CUT, celebrity chef Wolfgang Puck's award-winning steakhouse. Be warned, it's valet parking only at this hotel and it runs $40 a night. $$$$

For More Information

Beverly Hills Conference and Visitors Bureau. 239 South Beverly Dr.; (800) 345-2210; www.beverlyhillsbehere.com.

The Valleys

Did you think a trip to L.A. would be, like, uh, complete without a visit to the valleys? Think again, dude! The valleys are worlds unto themselves.

When you hear people talk about "the Valley," they are referring to the San Fernando Valley, home of more than a million people and bigger than metropolitan Chicago. You can get an overview of the valley from serpentine Mulholland Drive, which bisects the Santa Monica Mountains, the natural topographical separator of the Los Angeles Basin from the vast valley floor.

If you have time for an outdoor interlude, by all means explore the Santa Monica Mountains National Recreation Area. These chaparral-covered slopes, which stretch 55 miles from Griffith Park all the way to Point Mugu in Ventura County, have provided the backdrop for many a Hollywood movie. For instance, *M*A*S*H* (movie and TV show) was filmed at Malibu Creek State Park (alongside Las Virgenes Road/Malibu Canyon) and at Paramount Ranch, Agoura Hills, 1813 Cornell Rd. (805-370-2301). The latter, once owned by Paramount Studios, still has the fabricated western town used in dozens of films and TV shows. Horseback riding and nature walks through the canyons covering 2,400 acres also make for refreshing mini-escapes from the city's bustle.

The **Canyons**

Coldwater Canyon (which connects Beverly Hills to Studio City) and, about 10 miles to the west, Topanga Canyon (connecting Malibu to Woodland Hills) are sights to see. Topanga is a Chumash Indian word meaning "mountains that crash down to the sea." You'll see what the Chumash meant if you drive the length of the canyon. If you park your car along any of the turnouts along the road and look closely at the exposed mountain sides, you may well see fossils of ancient sea creatures—proof positive the whole area was once under water.

The intersection of Topanga and Old Topanga Canyon Roads is marked by the village of—no surprise here—Topanga, with its health-food stores, hippie feel, and more. One place you'll want to visit is the Will Geer Theatricum Botanicum, 1419 North Topanga Canyon Blvd., 5 miles from Highway 101 (310-455-2322 or 310-455-3723; www.theatricum.com), an open-air ancient Greek–style amphitheater that features first-rate performances of Shakespearean works and other classics and Kids Koncerts & Creative PlayGround from June to October. This outdoor theater offers more than culture. It occupies a natural setting with a youth drama camp, youth classes, and a variety of plays. Call ahead for seasonal schedule.

If you have more time, explore the stretch of miles-long Ventura Boulevard, which bisects Encino and Sherman Oaks. Together with Highway (the Ventura Freeway), "the Boulevard" is the valley's main artery. Of the two, Encino has the more up-market sections, whereas Sherman Oaks (along Ventura Boulevard) has a myriad of avant-garde establishments that your tweens and teens will love.

Burbank

Among the largest cities in California (population 100,000-plus) is Burbank, known as the home of major film and television studios, a bustling airport, and shopping malls. Many jokes have been made by television shows that emanate from here about "beautiful downtown Burbank," but you and your family will want to visit those studios.

Warner Bros. Studio VIP Tour (ages 8 and up)

3400 Riverside Dr., Gate 6, VIP Tour Center; (818) 972-8687; www.wbstudiotour.com. Tours generally Mon through Fri 9 a.m. to 3 p.m., with expanded hours in summer. Call for schedule. Reservations are required. $$$.

This is an insider's look at a very busy and famous motion picture and television studio— past and present. The tour begins with a short film highlighting the movies and television shows created by Warner Bros. talent. Then, via electric tour carts to the Warner Bros. Museum and from the museum, you visit backlot sets, soundstages, and craft/production shops. Routes change from day to day to accommodate production on the lot, so no two tours are exactly alike. Tours last approximately 2.5 hours. Deluxe Tours (5 hours) including lunch in the Studio Commissary ($$$$) are also available.

NBC TV Studios (ages 5 and up)

3000 West Alameda Ave.; (818) 840-3537 or (818) 840-4444. $$.

Escorted 70-minute walking tours are generally available on a first-come, first-served basis Mon through Fri, every hour on the hour between 9 a.m. and 3 p.m. The guest relations bungalow opens at 8:30 a.m. If you're lucky, you might see Jay Leno on the lot. Be sure to call for current tour schedules and fees, as many NBC shows are now filming at Universal Studios (owner of NBC).

Where to Eat & Stay

Marriott Burbank Airport Hotel & Convention Center. 2500 Hollywood Way; (818) 843-6000; www.marriottburbankairport.com. Located across the street from the Burbank Bob Hope Airport (the airport closest to Hollywood, Universal Studios, NBC, and ABC).

Free airport shuttle service. An excellent "home base" for exploring greater L.A., it has 488 comfortable rooms and 77 suites, 2 large heated pools, the Daily Grill restaurant, Starbucks in the lobby, and friendly staff to assist with your travel plans. $$$

Bob's Big Boy. 4211 Riverside Dr.; (818) 843-9334; www.bobs.net. Open 24 hours. Built in 1949, this iconic restaurant is the oldest remaining Bob's Big Boy in America. The towering 70-foot Bob's sign is an integral part of the building design and still is its most prominent feature. Breakfast at Bob's is served anytime you want it, but sometimes you just hunger for a Big Boy—the original double-decker hamburger with two all-beef patties on a grilled sesame-seed bun with crisp shredded lettuce, American cheese, special dressing, and relish—or a Bob's milkshake made 1950s-style with real ice cream and served in a silver tin goblet that comes with your order. Make sure your kids have this authentic experience—it's a tradition for us! $

For More Information

Burbank Chamber of Commerce. 200 West Magnolia Blvd.; (818) 846-3111; www.burbankchamber.org.

Valencia & Santa Clarita Valley

Just 30 minutes north of Burbank, discover Valencia in the Santa Clarita Valley—home to the Six Flags California Entertainment Complex, a not-to-be-missed area for your thrill-seeking family!

Six Flags Magic Mountain—The Xtreme Park

26101 Magic Mountain Pkwy.; (661) 255-4111; www.sixflags.com/magicmountain. The complex is located off I-5, from the Magic Mountain Parkway exit, 30 minutes north of downtown Los Angeles. Open daily from Mar through Sept; weekends and holidays the rest of the year. Call for exact schedule and opening and closing hours. $$$$.

Known worldwide as a thrill-ride haven, the 260-acre theme park features 16 roller coasters—the most on the planet—and more than a hundred rides, games, and attractions for the entire family. Enjoy such exciting thrill rides as SCREAM; X, the world's first and only 4-dimensional roller coaster; Deja Vu, the world's fastest and tallest suspended, looping boomerang coaster; Goliath, the coaster giant among giants; the Riddler's Revenge, the world's tallest and fastest stand-up roller coaster; Superman the Escape, towering 415 feet in the air; Colossus; Batman the Ride; Viper; and many more. For younger guests there is Bugs Bunny World, featuring rides and attractions that provide real thrills for kids and adults alike; Goliath Junior coaster; and Thomas the Tank Engine, Merrie Melodies Carousel, and Canyon Blaster Coaster for kids and parents together. In addition, meet your favorite Looney Tunes characters—Bugs Bunny, Daffy Duck, Yosemite Sam, and Sylvester. All this in one day!

Six Flags Hurricane Harbor

Located next door to Six Flags Magic Mountain; (661) 255-4100; www.sixflags.com/hurricane harborla. Open weekends May through Aug and daily Memorial Day through Labor Day. Call for exact schedule and times. $$$$.

This tropical-themed water-park attraction features more than 22 slides and attractions, including Tornado, a 6-story, 75-foot funnel, with two of the tallest enclosed speed slides in Southern California; Lizard Lagoon, a 7,000-square-foot pool for teen and adult activities; Bamboo Racer, an exciting 45-foot-tall, 6-lane racing attraction; Castaway Cove, an exclusive children's water-play kingdom; Shipwreck Shores, with water-play activities for the entire family; the Forgotten Sea wave pool; and the River Cruise lazy river. Way cool fun!

For More Information

Santa Clarita Valley Tourism Office. (661) 255-4318 or (800) 868-7398; www.visit
23920 Valencia Blvd., Suite 235, Santa Clarita; santaclarita.com.

Pasadena & San Gabriel Valley

Pasadena is the shining star of the San Gabriel Valley, just 11 miles northeast of downtown L.A. While the annual Tournament of Roses Parade (626-449-4100; www.tournamentof roses.com), held every January 1 since 1890, and Rose Bowl Stadium (626-577-3100; www .rosebowlstadium.com) have made the city famous, they reveal just a tip of the action taking place in a city studded with world-class art collections, vintage landmarks, and jacaranda-lined main streets and boulevards. Welcome to a city with 16 historical districts packed into 23 square miles!

Huntington Library, Art Collections
and Botanical Gardens

1151 Oxford Rd., San Marino (2 miles from Pasadena); (626) 405-2100; www.huntington.org. Open Mon, Wed, Thurs, and Fri noon to 4:30 p.m. and weekends 10:30 a.m. to 4:30 p.m.; closed Tues. $$.

Three art galleries and a library showcase magnificent collections of paintings, sculptures, rare books, manuscripts, and decorative arts. The botanical collection features over 14,000 different species of plants. A private, nonprofit institution, the Huntington was founded in 1919 by railroad and real estate developer Henry Edwards Huntington and opened to the public in 1928. At the 207-acre Huntington, you can walk through perfectly manicured gardens on your way to view a precious scrap of Emily Dickinson poetry or other historical documents and manuscripts. The library is home to many first-edition books, including a Gutenberg Bible. The wonderful exhibits bring history into perspective, reminding us how people managed to communicate before computers. The oil paintings, furniture, and decorative accessories are elegantly displayed. There's a restaurant, the Rose Garden Cafe (enjoy an English tea; 626-683-8131), and an excellent bookshop. The Helen and Peter Bing Children's Garden offers one acre of kinetic sculptures and activities for children ages 2 through 7.

Kidspace Children's Museum (ages 1 to 10)

480 North Arroyo Blvd., Pasadena, across from the Rose Bowl; (626) 449-9144; www.kid spacemuseum.org. Open Sept through May, Tues through Fri 9:30 a.m. to 5 p.m. and Sat and Sun 10 a.m. to 5 p.m. From June through Aug, open every day. Be sure to call for specific holiday hours and special event times. $$.

Features 20 world-class interactive exhibits and 2.2 acres of outdoor learning environments designed to encourage your kids to discover the excitement of learning while engaging in the creativity of play—such as unleashing an earthquake, feeding giant bugs, crafting art through nature, and climbing raindrops 40 feet into the air.

Rose Bowl Flea Market

The Rose Bowl, 1001 Rose Bowl Stadium; (323) 560-7469; www.rgcshows.com/rosebowl. It is held the second Sun of every month, rain or shine. $.

This is "America's Marketplace of Unusual Items," so prepare yourself for a feast of fabulous finds. Featuring over 2,500 vendors and 15,000 to 20,000 buyers each month. Your kids will probably whine about going until they see the variety of toys, food, and unique stuff!

Santa Anita Park (Seabiscuit's Home Stable)

285 West Huntington Dr., Arcadia; (626) 574-7223 or (626) 574-6677; www.santaanita.com. Open Dec through Apr. Free.

Located just a few miles east of Pasadena, Santa Anita Park is more than just a horse racetrack. The architecture is art deco, and the cuisine is outstanding. Thoroughbred racing is the main event at the track, but this 320-acre park is relaxing, exquisitely landscaped,

Old **Pasadena**

From downtown Los Angeles, head north on I-110; I-110 becomes Arroyo Parkway; continue on North Arroyo Parkway to Colorado Boulevard; when you arrive at Colorado Boulevard and Fair Oaks Avenue, you will be in the center of Old Pasadena. Beautifully renovated into an entertainment district showcasing over 200 vintage buildings that take you back to the 1800s, Old Pasadena covers 22 blocks with more than 200 businesses. This revitalized hot spot features art galleries, trendy boutiques, theaters, and an extraordinary choice of restaurants to satisfy every one of your family's desires. For more info, visit www.oldpasadena.org.

and worth the trip. The Seabiscuit tram tour includes riding by Seabiscuit's barn, looking at the locations where the movie *Seabiscuit* was filmed in 2003, observing the daily activities of the stable area, and more. Tours depart from the tram boarding area across from the receiving barn at 8:30 a.m. and 9:45 a.m. every Sat and Sun during racing season only. Clocker's Corner is open year-round for breakfast every day until 10 a.m. and parking and admission are **free.** If you are planning to take the Seabiscuit tram tour, come early and eat here first!

Raging Waters

111 Raging Waters Dr. (take the Raging Waters Drive exit off I-210), San Dimas (east of Pasadena), where the 10, 210, and 57 freeways meet; (909) 592-1457 or 24-hour information line, (909) 802-2200; www.ragingwaters.com. Open May through Sept. It is essential you call in advance as hours and days of operation constantly change. $$$$.

The 50-acre park, California's largest waterpark and ranked number 3 nationally by the Travel Channel in its top 10 ranking of US water parks, houses 50 million gallons of water and more than 36 water attractions for aquatic thrill seekers, including the new Dr. Von Dark's Tunnel of Terror, opened in 2010. And don't forget the Vortex, a 4-story tower with two enclosed, 270-foot-long, spiral body flumes, and the world's highest head-first water ride, the High EXtreme. For those not inclined to plunge from such heights or velocities, there are tamer options, including a children's activity pool and play area.

Where to Stay

The Langham Huntington Hotel and Spa. 1401 South Oak Knoll Ave., Pasadena; (626) 568-3900; http://pasadena.langham hotels.com. Formerly the Ritz-Carlton, this lovingly restored historic landmark first opened in 1907 and recalls the grace and elegance of a past era with all the 21st-century amenities your family needs. The hotel has 380 revitalized guest rooms, 2 restaurants, a full-service spa, 23 acres of gardens and grounds, and 8 guest cottages with working fireplaces. Special packages are available. $$$$

For More Information

Pasadena Convention and Visitors Bureau. 171 South Los Robles Ave.; (626) 795-9311 or (800) 307-7977; www.pasadena cal.com.

Coastal Los Angeles

After a few days spent driving, museum hopping, driving, stargazing, driving, shopping, and driving some more, you and the kids may begin to feel a little antsy. If you're starting to think "L.A.'s great, but . . ." then it's high time you hit the beach. Whereas in cities like Boston or New York there are only gradations of stress—it never totally dissipates—in L.A., stress can be lowered to tolerable levels thanks to the proximity of a long and stunning coastline and the beaches. And when it comes to beaches, you're truly spoiled with choices in Southern California. Three areas are absolute must-sees for families on vacation: Venice Beach, Santa Monica, and Malibu. While there are other beaches, none bear the singular L.A. signature as indelibly as these. (The Long Beach area is discussed separately and has its own charms!)

Venice Beach & Marina del Rey

Venice Beach lies due south of Santa Monica. Anything goes here, but with copious amounts of suntan oil.

While L.A. beaches are endowed with more than 22 miles of bicycle paths, the most colorful swath is Oceanfront Walk in Venice, where bikers, roller skaters, and zany in-line skaters all compete with pedestrians for maximum mobility. Add street performers—from jugglers and mimes to musicians and comedians—and you'll get an idea of the carnival-like atmosphere permeating the place. People come to Venice Beach not so much for the beach, which is actually quite nice, but to watch other people. A serious amount of body spotting goes on at Muscle Beach, a section of the sand where bodybuilders work out in the sun and flex their Schwarzenegger deltoids, pectorals, and biceps. If your kids are needling you for souvenirs, this is the place (and remember that when buying trinkets on the beach, tackiness is a virtue). For more information visit www.venicebeach.com.

Marina del Rey lies adjacent to Venice Beach, on the shore of the Pacific Ocean, 4 miles north of Los Angeles International Airport (LAX) and 3 miles south of Santa Monica. It boasts the world's largest human-made marina (with more than 6,000 vessels), and every conceivable type of water sport is offered here, from boats and watercraft you pedal, paddle, sail, or drive to windsurfing, sunbathing, swimming, and surfing. Other water-based options include boat charters, harbor cruises, whale watching, and ocean fishing. From "the Marina," bike, skate, walk, or run along a 22-mile coastal path that stretches from Malibu at the northern end through the marina and south to Torrance. Kid-friendly Mother's Beach, as the name implies, is a must for families; as is Fisherman's Village, a quaint area of shops, restaurants, and charter/cruise boat docks. "The Marina," as it's called by the locals, today is family friendly with a splash of waterfront excitement. Admiralty Way is the main drag, lined with most of the city's hotels and restaurants. Avenues with names like Fiji Way and Bali Way branch off from Admiralty, providing added waterfront dining and recreational options. Marina del Rey is a popular base for Los Angeles–area visitors due to its easy access to so many Southern California attractions.

Where to Eat & Stay

Tony P's Dockside Grill. 4445 Admiralty Way, Marina del Rey; (310) 823-4534; www.tonyps.com. Totally family-friendly waterfront casual dining. Open daily for lunch and dinner and on Sat and Sun for an all-American breakfast. Generous portions of steak, fresh seafood, pasta, and burgers at reasonable prices. The "Dinghy Club" kids' menu is one of the best we've seen for ages 10 and younger. Every kid gets a gift bag of little toys. What kid can resist a nonalcoholic "FooFoo drink" such as a piña colada or strawberry margarita? If kids clean their plate, they get a **free** dessert. $$

Marina del Rey Hotel. 13534 Bali Way, Marina del Rey; (310) 301-1000; www.marina delreyhotel.com. This full-service hotel offers the true feel of the Marina, located on a small peninsula, with boat slips and docks on three sides. The decor is casually elegant, with marina views from the pool, waterfront restaurant, and many guest rooms. $$$

The Sidewalk Cafe. 1401 Ocean Front Way and Horizon Avenue, Venice Beach; (310) 399-5547; www.thesidewalkcafe.com. Open daily from 8 a.m. to midnight. This iconic patio restaurant offers great people watching. The large covered patio sports tables with red-checkered tablecloths and a huge menu of American, Italian, and Mexican favorites, everything from burgers—they grind their own meat—to fajitas, soups, salads,

sandwiches, and pastas. Breakfast is served all day. $–$$

Venice Beach Suites. 1305 Ocean Front Walk, Venice Beach; (310) 396-4559; www .venicebeachsuites.com. On the boardwalk in the center of all the action, with 28 studio and oceanfront suites, some with fully equipped kitchens—making it easier on your family's budget. The style is turn-of-the-19th-century funky, with hardwood floors and exposed brick walls. Amenities include high-speed Internet access, parking, and beach toys and lounge chairs that you can check out. $$

For More Information

Marina del Rey Convention and Visitors Bureau. 4701 Admiralty Way; visitor information line: (310) 305-9545; www.visit marinadelrey.com.

Santa Monica

Santa Monica has been a favorite family hideaway since the early 1930s when wealthy Easterners came for winter respites and never left. Just 8.3 square miles and surrounded on three sides by Los Angeles (and the fourth side by the Pacific Ocean), the city's safe, eco-friendly environment is easy to navigate. Most of the major hotels, attractions, shopping, and dining outlets are conveniently located within a 14-block radius. Be sure to check out Palisades Park, a cliff-top 26-acre greenbelt overlooking the Pacific with miles of lush greenery and shady palms for walking, resting, jogging, picnicking, and bicycling. Three miles of coastline, two excellent beaches, historic Santa Monica Pier, hike-friendly mountains, and year-round warm weather in which to enjoy it all!

Santa Monica Pier and Pacific Park

The oldest pleasure pier on the West Coast, Santa Monica opened in 1909. The pier also features Heal the Bay's Santa Monica Pier Aquarium, the historic Hippodrome, and a handcrafted carousel (circa 1922) with 44 hand-painted wooden horses. Here you'll discover dining, amusement games, shops, and a fresh fish market. Year-round live entertainment is offered.

Pacific Park (310-260-8744; www.pacpark.com; $) is a traditional, small family amusement park. Hours vary by season, so be sure to call in advance. Admission to the park is **free,** with all 12 rides and dozens of games on a "pay-as-you-go" basis, or you can buy an all-day wristband for unlimited rides. The world's first solar-powered Ferris wheel offers stunning views from its 9-story height. A special Kiddy Zone has pint-size rides for kids less than 42 inches tall. Of course, there are bumper cars, a roller coaster, minigolf, a 9-story plunge tower, and a flying swing for the big kids.

Annenberg Community Beach House

415 Pacific Coast Hwy.; (310) 458-4904; beachhouse.smgov.net. Generally open daily. Call for seasonal hours of operation. The pool is open June through Sept. Pool admission: $$.

Free docent-led tours through the Marion Davies Guest House are offered at varying times throughout the year. Once the opulent beachfront estate of actress Marion Davies, this historic 5-acre oceanfront compound includes the original intricately tiled pool, a viewing deck, the Splash Pad fountain area for toddlers, gardens, changing lockers, a cafe, and the historic Marion Davies Guest House. The Annenberg Foundation (which provided a $27.5 million grant—hence the name), which paved the way for the site's rehabilitation, expanded public facilities and reopened in 2010.

Third Street Promenade

Third Street from Broadway to Wilshire Boulevard; (310) 393-8355; www.thirdstreet promenade.com.

In Santa Monica, some of the best times await families just a few blocks from the sand. Here you can shop in the sunshine or at night until midnight at this ultra-lively spot that begins at Broadway (actually at the Santa Monica Place mall) and stretches north to Wilshire Boulevard along Third Street. Now one of the hippest areas in L.A., the promenade overflows with shops, restaurants, entertainment centers, and street performers. The Farmer's Market on Wednesday and Saturday mornings (310-458-8712) is a great scene, and tasty, too! Wander and enjoy.

The Cove Skatepark

1401 Olympic Blvd.; (310) 485-8228; www.smgov.net/comm_progs/skatepark. $$.

Santa Monica is the recognized birthplace of modern skateboarding, and the 20,000-square-foot Cove Skatepark has been featured in numerous skateboarding videos. Watch the action or test your personal best on its state-of-the-art ramps, half-pipes, and bowls.

South Bay **Bicycle Trail**

Known to locals as "The Strand," this paved bikeway parallels the beach and is the "in spot" for in-line skating, cycling, and just hanging out. It has several rental shops for bikes and in-line skates and inviting beachfront eateries, too. The Strand begins north of Santa Monica at Will Rogers State Beach in Pacific Palisades and runs for 22 miles south to the city of Torrance. For more info, visit www.labikepaths.com.

Magicopolis

1418 4th St.; (310) 451-2241; www.magicopolis.com. $$$.

This 350-person, 2-theater club welcomes all ages to 90-minute magic shows on Sat and Sun. World-class magicians entertain at 2 and 8 p.m.

Where to Eat

Big Dean's Oceanfront Cafe. 1615 Ocean Front Walk, (310) 393-2666; www.bigdeans oceanfrontcafe.com. Open noon to 9 p.m. Mon; 11 a.m. to 9 p.m. Tues through Thurs; and 10 a.m. to 10 p.m. Fri through Sun. Tucked below the Santa Monica Pier, this is a rustic locals' favorite that looks as if it were straight out of a vintage movie—not surprising since it's been in the same spot since 1902. Burgers, beer, sports TV, and a Cheers kind of friendliness make it a memorable find and children are always welcome here. $–$$

Typhoon. 3221 Donald Douglas Loop South, at the edge of the Santa Monica Airport; (310) 390-6565; www.typhoon.biz. Kids can watch the airplanes land between bites of Pan-Asian cuisine, such as Vietnamese spring rolls, fried rice, and puffy bao buns. Also on the menu are insects! Yes, there are crunchy crickets, stir-fry crickets, giant mountain ants, and Thai-style crispy scorpions. Now that's a mouthful! Celebrities such as John Travolta have been known to fly their private planes to Typhoon, so be prepared for a stellar dining experience. $$$

Where to Stay

The Georgian Hotel. 1415 Ocean Ave.; (310) 395-9945 or (800) 538-8147 (toll-free reservations); www.georgianhotel.com. This distinctive turquoise and gold art deco gem, built in 1933 as a seaside getaway for the exclusive Hollywood set, has been beautifully restored and refurbished. Choose from 56 spacious rooms and 28 suites overlooking the city and Santa Monica Bay. A real historic treat for your family. $$$$

Loews Santa Monica Beach Hotel. 1700 Ocean Ave.; (310) 458-6700; www .santamonicaloewshotel.com. Open since 1989, with a $7 million renovation and remodeling venture in 2010 to keep things fresh. The hotel has an unbeatable location adjacent to Santa Monica Pier overlooking the Pacific, with excellent beach access out the ground-floor back doors. This casually elegant 342-room luxury property has an outstanding children's program that includes lending game libraries, special menus, tours, welcome gifts for children younger than age 10, and supervised recreational programs. Children younger than age 18 stay **free** in the same room as their parents. The spa, fitness suite, ocean-view pool, and whirlpool are perfect for relaxing after a hard day's touring. **Ocean and Vine** is the hotel's signature restaurant offering fresh California cuisine that highlights locally sourced ingredients and an abundance of produce from the renowned Santa Monica Farmer's Markets for dining throughout the day and evening. While the kids are occupied, take in Papillion Lounge with its breathtaking ocean views and signature drinks and tasty bites. $$$$

For More Information

Santa Monica Convention and Visitors Bureau. 1920 Main St., Suite B; (310) 319-6263 or (800) 544-5319; www.santamonica .com.

Malibu

Malibu is Beach Boys country, where a dozen or so beaches beckon alongside the Pacific Coast Highway (PCH) at the foot of the Santa Monica Mountains. Although part of Los Angeles County, Malibu is actually a separate city—and a funny-shaped one at that. Because of the area's geography, Malibu is barely 1.5 miles wide but some 27 miles long. PCH is the lifeline of this seaside community and the commuting route to Hollywood for the hundreds of celebrities who live in seaside villas and estates here. You might even bump into one or two on the beach—it happens all the time. And while the gated Malibu Colony is off limits (unless you have a friend with a home in this star-studded seaside residential enclave), everything else is wide open. Don't be surprised if the landscapes look familiar; you've probably seen them on the big and small screens, since Malibu has been favorite filming ground since moviemaking began in the early 20th century.

One of the finest stretches of sand is Malibu Beach, on either side of the historic Malibu Pier (you can't miss it). White sand, pounding surf, sun-bronzed lifeguards with fluorescent-colored zinc oxide on their noses—yes, and this is Malibu. Even in summer, the beach is not as crowded as those in Santa Monica and Venice, and there is less emphasis on people-watching. Malibu-ites know what's really important in life: surfing at the best point breaks of the day!

It's not all sand and surf here, with the 2006 reopening of the Getty Villa, a lavish art museum and outdoor theater complex owned by J. Paul Getty Trust.

Getty Villa

17985 Pacific Coast Highway, 1 mile north of Sunset Boulevard; (310) 440-7300; www.getty .edu. Open Thurs through Mon 10 a.m. to 5 p.m. Closed major holidays. Advance, timed tickets are required for each individual older than 5. Admission is free, but there is a per-car fee for parking ($$$).

Reopened in 2006 after a nine-year closure for extensive remodeling, the Villa presides on a hill overlooking the Pacific. There is 48,000 square feet of gallery space on 2 floors designed as a palatial country home in the time of the Caesars, with elaborate ponds, gardens, and fountains, and 23 rooms exhibiting 1,200 carefully collected and curated pieces depicting life at the beginning of civilization. The "Family Forum" features a hands-on experience for kids. Enjoy lunch in the cafe with tasty salads, sandwiches, and ocean views through the pine trees. A must-do, one-of-a-kind cultural attraction.

Where to Eat & Stay

Malibu Beach Inn. 22878 Pacific Coast Hwy.; (310) 456-6444; www.malibubeachinn .com. Look for the famous Malibu Pier and you have arrived at this luxurious forty-seven-room, nonsmoking inn on Carbon Beach (also known as Billionaire's Beach). This is the perfect getaway when you want to be lulled to sleep by seagull calls in four-star surroundings. Their popular restaurant, the **Carbon Beach Club,** has a patio for outdoor dining and an excellent selection of California-inspired cuisine and wines. Valet parking only at an additional charge daily. $$$$

Duke's at Malibu. 21150 Pacific Coast Highway; (310) 317-0777; www.dukesmalibu .com. Lunch and dinner daily. Named after Duke Kahanamoku, the "father of surfing," this is the ideal place for your family to get the feeling of the Malibu lifestyle, thanks to the magnificent stretch of windows overlooking the beach. The prices are reasonable, and the kids will like the exhibit of surfing memorabilia. You might remind them about the Beach Boys and all of those surfing movies from the 1960s. $$

The Reel Inn. 18661 Pacific Coast Hwy., Malibu; (310) 456-8221; www.reelinnmalibu .com. Open daily 11 a.m. to 9 p.m. Casual to the max, this roadside dining marker has been reeling in seafood fans for years! The menu is on a blackboard, and folks wait in line to order fresh fish from halibut and mahi-mahi to ahi tuna and orange roughy. There is a respectable kids' menu, and for non–fish eaters there are chicken and pasta. $–$$

For More Information

Malibu Chamber of Commerce. 23805 Stuart Ranch Rd., Suite 100; (310) 456-9025; www.malibu.org.

Long Beach

As its name indicates, life in Long Beach centers on things of a coastal nature, with more than 5.5 miles of sandy beaches and shorelines. Settled by the Spaniards in 1784, Long Beach has been a visitor-friendly place ever since. Though close to downtown Los Angeles, Long Beach has a distinctly different, somewhat lower-key feel. If you have the time, give yourself two full days here.

In Long Beach, you will find an array of peaceful beaches that invite sunbathing and sand-castle building. Thanks to a human-made breakwater, the beaches of Long Beach do not experience high surf and are therefore ideal for families with small children.

The 15-block stretch of Second Street in the Belmont Shore area has swimming, lots of boutiques, and restaurants that range from Indian to Chinese to New York–style bagel shops. A mile and a half away, down Ocean Boulevard, downtown activity hustles and bustles along revitalized Pine Avenue.

Long Beach Aquarium of the Pacific

100 Aquarium Way; (562) 590-3100; www.aquariumofpacific.org. Open daily 9 a.m. to 6 p.m. except Christmas. $$$.

When you see the full-scale model of a blue whale, you'll know you're at the Long Beach Aquarium, a 156,000-square-foot facility that covers 5 acres and includes 550 species and 12,500 specimens. After you've checked out the wonderful exhibits, including Sea Lion/

On the **Water**

Gondola Getaway. 5437 East Ocean Blvd., Long Beach; (562) 433-9595; www .gondolagetawayinc.com. The Getaway features Venetian-style gondolas that cruise through narrow canals in the "backyards" of affluent homeowners. Cruises last 50 minutes.

Alfredo's Beach Rentals. Long Beach and locations throughout L.A. and Orange Counties; (562) 434-6121; www.alfredosbeachclub.com. Boogie boards? Skates? Bikes? All of the equipment you couldn't get on the plane and in your car can be rented from Alfredo!

Harbor Breeze Cruises. Rainbow Harbor Dock #2; (562) 432-4900; http://2see whales.com. Double-deck 6-foot, 149-passenger sightseeing vessels.

Rainbow Rocket. (562) 43-ROCKET; www.rocketboat.net. A 124-passenger 200-horsepower speedboat that's family-oriented during the day (at night, it turns into a party boat—beware!) Fast fun for everyone!

Long Beach Sport Fishing. (562) 432-8993; www.longbeachsportfishing.com.

Offshore Water Sports. (562) 436-1996; www.owsrentals.com.

Pacific Sailing. (562) 590-0323; www.pacificsailing.net. Charters or learn to sail.

Spirit Cruises at Shoreline Village. (562) 495-5884; www.spiritmarine.com. Sail aboard a 90-foot motor yacht. Public dinner cruises, harbor cruises, whale watching trips, and private charters.

Seal Tunnel, Baja Gallery, Wetlands Discovery Lab, Pacific Gallery, Coastal Corner, Live Coral Discovery, Lorikeet Aviary, and the Shark Lagoon, head for Kid's Cove. A playground of the Pacific Ocean, Kid's Cove is a hands-on interactive aquarium experience for kids of all ages. The focus is on feeding habits, family structures, and the lives of the exhibit specimens. Dine at the Bamboo Bistro or Cafe Scuba. Behind-the-scenes tours and 90-minute ocean educational cruises aboard *The Conqueror* are real winners, too.

Where to Eat

Omelette Inn. 108 West 3rd St.; (562) 437-5625; www.omeletteinn.com. Locally owned and operated for more than two decades, serving traditional American diner food (featuring omelettes, of course) for breakfast and lunch every day from 7 a.m. to 2:30 p.m. $

Parker's Lighthouse. 435 Shoreline Village Dr.; (562) 432-6500; www.parkerslighthouse .com. Serves lunch and dinner daily. Just look for the lighthouse to find this family-friendly restaurant. The view is terrific from the patio: the *Queen Mary* and harbor. The down-to-earth menu includes fresh fish, mesquite-grilled with a choice of side sauces or blackened, seared, poached, or Cajun seasoned as well as sushi, and an Angus burger to satisfy any carnivores. $$$

Where to Stay

Dockside Boat & Bed. Rainbow Harbor; (562) 436-3111; www.boatandbed.com/ longbeach.html. Four private moored yachts to stay aboard overnight. All boats fully furnished; continental breakfast basket provided. Next to Aquarium of the Pacific and Shoreline Village. A highly recommended unique family-lodging experience with an extraordinary view you'll never have in a hotel. $$$$

Hotel Maya. 700 Queensway Dr.; (800) 738-7477 or (562) 435-7676; www.hotelmayalong beach.com. Inspired by Mayan architecture, this luxury, boutique resort–style hotel reopened in 2009 after a multimillion-dollar makeover. From the private balconies or patios of 195 plush guest rooms with both waterfront and garden views you'll see stunning vistas of the city skyline and the *Queen Mary*. Fuego, helmed by award-winning executive chef Jesse Perez, features coastal Latin cuisine, specializing in *mariscos* (fresh seafood), an extensive selection of *antojitos* (appetizers), and entrees made from both traditional and contemporary recipes. The restaurant is open for breakfast, lunch, and dinner daily and on Sun for its signature Fiesta Domingo Brunch. *Viva!* $$$$

For More Information

Long Beach Area Convention and Visitor's Bureau. 1 World Trade Center, 3rd floor; (562) 436-3645 or (800) 452-7829; www .visitlongbeach.com.

Queen *Mary*

There are many fun family attractions in Long Beach, but none as famous as the majestic *Queen Mary*. The world's largest luxury liner is permanently docked in the 55-acre Queen Mary Seaport, located at the end of the 710 Freeway. There are many hotels in Long Beach, but if this is your first visit, try the Hotel Queen Mary, 1126 Queens Highway; (562) 435-3511 or (800) 437-2934; www.queenmary.com. The ship has been converted into the 307-stateroom hotel. While aboard, you can take a Behind-the-Scenes guided tour or dine in one of the ship's restaurants. The Promenade Café is the Queen Mary's breakfast, lunch, and dinner diner, offering American favorites such as gourmet burgers, fresh seasonal salads, and comfort-food classics perfect for families. If you can't stay on the ship for a night or two, be sure to do the self-guided audio tour or an hour-long behind-the-scenes guided walking tour. Add a self-guided tour of the Soviet Foxtrot Submarine *Scorpion* anchored adjacent or do the Ghosts and Legends Show onboard for some paranormal fun if your kids like mysteries. $$$

San Pedro—Port of Los Angeles

Originally settled as a commercial fishing village in the 1800s, today San Pedro is home to the Port of Los Angeles, one of the world's largest deepwater commercial seaports. Here you also will find the World Cruise Center (located at Berths 91, 92, and 93A/B), point of embarkation for more than a million passengers annually sailing on vacations to Mexico, Alaska, Hawaii, and beyond onboard ships from Princess Cruises, Royal Caribbean, Silversea, and others. (Note that Carnival Cruise Lines docks in the adjacent Port of Long Beach.)

Located at the end of the 110-Harbor Freeway, San Pedro offers value-priced lodging, restaurants, and shopping options. It is easy to explore the attractions via the San Pedro Red Car Electric Trolley route currently stretching 1.5 miles along Harbor Boulevard with terminals at Swinford Street, Sixth Street, Ports O' Call Village, and Miner Street. Red Cars operate from noon to 9 p.m. Fri through Sun. A $1 all-day fare includes unlimited rides and is transferable for **free** rides on the shuttle bus to nearby Cabrillo Beach. For complete details, call (310) 732-3473 or visit www.railwaypreservation.com.

Los Angeles Maritime Museum

Berth 84, at the foot of 6th Street in John S. Gibson Park; (310) 548-7618; www.lamaritime museum.org. Open Tues through Sun 10 a.m. to 5 p.m. $.

Built in 1941, this "Streamlined Moderne" building was the base for an auto ferry. Saved and beautifully restored, it now houses the largest maritime museum in California. This 75,000-square-foot facility features more than 700 ship and boat models, a variety of navigational equipment, and an operating amateur radio station. Try your hand at tying any of the 64 types of seaman's knots on display.

Cabrillo Marine Aquarium

3720 Steven White Dr.; (310) 548-7562; www.cabrilloaq.org. Open Tues through Fri noon to 5 p.m., Sat and Sun 10 a.m. to 5 p.m. Free, but a suggested donation of $5 for adults and $1 for children is appreciated.

Featuring 38 aquaria, these innovative exhibits will teach kids about the plant and animal life of Southern California. The simulated tide-pool touch tank is a good place to start this aquatic journey. In addition, there are whale trips organized from December through March focusing on the Pacific gray whale. This museum predated the Aquarium of the Pacific in neighboring Long Beach by 65 years. Here's where it all started, and that's no whale of a tale.

SS *Lane Victory*

Berth 94 off Harbor Boulevard; (310) 519-9545; www.lanevictory.org. Open for tours daily 9 a.m. to 4 p.m. except for six daylong Saturday cruises each summer. $.

This operational World War II cargo ship with wartime armament was built in 1945 and saw service in World War II, Korea, and Vietnam. Decommissioned and fully restored, her 455-foot length and 10,000 tons are a marvel to behold. If your family is visiting the Los

Angeles area in the summer, make every attempt to secure reservations on one of the day cruises, where the seamen's lives will come alive as you sail. You will even be buzzed by attacking biplanes. This ship is a living memorial to all Merchant Marines.

For More Information

Port of Los Angeles. 425 South Palos Verdes St.; (310) SEA-PORT; www.portoflos angeles.org.

San Pedro Peninsula Chamber of Commerce. 390 West 7th St.; (310) 832-7272 or (888) 447-3376; www.sanpedrochamber.com or www.sanpedro.com.

Santa Catalina Island

Part of the chain of eight Channel Islands off the coast of southern California, Santa Catalina Island was first discovered by the European explorer Juan Rodriguez Cabrillo and claimed for Spain in 1542. Sixty years later, explorer Sebastian Viscaino reclaimed the island and gave it its current name in honor of Saint Catherine. You can easily sail away to the Mediterranean-like island, a relaxing 22-mile (one-hour) boat trip from Long Beach or San Pedro Harbor. You might want to spend a couple of days on this enchanted isle, where you won't need a car for a change (since they are restricted to residents). In our opinion, the best way to get to Santa Catalina is aboard Catalina Express high-speed vessels (with ports in Long Beach, San Pedro, and Dana Point; 310-519-1212 or 800-481-3470; www.catalinaexpress.com). You'll arrive at the green "Pleasure Pier" in the sun-splashed city of Avalon. With its restaurant- and boutique-filled streets and a population of around 3,000, it's Catalina's biggest town and your headquarters for fun.

Avalon is only one square mile, and everything is within easy walking distance. Your feet are the best mode of transportation once you arrive. In car-crazy California, Avalon is the only city authorized by the State Legislature to regulate the number and size of vehicles allowed to drive on city streets. Currently, there is a 14-year waiting list to own a car on Catalina, but you really don't need one to enjoy your visit here, really! You can rent a bicycle to go exploring or take a sightseeing tour in a comfortable motor coach or open-air tram. To enjoy the hills above the town, do what locals do—drive an electric golf cart and putt around—rental stands are all around downtown Catalina. Transportation Services (310-510-0025) offers door-to-door taxi, shuttle, and delivery services throughout Santa Catalina Island. So relax and enjoy this picturesque place sans gas-powered vehicle!

Catalina Casino

(310) 510-7428; www.visitcatalinaisland.com.

You can't miss this red-roofed Avalon landmark as you approach Avalon harbor. Never actually used for gambling, the casino is famed for its ballroom and the Avalon Theatre, the first designed for sound movies. Art deco murals of stylized underwater scenes grace the theater, which also has a full-scale pipe organ with 250 miles of wire. On the ground floor, visit the Catalina Island Museum, (310) 510-2414 or www.catalinamuseum.com, for tours and information.

Santa Catalina Island Company's Discovery Tours
(310) 510-2500 or (800) 626-1496; www.visitcatalinaisland.com. $$$.

Operating since 1894 and departing from Avalon and Two Harbors, Discovery Tours by Land include the Avalon Scenic Tour, Casino Tour, Skyline Drive Tour, and Inland Motor Tour (the most comprehensive at 4 hours). Discovery Tours by Sea include Undersea Tour, Glass Bottom Boat Trip, Seal Rocks Cruise, Sundown Isthmus Cruise, and the Flying Fish Boat Trip. Newly launched in 2010 is the Catalina Zip Line Eco Tour—the ultimate island interior tour on the only zip line in Los Angeles and Orange County, dropping from 500 feet to 60 feet above sea level traveling three quarters of a mile over five consecutive zip lines at speeds pushing 45 miles per hour. Beginning at the Hog's Back gate, high in the hills near Avalon and descending through Descanso Canyon, you will pause at several eco-stations along the way before continuing on your journey to learn about ecosystems and history you're zipping through until you reach Descanso Beach approximately two hours later. Reservations are required and tickets are limited. Do not miss this if you or any of your kids have a huge spirit of adventure. Money-saving combinations are the best way to tailor the tours to your family at a 25 percent discount off regular pricing. Reservations are recommended, especially during the busy times of weekends, holidays, and the summer season.

Catalina Adventure Tours
On the green Pleasure Pier; (310) 510-2888; www.catalinaadventuretours.com. $$$$.

Tours via modern air-conditioned buses include the Avalon Explorer, City Passport, City Botanical, and Inside Adventure (the most popular). On the water, tours include the SS *Nautilus* (a semi-submersible sub), Sea View (glass-bottom boat), Seal Rock Explorer Cruise, and a Scenic Harbor cruise. Village walking tours are also offered.

Where to Eat & Stay

Catalina Coffee & Cookie Company. 205 Crescent Ave., Avalon; (310) 510-2447; www.metropolemarketplace.com. Need a pick-me-up? Come here for an Eclipse, a fudge cookie dipped in white chocolate. Open daily at 5 a.m. year-round. $

The Cottage. 118 Catalina Ave., Avalon; (310) 510-0726; www.menu4u.com/thecottage. Totally traditional family breakfast, lunch, and dinner favorites served daily starting at 6 a.m., now offering full bar service, too. The Chef's

Mess omelet contains everything but the kitchen sink! Just about every breakfast item is available all day. $

Pavilion Lodge. 513 Crescent Ave., Avalon; (310) 510-2500 or (800) 626-1496; www.visitcatalinaisland.com. Reopened after an extensive renovation in 2010, but it is still just 14 steps from the beach. The charming 2-story property now features 71 upscale rooms all facing a huge garden courtyard—with ground-floor rooms featuring private

On the Island's **Wild Side**

Catalina now has a 4-hour off-road tour that is ideal for families. Visiting the "wild side" of the island on the Cape Canyon Tour, passengers ride in a four-wheel-drive vehicle driven by a Catalina Island Conservancy–trained guide. The tour features a scenic drive along a ridgeline overlooking coves of west Avalon, a guided tour of the American Bald Eagle Habitat at Middle Ranch, and a ride in Cape Canyon for stunning views of the Catalina outback. Lunch is included at the famous Catalina Airport-in-the-Sky. Reservations required; call (310) 510-2000 or visit www.visitcatalinaisland.com.

lanais as well as 2 ocean-view suites. Excellent values and packages; **free** continental breakfast, and kids under 12 stay **free.** $$

For More Information

Catalina Island Visitors Bureau and Chamber of Commerce. On the green Pleasure Pier in the center of town, P.O. Box 217, Avalon 90704; (310) 510-1520; www.visit catalina.org or www.catalinachamber.com.

Redondo Beach

Known as the South Bay (because the area is south of Long Beach), Redondo Beach is within a 45-minute range of Disneyland, Knott's Berry Farm, Universal Studios, Six Flags Magic Mountain, the La Brea Tar Pits, Catalina Island terminals, and the *Queen Mary*. Redondo has the Galleria at South Bay (with 150 stores), superb sport fishing, and charters at the Redondo Beach King Harbor Marina. If you should base the family here, you'll have the best of both worlds—the atmosphere of a small, seaside village and the accessibility of most of greater L.A.'s attractions. The oceanfront location places you but 6 miles from LAX and within walking distance of King Harbor, Seaside Lagoon, and the South Bay Bikeway, a 27-mile-long coastal walking and biking path passing through Venice, Santa Monica, and Malibu.

Where to Eat & Stay

Captain Kidd's. 209 Harbor Dr.; (310) 372-7703; www.captainkidds.com. Open for lunch and dinner daily, 11 a.m. to 9 p.m. Fresh-from-the-market fish and crab are prepared grilled, Cajun-style, charbroiled, or deep fried and come with two generous side dishes.

Check the Captain Kidd's Meal for choices all under $5. $$

The Fun Fish Market & Restaurant/ Fun Factory Amusement Center. 121 International Boardwalk; (310) 374-4277 or

(310) 374-9982; http://redondo.com/rff. The Redondo Pier has a big amusement center with dozens of arcade games and kiddie rides, which is good, but even more appealing around mealtime is Fun Fish, where fresh fish is served any way you like it. Kids will like selecting their fish from a tank. And don't forget the chowder! $$

Portofino Hotel and Yacht Club. 260 Portofino Way; (310) 379-8481 or (800) 468-4292; www.hotelportofino.com. The Portofino's 163 rooms include 90 with views of the Pacific. An assortment of complimentary family amenities is provided, from "baby joggers" and snugglies to high chairs and diapers. Breakfast, lunch, and dinner are served waterside at Baleen Los Angeles Restaurant and Lounge. Please call (310) 372-1202 for specific serving hours. $$$$

For More Information

Redondo Beach Chamber of Commerce and Visitors Bureau. 200 North Pacific Coast Highway; (310) 376-6911 or (800) 282-0333; www.redondochamber.org.

Orange
County

The land on which the visionary Walt Disney built his Magic Kingdom in 1955 was discovered more than 150 years earlier by a Spanish explorer. Gaspar de Portolá gazed upon the magic river bringing life to the fertile valleys and fields leading to the Pacific Ocean and named it Santa Ana. In 1857 German immigrants bought portions of the area, at the time a Spanish land grant, for a mere $2 an acre. They called their new settlement Anaheim, which means "home of the Ana." With cuttings from their native Rhineland, the settlers began growing California's first grapes and making wine. In the late 1880s, the vineyards of California's wine capital in Anaheim were devastated by blight. So the settlers decided to plant oranges instead, and the current name Orange County was created, now immortalized by television's infamous teen drama *The O.C.* and the reality-TV show *The Real Housewives of Orange County*.

Today's fastest-growing crops in the area are neither grapes nor oranges but amusement parks, sports attractions, and a galaxy of animated stars from Disney—all ready and waiting for the picking by you and your fun-starved entourage. If oranges thrive in this climate, so will you! Wintertime highs of 65 degrees rise to 79 degrees in summer, and overnight lows—even in winter's darkest hours—rarely dip below 45 degrees. December through February is what passes for the area's "rainy season," although total annual rainfall is only 13 inches. Days are sunny and mild, nights clear and cool—that's the forecast for your Orange County visit.

Casual clothing is the way to go for 90 percent of your family fun here. Be sure to pack shorts, T-shirts, cotton pants, skirts, and really comfortable walking shoes or sandals. Bring a sweater or light jacket for evenings—along the waterfront it may get nippy. Don't forget your bathing suit and shades (but never fear, you can always buy the latest beachwear and gear at one of the numerous malls or gift shops).

Your family can still visit the city of Orange itself, with its historic district featuring a 19th-century soda fountain; relax on the beaches of Newport and Laguna; check out the world-class surfing at Huntington Beach; shop 'til you drop in Costa Mesa; and see the swallows in Capistrano and the marine life in Dana Point. By popular kid demand,

ORANGE COUNTY

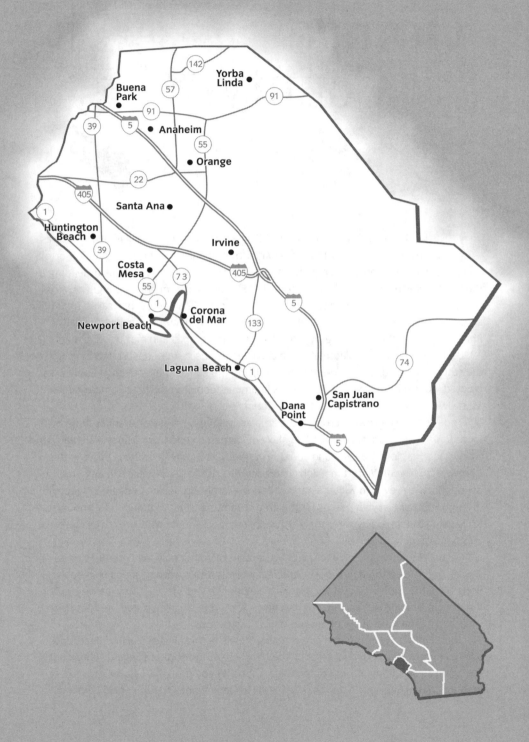

however, you will doubtless make your first Orange County stop in Anaheim at "Uncle Walt's place"—the unparalleled Disneyland Resort, which includes the original Disneyland and Disney's California Adventure parks, plus Downtown Disney shopping, dining and entertainment district.

Anaheim Resort Area

From Los Angeles drive south on I-5 to the city of Anaheim and vicinity, the family fun center of Orange County. Using Disneyland Resort as your Orange County starting point makes much sense geographically and economically. Family-style lodging and restaurants are plentiful and very affordable in Anaheim and neighboring Buena Park. Make room reservations as far in advance as you can, especially for summertime and holiday periods, since Anaheim attracts 20-million-plus visitors every year, including many who visit at the West Coast's largest exhibition center, the Anaheim Convention Center. Many hotels and motels provide package plans that include Disneyland Resort tickets (passports) as well as **free** breakfasts and transportation services.

Disneyland Park

1313 Harbor Blvd., at the intersection of I-5; (714) 781-4565; www.disneyland.com. Follow the signs to designated parking areas. Trams are provided to the Transit Plaza/Main Entrance for both Disney parks and Downtown Disney. Parking is $15 per car per day. During the fall, winter, and spring, hours are generally Mon through Fri 10 a.m. to 8 p.m., Sat 9 a.m. to midnight, and Sun 9 a.m. to 10 p.m. Summertime hours are usually 8 a.m. to midnight every day. Extended hours are in effect during holiday periods. Very important note: Hours are subject to change, so call ahead for exact opening and closing times on your preferred days to avoid disappointment. $$$$.

Since 1955, the magic of Disneyland has existed in eight "themed lands." Begin with your entrance on Main Street USA, a composite of America in the 1900s. Move along to **Adventureland,** housing Tarzan's Treehouse; the Indiana Jones Adventure (still one of our favorites); the Jungle Cruise; and the Enchanted Tiki Room (a good place we found to sit in a cool room for 20 minutes for the animated show). **New Orleans Square** features the classic Pirates of the Caribbean and Haunted Mansion. **Critter Country** has the wettest ride—Splash Mountain—and Many Adventures of Winnie-the-Pooh. **Fantasyland** is highlighted by the Disney Princess Fantasy Faire (complete with dress-up and meet royalty options), the iconic Sleeping Beauty's Castle, King Arthur's Carousel, Mr. Toad's Wild Ride, Peter Pan's Flight, and the breathtaking Matterhorn Bobsleds. Next comes **Frontierland,** with the Big Thunder Mountain mine ride and the chances to cruise on the Mark Twain riverboat or Sailing Ship *Columbia* around Tom Sawyer's Island. **Mickey's Toontown** is base camp for all your young ones' favorite Disney characters. See Mickey's and Minnie's residences and Goofy's Bounce House, and ride Roger Rabbit's Car Toon Spin and Gadget's Go Coaster. **Tomorrowland** is the launching pad for space-age attractions. Here you will thrill to classics such as Star Tours and Space Mountain, plus the Astro Orbitor, 3-D "Honey I Shrunk the Audience," "Buzz

Lightyear Astro Blasters," and the "Finding Nemo Submarine Voyage." The Disneyland Monorail, once the coolest ride in Tomorrowland, now just runs back and forth from Downtown Disney instead of around the park. The steam engine Disneyland Railroad still circumnavigates the park with stops at various lands. We recommend you take the full 20-minute circuit for a calming respite from all the excitement! Be sure to check the website and daily park schedules for special shows such as evening fireworks or laser light spectaculars.

Disney's California Adventure Park

1313 Harbor Blvd., at the intersection of I-5 (you can also exit at Disneyland Drive); (714) 781-4565; www.disneyland.com. Open year-round, generally Mon through Fri 10 a.m. to 8 p.m., Sat 9 a.m. to 10 p.m., and Sun 9 a.m. to 10 p.m. Extended hours during the summer and holiday periods. NOTE: Hours are very subject to change; call ahead for exact opening and closing times on your preferred days to visit. Admission fees are also subject to change. Many special packages and promotions are offered throughout the year. $$$$.

Opened in February 2001 and continually adding new rides and shows, this 55-acre theme park celebrates the great state of California—from Disney's imaginative perspective. You'll enter the park, affectionately known as DCA for short, from the promenade area under a replica of San Francisco's Golden Gate Bridge into the Sunshine Plaza fountain area to explore four distinct lands. **Paradise Pier** re-creates a beachfront amusement zone reminiscent of Santa Monica Pier or the Santa Cruz boardwalk. Check out California Scream-in'—a superfast steel roller coaster that loops you upside down around a Mickey Mouse head icon. Toy Story Mania! is a 4-D interactive attraction where you'll ride in vehicles that seemingly travel and twist along a colorful route while you play tag games. The 150-foot Sun Wheel Ferris wheel, Orange Stinger, Maliboomer, Mulholland Madness mini-coaster, and King Triton's Carousel get family fun points here, along with plenty of concessions and food vendors along the midway.

The second land, dubbed the **Hollywood Pictures Backlot,** has huge soundstages that hold attractions such as *Jim Henson's Muppet Vision* 3-D movie; Hyperion Theater's live hip musical/dance performances; and the Animation Center, featuring "Turtle Talk with Crush" from the movie *Finding Nemo*. The Twilight Zone Tower of Terror drops you 13 stories faster than the speed of gravity (do not eat before this one, really!). Monsters, Inc.: Mike and Sully to the Rescue is another 3-D attraction that re-creates the streets of Monstropolis from the animated film. The live show "Playhouse Disney" is where your kids can sing and dance along with fun Disney characters onstage (floor seating for 550 guests, so be ready to participate). Watch for the Pixar Play Parade featuring more "live" characters on the backlot streets.

The **Condor Flats area** features the must-do Soarin' Over California experience, where you will hang with feet dangling as you fly like an eagle—visually—around an 80-foot dome-shaped motion-picture screen filled with an amazing view of the best California scenery. Don't miss adjacent 8-acre Grizzly Peak Recreation Area with trees and trails leading to Grizzly River Run, a white-water-rafting ride that swirls you down two waterfalls (you will get wet).

Doing **Disneyland**

With three attractions—the original Disneyland (opened 1955), Disney's California Adventure, and Downtown Disney (both opened in 2001)—this trip can be a visual and physical overload for you and your family. We strongly advise a minimum two-night stay and three days to really enjoy all the fun available. (It's practically impossible to do both parks in one day; even one overnight and two full days can be very tricky, depending on your stamina.) For first-timers, begin with the original Disneyland early in the day. Take short break midday for lunch and naps, and then return for the afternoon and evening shows (such as the fireworks over the Magic Castle). You'll need a second full day to really explore DCA (Disney's California Adventure) because many of the activities are live stage shows and movies presented at specific times. On the third day, revisit favorite attractions at either park or get in some shopping and dining or a movie at Downtown Disney. Always check park operating hours and plan your visit around your kids' eat-sleep schedule. The best time-saving option is the **free** FASTPASS, a computerized ticketing system that allows you to reserve a time slot for the most popular rides. When you arrive at your designated time period with your computer-generated pass, you'll go to a special line and get on within minutes. Highly recommended!

A Bug's Land is a fourth area including five attractions inside Flik's Fun Fair and the comical 3-D movie *It's Tough to be a Bug*; Bountiful Valley Farm with its demonstration veggie and fruit gardens; Robert Mondavi's Golden Vine Winery, with wine tasting for us adults; and Pacific Wharf, where you can watch Boudin's Bakery make sourdough bread and Mission brand tortillas. Plenty of food and beverage options inhabit DCA, and be prepared to spend some gold nuggets to enjoy the diverse range of fare, ranging from traditional burgers, dogs, and fries to sushi, chowder, pizza, and Chinese and Mexican cuisine.

In 2010 the World of Color nighttime water spectacular debuted, combining water, color, fire and light into a kaleidoscope of sensory (over)load. More than 1,000 jets of water form incredible shapes in time to 25 minutes of music as Disney characters come to life on a shimmering veil of mist near Paradise Pier. Disney's California Adventure certainly embraces Walt's original promise: "Disneyland will never be complete as long as there is imagination left in the world."

Angel Stadium of Anaheim

2000 Gene Autry Way. Baseball season runs Apr through Sept; call (714) 940-2000 for a schedule and ticket prices; www.angelsbaseball.com. $.

The 45,000-seat stadium is home to Major League Baseball's Los Angeles Angels of Anaheim.

Anaheim **Gardenwalk**

Located at 321 West Katella Ave. at Clementine, just east of Harbor Boulevard and within walking distance of the Disneyland Resort; (714) 635-7400; www.anaheimgardenwalk.com. Open 11 a.m. to 9 p.m. daily, with restaurants and nightclubs with extended hours. GardenWalk is a unique 440,000-square-foot outdoor shopping and dining experience set among beautifully manicured walkways and gardens that first opened in 2008. GardenWalk includes "300," an upscale bowling lounge, a 14-plex theater, and various establishments including Aveda, Banana Republic, Bar Louie, Chico's, Harley Davidson, Heat Ultra Lounge, White House/Black Market, and XP Sports. Restaurants include national favorites California Pizza Kitchen, The Cheesecake Factory, McCormick & Schmick's Grille, P.F. Chang's China Bistro, and Roy's (Hawaiian Fusion Cuisine), plus the super-family-friendly Bubba Gump Shrimp Company, modeled after the 1994 hit movie *Forrest Gump*. This restaurant combines a casual, playful atmosphere with high quality and quantities of seafood, especially shrimp prepared myriad ways, tasty appetizers, humongous desserts, and a reasonably priced kids' menu featuring Bus Bench Burger, Hubba Bubba Popcorn Shrimp, and Yummy Smoothies (714-635-GUMP or www.bubbagump.com). We like GardenWalk for a nearby non-Disney respite!

Honda Center (formerly Arrowhead Pond)
2695 East Katella Ave.; (714) 704-2400; www.hondacenter.com.

This 18,900-seat enclosed arena—ranked number three entertainment venue in the world by *Billboard* magazine—hosts many events and concerts and is home to the National Hockey League's Stanley Cup Champion Anaheim Ducks, who skate from October through March (714-704-2000; http://ducks.nhl.com). Call for ticket prices and schedules.

Glacial Gardens Skating Arena
3975 Pixie St., Lakewood; (562) 429-1805; www.glacialgardens.com. Open daily, with varying times and fees for open figure skating, instruction, and hockey matches. $$.

This is the place to go if your family would rather participate in ice sports than watch the Anaheim Ducks. Head over to this triple-rink facility (Olympic size, NHL size, and a slightly smaller training rink), complete with a pro shop, snack bar, locker rooms, and skate rentals.

Children's Museum at La Habra (ages 2 to 10)

301 South Euclid Ave., La Habra, approximately 30 minutes from Disneyland; (562) 905-9793; www.lhcm.org. Open Tues through Fri 10 a.m. to 4 p.m.; Sat 10 a.m. to 5 p.m., and Sun 1 to 5 p.m.; closed major holidays. $$.

Opened in 1977 as California's first children's museum, this facility is located in a renovated 1923 Union Pacific train depot. It features 7 galleries and 14 different hands-on exhibits, outdoor dinosaur topiary and historic 1942 caboose, and a seasonal feature exhibit that changes 4 times per year.

MUZEO

241 South Anaheim Blvd.; (714) 956-8936; www.muzeo.org. Open 10 a.m. to 5 p.m. daily except holidays. $$$.

MUZEO means "museum" in the international Esperanto language. It opened in 2007 as part of a complex that includes Anaheim's original 1908 Carnegie Library surrounded by two courtyards that connect to apartments and stores to create a very user-friendly urban setting. MUZEO is a revolutionary 25,000-square-foot facility that combines high-tech innovations of today (state-of-the-art self guided audio podcasts, Wi-Fi access, and interactive displays) with incredible interchangeable exhibits of history, art, architecture, and natural science from yesterday and the future. There are three traveling exhibitions per year. In 2010, the center offered "State of the Blues: The Living Legend of the Delta"; "Frogs: A Chorus of Colors," featuring 15 live frog habitats; and "The Holy Art of Imperial Russia: Icons from the 17th Century to the Early 20th Century." Each special exhibit has programs,

Downtown **Disney**

Opened in January 2001, this 20-acre dining, shopping, and entertainment area is located between Disneyland and Disney's California Adventure and encircles 3 Disneyland Resort hotels. The district is free and open to the public year-round. It features lovely landscaped gardens and promenades interspersed with 300,000 square feet of retail shops, restaurants, and 12 AMC movie theaters. Some highlights: excellent pastries and espresso at La Brea Bakery; wood-fired pizza at Naples Ristorante; tapas at Catal Restaurant; Ralph Brennen's Jazz Kitchen for Cajun food; the House of Blues for live entertainment (the Sunday gospel brunch is inspiring!); Rainforest Cafe for tropical treats; and the ESPN Zone for a fantastic sports fix (live sports broadcasts, interactive games, and food). Shopping includes the ubiquitous Disney store and Build-A-Bear, plus plenty of other gift, souvenir, music, jewelry, and fashion emporiums. For more information call (714) 300-7800 or visit www.disneyland.com.

Anaheim Resort Transit—**The Car-Free and Carefree Way to Get Around!**

The newest, hassle-free way to navigate the Anaheim Resort Area and avoid parking fees and traffic (and reduce air pollution) is via ART (714-563-5287 or www.rideart.org), a fixed 16-route transportation system using zero-emission electric buses and clean fuel propane trolleys. Be sure to purchase an ART Pass before you get on the bus (or you'll be charged the $4 one-way cash fee). There are convenient ticketing kiosks at all the stops that accept major credit cards and you can also purchase online. The routes run to and from Disneyland Resort Transit Plaza/Main Entrance about every 15 to 20 minutes from all major hotels, the Honda Center, Angel Stadium, and the Amtrak/Metrolink Railway station (http://rideart.org/amtrak.html)—giving you a complete car-free option for arriving at the Magic Kingdom. A one-day unlimited ART Pass is $4 for adults, $1 for children ages 3 to 9, and free for children 2 and under. Multiple-day ART Passes are also readily available. We found ART extremely convenient in getting us back and forth between our Anaheim hotel and the Disneyland Resort. Highly recommended!

events and activities attached to it—which make it fascinating to visit no matter when your family is nearby.

Crystal Cathedral of the Reformed Church in America

13280 Chapman Ave., Garden Grove. Call the visitor center at (714) 971-4000 to check tour times or (714) 544-5679 to reserve tickets for the extremely cherished holiday pageants; www.crystalcathedral.org. Free tours are generally available Mon through Sat, but times are subject to change due to church services and events. Donations appreciated.

For some religious and architectural history, visit the dramatic, all-glass sanctuary designed by Philip Johnson, considered a dean of American architects. This incredible place features 10,000 glass panes covering a weblike steel frame resembling a four-point star. The 2,890-seat cathedral hosts the annual Glory of Christmas and Glory of Easter pageants, with live animals, flying angels, and incredible special lighting reflected from the 12-story glass walls and ceilings.

Nixon Presidential Library and Museum

18001 Yorba Linda Blvd., Yorba Linda. From Anaheim take the Riverside Freeway Route 57 northbound and exit Yorba Linda Boulevard, then travel about 5 miles east to the library, on the left-hand side (watch carefully for signs); (714) 993-5075 or (800) 872-8865; http://nixon.archives.gov and www.nixonlibraryfoundation.org. Open Mon through Sat 10 a.m. to 5 p.m. and Sun 11 a.m. to 5 p.m. $$.

The facility was first opened and dedicated on July 19, 1990, and inherited by the Federal government in 2007 from the private foundation that had previously controlled the library. Be sure to schedule at least half a day to let your family experience the political and world history depicted at this 9-acre site. You'll begin your tour in the auditorium, which shows vintage campaign films, news footage, and historically significant television appearances by President Nixon; then proceed to the permanent galleries displaying images, video, and artifacts related to President Nixon's career, family life, and volunteer service. One of our favorites details the space program during the Nixon presidency, featuring an astronaut's space suit, the telephone President Nixon used to call Neil Armstrong and Buzz Aldrin on the moon, and an actual moon rock. See a replica of the East Room of the White House as well as President Nixon's helicopter and birthplace. The exhibits portray America's 37th commander in chief right up until his death on April 22, 1994. Both President and Mrs. Nixon are buried here in the tranquil First Lady's Garden. You may visit the gravesite, the reflecting pool, and the white clapboard farmhouse where Nixon was born on January 9, 1913. It remains precisely as it was when Nixon and his family lived there, right down to the bed where he was born. The intimate museum store on the premises contains commemorative souvenirs, postcards, and a selection of Nixon's books.

Getting **in the Swing**

The ever-popular **Golf N' Stuff** is conveniently located across the street from Disneyland at 1656 South Harbor Blvd. (714-778-4100) and has two beautifully landscaped 18-hole miniature golf courses and an arcade center open seven days a week. Real golf enthusiasts can swing out under the instruction of PGA pros at the **Islands Golf Center,** 14893 Ball Rd. (714-630-7888; www.theislandsgolfcenter.com), on 18 acres of practice tees, greens, and a fairway on a 10-acre lake. There are more than 20 other Orange County golf options.

If your family wants to swing out with a racket, you can choose from 12 championship hard-surface tennis courts at the **Anaheim Tennis Center Inc.,** located at 975 South State College Blvd. (714-991-9090; www.anaheim tenniscenter.com). The center is open year-round and offers computerized, self-loading ball machines as well as professional instruction. More than 50 tennis courts can be found at hotels and in Orange County's public parks. Call (714) 771-6731, ext. 220 or (866) OC-PARKS, or visit www.ocparks.com for information on the county's 37,000 acres of parkland and open space including regional and wilderness parks, nature preserves and recreational trails, historic sites, harbors, and beaches.

Where to Eat & Stay

Disney's PCH Grill at Disney's Paradise Pier Hotel. 1717 Disneyland Dr.; (714) 999-0990. Open daily for breakfast, lunch, and dinner. Hours vary seasonally. PCH stands for Pacific Coast Highway, California's prime and celebrated coastal route. Dining in the PCH Grill for lunch and dinner celebrates all the foods and beverages that make up California cuisine. Menu maps plot your meal course by course and feature fresh seafood, pastas, oak-fired pizzas, burgers, and desserts. If you're looking for traditional American fare, this is probably not the best spot for you, but you know what they say: "When in California, eat like the Californians do," or something like that. Your best bet for the family at the PCH Grill is breakfast, because Disney characters make this a fun-filled Disney dining experience that also features a magic act onstage with Mr. Wizard. (Kids get to help perform tricks between bites.) You can order off the menu or cruise the buffet for your favorite breakfast items. $$$

Goofy's Kitchen at the Disneyland Hotel. 1150 Magic Way; (714) 778-6600. Your kids will not want to miss Goofy's, one of the nine restaurants on-site. Open every day—breakfast, lunch, and dinner. Call for specific hours as they vary seasonally. You can dine with Disney characters (and get your picture taken!), eat Disney Character Meals, try out the all-you-can-eat buffet, and receive a **free** souvenir button. Our kids insist on this "dining experience" every time! $$$

Disneyland Hotel. 1150 Magic Way; (714) 778-6600 or direct to reservations at (714) 956-6400. Just west of Disneyland and connected by the futuristic monorail, this hotel opened at the same time as the park in 1955 and has continued to evolve. It features 990 guest rooms and suites in 3 high-rise towers surrounding the magical Peter Pan–themed Neverland pool complex (with water slides, bridges, and shallow play areas); a kids' playground; and a sandy beach with rental pedal boats, remote-control tugboats, and dune buggies. There are 9 restaurants and lounges to choose from, plus 4 swimming pools, a hot tub, the Team Mickey Fitness Center, gift shops, and an 80-game video arcade. Nineteen guest rooms are highly themed to either Mickey Mouse or the regal Disney Princesses. These "Character Quarters" each feature 2 twin beds and are available adjoining a standard room. They are perfect for a family of five or more. (Of course, advance reservations are required for these high-demand lodgings.) This hotel is a destination

All-Suite Hotels **near Disneyland**

Like California wildflowers, an amazing variety of all-suite hotels have sprung up near the park in recent years. This trend really is a boon for traveling families like us, who like to have a private bedroom for the adults and a multifunction living room/dining area with hide-a-bed arrangements for the kids. Each suite hotel has varying amenities such as **free** breakfasts, kitchenettes, pools, and spas. You might want to investigate the Castle Inn & Suites (714-774-8111), the Peacock Suite Resort (714-535-8255), Carousel Inn & Suites (check out the rooftop pool; 714-758-0444), or Anaheim Portofino Inn and Suites (714-782-7600), as well as all the national chains.

within itself, and you should plan some time to enjoy all the amenities. Family-friendly features include no charge for children younger than age 17 staying in same room as parents; **free** roll-aways and porta-cribs, and baby-sitting referrals to licensed "grandmother types." Value-priced hotel and park package plans are prevalent and include early admission into both parks before the regular opening. Be sure to ask what's available when making reservations. Another great service is the Package Express, which delivers all your park purchases to your hotel room for **free.** $$$$

Disney's Grand Californian Hotel & Spa. 1600 South Disneyland Dr.; (714) 635-2300. Opened in February 2001, this AAA four-diamond rated luxurious 745-room hotel with its striking California Craftsman architectural design is located on the northwest corner of Disney's California Adventure. This hotel is the only one to offer direct access straight into the park, a wonderful time-saving feature for your family. Guest rooms come equipped with a choice of king, 2 queens, or a queen and a set of bunk beds—a real family-fun plus for us! The concierge level offers extra amenities including complimentary continental breakfast and evening wine and cheese and an array of recreational activities for the entire family. We adults savor the Mandara Spa with some precious pampering and personal service. We all enjoyed the Fountain Pool and the Redwood Pool with waterslide; and for ages 5 to 12, there is nothing better than Pinocchio's Workshop—an evening of arts and crafts, computer games, Disney movies, dinner, and snacks with a licensed supervisor. The storytelling hour in front of the massive lobby fireplace with kids in pint-size wooden rockers is a perfect example of the Disney detail you can expect for your family here.

From the moment you arrive (and are offered valet parking), you are treated with outstanding hospitality and service. Hotel dining options include 24-hour room service and the excellent Storyteller's Cafe with its tasty breakfast buffet and American cuisine for lunch and dinner daily (and visits from Disney characters such as Chip 'n Dale), plus the stunning Napa Rose Restaurant (with an open exhibition kitchen), Hearthstone Lounge, and White Water Snacks Poolside. We really like this property and feel the higher room rates are justified given the ease of park accessibility combined with the outstanding amenities and service. $$$$

Disney's Paradise Pier Hotel. 1717 Disneyland Dr.; (714) 999-0990 or direct to reservations at (714) 956-6400. This 15-story, full-service hotel overlooks the festive Paradise Pier area at Disney's California Adventure. Choose from 489 nicely furnished guest rooms and suites. There are 4 restaurants and lounges, an outdoor pool and spa deck, a game arcade, convenient indoor/outdoor parking, and gift shops. There is no charge for children younger than age 18 staying in the same room as parents. $$$–$$$$

For More Information

Anaheim/Orange County Visitor and Convention Bureau. 800 West Katella Ave.; (714) 765-8888 or (888) 598-3200; www.anaheimoc.org.

Buena Park

Now it's time to gear up for another round of great family adventure in nearby Buena Park—only 15 minutes from Anaheim and Disneyland. This area's development began in

1920, when Walter and Cordelia Knott and their three young children arrived and started farming on 20 acres of leased land. The Knotts set up a roadside produce stand on Beach Boulevard to sell their crops, and in 1932 Walter Knott started propagating a cross blend of raspberry, blackberry, and loganberry plants that he named boysenberry. In 1934, to help make ends meet during the Great Depression, Cordelia Knott began serving chicken dinners for 65 cents on her wedding china to passing motorists. Soon Knott's Berry Farm boysenberry fruits, jams, jellies, and pies, along with the Chicken Dinner Restaurant, became so popular that the family decided to build an attraction to keep waiting patrons amused. In 1940 Walter Knott began moving old buildings to the site from various ghost towns. The Calico Mine Ride followed in 1960, and a re-creation of Philadelphia's Independence Hall was constructed in 1966. In 1968 the amusement park area was enclosed, and for the first time a general admission fee was charged. Knott's Berry Farm forms the nucleus for many attractions in this commercial section of Orange County. Plan on spending at least two days here in order to do it all "berry good."

Knott's Berry Farm

8039 Beach Blvd. at the corner of La Palma Avenue; (714) 220-5200; www.knotts.com. Open daily except Christmas. Summer hours 9 a.m. to midnight. In winter the park operates weekdays 10 a.m. to 6 p.m., Sat 10 a.m. to 10 p.m., and Sun 10 a.m. to 7 p.m. Extended hours are offered during holiday periods. All admissions after 4 p.m. are reduced year-round. Parking across the street and accessed by a special walkway or tram is $12 per car. Be absolutely sure to call in advance for current ticket prices and schedules since all are subject to change without notice. $$$$.

Knott's Berry Farm was family-owned and -operated until its 1997 purchase by Cedar Fair Entertainment Company. It attracts more than 5 million guests each year to its entertainment park and marketplace, featuring 165 attractions, rides, live shows, restaurants, and shops. The lushly landscaped 160 acres have plenty of flowers, trees, waterfalls, and shady spots.

Five theme areas include the original **Ghost Town,** where you can pan for gold and go for a great log ride and take the Ghost Rider, the longest wooden coaster in the West; **Camp Snoopy,** the official home of the Peanuts gang, including Woodstock's air mail ride; and **Fiesta Village,** prowling ground for the Jaguar!, a 2,700-foot-long steel roller coaster that winds its way above the park and loops through Montezooma's Revenge (another thrilling coaster with its own 76-foot-high loop). The **Boardwalk** has Xcelerator, Perilous Plunge, Riptide, the Boomerang (ever been on a roller coaster that rolls backward? Definite queasy alert!), and Supreme Scream (312 feet of vertical excitement), as well as Sky Cabin and Wipeout. The Mystery Lodge is a magical multisensory show focusing on native North American culture located in the **Wild Water Wilderness.** Come here at the end of your day if you plan on riding Bigfoot Rapids. Speaking from personal experience, heed the warning signs: You will get wet on this ride—most likely drenched! It may feel great on a hot summer day, but squishy shoes and clothing can get mighty uncomfortable mighty fast. "Indian Trails" gives you a chance to dry off and watch Native American arts, crafts, and music. Don't miss the Pony Express coaster, a horseback relay launching at a speed of 0 to 38 mph in less than three seconds—speeds never imagined in the Old West! New at Knott's in 2010 was Snoopy's Starlight Spectacular, a continuous light show filled with Peanuts three-dimensional figures, themed music, sound effects, voice-overs, and colorful projections; plus a new Everyone Loves Snoopy ice-show extravaganza at the Charles M. Schulz Theatre.

Knott's Soak City U.S.A.—Orange County

Across the street from Knott's Berry Farm, 8039 Beach Blvd. at La Palma Avenue, adjacent to Knott's Independence Hall; (714) 220-5200; www.knotts.com. Open daily Memorial Day through Labor Day; open Sat and Sun in May, Sept, and Oct. Be sure to call for current schedule as it is subject to change seasonally. $$$$.

This California-beach-theme water park features 23 separate water rides and attractions, including tube and body water slides, a wave pool, a lazy river, a family fun house, restaurants, snack bars, a sand beach, a pier, and gift shops.

Adventure City (ages 2 to 12)

1238 Beach Blvd. between Cerritos Avenue and Ball Road, on the outskirts of Anaheim near Buena Park; (714) 236-9300 for current operating hours; www.adventurecity.com. Generally open daily in summer from 10 a.m. to 5 p.m. and in winter Fri through Sun, but hours are subject to change without notice. $$$.

Adventure City, "the Little Theme Park Just for Kids," resembles a storybook village designed and proportioned for children ages 2 to 12. For a wonderfully relaxing experience, consider visiting this 2-acre park with its ten kid-size rides that are quiet yet still zoom and thrill, as well as hourly puppet shows, a 25-foot climbing wall, live theater, storytelling, and face painting. Parent-child interaction is made easy here because the atmosphere is very casual and low-hype. There are plenty of park benches for parental units to sit and relax while the kids go brave the Kid Coaster or the carousel.

Medieval Times Dinner and Tournament

7662 Beach Blvd.; (714) 521-4740 or (888) WE-JOUST; www.medievaltimes.com. Open nightly year-round; call for specific show times (vary daily). $$$$.

You'll eat in an arena filled with more than 1,100 people, divided into 6 sections, wearing colored hats, waving streamers, and cheering their favorite knight on to victory over the course of a 2-hour 11th-century show. Included is a four-course meal of 21st-century food (appetizer, vegetable soup, chicken, ribs, baked potato slice, and apple turnover) in medieval style (no modern knife, fork, or spoon to assist you). Make sure you bring plenty of extra cash to buy banners to wave, souvenir programs, and photos taken during dinner. Beer, wine, sodas, and coffee are included in the admission price; however, these prices are subject to change and do not include gratuity for your hardworking serving wenches and serfs. Call the colorful castle for daily showtimes—advance reservations are required. Make sure you arrive at least one hour before your scheduled showtime to navigate the parking lot with your chariot and negotiate the check-in line.

This is outstanding family fun that is not to be missed—you and the kids can release all kinds of pent-up vocal energy as you yell for "your" knight in armor during a pageant of excellent horsemanship and tournament games of skill and accuracy. A pricey outing, but we think you definitely will agree that "your day's not over until you've seen those knights!"

Pirate's Dinner Adventure

7600 Beach Blvd., immediately off the 91 freeway; (714) 690-1497 or (866) 439-2469; www.piratesdinneradventure.com. Open daily; call for show times and specials. Doors open 90 minutes prior to the show for appetizers in the ship's "lounge." Showroom doors open 15 minutes prior to performance, and seating begins in an authentically replicated 18th-century Spanish galleon anchored in a 250,000-gallon indoor lagoon with 6 "audience ships" around the perimeter—each equipped with color-coded character pirate you are encouraged to cheer and interact with throughout the evening. Show is 90 minutes. $$$$.

At Pirate's Dinner Adventure up to 750 guests can enjoy this extravaganza, featuring an astonishing display of special-effects wizardry, aerial trapeze artistry, swashbuckling swordplay, pirate fights, and dynamic duels. While all this action is going on, you can eat your "Port of Call Feast," including garden salad, choice of beef or marinated chicken with seafood (shrimp and scallops), West Indies yellow rice with Caribbean seasonings, and steamed vegetables with warm apple cobbler a la mode for dessert washed down with a choice of soda, beer, or wine. Our recommendation: The show is geared for ages 10 and up, but there certainly are plenty of younger guests in attendance and participating in the pirates' activities during the show—it just seemed a bit too much excitement, noise, lights, and fights for a young child's activity. Ahoy!

Where to Eat

Knott's California Marketplace. Just outside the main entrance of Knott's Berry Farm, 8039 Beach Blvd. at the corner of La Palma Avenue; (714) 220-5200. This area is filled with shops and restaurants for your family's pleasure, but the best is Mrs. Knott's original Chicken Dinner Restaurant. Hearty American fare is served for breakfast, lunch, and dinner at very reasonable prices. The kids' menu comes complete with crayons and a coloring book. We recommend eating here for lunch (go early or late to avoid crowds). Don't plan on taking any rides at the theme park anytime near your consumption of that delicious chicken, mashed potatoes, and boysenberry pie. (We speak from experience here. Trust us!) $$

Where to Stay

Knott's Berry Farm Resort Hotel. 7675 Crescent Ave., adjacent to Knott's Berry Farm; (714) 995-1111; www.knottshotel .com. Its 320 units include a limited number of Peanuts theme rooms with nightly Snoopy character turndown service. **Free** Snoopy gift for kids at check-in. Outdoor kiddy pool, adult pool, whirlpool, fitness center, sauna, and steam room. Popular American-style family food at Amber Waves Restaurant with kids' menus and daily visits

from Snoopy to add to the fun. Check out the all-you-can-eat breakfast buffet as well as nightly specials (2010 saw Fri and Sat Prime Rib & Crab Leg dinners for $26.95!). **Free** parking. $$$

For More Information

Buena Park Convention and Visitors Office. 6601 Beach Blvd., Suite 200; (714) 562-3560 or (800) 541-3953; www.visitbuena park.com.

Orange

How would you like to find a slice of the Midwestern United States buried in the heart of Orange County? Look no further than the historic city of Orange, sandwiched between Santa Ana and Anaheim, the two largest cities in all of Orange County. Approach the city of Orange by way of eastbound Chapman Avenue, off I-5 or from Highway 57. As you enter downtown, cobblestone, tree-lined thoroughfares take you into the intersection of Chapman and Glassell Streets, where you will discover a circular central plaza. The "Plaza City" boasts a 1-square-mile historic district, where 19th-century architecture is preserved and cherished, and the appeal is decidedly homespun and friendly. Check out the living-history lessons presented in the myriad antiques shops scattered around the plaza.

Watson's Drugs and Soda Fountain

116 East Chapman; (714) 633-1050. Open Mon through Sat 6:30 a.m. to 9 p.m. and Sun 8 a.m. to 6 p.m. $.

The best place to soak up the flavor of Orange is on a stool at a joint that has been continuously serving heaping scoops of ice cream, traditional American meals, and remedies at its Plaza Square location since 1899. The root beer floats are so frothy you will wonder

A Card Game **Names a Town**

In 1869, Los Angeles attorneys Alfred Chapman and Andrew Glassell received 1,385 acres of land as payment for their legal services. They quickly subdivided it into a 1-square-mile town dubbed Richland with numerous 10-acre farm lots surrounding it. When attempting to register the name Richland in 1873, it was denied by the state clerk since there already was a Richland, California, in Sacramento County. Legend has it that Alfred Chapman (who wanted the name "Lemon"), Andrew Glassell (who liked "Orange"), and two other gentlemen (who preferred "Olive" or "Walnut") played a hand of poker, and the man that won the card game named the town. Glassell, the astute poker player born in Orange County, Virginia, was the ultimate winner, and the city hereafter and still today is called . . . Orange.

how you lived this long without one, and the malts are the real deal—hand-dipped ice cream with a scoop of malt and real milk. Sweet! Breakfast, lunch, and dinner daily, featuring a kids' menu for those ages 12 and younger. Go in anytime to see an authentic soda fountain in action and watch the servers in their period outfits and hairdos play soda jerks. The interior and exterior have been used to film many movies and commercials, including Tom Hanks's film *That Thing You Do!*

For More Information

City of Orange Chamber of Commerce.
439 East Chapman Ave., Suite A; (714)
538-3581 or (800) 938-0073; www.orange
chamber.com.

Santa Ana

Orange County's largest city is also the county seat of government and home to the John Wayne/Orange County Airport (SNA) (949-252-5200; www.ocair.com). Downtown Santa Ana combines Fiesta Marketplace, a bustling Latino-style pedestrian mall, with a contemporary $50 million civic center and about a hundred historic buildings that would make the Spanish explorer Portolá proud of the city he christened in 1796.

Bowers Museum of Cultural Art and Kidseum

2002 North Main St.; (714) 567-3600; www.bowers.org. Open Tues through Fri 10 a.m. to 4 p.m., Sat and Sun 10 a.m. to 6 p.m. Open holidays except Christmas, Thanksgiving, and New Year's Day. Closed Mon. $$.

A significant part of Santa Ana's past is found in its first museum, created in 1936 through a bequest from Charles and Ada Bowers to preserve the local history of Orange County. Through gifts and acquisitions, the Bowers' collections have grown over the years, and the museum has enlarged its space three times. It is now considered one of the finest cultural arts repositories in the West. The museum specializes in the arts of the Americas, the Pacific Rim, and Africa, along with its ongoing commitment to chronicle the story of Orange County. The museum store has unique art treasures, cards, and gifts not readily available in traditional museum gift shops.

In 1994 the 11,000-square-foot **Bowers Kidseum** opened 2 blocks away at 1802 North Main St. This amazing center has been competently designed for youths ages 6 to 12 as a place where children can learn about other cultures, music, art, and history through interactive, hands-on exhibits. Hours of operation for the general public run Tues through Fri from 1 to 4 p.m. and Sat and Sun from 10 a.m. to 4 p.m. Admission fees are identical and reciprocal with the Bowers Museum. Thematic "explorers' backpacks" covering various cultural differences are just one example of this outstanding opportunity for your kids to actually learn something valuable while vacationing. The Kidseum perfectly bridges the gap between amusement and education.

Heritage Museum of Orange County

3101 West Harvard St.; (714) 540-0404; www.heritagemuseumoc.org. Open to the public Fri 1 to 5 p.m. and Sun 11 a.m. to 3 p.m. Other days/times by appointment only. Closed major holidays. $.

This historic museum, located in the fully restored, 1898 Victorian Kellogg House, is your family's chance to step back in time to the 1800s. Kids can try on Victorian costumes, wash clothes on a scrub board, play a pump organ, or talk on a hand-cranked telephone. Recently restored, the Maag House, built in 1899, was the ranch house of citrus and nut grower John Anton Maag and his family. This is a very fun yet informative way to learn early California history. The 8-acre Nature Center has interpretive trails.

The Santa Ana Zoo at Prentice Park

1801 East Chestnut Ave.; (714) 835-7484; www.santaanazoo.org. Open daily 10 a.m. to 4 p.m., extended hours in summer. Closed only Christmas and New Year's Day. $$.

This charming zoo will calm your kids' animal urges with its 250 species of primates, other mammals, and birds. Tierra de la Pampas is a new, multi-species exhibit, showcasing ant-eaters, guanacos, and rheas. This exhibit celebrates and preserves one of the most highly endangered habitats in the world, the Pampas grasslands of South America. Refreshments are available in the food court, and vendors around the grounds sell snacks and ice cream. A playground, the Crean Family Farm (with interactive feeding), and Zoofari Express minia-ture train rides are offered. Call for current programs and times.

Discovery Science Center

2500 North Main St. (at the corner of I-5 and the Santa Ana Freeway); (714) 542-CUBE; www .discoverycube.org. Open daily 10 a.m. to 5 p.m. except major holidays. $$$.

"The Amusement Park for Your Mind" opened in 1998 in a 59,000-square-foot multistory facility with a cube on top devoted to sparking children's natural curiosity and increasing everyone's understanding of science, math, and technology. More than 120 highly interac-tive exhibits make you think, search for answers, and participate in the learning process. Themed areas include Perception, Dynamic Earth, Quake Zone, Showcase Gallery, Boeing Delta III Rocket, Air & Space, Techno Arts, and Digital Lab. Our personal favorite activities include the Shake Shack to experience an earthquake, lying down on a bed of nails (and not screaming), and dancing on the musical floor. New in 2010, Boeing Rocket Lab allows you to discover your inner astronaut for those who love all things space, and want to learn about the science of space, rockets, and engineering. "The Cube" is a marvelous family attraction that you should not miss! Highly recommended.

For More Information

Santa Ana Chamber of Commerce. 2020 North Broadway, second floor; (714) 541-5353; www.santanachamber.com.

Irvine & Costa Mesa

The city of Irvine is the largest master-planned community in the United States. It was first developed in 1959 as a site for the University of California-Irvine on an old Spanish land grant. Billboards, overhead power lines, and TV antennas are banned here in an area divided into 38 urban villages featuring a plethora of parks, all connected by greenbelts and bike paths. Shopping centers and services are all conveniently located nearby. The central corridor of high-rise buildings, such as the Irvine Spectrum and Koll Center, provide headquarters for plenty of Fortune 500 firms as well as some family fun.

The adjacent city of Costa Mesa, also home to many corporations as well as a popular residential community, became a player on the Orange County shopping and entertainment scene in 1967 with the opening of South Coast Plaza: dubbed the Ultimate Shopping Resort, a great place for your family to satisfy those shopping urges.

Irvine Spectrum Center

At the intersection of I-405 (exit Irvine Center Drive) and I-5 (exit Alton), Irvine. Open daily 10 a.m. to 9 p.m.; hours can vary for restaurants and during holiday periods and special events. Call (949) 753-5180 for more information or visit www.shopirvinespectrumcenter.com.

This premier plaza offers 21 IMAX movie cinemas, world-class restaurants, nightlife, 120 specialty shops from around the globe, a 108-foot-tall Giant Wheel (Ferris wheel), and a carousel. Opened in November 1995, it was one of the first in the country to be anchored by restaurants and entertainment venues—a "lifestyle center"—setting a precedent in the shopping center industry, and it attracts nearly 13 million visitors annually. Stores include Anthropologie, bebe, White House/ Black Market, Urban Outfitters, Brighton Collectibles, Ann Taylor Loft, Oakley "O" Store, Quiksilver Boardriders Club, Garys Island, Forever 21, Barnes & Noble, and many more.

Wild Rivers Waterpark (ages 3 and up)

8770 Irvine Center Dr., Irvine; (949) 768-WILD; www.wildrivers.com. Open daily from Memorial Day weekend throughout the summer season from 10 a.m. to 8 p.m.; call for early/ seasonal hours. $$$$.

Your high-tech children will definitely want to take advantage of this 20-acre park with more than 40 water rides, including the Edge, the Ledge, and the Abyss; two wave pools; kiddie wading pools; sunbathing areas; a water slide; log flumes; picnic areas; and a video arcade to complete the family-fun mix.

South Coast Plaza

3333 Bristol St., at the intersection of I-405 and Bristol Street, Costa Mesa; (800) 782-8888 or call the concierge at (949) 435-2034 for a current special-event and promotion schedule; www.southcoastplaza.com.

One of the largest retail centers in the USA, welcoming approximately 24 million visitors annually. In addition to shopping, it is also home to the Orange Lounge, a digital media-focused branch of the Orange County Museum of Art. Many ultra-luxury brands also call South Coast Plaza home, including French luxury design house Chloé, Rolex, Harry Winston, Tiffany's, Cartier, Montblanc, Louis Vuitton, Versace, Prada, Dior, Valentino, Chanel, Yves Saint Laurent, Gucci, Hermès, Barney's New York Co-Op, and Nordstrom. Restaurants include Lawry's Carvery, Charlie Palmer at Bloomingdales, and Vie De France (no food courts here!). Check out the valet parking, concierge services, and hot beverage service on those infrequent cool days, which make this one of the most upscale malls anywhere—your fashionista tweens and teens will revel here.

Trinity Christian City International

3150 Bear St. (across I-405 from the South Coast Plaza Mall); (714) 832-2950 or (714) 708-5405; www.tbn.org. Free.

This striking, classically inspirational building houses broadcast studios and the popular gift and bookshop of this Christian television network. The Virtual Reality Theater presents free motion pictures daily. Tour the Demos Shakarian Memorial Building, seen regularly on international television broadcasts. On special evenings join in during a free live television broadcast of the "Praise The Lord!" program. Call for current titles and show times. All ages are welcome.

Orange County Performing Arts Center

600 Town Center Dr., South Coast Plaza, Costa Mesa; (714) 556-2121 or www.ocpac.org for current events and admission charges. $$$$.

Opened in 1986, the 3,000-seat Segerstrom Hall is where major symphony concerts, operas, ballets, and Broadway musicals are presented year-round; joined in 2006 by the new 1,700-seat Renée and Henry Segerstrom Concert Hall and the intimate Samueli Theater. It is the home of four resident companies: Pacific Symphony, the Philharmonic Society of Orange County, Opera Pacific, and Pacific Chorale. In 2009–10, the Family Series of Events featured kid-friendly productions including *Jason and the Argonauts*, *The Man Who Planted Trees*, *Stellaluna*, *Pigeon Party*, and *The Story of Frog Belly Rat Bone*.

Orange County Fair and Event Center

88 Fair Dr., Costa Mesa; (714) 708-1567 or www.ocfair.com/ocf for current activities.

Discover a variety of fun family events, including swap meets, automobile and motorcycle speedway races, and concerts. In July, the Orange County Fair takes over, featuring top-name entertainment, livestock, carnival rides, rodeo, foodstuffs, arts, crafts, contests, and demonstrations.

For More Information

Costa Mesa Conference and Visitor Bureau. P.O. Box 5071, Costa Mesa 92628-5071; (866) 918-4749 or (714) 435-8530; www.travelcostamesa.com.

Irvine Chamber of Commerce Visitors Bureau. 2485 McCabe Way, Suite 150, Irvine; (949) 660-9112 or (877) IRVINE-7; www.irvinecvb.org.

Huntington Beach

Waterfront action or just plain relaxation (lack of action) will provide a respite from all your inland encounters. Orange County's beaches are part of the defining Southern California experience. Traveling along the Pacific Coast Highway, commonly known as PCH or just the Coast Highway in these parts, begin your waterside explorations at Huntington Beach, Orange County's third-largest city (after Santa Ana and Anaheim). It is growing into a thriving resort area with more than 8 miles of uninterrupted shoreline. Between Goldenwest Street and Brookhurst Street along PCH, the Bolsa Chica and Huntington Beaches provide plenty of area for safe swimming, picnicking, and surfing. Beach parking fees are charged and vary according to time and season.

Huntington is one of the surf capitals of Southern California, and it thus has been named "Surf City USA." Your kids will probably know this because of the mega-television coverage afforded the surfing championships and international competitions held here every summer. You can easily spend a day on the beaches of Huntington, just enjoying the beautiful surf, sand, and sea. (Do remember to use your sunscreen liberally. Ask any Huntington Beach surfer dude—sunburn is not cool!) The town's ambitious redevelopment efforts along Main Street, just off PCH, contain postmodern shopping plazas and condos alongside the original turn-of-the-last-century waterfront clapboards, which now house trendy clothing stores, beach shops, and bistros. Strolling the 1,856-foot municipal pier is a favorite pastime. Pier Plaza, on PCH at Main, hosts a farmers' market on Friday and live entertainment.

International Surfing Museum

411 Olive Ave.; (714) 960-3483; www.surfingmuseum.org. Displays, admission fees, and opening and closing hours change like the tides (well, not really that frequently!), so call for the current schedule and low admission donations, dudes. Free, but donations welcome.

An art deco–ish building downtown, home of radical exhibits, artifacts, and memorabilia ranging from vintage surfboards to surf wear and surf films, all preserving the heritage of "Surf City USA." Dedicated in May 1994, the Huntington Beach Surfing Walk of Fame marked an historic addition to "Surf City." Each inductee receives a granite stone placed in the sidewalk extending from the corners of Pacific Coast Highway and Main Street. Categories include Surf Pioneer, Surf Champion, Surfing Culture, Local Hero, Woman of the Year, and the Honor Roll.

Bolsa Chica Ecological Reserve and Interpretive Center

Between Warner Avenue and Goldenwest Street on the Pacific Coast Highway, just opposite the entrance to Bolsa Chica State Beach; (714) 846-1114; www.bolsachica.org. Open daily, dawn to dusk. Free.

It is both relaxing and educational to walk through this 300-acre reserve, one of the largest salt marsh preserves in Southern California. The reserve supports such rare migratory

Surfing HQ

Huntington Beach has lured legendary surfing icons such as Duke Kahanamoku, Corky Carroll, Pete Townend, Kelly Slater, Rob Machado, and Layne Beachley over the decades with some of the most consistent surf on the West Coast. The city hosts more than 30 national and international surfing championships each year, including the US Open of Surfing each July, the gnarliest of North American surfing events. Several surfing industry leaders consider Huntington Beach their home, such as Quiksilver, a worldwide clothing brand; Surfline.com, a website that monitors more than a hundred global surfing locations daily; the Association of Surfing Professionals (ASP); and the USA Surf Team. Jack's Surfboards (www.jacks surfboards.com) and Huntington Surf and Sport (www.hsssurf.com) are legendary surf and clothing shops headquartered in Huntington. Stop by and hang for some truly authentic culture—your surf rat progeny will love you for it!

waterfowl as avocets, egrets, plovers, and terns. A 1.5-mile walkway with explanatory signs leads the way throughout the ecosystem. Ask about the guided public tour schedule.

Shipley Nature Center at Huntington Central Park

17829 Goldenwest St. (south of Slater Ave.); (714) 960-8847; www.shipleynature.org. Center is generally open Mon through Sat 9 a.m. to 1 p.m.; park is open 5 a.m. to 10 p.m. Free admission.

For another view of plants and animals, check out this park, home to hundreds of bird species. For human guests there are picnic areas and playgrounds, plus walking and bicycling trails that wind past ponds, waterways, and woodlands.

Where to Eat & Stay

Dwight's at the Beach. On the Boardwalk, 1 block south of the pier; (714) 536-8083. Winter hours: weekends only, 9 a.m. to 5:30 p.m. Summer hours: Mon to Sun, 9 a.m. to 5:30 p.m. Since 1932, serving juicy burgers, hot dogs, ice cream, and famous cheese strips—tortilla strips and cheddar cheese topped with secret hot sauce. Dwight's at the Beach also rents bicycles, surfboards, boogie boards, sand chairs, and more. $

Lazy Dog Café. 16310 Beach Blvd., at Mac-Donald Avenue, just south of the 405 freeway near Huntington Beach in Westminster; (714) 500-1140; www.thelazydogcafe.com. Open daily for lunch and dinner. They're serious about food here, but they don't take themselves too seriously since they offer build-your-own pizzas for kids, a plate of delicious mini chili-cheese dogs, and even a dessert served in a dog bowl. The extensive children's menu, which is broken down into "Puppy Dogs" (children up to age 7) and "Big Dogs" (ages 8 to 12) is very creative and nutritious! $$

Hyatt Regency Huntington Beach Resort & Spa. 21500 Pacific Coast Highway; (714) 698-1234; www.huntingtonbeach.hyatt.com. Garden and ocean views from 517 guest rooms and 57 suites in Andalusian-inspired style. This luxurious hotel directly across from the beach via a pedestrian walkway features 3 restaurants (the Californian for fine dining, Pete Mallory's Surf City Sunset Grille, and Mankota's Grill poolside), the Village shopping plaza, and the 20,000-square-foot Pacific Waters Spa. Two Camp Hyatt children's programs are offered daily from 9 a.m. to 9 p.m. Campers receive a welcome gift upon arrival and a packet describing on-site activities. Kids ages 3 to 7 can become Camp Hyatt Beach Clubbers and make shell necklaces,

do beach sand art, and roast s'mores by the fire. The SophistiKids program for youth ages 8 to 12 includes cool pool and beach play, koi fish feeding, or surfboard making (www.camphyatt.com). Other options at the hotel include parents and kids shared spa treatments as well as Adventure Hyatt programs such as kayaking, learning to surf, and sport fishing tours. $$$$

For More Information

Huntington Beach Marketing and Visitors Bureau. 301 Main St., Suite 208; (714) 969-3492 or (800) 729-6232; www.surfcityusa.com.

Newport Beach Area

Just south of Huntington Beach along the glittering Pacific lies a city of villages, islands, and private enclaves first incorporated in 1906. The Newport Beach area comprises Balboa, Balboa Island, Lido Isle, Newport Heights, Harbor Island, Bay Shore, Linda Isle, and Corona del Mar. It includes one of the West Coast's largest and most famous yacht harbors, containing approximately 9,000 pleasure craft. In addition, a 6-mile "inland" beach lies along the peninsula between Newport Bay and the ocean. You and your family will discover what many believe to be the trendiest Southern California beach life here.

Balboa Pavilion

400 Main St., located at the Newport Bay end of Main Street, on the Balboa Peninsula; (800) 830-7744; www.balboapavilion.com. Open daily 10 a.m. to 10 p.m. Free.

Begin your exploration of the waterfront action at this classic building constructed in 1905 and now listed on the National Register of Historic Places. Here you will discover a marine recreation center offering ferries to quaint Balboa Island and Catalina Island and charter boats for sailing, whale watching, sightseeing, and sport fishing. The Fun Zone has a carousel, Ferris wheel, and arcade. Even more about Balboa Village can be discovered at www.balboavillage.com.

Cruising to Catalina **from Orange County**

The Catalina Passenger Service operates the *Catalina Flyer*, its 500-passenger catamaran vessel, from Balboa Pavilion in Newport Beach. It offers a round-trip 75-minute cruise daily to neighboring Santa Catalina Island, a pristine, unspoiled isle only 26 miles out to sea yet a world away. (See the Greater Los Angeles chapter for other Long Beach/San Pedro embarkation choices.) Fares and departure times are subject to change seasonally. Reservations are required. Phone (949) 673-5245 or (800) 830-7744 for current schedules or visit www.catalinainfo.com. $$$$

Davey's Locker Sportfishing

400 Main St., Balboa Pavilion, Balboa; (949) 673-1434; www.daveyslocker.com. Open daily; hours vary according to season. $$$$.

Your headquarters in Newport Beach for harbor excursions, whale watching, and half-, three-quarter, and full-day fishing excursions for catching yellowfin tuna, bonito, sand bass, and rockfish. Twilight fishing trips are offered in the summer, too. These folks are pros, and they will make you feel very comfortable and safe on the water.

The Newport Harbor Nautical Museum

In the heart of Balboa Peninsula's Fun Zone, 600 East Bay Ave., Newport Beach; (949) 673-3377; www.nhnm.org. Open Sun through Thurs 11 a.m. to 6 p.m., Fri and Sat 11 a.m. to 7 p.m. $.

This interesting museum gives a photographic history of the harbor, a fascinating ships-in-a-bottle exhibit, and a display of navigational instruments and model ships, including one made of bone and human hair, and one made of 22 karat gold and silver. The new East Wing has interactive exhibits, a multimedia space called Touch Tank, and temporary and visiting exhibits.

Hornblower Cruises and Events

2431 West Pacific Coast Highway, Suite 101, Newport Beach; (949) 646-0155; www.horn blower.com. Cruises on climate-controlled large yachts offered year-round. Evening and Sunday brunch cruise schedules vary according to season and demand for private charters. Brunch cruises sail for two hours and include an all-you-can-eat buffet with champagne for adults; children ages 4 to 12 half price. Gratuity and cocktails additional. $$$$.

Excellent service from nautically attired crew and California cuisine prepared fresh onboard make this an upscale cruising, dining, and sightseeing experience to remember. Recommended for older children; for our families, we like the Sunday brunch cruises best.

Shopping and More **with an Ocean View**

Luring you away from the Newport Beach and harbor area, but with the ocean firmly in sight, the 600-acre Newport Center, just above the Pacific Coast Highway between MacArthur Boulevard and Jamboree Road, is an office, luxury hotel, and entertainment complex built in 1967. It hosts a must-stop shopping center—the trendy Fashion Island. Call (949) 721-2000, the concierge contact number, or visit www.shopfashionisland.com for schedules of children's activities, fashion shows, and great promotions. Containing more than 200 major chain stores and regional specialty shops, Newport Center is also home to the luxurious AAA-rated five-diamond Island Hotel (949-759-0808; www.islandhotel.com), as well as 40 restaurants in the Atrium Court. This is where you and the kids can chill out after a hard day at the beach!

Newport Sports Museum

100 Newport Center Dr., Suite 100; (949) 721-9333; www.newportsportsmuseum.org. Open Mon to Sat from 10 a.m. to 5 p.m. Free admission always.

This 6,000-square-foot museum features one of the world's largest collections of sports memorabilia, assembled in 15 themed rooms containing 10,000 items. Highlights include jerseys from Michael Jordan, Larry Bird, Dr. J, and Wilt Chamberlain and autographed baseballs from every Cy Young winner. There's even a baseball park with actual seats from places such as Yankee Stadium and Wrigley Field! The collection started in 1953 when John W. Hamilton, at the age of 12, was given a "Look All-American Football" by a family friend. Hamilton has been collecting sports memorabilia ever since, with the majority of the items being personally given to him by athletes.

Sherman Library and Gardens

2647 East Pacific Coast Highway, south of Newport Beach in Corona del Mar; (949) 673-2261; www.slgardens.org. Gardens are open daily from 10:30 a.m. to 4 p.m. $.

This 2-acre cultural center has botanical gardens displaying tropical and subtropical flora in addition to its research library of southwestern US history. The touch-and-smell garden is a major wow for your kids; you will enjoy the respite in the Café Jardin for lunch served Mon through Fri (949-673-0033).

Where to Eat

Back Bay Bistro. 1131 Back Bay Dr., Newport Beach; (949) 729-1144; www.backbay bistronewportbeach.com. Lunch: Tues and Wed 11:30 a.m. to 3 p.m.; Thurs and Fri 11:30 a.m. to close; Sat and Sun 8 a.m. to close. Dinner: Thurs to Sun 5 p.m. to close. Saturday and Sunday brunch 9 a.m. to 2 p.m. Closed Mon. (Call for daily closing hours.) In the Newport Dunes Resort, the Bistro ideally overlooks the calm inland waters of Upper

Newport Bay as well as all the action at the adjacent boat launch/marina. Totally family friendly, casual, nautical atmosphere both indoors and out on the patio. California/American traditional foods with children's menu for the 10-and-under crowd. $$

Where to Stay

The Newport Dunes Waterfront Resort. 1131 Back Bay Dr., just off PCH and Jamboree Boulevard; (949) 729-3863 or (800) 765-7661; www.newportdunes.com. Overnight camping site and a 7-lane boat-launch ramp are open 24 hours. This 100-acre "Ritz of RV Parks" waterfront resort provides more than 400 hookups for recreational vehicles and campers, each separated by tropical vine-covered fences. A dozen basic studio cottages inland plus 24 beachfront cottages that sleep from 2 to 8 people and are equipped with kitchens and full baths make ideal family headquarters (the Kath family had a wonderful reunion here in 2007!). You can rent bikes, kayaks, windsurfers, paddleboats, and sailboats here for hours of fun. Lots of family activities planned for guests year-round, such as "movies on the beach" in summer. Call for current rates. $$

Hyatt Regency Newport Beach. 1107 Jamboree Rd., 0.5 miles from Pacific Coast Highway, Newport Beach; (949) 729-1234 or (800) 233-1234; www.newportbeach .hyatt.com. This 410-room California-casual property has 26 spacious acres of beautifully landscaped grounds. The value is here for your family, with package plans and special rates. There are 3 heated pools; a wading pool for the kids; a 9-hole, par-3 golf course; plus a fitness center if you're feeling flabby from lying on the beach. Two restaurants serve daily meals. You'll appreciate the shuttle service to nearby shopping and attractions. $$$

For More Information

Newport Beach Conference and Visitors Bureau. 110 Newport Center Dr., Suite 120; (949) 722-1611 or (800) 94-COAST; www .visitnewportbeach.com

Laguna Beach

Unspoiled by time or tide, the dazzling white sands of Laguna Beach, combined with its artist-colony heritage and year-round mild climate, add up to a unique Orange County destination resort worth exploring. All the major beach action along the Pacific Coast Highway can be found here—your kids will "dig" the sand and the playground at Main Beach downtown, while you stroll the art galleries, boutiques, and bistros that line the Pacific Coast Highway.

Festival of Arts and Pageant of the Masters

In Irvine Bowl Park, 650 Laguna Canyon Rd., near the ocean. The annual festival is staged in July and Aug. For a complete program and brochures, call (949) 494-1145 or (800) 487-3378; www.lagunafestivalofarts.com. $$$$.

The Festival of Arts features 150 of the area's most accomplished artists in a rigorously juried show requiring that all pieces on display or for sale be original, including paintings, sculpture, pastels, drawings, serigraphs, photographs, ceramics, jewelry, etched and stained glass, weaving, handcrafted furniture, musical instruments, model ships, and scrimshaw.

Each summer evening the park's natural amphitheater is the site of the Pageant of the Masters, a world-famous event, where amazingly faithful re-creations of famous artwork are presented on stage by live models. Narrators and a full orchestra make these *tableaux vivants* (living pictures) an extraordinary dramatic experience, particularly the finale—a stunning live portrayal of Leonardo da Vinci's *Last Supper*.

The Sawdust Art Festival Winter Fantasy

935 Laguna Canyon Rd.; (949) 494-3030 for this year's Winter Fantasy dates and nominal admission fees; www.sawdustartfestival.com. $.

This favorite Laguna Beach event is held on four consecutive weekends in November and December in a fragrant eucalyptus grove. Wander 3 acres of paths containing 150 booths filled with holiday arts and crafts while your kids play in the snow (trucked in daily!). A children's art workshop, food, and entertainment make this a wonderful addition to your wintertime vacation experience in Southern California.

Where to Eat & Stay

Hotel Laguna and Claes Restaurant. 425 South Pacific Coast Highway; (949) 494-1151 or (800) 524-2927; www.hotellaguna.com. This historic, 65-room property right on the

Crystal Cove **State Park and Beach**

The park is located off the Pacific Coast Highway between Corona del Mar and Laguna Beach; www.crystalcovestatepark.com. In contrast to much of the glitz and glamour surrounding it, Crystal Cove is best known for its rather rustic setting. Three beach areas below the bluffs include Reef Point with access to two coves; Pelican Point, which is a 3.25-mile trail; and Los Trancos, which offers access to a historic district featuring 1930s-style cottages, with 22 available for nightly rental (www.crystalcovebeachcottages.org). Just offshore is a 1,140-acre underwater park for snorkelers and scuba divers. On the southern edge of the park is El Moro, a 2,200-acre chaparral canyon with 18 miles of hiking, biking, and horse trails. Since the early 1920s this area has been used as a recreational refuge for people escaping the big city in this serene little cove, owned by the Irvine Company until 1979 when they sold the land to California for a state park. A One Day Pass (good anywhere in the park) is $15. While you're there, your family will enjoy the Beachcomber Café (949-376-6900) for breakfast, lunch, or dinner, or grab a famous Date Shake (make the kids try it) at Ruby's Shake Shack (949-464-0100).

sand in the absolute center of town was built in 1930. The 3-story old girl has undergone several face-lifts over the years but remains a favorite. Don't expect ultramodern furnishings but revel in the California-beach quirky atmosphere. Be sure to request a room on the ocean side because the street side is way too noisy. Private beach access, complete with your own beach chairs and food/drinks/towel attendant, make this the ultimate place to people-watch while the kids create sand castles. **Free** continental breakfast included. We really enjoy Claes Restaurant and the Terrace for lunch or early dinner (the bar gets a little hectic later on). You can dine overlooking the beach and all the action. Weddings and special events are pretty and magical at this deco-dame, too. (Laura's niece tied the knot here in 2008!) $$$

The Cottage Restaurant. 308 North Coast Hwy., (949) 494-3023; www.thecottage restaurant.com. Open for breakfast, lunch, and dinner 365 days a year. Call for current hours. This landmark "board and batten" style home has watched the ever-changing Laguna surf for more than a half century and began serving meals to the public in 1964. This is home-style cooking we love to find—especially like the "Laguna Omelette" with bay shrimp, snow crab, fresh dill, and Swiss cheese. $

For More Information

Laguna Beach Visitors and Conference Bureau. 252 Broadway (Highway 133); (949) 497-9229 or (800) 877-1115; www.laguna beachinfo.org.

Dana Point

At the turn of the 19th century, Dana Point (named after Richard Henry Dana, author and mariner) was the only major port between Santa Barbara and San Diego. Now this natural cove has picturesque and modern marinas hosting 2,500 craft. It is famous for its whale-watching cruises from late December through March. The town celebrates its annual Harbor Whale Festival in March with street fairs and plenty of outdoor activities.

Ocean Institute

24200 Dana Point Harbor Dr.; (949) 496-2274; www.ocean-institute.org. Open daily; hours vary by season. Closed major holidays. Ship tours are Sun from 10 a.m. to 2:30 p.m. Members **free,** public general admission (ages 13 and up) $6.50; youth (ages 3 to 12) $4.50; kids (2 years and under) **free.**

Be sure to investigate this fun place that has outstanding sea-life exhibits, tide-pool tours, and a hands-on aquarium touch tank. While you're there, take a tour of the tall ship *Pilgrim*, a replica of the vessel on which Richard Henry Dana, author of the book *Two Years Before the Mast,* sailed to Southern California in the 1830s. In July and August, musical and dramatic productions with a nautical theme are presented on the *Pilgrim*'s deck. Your kids will love the chance to really see sea life in action!

Where to Stay

Doubletree Guest Suites Doheny Beach. 34402 Pacific Coast Highway, across from Doheny State Beach, next to the Yacht Harbor; (949) 661-1100. This full-service, 196-suite hotel is located along a 10-mile stretch of beautiful white-sand beach. All suites have a bedroom and a sitting room (our fave floor plan) with a wet bar, microwave, fridge, 2 remote control TVs, and panoramic views to boot. If you get bored with the beach (heresy), you can always take a dip in the pool or work out in the fitness center. The casual restaurant Tresca has a California-beach fusion menu, open daily for all three meals and Sunday brunch. $$$

For More Information

Dana Point Chamber of Commerce and Visitors Center. 24681 La Plaza #115, Box 12, 92629; (949) 496-1555; www.danapoint chamber.com.

San Juan Capistrano

The village of San Juan Capistrano is just inland along I-5 north from Dana Point, set in rolling hills between the Santa Ana Mountains and the sea. It has many old adobe buildings, and the 1895 Santa Fe Railroad depot has been lovingly restored and is now an Amtrak station and restaurant. Since San Juan Capistrano is good enough for thousands of swallows to return to every year, you know you cannot go wrong here, or for that matter anywhere in Orange County—the ultimate family vacation destination.

Southern California **CityPass**

The Southern California CityPass is an outstanding money saver for you and your family. It includes a Disneyland Resort Park Hopper Ticket, valid for unlimited admission to both Disneyland park and Disney's California Adventure park for three days; a one-day visit to Universal Studios Hollywood; and ample time to motor down the coast to stunning San Diego to visit SeaWorld and your choice between the San Diego Zoo or San Diego Zoo's Safari Park. CityPass delivers the best of Southern California fun at a savings of 30 percent (almost $100 off) regular admission fees. Plus, you have 14 days to take it all in from the first day you use it! Purchase the Southern California CityPass at any of the participating attractions or online at www.citypass.com/southern-california.

Mission San Juan Capistrano and Cultural Center

Two blocks west of the junction of Highway 74 and I-5 at 31882 Camino Capistrano; (949) 248-2048; www.missionsjc.com. Open Daily: 8:30 a.m. to 5 p.m. Closed Thanksgiving and Christmas Day. Closed at noon Good Friday and Christmas Eve. $$.

This "jewel of the missions" was founded on November 1, 1776, by Father Junípero Serra and is 7th in his famous chain of 21 missions along the California coast. On your self-guided walk through history, you will first enter the Serra Chapel, the oldest building still in use in California; then tour the ruins of the Great Stone Church, which was destroyed by an earthquake in 1812; and view the padres' quarters, soldiers' barracks, an Indian cemetery, and the mission kitchen. You can also view the site of an ongoing archaeological dig as well as revel in the majestic gardens. Even the crankiest toddlers seem to unwind here. Recently added is a **free** Summer Kids Activities Program from mid-June through Aug from 10 a.m. to 12 p.m.; Tues is Craft Day; Wed is Garden Day; Thurs is Toy Day.

The mission is famous for the swallows that arrive around every March 19 (St. Joseph's Day) and leave around October 23. These remarkably constant birds fly approximately 6,000 miles from Goya, Argentina, to nest and rear their young in San Juan Capistrano. As early as 1777, a record of their return was first noted in the mission archives, spawning ceremonies and celebrations each year since (not to mention the celebrated song "When the Swallows Come Back to Capistrano").

Zoomars Petting Zoo

31791 Los Rios St.; (949) 831-6550; www.zoomars.com. Open daily 10 a.m. to 6 p.m. $.

Typical petting zoo animals (goats, pigs, sheep, horses, chickens) as well as exotic birds and llamas and more on this 3-acre historic family farm. There is also a little train (adults can ride it too) and pony rides for an additional small fee, plus you can buy fresh veggies to feed the animals. Bonus—there is a small playground and picnic area. Best for toddlers and younger kids.

For More Information

San Juan Capistrano Chamber of Commerce. 31421 La Matanza St.; (949) 493-4700; www.sanjuanchamber.com.

The
Inland
Empire
& Beyond

Residents of Greater Los Angeles often think of everything else in California—with the exceptions of San Francisco, San Diego, and a handful of other cities—as "the great outdoors." Indeed, the presence of gold (somewhere) in "them thar hills" aside, what makes California such a gold mine for the nature enthusiast is the wealth of opportunities for outdoor excitement afforded by its vast expanses of wooded mountains, pristine lakes, and other natural areas. As with so many other lifestyle considerations, when it comes to out-of-doors fun, Southern California truly has the edge.

Even those areas with the most striking natural beauty, however, have rich cultural heritages stretching back to the days of the Spanish explorers and Native Americans before them. A wide variety of museums—many geared toward children—sprinkle the scenic splendor of the Southern California wilds. The combination of history, festive special events, and, towering above it all, those glorious mountain peaks makes for an unforgettable family adventure.

When considering which areas to travel to or through, it helps to think like a native Southern Californian: In other words, think big! We tend to take wide-open spaces for granted, but in a state where many counties are bigger than other entire states, can you blame us? We like to drive, and we consider many areas easily within the orbit of Greater L.A. These include, among others, the sizable chunks of San Bernardino and Riverside Counties east of L.A. (a 28,000-square-mile region known as the Inland Empire); vast Kern County north of the city, with its celebrated Kern River; Tulare County, farther north, gateway to Sequoia and Kings Canyon National Parks; and the ski resort of Mammoth, at the southern end of the Sierra Nevada range. The latter areas may seem more central than Southern California, but a true Californian just hops in the car, puts the top down, and goes. Getting there is easy, and with landscapes like these, easily half the fun.

It is California's Inland Empire that furnishes many archetypal images of the Golden State: acre upon acre of lush orange groves guarded by snowcapped mountains in the not-so-far-off distance. To the East Coast eye—that is, one accustomed to cities arranged on neat grids and self-contained countryside speckled with small towns—the

THE INLAND EMPIRE & BEYOND

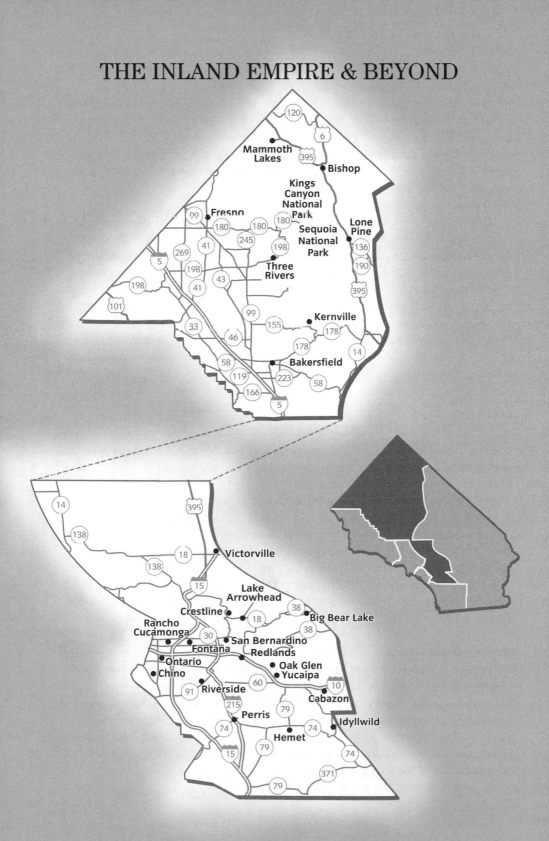

Inland Empire can be a bit overwhelming. The valley floor is an immense patchwork of farmlands and small cities. It's sometimes hard to tell where one town ends and another begins. Malls, museums, and roadside fruit stands all vie for the motorist's attention. There are more than 660,000 acres of National Forest land. All this makes for a slightly rough-and-tumble atmosphere, but a relaxed one, too. Though still growing, the palm-studded Inland Empire is a less pressured kind of place than adjacent L.A. and Orange counties. It's about as far away from stuffy as you can get—and that's very Southern California.

If the sight of citrus crops right and left is quintessential Southland, those snow-capped mountaintops house a part of the state perhaps less well-known to the visitor. Mountain vacation spots such as Lake Arrowhead and Big Bear, with its 7,000-foot-high lake, are like old-fashioned New Hampshire lakeside resorts à la California. They offer calm, cool respite from the hustle and bustle of L.A. and the beaches—and the surrounding valleys and loads of outdoor activities range from the simple to the simply adventurous. But to really appreciate the roominess of the Inland Empire, we recommend that you make stops along the way. Those who value the journey as well as the destination won't be disappointed, and during road trips kids need as much stretch-run-and-have-fun time as itineraries allow.

Ontario Area

If, like most people, you enter the Inland Empire via I-10 heading east out of Los Angeles, you'll want to make a couple of stops in the Ontario area. With its bustling international airport, Ontario is the hub of this region within a region.

The **Ontario International Airport (ONT)** can be a terrific gateway for families on the grand Southern California tour route. The airport is serviced by all the major carriers. You can start your itinerary from here without the enormity that is its sister airport, LAX. Ontario's state-of-the-art terminal is a major link in Southern California's air transportation network. You can easily rent a van or car from here and head for the hills, mountains, deserts, and beyond. The neighboring town of **Chino,** founded in 1887 on a Spanish land grant, is a prosperous community today of more than 68,000 residents with some family-minded attractions as well.

Graber Olive House

315 East 4th St., Ontario; (909) 983-1761 or (800) 996-5483; www.graberolives.com. Open Mon through Sun 9 a.m. to 5:30 p.m. except major holidays. Free admission.

This is a fitting place to visit just in case the area's warm Mediterranean-like breezes have put thoughts of—what else?—olive oil in your mind. They've been doing wonderfully delicious things with homegrown olives at Graber House since 1894. An on-site olive processing and packing plant and a museum will enlighten kids and adults alike. Be sure to purchase some for snacking and gifts, too!

Mall **Break!**

If you have visions of a megamall, with everything the kids could ever imagine (more than 200 shops, including Disney Store Outlet, Off 5th/Saks Fifth Avenue, plus 30 AMC Theatres, KB Toys Outlet, and Game Works), you'll be glad to know that the **Ontario Mills** (1 Mills Circle; 909-484-8300; www .ontariomills.com), Southern California's largest outlet mall, is open seven days a week. At the intersection of I-15 and I-10, Ontario Mills has it all. It's mere minutes from the airport, 30 minutes from Disneyland, and 40 minutes from downtown L.A. Start with a noisy lunch at the Rainforest Cafe (909-941-7979), where you'll find animated wildlife, environmental education, and a spunky menu with hamburgers, salads, and more. You'll hear the sounds of the rain forest as you dine. Dave & Buster's (909-987-1557) is another hit here with state-of-the-art interactive games and simulators. Snackers will like the humongous food court. Parents will love the smooth-as-silk cheesecake in more flavors than you thought possible at the Cheesecake Factory Cafe. Dig in!

Planes of Fame Air Museum

7000 Merrill Ave. #17, at the corner of Cal Acro Drive, Chino (just south of Ontario on Highway 60); (909) 597-3722; www.planesoffame.org. Open every day of the year, with the exception of Thanksgiving, Christmas, and occasional special events. Normal hours are Sun through Fri 10 a.m. to 5 p.m. and Sat 9 a.m. to 5 p.m. $$.

This museum houses a very impressive collection of more than 150 vintage airplanes from around the world and military aviation memorabilia. It's a vivid reminder of the pivotal role the aviation industry plays in California's history. The museum spans the history of manned flight from the Chanute Hang Glider of 1896 to the Space Age of Apollo shuttles.

Yanks Air Museum

7000 Merrill Ave., Hangar A270, Box 35, Chino; (909) 597-1734; www.yanksair.com. Open Mon through Sat from 8 a.m. to 4 p.m.; Closed Sun. $$.

Located just east of Planes of Fame, this museum focuses exclusively on American aviation history and technology. The collection now numbers more than 120 aircraft and continues to grow. The scope of the collection covers the entire history of American aviation, from Jennies to Jets. Impressive!

Where to Stay

Doubletree Hotel Ontario Airport. 222 North Vineyard; (909) 937-0900 or (800) 222-8733; www.doubletree.com. The hotel is next to the Convention Center and boasts

484 guest rooms, 2 restaurants, a pool, and a spa. $$$

Ontario Airport Marriott. 2200 East Holt; (909) 975-5000 or (800) 228-9290; www .marriottontario.com. This 293-room property is within walking distance of the Ontario Convention Center and restaurants and is close to the Ontario International Airport. Free 24-hour airport shuttle. $$

For More Information

Chino Valley Chamber of Commerce. 13150 Seventh St.; (909) 627-6177; www .chinovalleychamber.com.

Ontario Convention and Visitors Bureau. 2000 Convention Center Way; (909) 937-3000 or (800) 455-5755; www.ontariocvb .com.

Rancho Cucamonga

Along historic Route 66 (the famed road running from Chicago to L.A.; www.historic66 .com), Rancho Cucamonga, northeast of Ontario, has a name kids love to make fun of. But there's also fun to be had in the town. There's a monument here to Jack Benny (you'll have to explain to the kids who Jack Benny was), as he often mentioned Rancho Cucamonga on radio and television shows. For more current civic information, access the Chamber of Commerce at www.ranchochamber.org.

Fontana is **Motor Racing HQ**

Rev it up at the famous 5,680-acre Auto Club Speedway, which opened June 20, 1997, and is still going strong. You can hear the cars getting into high gear from miles away. NASCAR returns here for major spectator events with two races a year, in Feb and Oct. Motorcycle races, such as AMA Super Bike Challenge and races with historic sports cars, take place here. The speedway is also home of the quarter-mile NHRA-sanctioned drag strip, known to all drag fans as the Auto Club Dragway. This is recognized as "America's ultimate race place" and for good reason. The grandstand can seat 92,000, plus there are 63 terrace suites overlooking the pit road. For the ultimate view there are 28 luxury skybox suites. As for size, 1,800 RVs can be accommodated in the infield! All vehicle parking is free at the speedway and gates open approximately one hour before admission gates to the track open. If you and your family are motor racing fans, this is definitely a place you can't miss. It's located at 9300 Cherry Ave., Fontana, in the center of the Inland Empire; (800) 944-RACE (7223), or for tickets call (800) 944-7223; www.auto clubspeedway.com.

Where to Eat

Red Hill Coffee Shop. 8111 Foothill Blvd., Suite C; (909) 985-3816. Open daily, usually 6:30 a.m. to 12:30 p.m.—call to confirm as times can change. Opened in 1943 and still serving massive portions of comfort food, this is authentic Route 66 roadside hospitality as it was before the onset of fast food and drive-through. Stop in for huge burgers, omelets, or just a good cup of coffee as you're driving along this stretch of an important chapter in America's travel history. $

Magic Lamp Inn. 8189 Foothill Blvd.; (909) 981-8659; www.themagiclampinn.com. Open Tues to Sun—must call for daily hours. If you want to get more kicks on Route 66 when hunger sets in, visit this legendary, classic 1955 restaurant with its comfortable red banquettes and the look and feel of the mid-century. The menu includes old favorites such as chicken marsala and roast prime rib of steer au jus. $$$

Sycamore Inn. 8318 Foothill Blvd., Bear Gulch; (909) 982-1104; www.thesycamoreinn.com. Open every evening (7 nights a week); Mon to Sat at 5 p.m., Sun at 4 p.m. Call for closing hours. Reservations suggested. This rustic inn, just across the street from the Magic Lamp, opened in 1848. The children's menu includes the Hot Dogger, Burger Master, Mr. Chicken, and the Big Cheese. Tell your kids this restaurant was in business a long time before McDonald's and Burger King—even before the California burger was invented. $$

San Bernardino

Nestled at the base of local mountain resorts and at the crossroads of the I-215 and I-10 Freeways, "San Berdoo," as it's called locally, offers pleasures of a more municipal, but certainly no less stimulating, nature. It is the gateway to the mountain resorts of Big Bear and Lake Arrowhead. San Bernardino is home to year-round sports such as the Class "A" affiliate of Los Angeles Dodgers, the Inland Empire 66ers, and the Western Region Little League Tournament. The historic California Theater in downtown San Bernardino features Broadway plays, musicals, and cultural shows from the San Bernardino Symphony Orchestra. For a large variety of restaurants, cuisine, lodging, and shopping, visit Hospitality Lane, located right off the I-10 freeway.

Historic Site of the World's First McDonald's

1398 North E St. Open daily 10 a.m. to 5 p.m.

In 1948, brothers Dick and Mac McDonald opened their original namesake restaurant on this site on the business district loop of Route 66. It sold hamburgers, cheeseburgers, fries, soft drinks, and milk shakes at low prices and became very popular with residents and tourists. Ray Kroc encountered the restaurant in 1954 when he was working as a food-mixer salesman, and proposed and managed a plan to open franchised McDonald's around the USA. The McDonald brothers eventually sold the company to Kroc in 1961 for $2.7 million. Their original building has been razed, but there is a display of early McDonald's memorabilia—an homage to the American Dream. Ironically, it is now the headquarters for the Juan

Pollo fast-food chain (909-885-6324). Another fun factoid: Taco Tia, Taco Bell, Del Taco, and Der Weinerschnitzel fast-food chains also all started in San Bernardino!

Glen Helen Regional Park

2555 Glen Helen Parkway; (909) 887-7540; (909) 880-6500 for concert information.

The "jewel in the crown" of the area's regional parks, 1,425-acre Glen Helen comes complete with a half-acre swimming lagoon, a 350-foot water slide, and a beach. And proof positive that Southern Californians think big, the park also boasts the Glen Helen Hyundai Pavilion (909-88-MUSIC; www.hyundaipavilion.com) outdoor concert venue, the largest amphitheater in the United States (total capacity is 65,000). The adjacent Glen Helen Raceway (18585 Verdemont Ranch Rd.; 909-880-3090; www.glenhelen.com) features the best in motocross events.

National Orange Show

NOS Events Center, 689 South E St.; (909) 888-6788; www.nationalorangeshow.com. Held from Thurs through Mon (Memorial Day weekend). Admission is free.

Here's an event you'll never find in Kansas. Started way back in 1911, the show has been getting juicier ever since. Today it features fireworks, top entertainment, a rodeo, livestock shows, art exhibits, kid-friendly rides, and, of course, a broad range of oranges and orange food products.

Stater Bros. **Route 66 Rendezvous**

If you're up for a healthy dose of nostalgic honky-tonk (more than 500,000 were in 2009), check out this four-day affair that kicks off every year in mid-September. Southern Californians have always had a special relationship with their automobiles; what wine is to the French, cars are to us—sacred objects, worthy of adulation. This is clearly in evidence as squeaky-clean Corvettes, Cobras, and Chevys limited to 1,900 pre-1974 classics, customs, hot rods, and other vehicles receive an assigned reserved parking space for the four-day event. Vehicles cruise a 36-block area of downtown San Bernardino while visitors enjoy the beautiful cars, food, vendors, sponsor displays, and live entertainment. Drag races, an auto sound challenge, and an antique performance parts swap are also on the annual activity roster. Dozens of vendors hawk their wares, which range from antique milk caps and Elvis clocks to new stereo equipment. And to put a little honk into the tonk, celebrities come to life via ongoing Legends in Concert performances. The Rendezvous, which is free to spectators, is sponsored and produced by the San Bernardino Convention and Visitors Bureau. For more information, call (800) 867-8366 or visit www.route-66.org.

Where to Eat & Stay

For a large variety of restaurants, cuisine, lodging, and shopping in San Bernardino, check out the Hospitality Lane exit located right off the I-10. Be sure to call for hours of operation first. Here are a couple of our favorites there:

Guadalaharry's. 280 East Hospitality Lane; (909) 889-8555. Open daily for lunch and dinner and Sunday brunch. Specializing in fajitas, Guadalaharry's is also known for its fried ice cream dessert. Yum yum. $–$$

Hilton San Bernardino. 285 East Hospitality Lane; (909) 889-0133 or (800) 445-8667; www1.hilton.com. The largest full-service hotel in the city with 250 rooms, heated outdoor pool and whirlpool, and Manhattan's Restaurant serving breakfast, lunch, and dinner. Located off I-10 at the North Waterman exit. As the street name suggests, this area of San Bernardino is very visitor-friendly. $$$$

For More Information

San Bernardino Convention and Visitors Bureau. 1955 Hunts Lane, Suite 102, San Bernardino; (909) 889-3980 or (800) 867-8366; www.sanbernardino.travel.

California Welcome Center–Inland Empire. 1955 Hunts Lane, Suite 102, San Bernardino; (909) 891 1874; www.cwcinland empire.com.

Redlands

Quiet little Redlands, named for the color of the local soil and home of the eponymous and highly regarded university, awaits exploration just a few minutes east of San Bernardino on I-10. In the latter part of the 19th century, Midwesterners and East Coasters of certain means began a time-honored tradition of wintering in Southern California, and one of their favorite spots was Redlands. Among the city's attractions are several mansions that bear witness to the Golden State's brief Victorian renaissance.

San Bernardino County Museum

2024 Orange Tree Lane, near the California Street exit from I-10; (909) 307-2669 or (888) BIRD-EGG; www.co.san-bernardino.ca.us/museum. Open Tues through Sun 9 a.m. to 5 p.m. $, children younger than 5 free.

This local landmark is easily recognized by its large geodesic dome (actually a seminar room). Here you'll find exhibits on early Californian ranch life and the Native Americans who once lived in these parts. But the real strong suits of the museum are the earth and biological science exhibits, which also happen to be among the most popular with younger children. For starters, there are more than 40,000 birds' eggs, the state's only dinosaur tracks, a dazzling collection of minerals and gemstones, and the Exploration Show. Kids are captivated by the live insect, reptile, and amphibian displays. Both kids and adults can contemplate the forces that formed the Inland Empire's beautiful mountains by keeping an eye on the always-on seismometer.

Kimberly Crest House and Gardens

1325 Prospect Dr.; (909) 792-2111; www.kimberlycrest.org. Open Thurs through Sun 1 to 4 p.m. Sept through July. Closed Aug. $.

With its commanding views of the San Bernardino Valley, this 6-acre estate, purchased in 1905 by J. Alfred Kimberly (of Kimberly-Clark fame) and his wife, Helen, features Louis XVI decor on the inside and formal Italian gardens and lush orange groves on the outside. See if you can spot the great southern magnolia, for years it's been the Kimberlys' outdoor Christmas tree. The most impressive of the city's mansions, this French château-style home is off I-10 at the Ford exit. It is California Registered Historic Landmark No. 1019.

The Frugal Frigate

9 North 6th St.; (909) 793-0740. www.frugalfrigate.com. Open Mon, Tues, Wed, Fri 10 a.m. to 6 p.m.; Thurs 10 a.m. to 5:30 p.m.; and Sat 10 a.m. to 3 p.m.

A delightful source for "carefully chosen children's classics," this unique bookstore is located in historic downtown Redlands and has plenty of special events your kids will enjoy. Call for schedule.

Where to Eat

Doughlectibles and the Eating Room. 107 East Citrus Ave.; (909) 798-7321 or (909) 792-5400; www.allmarthagreen.com. The bakery has all varieties of fresh pastries and breads. The restaurant serves breakfast and lunch. The French toast is worth the calories. Lunch choices include a great patty melt. $

The Gourmet Pizza Shoppe. 120 East State St.; (909) 792-3313; www.gourmetpizzas.com. Hours: Tues through Sat 11 a.m. to 9 p.m.; Sun 12 p.m. to 8 p.m.; closed Mon. Here you'll find 90 different combinations of pizza, including peanut butter and jelly! The beverage list features sodas from all over the world, including cream sodas, root beers, black cherry sodas,

and 6 varieties of orange soda. You won't find noisy arcade games or a TV in the dining room—instead; children's books are available for kids to read while they wait. $$

Oscar's Mexican Restaurant. 19 North 5th St.; (909) 792-8211. Oscar's is an institution in downtown Redlands, serving great Mexican food that is sure to satisfy your appetite. They have great "lite combos," too. $

For More Information

Redlands Chamber of Commerce. 1 East Redlands Blvd.; (909) 793-2546; www.red landschamber.org.

Alpine Paradises

You've taken in a bit of culture, shopping, and attractions, mixed in a bit of sunshine, and are ready to hit some elevation. There are three main resort areas in the mountains framing the northern tier of the Inland Empire: Crestline, Lake Arrowhead, and Big Bear. Choose according to Old Man Time: a day for a detour, two or three for a mini-vacation, or a week for some really relaxing family fun.

Crestline

A 20-minute drive from the San Bernardino Valley via State Highway 18 (a nationally designated scenic byway know as "Rim of the World Highway"), you'll encounter Crestline, a smallish (population 10,000), rather funky, no-nonsense mountain village that lures passersby in for a meal or a lakeside stroll (http://crestlineca.net). The 86-acre Lake Gregory is Crestline's center piece, a popular though rarely crowded spot for swimming, shore fishing, and paddle-boarding. Some scenes from Disney's *Parent Trap* movie were filmed here as well. From May through September, Friday night in Crestline means Lakeside Family Market Night that features not only plenty of food and fresh produce but also kids' rides, crafts vendors, and entertainment. Lake Gregory County Regional Park is located at 24171 Lake Dr., off Highway 18; (909) 338-2233; www.co.san-bernardino.ca.us.

Lake Arrowhead

This mountain community 90 miles east of downtown Los Angeles puts you at an altitude of 5,106 feet with 782-acre Lake Arrowhead, at 782 acres, as the center point. The San Bernardino Mountains offer a four season climate paradise. **Lake Arrowhead Village** is on the lakefront on Highway 189—a hundred-year-old resort named for the arrowhead landmark at the base of the San Bernardino Mountains. No one knows exactly how the 1,115-foot-tall, 396-foot-wide geological imprint got there, but it certainly helps those with a less-than-stellar sense of direction. Virtually every imaginable aquatic activity—swimming, waterskiing, fishing, sailing—is available on the lake, which is ringed by accommodations ranging from camping facilities to deluxe hotels and private residences. In the winter, this elevation welcomes snow sports and recreation. That's the basic plan of Lake Arrowhead, a pristine mountain community perfect for year-round recreational pursuits or just sheer relaxation. A true wonderland only two hours from the beach!

The *Arrowhead Queen*

Lake Arrowhead Village; (909) 336-6992. Buy your tickets at 28200 Highway 189, Bldg. C100, at the waterfront next to the dock.

This 50-minute cruise aboard a Louisiana-style paddlewheel boat takes you by architectural points of interest and historical sites, all narrated by the ship's captain. This delightful cruise provides the ideal introduction to the beauty of Lake Arrowhead and serves as a starting point for your excursions.

The Ice Castle International Training Center

401 Burnt Mill Rd.; (909) 337-0802; www.icecastle.us. The world-famous training center for ice skaters is also open to the public year round for $8 plus skate rental.

Your aspiring kid skaters will find this landmark worthwhile to visit even if they can only spend a few hours here. You can even take one skating lesson if that is all the time you have. Olympic medalist Michelle Kwan skated here; the rink even flies the Olympic flag.

The Mountain Skies Astronomy Village

2001 Observatory Way off Highway 18 in Lake Arrowhead between Daley Canyon and Rim of the World High School; (909) 336-1299; www.mountain-skies.org. Call for current hours of operation and events.

Don't miss these informative two-hour sessions that are scheduled throughout the year, covering topics from "Stars to Star Dust" to "Meteorites, Alien Rocks from Space" and more. Call and reserve your preferred session in advance; note that the sessions take place weather permitting. Gift shop and observation area also available.

Where to Eat

Belgian Waffle Works. 28200 Highway 189, Lake Arrowhead Village, dockside; (909) 337-5222; http://belgianwaffle.com. Generally open daily at 8 a.m.—call for seasonal closing hours. Breakfast, lunch, and dinner since 1982—they use an exclusive waffle mix that is so delicious. This family-style restaurant is a tradition here. $

Woody's Boathouse. Lake Arrowhead Village, lower level; (909) 337-2628; www.woodysboathouse.com. Dockside merchants offer another view of the lake, so spend some time exploring this corner of the village. If you are a fan of the Chris Craft boats of the 1950s, you must stop by Woody's for breakfast, lunch, or dinner. Woody's has a salad bar in a boat, a separate kids' menu, and fair prices. Beautifully restored Chris Craft boats serve as booths and your platform for viewing the lake. $$

Where to Stay

Arrowhead Pine Rose Cabins. 25994 Highway 189, Twin Peaks, at Grandview; (909) 337-2341 or (800) 429-PINE; www.pinerose.com. Individuality reigns supreme at this great base camp for sightseeing. It's centrally located between Lake Arrowhead and Lake Gregory. Scattered around 5 forested acres are 17 cabins (1, 2, and 3 bedrooms) and two 4- to 7-bedroom lodges. No charge for cribs. Children very welcome and stay **free** in same cabin as parents. $$

Lake Arrowhead Resort & Spa. 27984 Highway 189, Lake Arrowhead Village; (800) 800-6792, (909) 336-1511; www.laresort.com. The ideal 173-room property where you can experience the best of Lake Arrowhead complete with a perfect location, ample **free** parking, its own private beach, outdoor swimming pool, and easy access to skiing, golf, and shopping. The resort's Bin189 is considered the best restaurant for fine dining in Lake Arrowhead. The resort's Spa of the Pines is a serious full-service operation with a fitness studio, cardio theater, Pilates, and ongoing fitness classes. $$$$

For More Information

Lake Arrowhead Communities Chamber of Commerce. P.O. Box 219, 92352; (909) 337-3715; www.lakearrowhead.net.

Lake Arrowhead Village. P.O. Box 640, 28200 Highway 189, Suite F-240, 92352; (909) 337-2533; www.lakearrowheadvillage.com.

Big Bear

If you follow Highway 18 east from Lake Arrowhead to Big Bear Lake, you'll be cruising along the Rim of the World Scenic Byway, with its spectacular vistas of thick forests and the sprawling valley below. Big Bear is many things to many people. The area includes the city of Big Bear Lake, as well as the smaller communities of Fawnskin, Big Bear City, and Moonridge. In the spring, summer and fall, some come for the great water sports (23 miles of shoreline), others for the chance to see the stars and meteor showers during the refreshingly cool nights, and others for the hiking opportunities. And you know what they come for in the winter—snow sports! This alpine paradise is surrounded by the majesty of the San Bernardino National Forest, ranging in altitude from 6,750 to 9,000 feet. Home to Southern California's premier ski resorts, this pristine dot on the map also has a sunny side. During the spring, the welcome mat rolls out carpets of wildflowers (there are 30 varieties), and mountain biking and fishing enter the scene. During June those challenged by Southern California's "June gloom" syndrome (coastal fog, for the uninitiated) flock here because Big Bear is above the marine layers that are the culprit, causing dreary, grey skies. Trailheads throughout the Big Bear Valley present fun challenges for those who treasure a pure hiking adventure. Fishing fans, especially those who prize trout, will find Big Bear Lake impressive. You've probably seen Big Bear in many movies, and didn't know it! *Old Yeller* (1957), starring Fess Parker, was filmed here, along with *Magnolia* (1999), starring Tom Cruise. If you ever chance to see vintage films such as the *Northwest Mounted Police* (1940) or *North to Alaska* (1960), you're looking at Big Bear!

Big Bear Discovery Center

San Bernardino National Forest, 40971 North Shore Dr. (Highway 38), P.O. Box 66, Fawnskin 92333; (909) 866-3437; www.bigbeardiscoverycenter.com.

Get your family to the marvelous Big Bear Discovery Center before you make any decisions on where to go and what to do. Try one of the tours, such as the Grout Bay Canoe Tour, Mountain Mining Tour, or Woodland Trail Tour; children are welcome. The USDA Forest Service has made great strides in opening this area to tourists. There is an orientation video, a gift shop, cafe, exhibits, an amphitheater, and information on more than 50 activities, from horseback riding, hiking, and backpacking to fishing and bird-watching. Ask about the Children's Forest, a 3,400-acre site on Highway 18 between Running Springs and Big Bear Lake, where kids learn about the preservation of our magnificent wildlands.

Miss Liberty **Paddlewheel Tour Boat**

400 Pine Knot Ave.; (909) 866-8129; www.pineknotmarina.com. Times and hours of operation vary. $$.

All aboard Southern California's newest and largest one-of-a kind boat on Big Bear Lake. The 2 p.m. narrated cruise departs daily for a 90-minute tour that reveals Big Bear's rich history. Arrivals are requested at least 15 minutes prior to departure.

Big Bear Lake Pirate Ship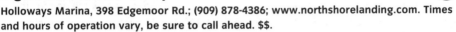

Holloways Marina, 398 Edgemoor Rd.; (909) 878-4386; www.northshorelanding.com. Times and hours of operation vary, be sure to call ahead. $$.

This one-third-scale replica of a 16th-century Spanish galleon is complete with four masts (for landlubbers that's the sprint, fore, main, and mizzen) and has sails that are square on the first three masts. The 1.5-hour tours are narrated by the "pirate captain." Shipmates take note: the maximum number of sailors is 25, so reserve in advance!

Big Bear Charter Fishing

Holloway's Marina, 398 Edgemoor Rd., Big Bear Lake; (909) 866-2240; www.bigbearfishing .com.

You can easily charter a pontoon or bass boat and fish to your heart's desire. Fully loaded with gear, poles, reels, bait, and lures, get set to catch trout, bass, catfish, crappie, and bluegills with a fish- friendly guide. The bass boat accommodates up to four people, and the pontoon handles up to 10 people at a time.

Big Bear Parasail & Watersports

400 Pine Knot Ave.; (909) 866-4359; www.bigbearparasail.net. The season is from late May to mid-Sept. Call for availability and rates.

A thrill ride that will take you 7,000 feet up, up, and away. The bird's-eye view of Big Bear Valley is amazing. You'll sail right over the lake with the clear blue sky as a backdrop. The company has been offering New Zealand–style jet boat rides since 2010.

Moonridge Animal Park

432 Goldmine Dr.; (909) 880-4200; www.bigbearzoo.com.

Check out the alpine wildlife collection of over 160 animals, which of course includes the legendary "Big Bear." Your family will enjoy events throughout the year such as a Bear Country Fair in May and the Boo in the Zoo in October.

Alpine Slide at Magic Mountain

800 Wildrose Lane, Big Bear Lake; (909) 866-4626; www.alpineslidebigbear.com.

Custom-made for families and lots of fun, this Magic Carpet Ride is Southern California's only authentic winter-time bobsled experience. The track is a quarter-mile long. During the summer, there's a double water slide guaranteed to cool you off. Making a few hours even

A Winter **Playground**

Be sure to stay on high alert for treacherous driving conditions and be safe on mountain roads during the winter season. Even when tire chain restrictions are in effect, roads leading to Big Bear are still open.

Now, here's where to play in the snow! In Big Bear, skiing is an affordable sport for your family thanks to the Big Bear Lake Resort Association and their seasonal deals at Big Bear Mountain Resorts (www.bigbearmountain resorts.com). There are two full-service winter resorts here: **Bear Mountain,** 43101 Goldmine Dr., (909) 866-5766, and **Snow Summit,** 880 Summit Blvd., (909) 866-2052—both have complete ski and snowboard facilities and schools, full-service rental shops, and 100 percent snowmaking capabilities.

Snow Summit is advised for everyday skiers and snowboarders seeking a more laid-back winter playground. "The Park" at Bear Mountain is the first full-service mountain resort in the world that is almost entirely devoted to an innovative freestyle terrain that includes 150 jumps, 80 jibs, and 2 pipes on 195 acres. It is also the site of the only superpipe in Southern California. An interchangeable ticket for the two areas will put you on the mountain with more than 435 skiable acres, 4 high-speed chairs, 26 lifts, and 200 terrains featuring several types of jumps, fun boxes, and rails. Note that Big Bear is proud owner of two of the largest snowmaking technology facilities in the region. If you require ski equipment, there are quality outfitters and full-service rental shops nearby. Snow is known as "white gold" in Big Bear; when it rains in Southern California chances are it is snowing in Big Bear on Bear Mountain! Remember, Bear Mountain and Snow Summit are open year-round—call for current snow conditions. Other months, enjoy golf, hiking, mountain biking, and sky chair rides as well as concerts and parties. Big Bear really is your four-season family fun destination.

more enjoyable are go-karts and an 18-hole miniature golf course (available only in summertime, of course).

Where to Eat & Stay

Goldmine Resort. 42268 Moonridge Rd., 0.5 mile east of Big Bear Boulevard, Big Bear Lake; (909) 866-5118; www.bigbear-gold mine-lodge.com. Open year-round and only 1 mile to Snow Summit and Bear Mountain. Lodge rooms, 1- and 2-room suites, and cabins. Vacation-home rentals also offered. Large playground, horseshoe pit, and fireplaces; family reunions and weddings welcomed. $$

Northwoods Resort. 40650 Village Dr., Big Bear Lake; reservations: (800) 866-3121; www

.northwoodsresort.com. This 1930s-style, 148-room mountain lodge is great for families; there are comfortable connecting rooms, heated outdoor pool and spa with poolside food service, fitness room, and Wi-Fi and Nintendo for those who can't quite disconnect. The year-round heated outdoor pool (the only one in Big Bear) is a popular gathering place along with the fitness center and sauna. You are right at the village, where there are inviting shops and restaurants, all amid those enchanting whispering pines. **Stillwell's Restaurant** serves breakfast, lunch, and dinner in this unique, rustic mountain atmosphere. $$$

Old Country Inn. 41126 Big Bear Blvd., Big Bear Lake; (909) 866-5600. Call for hours.

Serving comfort food for over 30 years, this cozy restaurant boasts hearty breakfasts, lunches, and dinners. The cooking is home-style and you'll find it all "on the sunny side of the boulevard." Check out the patio for outdoor dining, from which you can enjoy the marvelous mountain air and get into the swing of the relaxing mountain lifestyle. $–$$

For More Information

Big Bear Lake Resort Association and Visitor Center. 630 Bartlett Rd., Big Bear Village, P.O. Box 1936, Big Bear Lake 92315-1936; (909) 866-6190 or (800) 4-BIG-BEAR; www.bigbear.com.

Victorville

In southwestern San Bernardino County, if you take I-15 a bit north (another section of the Historic Route 66 Corridor), before you get too far into the Mojave Desert you'll come across the city of Victorville, population around 100,000 and growing. In addition to its role as a gateway to the Mojave, it has a few worthwhile stops.

California Route 66 Museum

16825 D St. (take exit D off I-15); (760) 951-0436; www.califrt66museum.org. Open Thurs through Mon 10 a.m. to 4 p.m. Free.

The museum was established in Old Town Victorville, in 1995, along a stretch of the old Mother Road. The museum building itself was once a Route 66 roadhouse, the Red Rooster Cafe. In fact, the movie *The Jazz Singer*, starring Neil Diamond, was filmed here. Kids may not appreciate the incredible array of memorabilia gathered by Route 66 fans, but this museum will make them wonder and ask questions about what travel was like before freeways. That alone is worth making the stop. The high desert landmark called Hulaville (once an open-air museum along Route 66 on Victorville's southern fringes built by an eccentric ex-carny) and the curiosities displayed here reveal an era of American travel left to the pages of history. Just a refresher—Route 66 debuted in 1926, connecting Chicago to L.A. (Santa Monica).

Check out the historical exhibits, contemporary gallery, research library, and loads of travel info. "Get your kicks" here, on Route 66!

Mojave Narrows Regional Park

18000 Yates Rd., off Bear Valley Road; (760) 245-2226; www.county-parks.com.

This picturesque, not-quite-yet-the-desert site spans 840 acres and overlooks the Mojave River. With an 87-unit campground (with 38 full utility pads), year-round fishing, and rowboat rentals, the park is well equipped for families interested in a little communing with nature. This is the home to the **Huck Finn Jubilee** during Father's Day weekend (http://huckfinn.com). This festival is loaded with toe-tappin' bluegrass music, a watermelon seed spittin' contest, arts and crafts booths, and a catfish derby.

For More Information

Victorville Chamber of Commerce.
14174 Green Tree Blvd.; (760) 245-6506;
www.vvchamber.com.

Riverside & Environs

If one views the Inland Empire as a vast stage, its myriad outdoor attractions tend to steal the show. Maybe that's why so few people seem to know much about Riverside, the city built on oranges. By 1895 more than 20,000 acres of navel orange trees had made then-sleepy Riverside into the nation's wealthiest city per capita. This distinctly Californian heritage is still evident, thanks to the presence of a handful of old California-style structures: the old City Hall (3612 Mission Inn Ave.); restored 1892 Heritage House (8193 Magnolia Ave.), the finest example of Victorian lifestyle in the West; and the city's landmark, the restored Mission Inn (3649 Mission Inn Ave.). Originally a 12-room adobe built in 1875 (a very long time ago by Californian standards), this grand hostelry expanded along with the town. Showcasing the Victorian lifestyle with a western spin made Riverside into an important center of agriculture and trade. Riverside is accessible via Highway 60 or Highway 91, both just south of I-10.

Riverside Metropolitan Museum

3580 Mission Inn Ave.; (951) 826-5273; www.riversideca.gov/museum. Open Mon 9 a.m. to 1 p.m., Tues through Fri 9 a.m. to 5 p.m., and Sat and Sun 11 a.m. to 5 p.m. Admission is **free**; donations suggested.

The area's roots are on display at this museum, with its large collection of Native American artifacts and early citrus-industry exhibits in the former 1912 Post Office.

California Citrus State Historic Park

Take Riverside Freeway (Highway 91) to Van Buren Boulevard at 9400 Dufferin Ave.; look for the big orange; (951) 780-6222; www.parks.ca.gov. Open Mon to Fri 8 a.m. to 5 p.m.; Sat and Sun 8 a.m. to 7 p.m.; Visitor Center 10 a.m. to 4 p.m. on Wed and weekends. Parking fees are $8 per vehicle.

This California state park was built to celebrate one hundred years of citrus production in Riverside with support from Sunkist growers. Located on the 377 acres are the Varietal Grove, which has a hundred different species of citrus; an outdoor amphitheater where concerts are held on Friday evenings during summer (the last concert is the first Fri in Aug); and a visitor center. As you walk around the park, you will encounter interpretive displays and picnic areas.

Botanic Gardens at University of California—Riverside (UCR)

University of California at Riverside; (951) 787-4650; www.gardens.ucr.edu. Open daily from 8 a.m. to 5 p.m. Admission is free, although donations are appreciated.

These gardens are nestled in the foothills of the Box Springs Mountains in East Riverside and cover 40 hilly acres. The gardens boast more than 3,500 plant species from around the world. More than 200 species of birds have been observed in the gardens. From Highway 60/I-215, exit at Martin Luther King Boulevard and turn right. Turn right again at Canyon Crest Avenue and enter the UCR campus. Follow signs to the gardens and park in Lot 13.

Rancho Jurupa Park

4600 Crestmore Rd.; (951) 684-7032; www.riversidecountyparks.org.

There are 35 parks in Riverside County's Regional Park and Open Spaces system. Rancho Jurupa Park is located just outside the city limits of Riverside and provides fishing, biking, hiking, and equestrian trails as well as camping. Don't forget to stop in the Luis Robidoux Nature Center on the park grounds. Only a mile (as the crow flies) from Rancho Jurupa is the Jensen-Alvarado Ranch. This was the first non-adobe building in the Riverside area. Many school groups come to learn how to make homemade ice cream and tortillas (on a potbellied stove!). The Jensen-Alvarado Ranch is located at 4307 Briggs St. in Riverside. Take Freeway 60 west from Riverside, exit at Rubidoux Boulevard, drive south to Tilton Avenue, and head west on Briggs.

Castle Amusement Park

3500 Polk St.; (951) 785-3000; www.castlepark.com. Open daily; call for hours. No admission fee; ride tickets and game tokens can be purchased inside the park.

This 25-acre park has it all. It was built in 1976 to be the "Ultimate Family Entertainment Park." The three-level castle houses more than 400 state-of-the-art games. The rare Dentzel carousel (built in 1898) is one of the oldest in America and has 52 hand-carved, brightly painted animals and 2 sleighs on highly polished brass poles. Add to these 4 world-class, 18-hole, championship miniature par 4 golf courses surrounded by gorgeous palm trees. The Big Top Restaurant has everything from a salad bar to super sundaes, and Plaza Café and Snack Bar are two more kid-friendly options.

Where to Eat

Anchos Southwest Grill and Bar. 10773 Hole St.; (909) 352-0240; www.anchos.net. Open daily at 11:30 a.m., generally closed at 9 p.m. (call to confirm). Delicious Mexican and Southwestern cuisine. Watch the flour tortillas being made and rotating in the warmer. $

Mario's Place. 3646 Mission Inn Ave.; (951) 684-7755; www.mariosplace.com. Some of the most savory Italian dishes available. The Palagi family has made Mario's Place a landmark in Riverside. $$–$$$

Where to Stay

The Mission Inn Hotel & Spa. 3649 Mission Inn Ave.; (951) 784-0300; www.mission inn.com. This full-service, beautifully restored 1902 European-style hotel encompasses an entire city block in downtown Riverside. Come stroll the halls of this great inn, which has hosted several of our nation's presidents. There are 239 elegant rooms and suites, no two alike. Today, there's a European-inspired spa, and a Sunday buffet reminiscent of what you would find on a world-class cruise ship. Five restaurants will serve you classic California cuisine. The Mission Inn Foundation/Museum offers walking history tours (www.missioninnmuseum.com; $, children under 12 **free**). $$$$

For More Information

Greater Riverside Chamber of Commerce. 3985 University Ave.; (951) 683-7100; www.riverside-chamber.com.

Riverside Convention & Visitors Bureau. 3750 University Ave., Suite 175; (951) 222-4700 or (888) 748-7733; www.riversidecb.com.

Perris

For a taste of the real Riverside County, you have to delve in deep—in other words, let the country roads be your guide. If you take I-215 south from Highway 60 (which runs right through Riverside), in about 20 traffic-free minutes you'll come across the town of Perris, population 46,000. The city is named in honor of Fred T. Perris, chief engineer of the California Southern Railroad. The California Southern was built through the future town site in 1882 to build a rail connection between the present day cities of Barstow and San Diego. The locals always say there's nothing like Perris in the springtime—a reference to the California golden poppies and other wildflowers that carpet these parts round about April. Even if your visit doesn't happen to coincide with the annual flora show, Mother Nature won't disappoint.

The Perris area is well known for the outdoor activities afforded by its laid-back country setting. The early morning and late evening stillness, coupled with mild temperatures, spells paradise for aviation buffs. Hot-air-balloon, sailplane, hang glider, and even skydiving outfitters (Skydive Perris; 800-SKY-DIVE; www.skydiveperris.com) abound in the area. It can be quite a spectacle simply to watch these folks in action at the private Perris Valley Airport (www.airnav.com/airport/L65). The skydiving scenes in *The Bucket List*, starring Morgan Freeman and Jack Nicholson, were filmed near Perris. At ground level, campers, swimmers, boaters, fishers, hikers, and bikers will enjoy a detour to the Lake Perris State Recreation Area (LPRA), 1781 Lake Perris Dr. (951-657-0676; www.parks.ca .gov). Visit the YA-I Heki Museum, located at LPRA, for information on Native American history of the area.

Orange Empire Railway Museum

2201 South A St.; (951) 657-2605; www.oerm.org. The grounds are open every day from 9 a.m. to 5 p.m. The Reception Center/Museum Store is open from 9:30 a.m. to 4:30 p.m. weekdays and 9:30 a.m. to 5 p.m. on weekends. Free admission, $$ for trolley and train rides.

This is the West's biggest railway museum, with electric cars, buildings, and other artifacts. The museum covers 60 acres, so there is plenty of room for a family picnic among streetcars, trains, and municipal buses from yesteryear.

More than 150 historic train cars, locomotives, and streetcars are on display indoors and outside. Are you ready to ride the rails, kids? Each Sat and Sun from 11 a.m. to 5 p.m., vintage streetcars circle the museum property (it takes about 7 minutes), and antique Southern Pacific train cars make a 10-minute trip to the Perris Depot and back.

Hemet/San Jacinto Valley

If you're heading from the Perris area east to Hemet or Idyllwild (more on that next), you could take either Highway 74 east or drive along the Juan Bautista de Anza National Historic Trail. This scenic corridor, which skirts Lake Perris, dairy farms, and other quiet farmlands, follows the tracks de Anza made when he explored the region for Spain in 1775. For more information call (951) 658-3211 or visit www.hemetsanjacintochamber.com.

Ramona Outdoor Play

2400 Ramona Bowl Rd.; (951) 658-3111 or (800) 645-4465; www.ramonabowl.com. The play runs on weekends from 3:30 to about 6:30 p.m. in late Apr and early May.

Performed by more than 400 of the town's residents, the play is adapted from the 1884 novel *Ramona*, which depicts the romantic spectacle of early California. It has been an annual event since 1923, earning it the designation as the official outdoor play of California. Not to be missed. Other productions are performed throughout the year here at the Ramona Bowl; for example, look for *A Christmas Carol* in December and a summer concert series as well.

Diamond Valley Lake

Visitor center located next to the Western Center for Archaeology and Paleontology (www .westerncentermuseum.org), 2325 Searl Parkway, Hemet; (951) 765-2612; www.dvlake.com. Open Thurs through Sun; 10 a.m. to 4 p.m. Free.

These 4,000 square acres of water storage and recreational land are the great attraction of the Hemet Valley. Inside the visitor center you can see the mastodon exhibit as well as other artifacts retrieved from excavations made as this lake began to fill in 1999. Diamond Valley Lake is embarking on a substantial trail system that will allow families to hike and ride through the hill surrounding the reservoir. The first sets of trails are along the north hills overlooking the lake, and another circumnavigates the lake. Other amenities at the east dam area include a swimming pool and soccer and other sports fields.

Idyllwild

Take Highway 74 east out of Hemet to Highway 243, which leads to the hamlet of Idyllwild. You will be traveling on the **Palms to Pines Scenic Highway,** and as the name indicates, you'll observe desert palm and oak trees giving way to pine and fir forests as the elevation increases. Idyllwild, which looks like a village from the Swiss Alps, dropped into the heart of the **San Bernardino National Forest,** makes for one of the most enchanting detours in the Inland Empire, especially in winter. This town, at an altitude of 5,400 feet with zero days of smog, is a mile-high oasis nestled in the San Jacinto Mountains and a favorite choice for a well-balanced family vacation in Southern California. It is devoid of fast-food joints but the exceptional opportunities for family recreation more than compensate. Since the town has a high elevation, Idyllwild nights are cool and crisp, even in the summer. Idyllwild is home to more than a dozen art galleries and estimated 30 art events annually. Get ready to tackle the great outdoors by ordering up a savory Belgian waffle first—any time of day—at the **Idyllwild Cafe,** 26600 Highway 243 (951-659-2210; www .idyllwildcafe.com) next to Idyllwild School.

Highland Springs Resort
and Guest Ranch

This 900-acre ranch, at 10600 Highland Ave. in Cherry Valley north of Beaumont off I-10, offers horseback riding, cookouts, hayrides, and barbecues. Once a stagecoach stop for gold panners headed for the Colorado River, this rustic resort, at 3,000 feet in elevation, has been a good choice for a family vacation since 1884. It is also the home of popular Camp Highland Outdoor Science School (www.camphighland.net). Palm Springs is 30 miles east, and Idyllwild is 20 miles south; so you're really in the center of Riverside County attractions. Call (951) 845-1151 or visit www.highlandspringsresort.com.

Idyllwild Arts

P.O. Box 38, 92549 (52500 Temecula Rd., located at the end of Tollgate Road); (951) 659-2171; www.idyllwildarts.org. $$$$.

Idyllwild Arts offers a family camp in late June and early July. There are separate activities for children, teenagers, and adults, including hiking, wilderness activities, swimming, and just relaxing. Evening activities include concerts, folk dancing, and family talent night.

Where to Stay

Quiet Creek Inn. 26345 Delano Dr.; (951) 659-6110 or (800) 450-6110; www.quietcreek inn.com. Deluxe cabins with fireplaces, spas, and private decks overlooking Strawberry Creek will immediately relax you and your family. Owner also offers vacation rentals. Recommended by *Sunset* magazine. $$$$

For More Information

Idyllwild Chamber of Commerce. 54295 Village Center Dr.; (951) 659-3259 or (888) 659-3259; www.idyllwildchamber.com.

Oak Glen

Washington State doesn't have a monopoly on apples. Oak Glen, just north of Yucaipa, is the core of the Inland Empire's tranquil apple country, which both tourists and natives are often surprised to find. September through December means apple-picking time at the 900-acre **Los Rios Rancho,** 39611 Oak Glen Rd. (909-795-1005; www.losriosrancho.com), and **Parrish Pioneer Ranch,** 38561 Oak Glen Rd. (909-797-1753; www.parrishranch.com).

In the summer, you can pick raspberries instead—not a bad alternative. The New England atmosphere of Oak Glen is particularly strong in wintertime, when snow often coats the apple orchards. But any time of year, the place is simply charming. Contact the Oak Glen Apple Growers Association at www.oakglen.net or call (909) 797-2364 for the latest news on this year's crop and the annual Apple Blossom Festival.

The town of Oak Glen is like a West Coast version of Sleepy Hollow, with its antiques stores and scent of fresh apple pie wafting out of the windows of little restaurants. The pace is slower up here, and residents seem to like it that way.

Riley's Farm and Orchard

12261 South Oak Glen Rd.; Oak Glen; (909) 790-2364; www.rileysfarm.com. Open Mon through Sat 10 a.m. to 4 p.m.

"Villagers and country folk" are cordially invited to "come and be one hundred years behind the times" at the Old Packing Shed Bakery and Grill and the Hawk's Head Public House for victuals like chicken pot pie and corn chowder or bottles of vintage sodas. During apple season you can take the kids on a hayride that includes a farm tour, cider pressing, and hot-caramel-dipped apples. Check out their summer tours, dinner events, and Colonial Farm Life Adventure Trips.

Dinosaurs, Fruit, and Shopping

As you drive along I-10, the kids will make you pull over the instant they see two hulking dinosaurs stalking drivers in Cabazon (population 2,200). Exit at Main Street; actual Dinosaurs address is 50770 Seminole Dr., Cabazon. They are open daily from 9 a.m. to 7 p.m.; closed Thanksgiving and Christmas Day. The first dinosaur is an *aptosaurus* (Dinny) with a mini-museum and gift shop tucked into his belly. His friend is a not-too-friendly-looking *Tyrannosaurus rex* named Mr. Rex. Like Pee Wee Herman in *Pee Wee's Big Adventure* (if you haven't seen it, your kids probably have), you can climb up to the dinosaur's jaw to take in the view. These Jurassic monstrosities are California kitsch at its best. They seem to be made expressly for family vacation fun. For more information, call (951) 922-0076 or visit www.cabazondinosaurs.com.

Next door to the dinos, you can fill up at the Wheel Inn diner (50900 Seminole Dr.; 951-849-7012), serving great grub 24/7 since 1964. We love this roadside classic, especially the pies!

And adjacent to the dinos and diner, there are other attractions in Cabazon, easily visible from I-10. The first is Hadley's Fruit Orchards (888-854-5655; www.hadleyfruitorchards.com), an all-natural dried fruit and produce emporium famous for its deliciously frosty date shakes. The others are Desert Hills Premium Outlets (48400 Seminole Rd.; 951-849-6641; www.premium outlets.com) and Cabazon Outlets (48750 Seminole Rd.; 951-922-3000; www .cabazonoutlets.com), three rambling retail complexes. If your kids have been pining for a new pair of Nikes, or you have designs on some off-price Ralph Lauren apparel or home furnishings, you've hit the jackpot. And this isn't even Las Vegas; it just may feel like it with the combination of attractions!

Where to Eat

Parrish Pioneer Apple Ranch. 38561 Oak Glen Rd., Yucaipa; (909) 797-4020; www .parrishranch.com. Home to Apple Dumplin's Restaurant. Stop in for lunch (they have a great selection of sandwiches) and hot apple pie à la mode daily from 10 a.m. to 6 p.m. Ranch shops sell plenty of food and gifts. $

Kern County

Unlike many other states, California never quite seems to end (of course, it does end at its westernmost border, the Pacific Ocean!). If you thought the sweeping vistas stopped after the San Bernardino Mountains, think again—of Kern County, a rectangular region of 8,073 square miles sharing its eastern edge with San Bernardino County, its southern edge with Los Angeles County, and its western edge with San Luis Obispo County. North of Kern County are Kings and Tulare Counties, the gateways to the Sequoia National Parks (more about them later). Kern is the third-largest county by area in California and is as large as the entire state of Massachusetts. It forms the southern tier of the agriculture- and oil-rich California Central Valley, the one of *Grapes of Wrath* fame, acre for acre the richest in the world. No matter what time of year you happen to be driving through, you'll see boundless fields of grapes, almonds, carrots, apples, watermelons, tomatoes, and more. The fruits and vegetables grown here are shipped all over the world, but you can sample them first at any of the numerous roadside farmers' markets.

Kern County's geography offers a wide variety of outdoor recreational options for your family including horseback riding, water skiing (Lake Buena Vista, Lake Ming, and private ski ranches), off-road biking and dune buggies (Jawbone Canyon, California City, and Randsburg), auto racing, paintball courses, white-water rafting, Olympic quality kayaking, hiking, biking (trails, paths, and roads), camping, fishing, and more. It was the Kern River, in fact, that put the region on the map: Gold was discovered in the riverbed in 1851. While the west side of the county is often associated with the oil industry today, it was an 1899 discovery along the Kern River, today part of the giant Kern River Oil Field, that was the breakthrough in Kern's oil production. The county today contributes more than three-quarters of all the oil produced onshore in California. There is plenty to explore, but basically the region is less tourist intensive than the California that lies farther south. It is, above all, a place to appreciate the great outdoors, slow down a bit, and smell the forest.

Kernville

Have you been contemplating a white-water river-rafting adventure for your family? If so, you're in the right place. From its headwaters at Lake South America in the Sierra Nevada (elevation 11,800 feet), the Kern River falls more than 12,000 feet in 150 miles. That makes it one of the fastest-falling rivers in North America. But the pace of the rapids ranges from wild to mild. According to the International River Classification System, rapids ratings range from Class I—very easy, like a swimming pool with a current—all the way up to Class VI, which is virtually unrunnable. Class I and II rapids are perfectly suitable for most children; older ones who enjoy a good soaking can take on Class III. The important thing to remember is that you don't just drive up to the river and hop in with an inner tube. There are several professional rafting outfitters whose sole purpose is to orchestrate a fun, safe time for everyone who signs up.

Most of these outfitters are based in Kernville, the traditional jumping-off point for rafting trips. If you've never done this kind of thing before, ask them about one-day instruction sessions.

If you happen to be in Kernville in late February (before the rafting season kicks in), enjoy the carnival atmosphere of **Whiskey Flat Days,** when the town travels back in time to the gold-rush days. With a parade, rodeo, whisker and costume contests, and frog races, the event is designed for families in search of a little quality fun time. Call (760) 376-2629 or visit www.kernvillechamber.org for dates and other information.

Kernville straddles the northern end of **Lake Isabella,** built in 1953 for flood control and as a hydroelectric source and reservoir. It is Southern California's largest freshwater lake. With up to 11,000 surface-acre feet, it also happens to be a prime body of water for Jet Skiing, waterskiing, windsurfing, sailing, and fishing.

The region around the lake is surrounded by the **Sequoia National Forest;** for camping information and details about other outdoor activities stop by the USDA Forest Service's visitor center off Highway 155, just south of the lake's main dam, at 4875 Ponderosa Rd. (760-379-5646; www.fs.fed.us/r5/sequoia).

Sierra South Mountain Sports Outfitters

11300 Kernville Rd.; (760) 376-3745 or (800) 376-2082; www.sierrasouth.com. Prices vary.

This company offers a wide range of rafting and kayaking excursions, including a 2.5-hour Lickety-Blaster run. On this eminently manageable aquatic jaunt, rafters experience Class II and III rapids. Lake kayaking is an alternative to river rafting for those traveling with kids younger than 12, say the folks at Sierra South, because it is more relaxed and there is swimming at Lake Isabella. It's a family paddle adventure at a mellow pace. Sierra South is a permittee of Sequoia National Forest, US Forest Service.

Whitewater Voyages

11252 Kernville Rd.; (800) 400-RAFT; www.whitewatervoyages.com. Open daily May through Aug. $$$$.

Since 1975, this outfitter has offered Class I and II family trips that accommodate kids as young as age 4. Whitewater's guides were stunt doubles for Meryl Streep and Kevin Bacon in the movie *The River Wild*.

Kern Valley **Turkey Vulture Festival**

Just when you think you've heard about the most unusual festival imaginable (for instance, the tobacco-spitting competition in Calico), along comes this one. Held between September 1 and October 31, depending on when the big birds decide to fly through Kern Valley, the festival offers such activities as a turkey vulture slide show, workshops on raptor rehabilitation, a bird-banding demonstration, and an official Turkey Vultures Lift-Off. There are turkey vulture T-shirts to buy and enough information to satisfy the most rabid bird-watcher (or turkey vulture buff). The festival takes place in Weldon at Audubon's Kern River Preserve. Contact Kernville Chamber of Commerce; (760) 376-2629 or (800) 350-7390; http://kern.audubon.org/tvfest.htm.

Mountain and River Adventures

11113 Kernville Rd.; (760) 376-6553 or (800) 861-6553; www.mtnriver.com. $$$$.

Offers mountain-biking and rock-climbing rambles in addition to white-water rafting trips—all under expert supervision by guides who know the lay of the land (and water) inside out. There's also a tent campground on-site.

Where to Eat & Stay

Cheryl's Diner. 11030 Kernville Rd.; (760) 376-6131. Open from 6 a.m. to 9 p.m. Breakfast, lunch, and dinner served at family-friendly prices. $

The River View Lodge. #2 Sirretta St., P.O. Box 887, Kernville 93238; (760) 376-6019. This historic 11-room inn welcomes families and pets. You'll find refrigerators in every room and a picnic area, too. The country-style rooms with 2 queen-size beds are ideal for families. $$

For More Information

Kernville Chamber of Commerce. 11447 Kernville Rd., P.O. Box 397, 93238-0397; (760) 376-2629; www.kernvillechamber.org.

Bakersfield

In 2008, the city's population was estimated to be more than 300,000, making it the 11th largest city in California. Approximately 100 miles north of Los Angeles via I-5 or Highway 99, Bakersfield's northern city limits extend to the Sequoia National Forest, at the foot of the Greenhorn Mountain Range and at the entrance to the Kern Canyon. To the south, the Tehachapi Mountains feature the historic Tejon Ranch. To the west is the Temblor Range, behind which are the Carrizo Plain National Monument and the San Andreas Fault (see Central Coast chapter for details on that earth-shaking attraction). There are several more-stable attractions in and around the city, Kern's county seat.

Kern County Museum and Lori Brock Children's Discovery Center

3801 Chester Ave.; (661) 852-5000; www.kcmuseum.org. Open Mon through Sat, 10 a.m. to 5 p.m.; Sun 12 p.m. to 5 p.m. Closed Federal and state Holidays. $$.

This museum provides more than a glimpse into the history of Bakersfield and its environs. Kids have room to roam here, for it's a 16-acre walk-through site with more than 60 historic and refurbished structures, ranging from the Havilah Courthouse and Jail (1866) and the Calloway Ranch Blacksmith Shop (circa 1880) to an 1898 Southern Pacific locomotive. The Spanish Mission–style main museum building houses permanent and changing exhibitions that chronicle Kern County's history, natural history, and culture. The Lori Brock Children's Discovery Center, since 1976, has provided hands-on displays and activities for kids on the premises. Black Gold: The Oil Experience is a permanent $4 million science,

Vroom **Vroom**

If you and your kids are feeling the need to see some speed, feel the roar, and taste the dust, Kern County is renowned for its racetracks. Here's where the action is!

- **Auto Club Famoso Raceway.** 33559 Famoso Rd., McFarland; (661) 399-2210, info line: (661) 399-5351; www.famosoraceway.com. Quarter-mile drag strip featuring the Good Guys Nostalgia March Meet, the NHRA FM series in April, and the NHRA CHRR IX in October.

- **Willow Springs International Motorsports Park.** 3500 75th St. West, Rosamond; (661) 256-2471; www.willowspringsraceway.com. Races held every weekend; 5 circuits available. Car, motorcycle, go-kart driving, and racing schools.

- **Buttonwillow Raceway Park.** 24551 Lerdo Hwy., Buttonwillow; (661) 764-5333; www.buttonwillowraceway.com. Three-mile road-racing track. Indy cars, sports cars, motorcycles, and go-karts go here.

technology, and history exhibition. The refurbished Kid City is a self guided tour that features the basics of any town—a library, a bank, a doctor's office, a restaurant, a park, a theater, an ambulance, and fire department, among others, so kids can explore career options.

California Living Museum (CALM)

Just north of Bakersfield, 14000 Alfred Harrell Hwy.; (661) 872-2256; www.calmzoo.org. Open daily 9 a.m. to 5 p.m.; closed major holidays. $.

Whereas the Kern County Museum focuses on the human history of the area, the natural environment occupies center stage here. This is an ideally situated spot for a family-oriented wildlife experience. The 13 acres house a botanical garden, petting zoo, and natural history museum. The animal exhibits assemble fauna native to California: coyotes, desert tortoises, shorebirds, and birds of prey, including hawks, raptors, owls, and eagles. The Mammal Round exhibit features mountain lions, raccoons, foxes, and bobcats—yes, all native to the Golden State! The Living Museum merits at least a 90-minute visit.

Tule Elk State Reserve

Twenty-seven miles west of Bakersfield, 4 miles west of I-5, and off the Stockdale Highway, south of Buttonwillow; (661) 764-6881 or (661) 248-6692; www.parks.ca.gov. Open daily 8 a.m. to sunset. $$.

For a slightly wilder look at the wild kingdom, head to this 953-acre site. Tule elks were once as common in California as the antelope of South Africa are today, but they are now

Home on the Ranch

If your kids spot some elk, they may be disappointed to learn that no, they can't ride or even pet them. However, they can pet and ride horses to their hearts' content at **Rankin Ranch,** minutes north of Bakersfield in Walker's Basin. To get there, take I-5 north to the Lamont–Lake Isabelle exit. The ranch is 38 miles from the exit, past the town of Caliente. Members of the Rankin family have been ranching at their Quarter Circle U since 1863, and they've got the western way of life down pat. This is a working, 31,000-acre cattle and guest ranch where kids and adults can help out with farm chores and horseback ride at their leisure. Fourteen cozy cabins with no room phones or TV. Family-style meals, horseback riding, swimming, and hiking. The seasonal supervised children's program is first-rate. Open in spring, summer, and fall. Call for current rates (which include riding, lodging, and 3 meals a day) and other information at (661) 867-2511, or visit www.rankin ranch.com.

a rare species. The State Division of Beaches and Parks keeps a herd of about 30 adult elk at the park, which is equipped with a shaded picnic and viewing area. With the sweeping grassland forming a backdrop, gawking at the elks' regal antlers (which only the males have) is rather like taking a mini-safari. The best times to view the elk are in summer and fall.

Fort Tejon State Historic Park

I-5, 36 miles south of Bakersfield. Exit off I-5, 70 miles northwest of Los Angeles at the top of Grapevine Canyon; (661) 248-6692; www.parks.ca.gov. Living-history programs held the first Sunday of each month; Civil War reenactments, third Sunday, Apr through Oct. $.

Listed on the National Register of Historic Places, the fort is well worth a few hours' stop, especially for a realistic perspective of life in the 1850–60s, an era when the fort was an active US Army outpost. The fort's strategic location guarded Bakersfield and the San Joaquin Valley from the south and east. Its mission was to suppress stock rustling and protect settlers from attacks by Native American tribes.

Buck Owens' Crystal Palace

2800 Buck Owens Blvd.; (661) 869-BUCK; (661) 328-7500 for dinner reservations. Call (661) 328-7560 or (808) 855-5005 for show reservations; www.buckowens.com. Daily free tours are available. Dinners Tues through Sat and brunch on Sun. Closed Mon except for special concerts and events.

Opened in 1996, this all-in-one restaurant, museum, and theater is a must-see! Even if the kids are unaware that Buck Owens starred in *Hee Haw*, they'll love the smashingly sensational decor. You'll be amazed by what's above the 50-foot-long bar: the car Elvis never drove, a vintage 1970s Pontiac land yacht, studded with silver dollars! It's mounted at a tilt so you can check out its luxurious interior. Buck Owens passed away in March 2006, but his friends still perform country favorites evenings, matinees, and weekends. State-of-the-art sound, lighting, and giant screens throughout make this a visual marvel. And we haven't even mentioned the 35-foot mural showing Buck's rise from the cotton fields to Carnegie Hall to entertaining presidents at the White House. Country music and cuisine has found a honky tonk home in Bakersfield.

Where to Eat & Stay

Dewar's Candy and Ice Cream Parlor. 1120 Eye St.; (661) 322-0933; www.dewars candy.com. (Another branch is at Riverlakes Mall, 9530 Hageman Rd. # K, 661-587-2056.) Savor sweet confections and ice cream from the Dewar's family recipes, originating in 1909, still operated by the fourth genera-tion of Dewar's today. You can see the daily

Basque in this **Culinary Surprise**

Bakersfield has an unexpected culinary surprise: numerous Basque restau-rants. One of the largest Basque communities outside the Pyrenees is in Kern County, and any chance to sample this special cuisine should not be missed. A highlight of the meal is the scrumptious Basque salsa, made of chopped tomatoes, yellow and jalapeño chiles, garlic, onion, and salt. Here are some great places to experience Basque for you and your family. (Family-style ser-vice is also very popular with this cuisine . . . *Ongi etorri!*)

- **Benji's French Basque Restaurant,** 4001 Rosedale Hwy.; (661) 328-0400.

- **Chalet Basque,** 200 Oak St.; (661) 327-2915.

- **Wool Growers,** 620 East 19th St.; (661) 327-9584; www.woolgrowers.net.

- **Pyrenees Cafe,** 601 Sumner St.; (661) 323-0053.

- **Noriega Hotel,** 525 Sumner St.; (661) 322-8419. www.noriegahotel.com. One seating at noon and one seating at 7 p.m. Our favorite Basque family-style dining spot. Make sure you know how to get there, as first-timers have some trouble. Hungry diners sit at long tables (you may not know who'll be next to you), sharing up to 7 courses of hearty Basque food. No set menu. We've tried soup, salad, chicken, ribs, fresh-cut French fries—all excellent. The ambience is, well, very plain, but the service is efficient and the fare is robust. Only the most ravenous will have room for dessert.

production of ice cream and taffy chews at the original shop Tues to Thurs at 10:30 a.m. by appointment. Yes, yum. $

Red Lion Hotel Bakersfield. 2400 Camino Del Rio Court; (661) 327-0681; reservations: (800) RED-LION; www.bakersfieldredlion.com. There are 165 rooms and suites, some with Jacuzzis. Prime location at junction of Freeway 99 and Highway 58 (Rosedale Highway exit) for all your family's Kern County adventures. Smokin' Joe's Beach Bar & Woodfired Cuisine restaurant on-site. $$$

For More Information

Greater Bakersfield Convention and Visitors Bureau. 515 Truxton Ave.; (661) 325-5051 or (866) 425-7353; www.bakersfield cvb.org.

Kern County Board of Trade and Tourist Information Center. Mailing address: P.O. Bin 1312, Bakersfield 93302; street address: 2101 Oak St., Bakersfield; (661) 861-2367 or (800) 500-KERN; www.visitkern.com.

Tulare County

Encompassing 4,863 square miles (slightly larger than Connecticut) in the San Joaquin Valley, Tulare County is nestled between the Sierra Nevada to the east and the Coastal Mountain Range to the west. Tulare County's extensively cultivated and very fertile valley floor is the second-leading producer of agricultural commodities in the United States. The rest of the county is composed of foothills, timbered slopes, and high mountains ranging in elevations from 270 feet to 14,495 feet (the top of Mt. Whitney, the highest point in the continental United States). There are more than 110 mountain peaks in eastern Tulare County, which furnish a backdrop of scenic wonder. Tulare County is home to Sequoia National Park as well as Inyo and Sequoia National Forests—offering an amazing array of dining, lodging, camping, winter sports of all kinds, fishing, boating, backpacking, hunting, hiking, and waterskiing options that attract thousands of visitors annually.

Sequoia and Kings Canyon **Junior Ranger Program**

Kids of any age can participate in this program. Kids ages 5 through 8 earn the Jay Award. Those ages 9 through 12 work for the Raven Award, and kids ages 13 through 103 can earn the Senior Patch. To get started, purchase a Junior Ranger booklet at any visitor center. Follow the instructions and have fun! Here's something we learned. When first set aside, what is now Sequoia and Kings Canyon National Parks were less than one-ninth of their present size. Over the last century, Congress has made seven major additions to the parks—the last being the Mineral King area in 1978.

Sequoia National Park and Kings Canyon National Park

Office of the Superintendent, 47050 Generals Hwy., Three Rivers; general visitor information: (559) 565-3341; www.nps.gov/seki. The two main entrances, Ash Mountain on Highway 198 and Big Stump on Highway 180, are open daily year-round. Certain areas of the park are open part of the year: The Mineral King area is open late May through Oct 31 in Sequoia National Park, and the Cedar Grove area in Kings Canyon is open mid-Apr through mid-Nov. Crystal Cave, some campgrounds, and several side roads close for the winter. The main park road, the Generals Highway, may close between Lodgepole and Grant Grove during and after storms for plowing. The highest visitation is in July and Aug. It can be difficult to find a campsite at popular campgrounds on summer Saturdays. Driving times: To Sequoia Park Ash Mountain entrance from Highway 99 at Visalia, take Highway 198 east for approximately 1 hour. To Kings Canyon Park Big Stump entrance from Highway 99 at Fresno, take Highway 180 east approximately 1.25 hours. Admission per vehicle: $20 for a 7-day pass, $30 for annual vehicle pass. Note: Gasoline is not sold within park boundaries, but it is available at locations near the park boundaries. Be sure to fill up in one of the towns near the park entrances or at one of three locations in the national forest that border parts of the park. Entrance Fee-Free Days are June 5 and 6, National Trails Day; Sept 25, National Public Lands Day; and Nov 11, Veterans Day.

Tulare County is best known as the home of these parks. Even though it's part of Fresno County, Kings Canyon shares its east-west boundary with Sequoia, and the two parks are generally referred to together. If the wooded retreats of Big Bear and Lake Arrowhead in the Inland Empire are imbued with an "escape from the city" atmosphere, up here you'll really feel a zillion miles away from it all. This is nature at its most unbridled, God's country with a very capital G. With more than 800 miles of marked hiking trails and 1,200-plus campsites and other lodging options, it's no wonder Sequoia and Kings Canyon are a California family favorite for camping and nature trips.

The biggest attractions are trees. Autumn in New England may be prime leaf-peeping time, but the trees of the central Sierra Nevada are marvels to behold any time of year. This is mainly due to their gargantuan size. Of the 37 largest sequoia trees in the world, 20 giants roost here in Sequoia and Kings Canyon. You'll find the most stupendous grove of sequoias in the Giant Forest, longtime home of the General Sherman Tree. Weighing in at 2.7 million pounds, the 275-foot-tall tree is the largest living thing in the world. At more than 2,300 years, it's also one of the oldest. Each year the venerable Sherman grows enough wood for another 60-foot-tall tree. Imagine the tree-house possibilities! For an easy, rewarding hike the whole family will enjoy, try the 2-mile, 2-hour Congress Trail, which begins at the Sherman and circles around the grove.

Kings Canyon is where the General Grant Tree, the earth's third-largest, has its roots. It's also known as the "Nation's Christmas Tree." Annual Noel celebrations are held beneath its considerable and magnificent canopy. Walk along the easy 0.3-mile-long trail, marked with informative signposts, to learn more about trees and the peoples who lived here.

Conservationist John Muir called Kings Canyon a rival to Yosemite, and it's not hard to see why. The depths of the canyon at Cedar Grove, where the Kings River gushes between sheer granite walls, bottom out at 8,000 feet. Both Sequoia and Kings Canyon offer incomparable vistas, hiking trails, camping, and other natural wonders, including more than a hundred caves.

There are several excellent visitor centers throughout the parks that offer **free** information, weather updates, naturalist programs, slide shows, maps, and services. **Grant Grove Visitor Center** in Kings Canyon (559-565-4307) is open daily. **Lodgepole Visitor Center** in Sequoia (559-565-4436) is open daily in summer and on weekends only in winter. **Cedar Grove Visitor Center** (559-565-3793; 30 miles east of Kings Canyon park entrance) is open daily during the summer only.

The **Giant Forest Museum** in Sequoia (559-565-4480) is open daily and should not be missed. It is housed in a historic log building in the Giant Forest sequoia grove at 6,500 feet elevation, 16 miles from the Ash Mountain entrance on Highway 198. Wonderful interactive exhibits tell the story of the sequoias of Giant Forest, and what we have learned about how to protect them.

Activities vary according to season, but no matter the time of year, the best way to get into the park is to get out of the car. "Don't leave until you have seen it," advised 1920s park superintendent Col. John R. White, "and this you cannot do from an automobile." In summer, rangers lead walks and talks in the foothills, the sequoia groves, and the high country. Take a tour of the exquisite Crystal Cave. There are rivers to enjoy—carefully—and pack stations offer horseback riding.

Come winter, cross-country skis or snowshoes can be rented to explore the sequoia groves beyond the roads, and there are ranger-guided snowshoe walks. Wolverton is a wonderful free-terrain snow-play area (sometimes even in April). If you prefer warmer activities, trails in the foothills are usually snow-free, and by February they are graced with wildflowers. Check bulletin boards and visitor centers to find what activities are being offered.

Where to Eat & Stay

Cedar Grove Lodge. Operated by Sequoia–Kings Canyon Park Services Company, (559) 335-5500; www.sequoia-kingscanyon.com. Open late Apr through Oct. Twenty-one motel rooms in Cedar Grove Village, deep in the canyon of Kings Canyon Park. Restaurant, market, and gift shop also in building. $$

Grant Grove Village. Operated by Sequoia–Kings Canyon Park Services Company, (559) 335-5500 or (866) JON-MUIR; www.sequoia-kingscanyon.com. Open all year. Here you will find the two-story John Muir Lodge, 30 modern hotel rooms with forest views, and more than 40 rustic tent and housekeeping cabins, all in the Grant Grove area of Kings Canyon Park, only a half-mile stroll to a sequoia grove. Casual dining on American fare (breakfast, lunch, and dinner daily) at Grant Grove Village Restaurant, next to the visitor center; market/general store; gift shop; and post office. $$$

Montecito–Sequoia Lodge. Privately owned by founder Dr. Virginia Barnes and family since 1946; in January 2007, acquired and now operated by the Dally family. (559)

565-3388 or (800) 843-8677; www.mslodge
.com. Open year-round. Located on its own
Lake Homavalo in Sequoia National Forest,
adjacent to Sequoia and Kings Canyon National
Parks. This rustic property functions as a
weekly family vacation camp in summer and
a cross-country ski center in the winter. There
are 36 basic lodge rooms with private baths
and 13 cabins with nearby bathhouses. Reasonable rates vary according to season and
include all meals, which are served buffet style
in the lodge. On-site summer and children's
activities include canoeing, sailing, waterskiing,
swimming, horseback riding, tennis, archery,
trampoline, riflery, fencing, nature, stream fishing, arts and crafts instruction, theme nights,
dances, sing-along campfires, variety shows,
water carnivals, fort building, junior gymnas-
tics, and pony rides. $$$

Wuksachi Village & Lodge. Operated by
Delaware North Park Services, in Sequoia
National Park, 4 miles from the Giant Forest
and 23 miles from Sequoia Park entrance.
(559) 253-2199 or (888) 252 5757; www
.visitsequoia.com. Open all year. Opened in
1999, the striking log lodge forms the center
of the village and houses the full-service din-
ing room (breakfast, lunch, and dinner daily),
cocktail lounge, gift shop, and conference
rooms, where naturalist-led programs are
held (**free** and not to be missed). There
are 102 modern rooms housed in 3 separate
log buildings up on the hillside (ask for the
Sequoia building for the best views of Mt.
Silliman and Silver Peak). The 18 large fam-
ily suites have sofa sleepers in alcove sitting
areas—ideal for your clan. Reserve early,
especially in summer and on weekends. $$$

Mammoth Lakes Area

The Mammoth Lakes area is California's answer to the Alps. Southern Californians have
been known to schlep their ski equipment to locales as far off as Chile and Chamonix, but
most will agree that some of the best skiing anywhere is found 300 miles north of Los
Angeles at **Mammoth Mountain Ski Area** in the heart of the Eastern Sierra Nevada.
(Yes, on the map, Mammoth looks like it should be a Northern California attraction—but
let's be honest—Northern Californians go to the Tahoe area for snow—and Mammoth has
always been somewhat of a Southern Californian hang-out!) The statistics bespeak world-
class thrills: an 11,053-foot summit, a 7,953-foot base, 30 lifts, 150 trails, and 3,500 acres
of skiable terrain. The ski season often extends as late as July. Don't let the fact that the US
Ski Team trains at Mammoth each spring deter you from coming: Fully 30 percent of the
ski runs are rated for beginners. Plus, Mammoth boasts one of the finest ski schools in the
country, with family lessons and a children's ski school offered regularly.

Throughout the Mammoth Lakes region, not only will your family groove on skiing
and snowboarding but also at cross-country ski centers, on snowmobile rentals, sledding,
tobogganing, outdoor ice skating, and snowshoeing. Summer means even more activities
to keep the family fit. In the summer, enjoy mountain biking, hiking, jazz and art festivals,
swimming, picnicking, fishing, boating, hot springs, and canoeing, kayaking, or riding your
Jet Skis and Wave Runners at Lakes Topaz, Klondike, Grant, Diaz, Walker, and Crowley. Or
check out national monuments—visit Devils Postpile, formed more than 100,000 years
ago, or Rainbow Falls, where the San Joaquin River drops more than 100 feet. How about

a horseback ride—most of the major canyons in the Eastern Sierra have pack stations, offering anywhere from one-hour to full-day or multiday trips. Your family will discover endless choices for accommodations (condos, chalets, hotels, cabins, inns), for dining (from fast food to continental cuisine), and for shopping (from trinkets to fine art), and a shuttle route connects all the fun year-round! Mammoth is one of the best choices for a family vacation—summer or winter.

Inyo National Forest

Headquarters, 351 Pacu Lane, Suite 200, Bishop; (760) 873-2400; www.fs.fed.us.

The name "Inyo" comes from a Native American word meaning "dwelling place of the great spirit." The Inyo National Forest was named after Inyo County, in which much of the forest resides. Here you'll find more than two million acres of clean air, crystal-blue skies, mountain lakes and streams, challenging trails, high mountain peaks, and beautiful views. The Inyo National Forest is home to many natural wonders, including Mt. Whitney, Mono Lake, Mammoth Lakes Basin, and the Ancient Bristlecone Pine Forest, as well as seven congressionally designated wildernesses, comprising more than 650,000 acres of land. Recreational opportunities include camping, picnicking, hiking, backpacking, equestrian use, and off-highway vehicle use. More than 100 miles of trails are groomed for multiple-purpose winter use (snowmobiling, skiing, and hiking), and approximately 45 miles of trails are groomed for cross-country skiing.

Mammoth Mountain Ski Area

1 Minaret Rd., Mammoth Lakes; snowphone: (760) 934-6166 or (888) SNOWRPT; general information: (760) 934-0745 or (800) MAMMOTH; www.mammothmountain.com. Open year-round. $$$$.

Mammoth Mountain is the leading four-season mountain resort in Southern California, encompassing 4 day lodges, 10 sports shops, 12 rental/repair shops, 1 on-hill snack bar, 4 food courts/cafeterias, a ski and snowboard school, a race department, lockers, 4 hotels (Tamarack Lodge, Mammoth Mountain Inn, the Village Lodge, and Juniper Springs Resort) as well as condominium accommodations, 5 restaurants, 7 bars, child-care services (www .mammothmountain.com), and game room. Rates for lodging, dining, and attractions are available in a wide range to fit any budget or taste.

Mammoth Kids Ski Schools

Infoline: (800) MAMMOTH; www.mammothmountain.com.

Mammoth has three learning centers where instructors specialize in working with kids: Woollywood at Main Lodge, Canyon Kids at Canyon Lodge, and Eagle Lodge Ski and Snow-board School. Mammoth Kids programs feature instruction, child care, and combination packages. The school is divided into Mammoth Explorers (ages 4 to 6 and 7 to 12), the Big Kahuna Snowboard Club (7 to 12), children's private lessons (4 to 12), the Custom Kid's Camp (7 to 12), and a three-day ski/snowboard camp. Helmets are required for ages 4 through 12.

Manzanar National Historic Site

During World War II, Manzanar Relocation Center, just off US 395, 12 miles north of Lone Pine, was one of ten camps where Japanese-American citizens and Japanese aliens were interned. Located at the foot of the imposing Sierra Nevada in eastern California's Owens Valley, Manzanar has been identified as the best preserved of these camps. A 20-minute film shows at the Interpretive Center between 9 a.m. and 4:30 p.m. daily. Open all year during daylight hours with **free** admission.

There is a 3.2-mile-long self-guided auto tour of the camp, with a tour description and map available at the camp entrance. A walking tour of the Manzanar Camp takes one to two hours. A self-guiding walking-tour booklet is available at the Interagency Visitor Center in Lone Pine and at the Eastern California Museum in Independence. For more information call (760) 878-2194 or visit www.nps.gov/manz.

Red's Meadow Pack Stations

P.O. Box 395, Mammoth Lakes 93546; (760) 934-2345 or (800) 292-7758; www.redsmeadow .com. $$.

If you're in the market for a modern A-frame cabin, these newer but rustic cabins are furnished with butane heating, running water, large bathrooms with showers, gas ranges, and refrigerators. There are also motel units, a grocery store, and cafe—both open 7 a.m. to 7 p.m. daily. From Red's Meadow there are various group riding and hiking trail trips to such places as the John Muir Wilderness, Bishop to Bodie (camping along the old stagecoach route via saddle horse, mule, and wagon), and other off-the-beaten-path tours your family will long remember. These tours begin in late May and end about the first of Oct. If you're into more comfort, reserve a condominium in Mammoth for the family and take the shuttle bus into Red's Meadow.

Tamarack Lodge & Resort and Cross-Country Ski Center

Located 2 miles from the town of Mammoth in the Mammoth Lakes Basin on Twin Lakes Road; (800) 237-6879; www.tamaracklodge.com. $$$$.

A great bet for families, with its 19 miles of groomed trails that weave through pine forests (open Nov through Apr). The resort has been welcoming guests since 1924—with cabins and lodge rooms from rustic to deluxe—and serving hearty lunch and dinner meals at the Lakefront Restaurant. Boat and canoe rentals are available summertime at the lodge. You can fish from Tamarack's front yard in Twin Lakes (Apr through Oct); or hike around one of the many trails in the nearby Lakes Basin.

Mammoth Dog Teams

(760) 934-6270 or (800) MAMMOTH; www.mammothdogteams.com. $$$$.

Tours (on an honest-to-goodness dogsled) mush off from the Main Lodge at Mammoth Mountain Inn. Rides in the winter, kennel tours in the off-season. The dogs also have a mushing museum and an art gallery. There is a sled workshop and even a classroom where you can take lessons on dog care and health, team dynamics, and the history of mushing. Call in advance.

For More Information

Mammoth Lakes Visitor Bureau. 2520 Main St., Box 48, Mammoth Lakes, 93546; (760) 934-2712 or (888) GO-MAMMOTH (888-466-2666); www.visitmammoth.com.

Mono County Tourism & Film Commission. P.O. Box 603, Mammoth Lakes, 93546; (760) 924-1700 or (800) 845-7922; www.monocounty.org.

Lone Pine

How can you not stop in Lone Pine, in southern Inyo County, once you realize you can explore one of the earth's oldest geological formations by car? Among others, these phantasmagoric formations resemble a bullfrog, a polar bear, Hannibal the Cannibal, and an owl. Hundreds of rock sculptures can be imagined in these bizarre hills, and you can drive the route in about half an hour.

You're on historical turf here; this is where Republic Pictures filmed dozens of spaghetti Westerns during the 1940s and '50s. Chase scenes from these cowboy flicks, with such stars as Hopalong Cassidy, were immortalized in this stunning landscape. Scenes for *Maverick* (starring Mel Gibson) were shot here. If you see *The Shadow* with Alec Baldwin, you'll recognize the Alabama hills backdrop. Many stars return for the mid-October Annual Lone Pine Film Festival. Spend a few hours or a few days here, within view of the majestic Mt. Whitney, at 14,494 feet high, the tallest mountain in the continental United States, 13 miles west of town on Whitney Portal Road. The summit is 11 miles up by strenuous trail from the end of the road; permits are required year-round (760-873-2483).

Where to Eat & Stay

Best Western Frontier Motel. 1008 Main St. at US 395, 0.5 miles south of Lone Pine; (760) 876-5571, (800) 528-1234; http://bestwesterncalifornia.com. Rates include continental breakfast at this simple, clean, 73-room property. Beautiful mountain views from the lawn. $$

Mt. Whitney Restaurant. 227 S. Main St., corner of Highway 395 and Whitney Portal Rd.; (760) 876-575. Serving breakfast, lunch, and dinner daily. Open 6:30 a.m. to 9 p.m. Comfort food, family setting; check out the burger selection including venison, buffalo, ostrich, and veggie. Game room in the back and a 50-inch big screen TV (a bit of a rarity in these parts!).

For More Information

Lone Pine Chamber of Commerce. 126 South Main St.; (760) 876-4444 or (877) 253-8981; www.lonepinechamber.org.

Bishop

Chances are quite good you'll pass through the town of Bishop on your way to or out of the Mammoth Lakes area. You'll see why Bishop calls itself the Mule Capital of the World if you arrive during Memorial Day weekend's annual Mule Days (www.muledays.org), when the streets are abuzz with mule and chariot races, jumping events, and myriad other equine-related activities. Approximately 40,000 mule lovers gather for what the Guinness Book of World Records called (in 1994) the world's longest-running nonmotorized parade. Call (760) 872-4263 for more information.

September in Bishop is a special event in itself thanks to the Millpond Traditional Music Festival (760-873-8014 or 800-874-0669; www.inyo.org) that takes place at Millpond County Park, sponsored by Inyo County and the Inyo Council for the Arts. Featured are top performers of bluegrass, folk, and country music. Families will find this musical weekend ideal for picnics and outdoor adventures.

Laws Railroad Museum and Historic Site

Half mile north of Bishop, off US 6; (760) 873-5950; www.lawsmuseum.org. Free; donations welcome.

This 11-acre indoor/outdoor museum harks back to the rough-and-tumble pioneer days in the Owens Valley. Kids can climb into the cab of Locomotive 9 to ring the bell, and explore the compartment cars of the 1883 Slim Princess narrow-gauge train, which, says the sign, began nowhere, ended nowhere, an' stopped all night to think it over. The museum is on the National Register of Historic Places. Check out the bell rack, featuring antique bells from Bishop-area schools; the Original Laws School, refurbished with local artifacts; and a country store with old-time school items and supplies on display.

Erick Schat's Bakery

763 North Main St.; (760) 873-7156; www.erickschatsbakery.com.

This is a local institution. Home since 1907 of the original "sheepherder bread," a hearty country loaf, Schat's also has delicious sweet rolls and scrumptious sandwiches. You'll leave well fortified and ready to tackle another stretch of scenic California.

For More Information

Bishop Area Chamber of Commerce and Visitors Bureau. 690 North Main St.; (760) 873-8504 or (888) 395-3952; www.bishopvisitor.com.

The Deserts

The California deserts conjure up different images for different people. To some, they suggest glittering resort cities, brilliant skies, mid-century (1950s) architectural marvels, and the verdant greens of impressive Palm Springs golf courses. To others, they raise thoughts of a barren, even desolate, landscape of boulders, sand, and cacti lining the freeway from Los Angeles to Las Vegas. To yet others, they inspire thoughts of pioneer history, rustic ghost towns, and abandoned gold mines. Vast opportunities for family fun endure under the desert sun! Whatever desert-related pictures may come to mind, however, one fact is indisputable: The desert is big. It is immense—stretching from the Mojave Desert and ultra-arid Death Valley National Park in the north to the Colorado Desert area that reaches south to the border of Mexico.

Although the region is strikingly—or starkly—beautiful, much of it is what some might call wasteland or others environmentally pristine. Either way, a good portion is off-limits to nonmilitary personnel. These two attributes certainly make it simpler for families who want to catch the desert's highlights but lack the time (or inclination) to explore every gully or gulch. As a matter of fact, vast tracts of the desert have no highways, and if something akin to a "road" exists, it can be rock-strewn, meandering, signless, and dusty, leading you and your clan (best-case scenario) to an old ghost town or some other remnant of long-gone Wild West days, or (worst-case scenario) to nowhere, nowhere at all.

If you are willing to take a modest chance, to be marginally adventuresome in checking out a few of the desert's endless nooks and crannies, you'll find that here, too—the Golden State is indeed a land of contrasts.

As its name suggests, Death Valley—at 282 feet below sea level, the lowest land surface in the Western Hemisphere—is about as dry and hot as a place can get. In sharp contrast, much of Palm Springs and other resort communities of the Coachella Valley, some 150 miles to the south of Death Valley, are as verdant and lush as a tropical oasis—primarily because of irrigation, but partly because of cool mountain streams that have flowed into the area for centuries. Even in summer, when 110-plus-degree temperatures expose the desert's true personality, it's still a great time to visit. During the summer months,

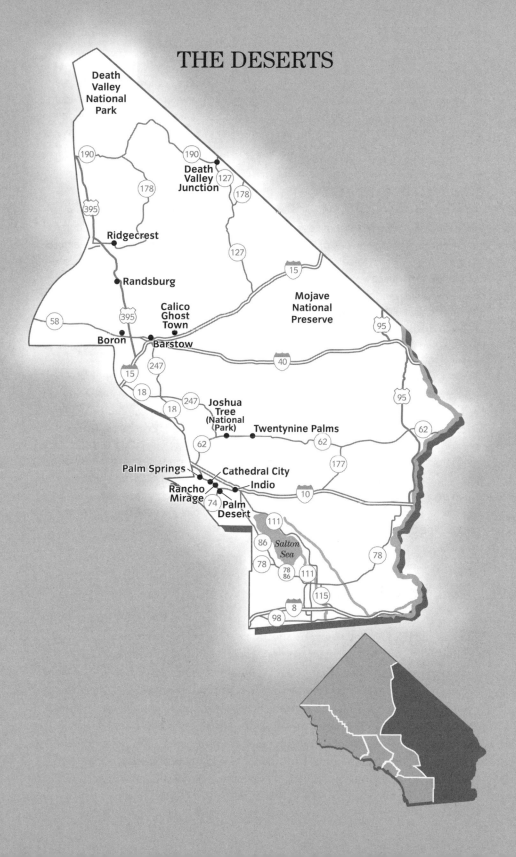

THE DESERTS

Death Valley National Park

190

190

Death Valley Junction

127

178

178

395

Ridgecrest

127

Randsburg

15

Mojave National Preserve

58

395

Calico Ghost Town

95

Boron

Barstow

15

247

40

95

18

247

18

Joshua Tree (National Park)

Twentynine Palms

95

62

62

62

177

Palm Springs

Cathedral City

Indio

Rancho Mirage

74

Palm Desert

10

111

86

Salton Sea

78

78

78 86

111

78

115

8

98

many Palm Springs–area hotels reduce their rates 50 percent or more. And throughout the desert, summer seems to go by a little slower than elsewhere in California. Of course, the sun certainly shines brighter. It's almost as if nature is telling you to enjoy the offerings of the desert at a pace that suits you—and reminding you to bring along plenty of water to drink and your sunscreen!

Palm Springs

Approximately 100 miles east of Los Angeles via I-10 lies the **Coachella Valley,** home to the desert resort communities of Palm Springs, Cathedral City, Rancho Mirage, Palm Desert, Indio, Indian Wells, Desert Hot Springs, and La Quinta. The other nearby high-desert destinations are Yucca Valley, Morongo Valley, Twentynine Palms, and Joshua Tree. Seen from an airplane window or hot-air balloon, these cities appear as rather artificial patches of green against a flat, arid landscape framed by mountain ridges.

If you drive into the Coachella Valley from L.A., however, the first things you'll notice are rows and rows of windmills protruding sentry-like from the hillsides. These are actually working wind turbines that generate electricity for nearly 100,000 homes.

Other desert areas may be more scenic (read: more barren), but the Coachella Valley (estimated local population 400,000, which swells to 800,000 during the peak visitor season from Jan through Apr) has the monopoly on recreational attractions and leisure opportunities. Just consider a few valley stats: an estimated 600 tennis courts, 16,200 hotel rooms in 130 hotels, and 111 golf courses, meaning more than one golf course per square mile in the desert resort area. Add 40,000 swimming pools, probably a zillion whirlpool spas, and 300-plus days of fun in the sunshine to the recipe, and it's a no-brainer why 3.5 million people visit the area every year. But the valley never seems crowded, even during the peak season, because things are so naturally spread out. To see how vast the desert really is, ride the Palm Springs Aerial Tramway for a "natural high."

Just Like **Home . . .**

An alternative to a hotel is this desert discovery called **Vacation Home Rentals,** a Coachella Valley company specializing in upscale condos and furnished homes with private pools and whirlpool spas (with 1 to 8 bedrooms). If you've been dreaming of that perfect Palm Springs family retreat with a magnificent mountain view surrounded by swaying palm trees, this is the easiest way to make that happen. Rentals are near entertainment, attractions, dining, and shops, plus some are pet friendly, too. Ask about Wi-Fi Internet access in case you or yours cannot give up being connected. Rentals are available nightly, weekly, and monthly. The main office is open seven days a week at 1276 N. Palm Canyon Dr.; (760) 778-7832; www.vacationpalmsprings.com.

World-famous as "America's Premier Desert Resort," Palm Springs has ranked high on everybody's Coachella Valley must-visit list since the 1930s, when the small town (current population est. 47,000) was a favorite playground for California's unofficial royalty—movie stars. Gone but not forgotten are Frank Sinatra and Liberace, who once had estates here. Barry Manilow, Carol Channing, Jack Jones, Suzanne Somers, Keely Smith, and Dick Van Patten still call the desert home for at least part of the year. It doesn't take a rocket scientist to understand the valley's appeal. Average winter temperatures in the mid-70s are enough to turn even Los Angelinos green (as in putting green) with envy. And the restaurants and resorts are truly world-class.

The *Desert Entertainer* (760-776-5181; www.desertentertainer.com) is published weekly, **free** of charge; you can pick it up on news racks all over town. It's a useful source for desert happenings. Listings include such items as local hikes, museums, various valley attractions, a daily calendar, and information on family-oriented events. That Little Family Book (www.coachellavalleykids.com), written by a busy area father of three, is a **free** monthly publication designed for parents and grandparents looking for the latest kid friendly options, events, and deals and discounts on restaurants and attractions in the area.

Elite Land Tours

540 South Vella Rd.; (760) 318-1200 or (800) 514-4866; www.elitelandtours.com. Call for current schedule and options. $$$$.

All tours conducted in fully air-conditioned, best-in-class all-terrain vehicles—the Hummer H2—accommodating up to five passengers plus professional guide. Owner Mark Farley and his team of experts can take you on a scheduled or customized tour of Palm Springs, from celebrity homes to a trek through the Indian canyons. Tours are available daily, either half- or full-day, and include resort/home pickup (door-to-door service), admissions, gourmet snacks, and assorted refreshments. Gourmet picnic lunch optional. Tour destinations include visits to the San Andreas Fault; Covington Flats, to see the world's largest Joshua tree; Mojave and Colorado/Sonora Desert trails; a Night Vision experience; the Salton Sea; the Spirit of the Indian Canyons; or a wind farm. Featured on the Travel Channel and in *Condé Nast Traveler*. A one-of-a-kind experience not to be missed.

Moorten Botanical Gardens

1701 South Palm Canyon Dr., corner of East Palm Canyon; (760) 327-6555; www.palm springs.com/moorten. Open 9 a.m. to 4:30 p.m.; closed Wed. Self-guided tours. $.

Kids will learn about the diversity of desert flora at the world's first "cactarium," where 3,000 varieties of cacti flourish in a natural setting. Established in 1938, this unusual botanical garden bristles with cacti in all shapes and sizes. Ask the kids to look for colorful desert flowers because there's "always something in bloom."

Palm Springs International Film Festival

1700 East Tahquitz Canyon Way, Suite 3; (760) 322-2930; www.psfilmfest.org.

Held annually since 1989, this film festival has become a mecca for buyers seeking films for distribution. Films screened here include comedy, romance, experimental, animation, period pieces, suspense, and thrillers. The 2010 festival screened more than 200 films, with an impressive representation of family films as well. Plan ahead for family-friendly films by ordering tickets in advance.

Palm Canyon Theatre

538 North Palm Canyon Dr. at corner of Alejo (in Frances Stevens Park); (760) 323-5123 (box office); www.palmcanyontheatre.org. Box office hours Tues through Sat 10 a.m. to 5 p.m. Closed June through Aug, but a special 5-week children's camp is offered then. $$.

This Palm Springs theater group, celebrating its 13th season in 2010–11, is located in a former school gym, now a 230-seat banked stadium-style proscenium theatre. Family-type plays such as *Cats*, *Annie*, or *Annie Get Your Gun* make this an ideal choice for an all-ages experience. This is the valley's only Equity theater, assuring high quality, professional, and affordable performances. **Free** parking on-site and ample refreshments between acts.

Palm Springs Celebrity Tours

67555 East Palm Canyon Dr., Suite C111, Cathedral City; (760) 770-2700; www.thecelebrity tour.com. Call for current schedule and times (reservations required). $$.

All tours are made in air-conditioned coaches starting from the tour office. See the area's largest mushroom (maybe), the House of Wax, an air conditioned dog house, the "Gum House," the "Never Elected President" headquarters, Palm Springs' smallest house, a home in a hole, "two homes or one," Clark Kent's changing room, a property guarded by Transformers, and so much more. Enjoy an area secret so well guarded the locals aren't even aware of it. Oh yeah, did we forget to mention stars' homes, and lots of them?

Well-rehearsed guides tell all, and you won't want to miss a word of their entertaining narrative. This is far better than a self-guided tour through the quiet neighborhoods of vined walls and winding streets—and it's the only way to get the lowdown on how Hollywood established itself in the desert.

Golf Courses

If in L.A., the celebrities are all on the beach in Malibu, in Palm Springs, they're probably on the golf course. Although many clubs are private, there are several beautiful courses

Stand-by Golf

Amateurs to seasoned duffers rave about **Stand-By Golf** service, making it possible for golf-motivated parents and kids to play on 40 of the desert's best courses with discounts between 5 and 50 percent depending on the golf course and date of play. Tee times are guaranteed and you can schedule them today, tomorrow, or 30 days in advance! Open seven days week from 7 a.m. to 9 p.m. Call (760) 321-BOOK (2665), or even book online at www.standbygolf.com.

open to the public. Remember, a licensed driver is required for any golf cart, and only two are allowed people per cart. Greens fees are substantially reduced at most desert courses in the summer.

- **Cimarron Golf Club.** 67–603 30th Ave., Cathedral City; (760) 770-6060; www .cimarrongolf.com. Golfers of all ages will find the 36 holes at this club sheer paradise. There is a short (Pebble) and a long (Boulder) course. Inquire about golf clinics and other events. Tee times can be booked up to 120 days in advance. Children under 15 are eligible for discount rates. $$$$

- **Desert Dunes Golf Club.** 19300 Palm Dr., Desert Hot Springs; (760) 231-5370; www .desertdunesgolf.com. Designed by world-renowned golf course architect Robert Trent Jones Jr. Ages 16 and under receive discount rates. $$

- **Desert Willow Golf Resort.** 38–995 Desert Willow Dr., Palm Desert; (760) 346-0015 or (800) 320-3323; www.desertwillow.com. Junior golfers from 6 to 12 years old will find Fairway Kids Academy the ultimate in early golf eduation with camps offered during winter and spring vacations Mon through Fri (8 a.m. to 3:30 p.m.) and lunch is included. For the more advanced juniors, there is a program whereby they can play 9 holes if they are able to carry their own golf bag. $$$

- **The Golf Resort at Indian Wells.** 44–400 Indian Wells Lane; (760) 346-GOLF; www .indianwellsgolfresort.com. Two Ted Robinson–designed championship courses. Home of the LG Skins Game and the only 36-hole facility in California with both courses ranked in the Top 20 "Best Courses You Can Play" in California by *Golfweek* magazine. $$$$

- **Tahquitz Creek Palm Springs.** 1885 Golf Club Dr.; (760) 328-1005 or (800) 743-2211; www.tahquitzcreek.com. Here is the place to enjoy resort golf "without paying for the rest of the resort." The club has two Arnold Palmer–managed courses, Resort and Legend, both rated four-stars by *Golf Digest* magazine. All-inclusive golf packages feature breakfast, lunch, greens fees, cart, and more. $$$

- **Tommy Jacob's Bel Air Greens.** 1001 South El Cielo; (760) 322-6062. Family-style golf during the season (Jan through Apr). Eighteen short holes on a beautiful course for adults and kids (they call it a putt-putt course). This is an all par 3 layout. The 9-hole Executive Course is ideal for juniors and adults. Children ages 17 and younger pay $7.50 for 9 holes of golf. $$

Indian Canyons

Indian Canyons & Tahquitz Visitor Center, 500 West Mesquite, west of Palm Canyon River in downtown Palm Springs; (760) 416-7044; www.tahquitzcanyon.com. Open daily from Oct to July from 7:30 a.m. to 5 p.m. From July to Sept, open Fri to Sun 7:30 a.m. to 5 p.m. Admission fee to enter canyon, plus additional fees for guided tours. Be sure to call for specific times/tours since prices and hours are subject to change. $$–$$$.

This is one of the most culturally sensitive areas of the Agua Caliente Indian Reservation, and you should take time for a narrative video that reveals the legend of Tahquitz Canyon

Agua Caliente Indians

The first people to fall under Palm Springs's spell were ancestors of the Agua Caliente band of Cahuilla (Kaw-we-ah) Indians, who developed communities in the palm canyons at the foot of the San Jacinto Mountains. These canyons, along with other chunks of the Coachella Valley, were deeded in trust to the Indians in 1876. The Cahuillas control 42 percent of the valley, making them the wealthiest tribe in North America. Visit www.aguacaliente.org for more information.

(shown in the Visitor Center) There are self-guided tours, but the ranger-led 2.5-hour interpretive hikes give you an insider's perspective on this historic canyon.

Revenues from the canyons help fill the Agua Caliente tribe's coffers, but this cluster of oases is a priceless natural jewel that you really don't want to miss. With some of the thickest concentrations of palm trees in the world, thanks to the cool mountain streams that flow through them, the site provides a refreshing refuge from the heat of the desert. There are actually four separate canyons, comprising 32,000 acres: Tahquitz, Palm, Murray, and Andreas. All have trails for walking or hiking. The unusual rock formations in Andreas Canyon are the repository of ancient Cahuilla rock art. The Tahquitz Canyon Trail leads to Tahquitz Falls and back. From the Visitor Center to the falls, you will be gaining 350 feet in elevation. The trail is steep and rocky with many rock steps as high as 12 to 15 inches to climb. This canyon has very little shade, no restroom facilities, and no water fountains. Note that the entrance for Palm, Murray, and Andreas Canyons is at 38520 South Palm Canyon Dr. Call (760) 323-6018 for more details.

Agua Caliente Cultural Museum

219 South Palm Canyon Dr.; (760) 778-1079; www.accmuseum.org. Open Labor Day through Memorial Day, Wed through Sat 10 a.m. to 5 p.m. and Sun noon to 5 p.m. Summer hours Fri, Sat, and Sun 10 a.m. to 4 p.m. Free.

This museum displays artifacts and historical photos from the early Cahuilla era that preserve the native spirit of the desert, permanent collections on local history, and changing exhibits (such as Cahuilla basketry), plus two shops with jewelry, clothing, music, and assorted Indian arts and crafts from tribes nationwide.

Palm Springs Aerial Tramway

Entrance on the north edge of town, at the end of Tramway Road, off Highway 111; (760) 325-1449 or (888) 515-TRAM; www.pstramway.com and www.summerrideanddine.com. Tram rides depart on the half hour, starting at 10 a.m. Mon through Fri, 8 a.m. weekends and holidays. Last ride down at 9:45 p.m. There are two rotating tram cars with breath-stopping views. Schedules subject to change without notice. Please call ahead for current times and weather conditions. Children under 3 ride free. $$$$.

Home on **the Ranch**

It's "home on the range" Palm Springs–style at the historic **Smoke Tree Ranch.** Best defined as friendly, casual, and understated, this is one of the most perfect family vacation choices in the Coachella Valley. Enjoying a history as old as Palm Springs, this approximately 400-acre ranch, home to 85 "colonists" (the residents, actually), is the desert's best-kept secret. There are 20 acres are devoted to 49 comfortable guest (visitor) ranch cottages where you can indulge in activities including tennis at first-rate facilities, hiking, birding, nature trails, swimming pool, hot tub, fitness center, 3-hole practice golf course, and, best of all, organized activities for kids at Camp Kawea. Adding to the vintage ambience is an old-fashioned playground.

Ranch guests savor cookouts in the nearby Indian Canyons, marshmallow roasts, cowboy crooners (remember those soothing sounds?), scavenger hunts, and even bonfires. Breakfast rides and cookouts are on the calendar of events, too. The bountiful buffets will keep the family energized, and that's what is needed to explore this pristine desert paradise. The Indian Canyons location reveals a peaceful sanctuary the entire family will find refreshing, reflective of a time when fast food and freeways were not part of our lives. Some more surprises are here: Check out Disney Hall for a collection of Disney memorabilia, since Walt Disney was one of the original colonists.

Check out the multi-bedroom cottages and family units, which are combinations of cottages merged into 2-, 3-, 4-, and 5-bedroom suites. Each unit has remote control cable TV, DVD player, telephone with voice mail and Internet access, refrigerator, down pillows, plantation shutters, and private patio; parking is complimentary. It may be a ranch, but the luxuries are evident! The rates are based on the full American plan, which includes breakfast, lunch, and dinner daily in the dining room. The breakfast plan is just that, breakfast only. Rate plans are based on discounts for kids ages 5 to 11, and adults are considered anyone age 12 and over. No charge for children under age 5. For additional information and reservations: 1850 Smoke Tree Lane; (760) 327-1221 or (800) 787-3922; www.smoketreeranch.com.

If you'd like to know where all those mountain streams come from, take a ride on the spectacular tramway, a thrilling and manageable adventure for the whole family. Two suspended cable cars whisk you from the parched desert floor nearly 6,000 feet up Chino Canyon to the top of 10,800-foot Mt. San Jacinto (San Yah'-sin-toh) in a mere 15 minutes. Up here, there's not a palm tree in sight: This is pine tree country, some 40 degrees cooler than the valley below. Really! What a relief in the summer!

At the Mountain Station, Peaks Restaurant offers fine contemporary California cuisine (760-325-4537 for information and reservations), and the Pines Café, a cafeteria-style restaurant, offers a variety of menu selections. A special Ride 'n' Dinner combination ticket is a great value at the Pines Café. The Lookout Lounge is a full cocktail bar offering a variety of alcoholic beverages and appetizers and is located on the same level as the restaurants..

From here, there are breathtaking views of the sprawling valley floor and, off to the left, the unmistakable imprint of the San Andreas Fault. The station is at 8,516 feet and also has a fun gift shop, museum, and hiking/cross-country skiing trails leading out into the backcountry. Don't miss this desert/mountain adventure. Do it in every season—in the winter, we like playing in the snow on top and 2 hours later, basking in bathing suits poolside!

Mount San Jacinto Wilderness State Park
(951) 659-2607; www.parks.ca.gov.

Behind you at the top of the Palm Springs Aerial Tramway is this 13,000-acre park, with 54 miles of hiking trails. If it's winter, chances are you'll be able to cross-country ski, too. The Adventure Center, open Nov 15 through Apr 15, rents equipment for adults and kids. In Long Valley, a short walk from the tram car station, you will find the Long Valley Ranger Station, a picnic area with barbecue stoves and restrooms, a ski center, a self-guided nature trail, and the Desert View Trail, which offers panoramas of the high country including several peaks over 10,000 feet in elevation. You can also enter the hiking trail system from this point as well as the Pacific Crest Trail—the jewel in the crown of America's scenic trails, spanning 2,650 miles from Mexico to Canada through three western states. If you want to spend a night or two camping up here, make reservations at www.reserve america.com.

Desert Adventures (ages 6 and up)
Administrative Offices at 74-794 Lennon Place, Suite A, Palm Desert; (760) 340-2345 or (888) 440-JEEP; www.red-jeep.com or http://desertadventures.rezgo.com. Tours operate year-round. Call for current schedule, pick-up/drop-off locations, and specific rates (all subject to change). $$$$.

Desert Adventures' famous guided tours in seven-passenger, four-wheel-drive red jeeps are a great way for families to explore this area. Here are some options that were offered in 2010—be sure to call or go online for new ones: 2-hour San Andreas Faultline Express and 3-hour Eco-Tour (learn about geology, earthquakes, and the desert's history, plants, and animals on this visit to the San Andreas Earthquake Fault). A 3-hour Nightwatch Jeep Tour adds stargazing to the popular San Andreas Fault Jeep Eco-Tour. The 4.5-hour Joshua

Tree Extreme Jeep Tour is a back-country ride up rugged trails through 2 deserts and the transition zone between 2 eco-systems as you climb into the Joshua Tree National Park. Customized tours with guides are also available; be sure to inquire.

Smoke Tree Stables (ages 7 and up)

2500 Toledo Ave.; (760) 327-1372; www.smoketreestables.com. Kids age 7 and older can ride their own horse, led by a guide. Open year-round 8 a.m. to 4 p.m. (when days are longer, open until 6 p.m.) Call for current times. Reservations highly recommended but you can also hire a private guide and horses for a custom ride. $$$$.

It's Coachella Valley horseback riding at its best. Overnight packages available at adjoining historic Smoke Tree Ranch.

Dollsville Dolls & Bearsville Bears

296 North Palm Canyon; (760) 325-2241, (800) CAL-DOLL, or (800) CAL-BEAR; www.dolls ville.com.

This charming shop is full of teddy bears and an astounding variety of Barbie collectibles. Kids will love visiting this Palm Springs classic, a treasure chest of dolls and bears that go

Palm Canyon Drive & Walk of Stars

For many families, the most enjoyable aspect of Palm Springs is taking a stroll on palm tree–lined Palm Canyon Drive, running through the historic center of the city. This celebrated stretch of pavement is flanked by a seemingly endless array of cafes, restaurants, boutiques, and theaters (www.palm canyondrive.org). While you're strolling along, stop by Ruddy's 1930s General Store Museum at 221 South Palm Canyon Dr., on the Village Green (children under 12 are free) and make sure the kids take a look at what shopping was like before Costco and Wal-Mart! Have them view authentic wood and glass showcases, fixtures, signs, and products from sewing notions and hairnets to soapsuds. This delightful museum reveals the charm of an authentic general store; don't miss this step back into time when you're stepping out here.

Watch where you're stepping while you're strolling along Palm Canyon Drive, and notice more than 300 celebrity stars on the sidewalks. They include such old notables as Elvis Presley, Frank Sinatra, Sophia Loren, Elizabeth Taylor, and Pamela Price (co-author of this book; at the corner of Palm Canyon Drive and Tahquitz)! There seems no end to the Palm Canyon "star placing" ceremonies throughout the year. We've often encountered a ceremony going on in front of one of the stores. Of course, passersby are welcome to watch the festivities. It ain't Hollywood Boulevard, but it's still a kick (www.palmspringswalkofstars.com).

The **Corridor**

At the corner of North Palm Canyon and Alejo Road, discover the Corridor. You'll know you're in the right place when you see a new mid-century-inspired sign in flashy tones of blue, coral, and brown that says "Just Fabulous," marking a Palm Springs original bookstore hosting books signings with panache. This independent bookstore has an imaginative selection of titles, Palm Springs–related publications, souvenirs, and music. The Corridor is quite the Palm Springs landmark where you can take a break for conversation, fashion, and world class chocolate at Café Chocolat; shop Diggs for home decor; and boost your caffeine quotient at the irresistible Koffi—featuring an appetizing display of freshly baked cookies, brownies, cupcakes, cinnamon rolls, and everything that goes well with coffee and teas, iced and hot. You'll find mountains of local tourist publications and the local newspapers for browsing; their dog friendly patio proves a magnet for locals and tourists alike.

back generations. Exhibits of beloved dolls and bears will captivate children of all ages. As much a museum as a shop, this desert landmark continues to charm all who enter.

The Fabulous Palm Springs Follies (ages 6 and up)
At the Plaza Theatre, 128 South Palm Canyon Dr.; (760) 327-0225; www.psfollies.com. Evening and matinee performances beginning in Nov and running through May. $$$$.

A Palm Springs original since 1991, this 3-hour revue has a cast all older than 50 years of age, and they kick up a storm. Kids of all ages will get a kick out of "The Follies Man, Riff Markowitz," as he shuffles through puns and tales. This colorful, always humorous vaudeville-style program gives kids a feel for what showbiz used to be all about, despite a few harmlessly off-color jokes now and then. Stars change with the season. Vintage performers will ring a bell with anyone 50-plus for sure, such as The Four Aces (hint: they sang "Love is a Many Splendored Thing" and "Three Coins in the Fountain"). It's a far cry from Madonna or Lady Gaga, but a fine way to share a moment of intergenerational nostalgia with the kids.

Villagefest
Palm Canyon Dr., between Baristo and Amado Roads; (760) 320-3781; www.villagefest.org. Open every Thurs, Oct through May, 6 p.m. to 10 p.m. and June through Sept, 7 p.m. to 10 p.m. except major holidays. Free.

This street fair transforms Palm Springs's main thoroughfare into a lively bazaar with street entertainers, live bands, food booths, 150 arts and crafts vendors, a farmers' market, and pony rides. This is your chance to buy anything from a quilted comforter that doubles as a pillow to scrumptious fudge. If you need to park, go early. Villagefest operates rain or shine.

Palm Springs Art Museum

101 Museum Dr.; (760) 322-4800; www.psmuseum.org. Open Oct through May. Closed Mon and major holidays. Tues, Wed, Fri, Sat, and Sun 10 a.m. to 5 p.m.; Thurs noon to 8 p.m. Free public admission every Thurs from 4 to 8 p.m. during downtown Villagefest. $$; youths under 17 free at all times.

The Palm Springs Art Museum was founded as a one-room facility in 1938 and has grown to the current 125,000-square-foot museum that has become the center of the desert's artistic community. This extraordinary museum that hints of New York with its ongoing openings of world class artists, photographers, glassmakers, and architects is family friendly too, offering programs for children on the fourth Thursday of each month, free of charge. The Annenberg Theater on the lower level has ongoing plays, concerts, and lectures. Stay for lunch at the Muse Café and visit the gift shop, which locals and tourists find a fascinating art adventure with designer-inspired jewelry, gifts, and handbags.

Palm Springs Air Museum

745 North Gene Autry Trail; (760) 778-6262; www.palmspringsairmuseum.org. Open year-round 10 a.m. to 5 p.m. $$, children under 6 free.

Visit the Air Museum for a close-up look at propeller-driven aircraft from an era your kids will know only from old movies, documentaries, and (perhaps) their history books. Vintage planes, many colorful and perfectly restored, recall the World War II era. The second floor has flight simulators (arrange to use them in advance) and a library. The gift shop carries a treasure trove of aviation gifts, books, and jewelry.

Stay in History and **Make Your Own**

The Historic Inns of Palm Springs, a free guide published by the Palm Springs Bureau of Tourism, reveals over 25 historic hideaways all independently owned and operated—in other words, no cookie cutter rooms among this distinctive group. A map of downtown Palm Springs indicates where these local treasures can be found and lists those that are child- and pet-friendly. Each property has its own ambiance and character with charm and friendliness. Expect lovely landscaping and sparking swimming pools amidst architectural preservation. From the chic Willows Historic Palm Springs Inn, a true Hollywood hideaway, to the Chase Hotel, with spacious apartments perfect for your kin, we think you might enjoy staying around some heritage.

Knott's Soak City Palm Springs

1500 South Gene Autry Trail; (760) 327-0499; www.knotts.com. Open daily mid-Mar through Labor Day and weekends only through Sept. Call for specific hours and promotions. $$$$.

Museums and movie stars aside, here's why kids flock to Palm Springs. The park is an immaculately clean fantasy playground where water reigns supreme—the largest and coolest water adventure park in the desert with 21 waterlogged acres featuring 18 of the most intense water rides this side of the Mississippi River. Start at the Pacific Spin, an exciting multi-person raft ride with a 132-foot-long tunnel dropping riders into another 75-foot, 6-story tunnel! After riders are confronted with 5,500 gallons of swirling water the ride has a finale: the waterfall splash. Hang on to your hat and sunglasses at the Tidal Wave Tower for a 7-story speed slide. The little ones will find consolation at the Gremmie Lagoon where pint-sized water slides and a splash pool prepare them for the more challenging water experiences when they're older. California's largest wave-action pool, Ripple Reef, is an 800,000-gallon pool that starts out calm, but don't be fooled—the water churns away every 10 minutes, making you feel like the surf is at your feet. Tired out? Take yourself to the Sunset River and float lazily on your inner tube. Wow—it feels like a tropical paradise, only you're smack dab in the middle of the desert!

Where to Eat

Manhattan in the Desert. 2665 East Palm Canyon; (760) 322-DELI. Open Sun through Thurs 7 a.m. to 9 p.m. and Fri and Sat until 10 p.m. **Free** parking. This deli restaurant has as much panache as a Paris bistro. The upbeat, albeit noisy, ambience is pure deli-lightful, and there is something on the 12-page menu for everyone, including light eaters. There are marvelous soups, from cold borscht to sweet and sour cabbage, and a terrific home-style chicken soup (with choice of rice, noodles, or matzo ball). Try Super Combo Number 12—brisket, pastrami, and Jack cheese served on an onion roll with lettuce and tomato. The "Just for Kids" menu (ages 10 and under) features a $5.95 lunch special with a choice of tuna, egg salad, or grilled cheese sandwich or hamburger, hot dog, or chicken strips; French fries or applesauce; milk or fountain drink; and a yummy sprinkle cookie. With fair prices and friendly service, this Manhattan-style deli is worth a visit. $

Sherman's Deli & Bakery. 401 East Tahquitz Canyon Way; (760) 325-1199; www.shermansdeli.com. Part of the Palm Spring's deli culture, the corn beef and pastrami here are tops, and the bakery display case is worthy of a painting. Constantly

Bus Around!

The SunBus will take you to most of the attractions we've tried and tested, from the Art Museum to the movies, malls, and more. Rides cost $1 (transfers 25 cents); $3 for a day pass for unlimited rides. Call 2009 EPA Clean Air Excellence Award-winning SunLine Transit for **free** personalized trip planning and information at (760) 343-3451 or (800) 347-8628 or visit www.sunline.org.

busy with locals and tourists, breakfast, lunch, and dinner are served daily, and the service is always friendly and efficient. You might say this is the nerve center of Palm Springs; it's been a favorite meeting place for decades. $–$$

Tyler's. 149 South Indian Canyon Dr.; (760) 325-2990. Open Mon through Sat 11 a.m. to 4 p.m , lunch only. This tiny hamburger haven was once a bus station and then an A & W root beer stand. It reopened as Tyler's, serving, as far Pamela is concerned, the best hamburgers in town. The half-pound burger is $5.50 and worth every cent. Kids will like the sliders, three mini hamburgers that can be decorated with hot sauce, pickles, grilled onions, and ketchup. The menu is small, but the essentials are there, from chili dogs and egg salad sandwiches to homemade potato salad and coleslaw. Before noon every bar stool along the counter is taken by serious foodies. The root beer floats ($2.50) are divine, and the fresh lemonade ($1.50) is like Grandma used to make. During winter, Diana, the proprietor, prepares soups you dream about, from red pepper to fresh mushroom. On Friday, ask for the clam chowder. There is a small patio in the back, but it's advisable to arrive early because this landmark beacon of comfort food, par excellence, fills up fast. You might try the take-out service if there is a long wait. And be sure to tell Diana, a whirlwind, that Pamela Price sent you. $

Where to Stay

Holiday Inn Resort Palm Springs. 1800 East Palm Canyon Dr.; (760) 323-1711 or (800) 245-6907; www.hipalmsprings.com. At last, a comfortable, affordable, family-friendly hotel downtown. The 229-room (plus 20 suites with living room; one family suite has bunk beds!), 100 percent nonsmoking property welcomes kids and canines! At Billy D's kids dine, compliments of the hotel, from the Pit Stop PS menu; all meals are **free** for registered guests 12 and under (limit 4 kids per family). More amenities include outdoor pool, splash pad, whirlpool, **free** parking, and **free** shuttles to the airport. Kids will love the nightly dive-in movies by the pool year round. $$$

Casa Cody, A Country Bed & Breakfast Inn. 175 South Cahuilla Rd.; (760) 320-9346 or (800) 231-2639; www.casacody.com. Historic and charming, this 23-room inn reflects all that made this desert destination resort a living legend. Founded in the 1920s by Harriet Cody, cousin of famous Buffalo Bill Cody, accommodations are in early California–style adobe bungalows framed by bougainvillea and citrus-filled courtyards. The 1910 adobe, recently restored, was the getaway of Lawrence Tibbett, the bon vivant Metropolitan baritone turned movie star, and his good friend Charlie Chaplin. Children and pets always welcome here. $$$$

For More Information

Palm Springs Visitor's Center. 2901 N. Palm Canyon Dr., Palm Springs; (760) 778-8418 or (800) 347-7746; www.visitpalm springs.com. Open seven days; call for seasonal hours. Your one stop for exploring the desert is right here! This Palm Springs landmark was once known to all who passed by as the Tramway gas station. Designed by Albert Frey, the architect who made world-famous the inimitable mid-century style reflected in residential and commercial buildings throughout the desert, this distinctive structure with its amazing roofline now puts out the welcome mat for tourists from around the world with exhibits, complimentary maps, and brochures, plus a marvelous rack of postcards from the mid-century showing movie star homes, among other well chosen souvenirs. Make this space age tourist center your first stop!

Cathedral City

Cathedral City is one of seven distinct Coachella Valley communities that you will pass on Highway 111 heading east out of Palm Springs. You'll know you've arrived when you see a complex of colorful yellow structures, all loosely connected. There is a small but marvelous mini-park where the most amazing mosaic fountain attracts kids of all ages. Once a sleepy, nondescript community on the way to somewhere else, Cathedral City has grown rapidly every season and now offers many reasons to stop and spend a day. There is a new shopping arcade and a growing population of 54,000-plus people. Check out the website www.ccisvalue.com for more than 50 discount offers!

Big League Dreams Sports Park

33–770 Date Palm Dr.; (760) 324-5600; www.bigleaguedreams.com. $$.

Ever imagined visiting Yankee Stadium, Fenway Park, and Wrigley Field all in one day? It's possible at this 30-acre park with replicas of those three famous fields. Sports enthusiasts will go for the batting cage stations and the sand volleyball courts, plus soccer fields, horseshoe pits, and the Stadium Club restaurant. There's a Tot Lot for the younger set.

Desert IMAX Theater

68–510 East Palm Canyon Dr. at Cathedral Canyon Boulevard; (760) 324-7333; www.desert imax.org. Free parking at the Cathedral City Civic Center. $$.

The big news in Cathedral City is the big screen—and we mean big. It's 52 by 70 feet—that's 6 stories high! Kids love "Learning at the Edge of Your Seat" here. Show times are subject to change, so call ahead. Adjacent to the theater are several eateries including Big Mama's Soul Food, Picanha Churrascaria, Trilussa Italian, Red Tomato/House of Lamb, El Gallito, Dragon King, La Tablita, Checkpoint, Sunshine Cafe, and other fine restaurants.

Where to Eat

El Gallito Mexican Restaurant. 68820 Grove St.; (760) 328-7794. A desert classic near the Cathedral City Hall complex owned and operated by Petra Cantu. The homemade cuisine includes chicken or beef tacos or taquitos, authentic rice, beans, and fresh guacamole, with family-friendly service for lunch and dinner. Call for days and hours of operation. $

Rancho Mirage

Known as the "Realm of the Desert Bighorn," the city of Rancho Mirage seems larger than 25 square miles. Its population of 17,000 does not include the "snowbirds" (seasonal residents) that flock here to participate in and enjoy the high-profile charitable events that dominate the January-to-May social-season calendar. Rancho Mirage's main attraction is golf, and the city is home to many private country-club communities, such as Tamarisk, Mission Hills, Thunderbird, and Morningside. Don't be discouraged—many of these emerald green courses are open to the public or have reciprocal agreements with hotels. Ambassador and Mrs. Walter H. Annenberg made their home here, calling it Sunnylands. It will open to the public in 2011 as the Education Center at Sunnylands with tours, a focus on mid-century modern architecture, and a garden showcasing water conservation and desert landscaping. Many streetsare named for vintage celebrities (all pre–Madonna and Brad Pitt) such as Frank Sinatra, Dinah Shore, Dean Martin, and Ginger Rogers. President Gerald Ford lived here—and his street intersects with Bob Hope Drive!

Children's Discovery Museum of the Desert

71–701 Gerald Ford Dr.; (760) 321-0602; www.cdmod.org. May through Dec Tues to Sun 10 a.m. to 5 p.m. (Closed Mon and select holidays) and Jan through Apr open every day 10 a.m. to 5 p.m. $$.

This 8,000-square-foot facility with more than 50 hands-on exhibits encourages kids to touch, explore, and discover. Youngsters can paint a Volkswagen Beetle, dig for Cahuilla Indian treasures, or make a pretend pizza in the Pizza Place. An ideal museum for children and parents who enjoy experiencing hands-on activities. Upstairs there are trunks and suitcases full of costumes and hats for kids to play dress-up—this is a good photo opportunity!

Tolerance Education Center

35147 Landy Lane; (760) 328-8252; www.toleranceeducationcenter.org. Open 9 a.m to 6 p.m. Mon to Fri. Free admission and parking.

A small space (4,000 square feet) with a big message focused on learning the impact of prejudice and intolerance. This worthwhile educational experience includes a media room with films and revolving exhibitions such as one featuring Polish artist Kalman Aron, who survived seven concentration camps. The center was founded by Earl Greif, a Holocaust survivor.

The River at Rancho Mirage

71–800 Hwy. 111, corner of Bob Hope Drive; (760) 341-2711; www.theriveratranchomirage .com. Call for seasonal hours of operation.

A 30-acre waterfront entertainment, dining, and shopping center, the River offers a pedestrian-friendly ambience. It is considered the downtown of Rancho Mirage and is anchored by the 3,114-seat Cinemark Century Theater complex. It's the desert, but there's water everywhere at this outdoor mall. Fascinating shops and pushcarts loaded with everything from designer togs for dogs to funky accessories will keep kids busy before and after breakfast, lunch, or dinner and a flick. For the best family dining in this 200,000-square-foot complex, check out Piero's Acqua Pazza, the Cheesecake Factory, Baja Fresh, Babe's Barbecue, Yard House, and Ben & Jerry's.

Where to Stay

Westin Mission Hills Resort & Spa.
71–777 Dinah Shore Dr., at the corner of
Dinah Shore and Bob Hope Drive; (760) 328-
5955 or (800) 544-0287; direct line to Kids
Club (760) 770-2181; www.westin.com. The
Westin Kids Club Discovery Room program,
designed for children ages 4 to 12, offers a
good mix of arts, crafts, scavenger hunts, Wii
tournaments, and games. Hours are 9 a.m.
to noon and 1 to 4 p.m.; rates are $45 per
child for 3-hour sessions, including snacks.
Kidz Night is scheduled for Saturday evenings
year-round with age-appropriate activities.
Kids love the 60-foot, S-curved water slide and
basketball, softball, and bicycle rentals. Then
there are 2 golf courses and tennis courts.
Inquire about special family packages. $$$$

For More Information

**Palm Springs Desert Resorts Conven-
tion and Visitors Authority.** 70–100 Hwy.
111, Rancho Mirage; (760) 770-9000 or (800)
41-RELAX; www.palmspringsusa.com Open
Mon through Fri 8:30 a.m. to 5 p.m. This
office consolidates the tourism information
for the 8 desert communities of Palm Springs,
Cathedral City, Rancho Mirage, Palm Desert,
La Quinta, Indian Wells, Indio, and Desert Hot
Springs. Be sure to ask for your **free** recent
edition of the *Palm Springs Desert Resorts
Vacation Planner,* featuring hotels, restaurants, attractions, golf, and spa and map
information.

Palm Desert

In recent years Palm Desert, "where the sun shines a little brighter," has been something
of a boomtown with a growing population of 50,000-plus, with shopping and dining opportunities to rival—some would say surpass—those of Palm Springs. The city of Palm Desert
helps makes the Coachella Valley the "golf capital of the world," not only on account of the
many courses it boasts but also because golf carts are legal transportation on several city
streets. There's even a **Golf Cart Parade** every November, in which a hundred carts decorated as floats parade along El Paseo, the "Rodeo Drive of the Desert."

Palm Desert is home to one of the most interesting street fairs in Southern California.
Look for the **College of the Desert Street Fair,** 435 Monterey Ave. in Palm Desert—
there's plenty of **free** parking. Kids will love wandering through the farmers' market and
checking out the endless vendors selling original art, jewelry, T-shirts, designer eyeglass
frames, and faux designer purses. You name it . . . it's for sale here somewhere. Open Sat
and Sun year-round. Don't miss it! And now, we will go from simple to "simply elegant"
shopping, from the street fair to El Paseo.

The undisputed style center of the desert is El Paseo, a 7-block drive between Highway
74 and Portola Avenue.

Living Desert

**47–900 Portola Ave.; (760) 346-5694; www.livingdesert.org. Open daily from Oct 1 through
May 31, 9 a.m. to 5 p.m., last admission at 4 p.m. During the summer—June 1 through Sept
30—plan to visit between 8 a.m. and 1 p.m.; hours are shortened because the temperature**

rises to over 100 degrees Fahrenheit during the summer, making dehydration common. Be sure to bring sunscreen, sunglasses, and comfortable walking shoes for this desert expedition that is safer than the wilds! $$.

It's worth spending the entire day at this 1,200-acre showcase of nature, which has the distinction of being the only American zoo and botanical garden dedicated to the deserts of the world. Scenic hiking trails surround this surreal setting, which features various exhibits for animal admirers of all ages. There are tempting gift shops and a superb cactus garden with many species of desert plants for sale. If you have at least one full day to indulge in desert pursuits, spend it here at the Coachella Valley's home to over 450 animals and more than 1,600 varieties of plants native to the world's deserts. Open- air exhibits in this natural setting reveal how diverse the desert can be with an astounding collection of animals ranging from giraffes and bighorn sheep to golden eagles and hawks. You can slither over to the Reptile House where local snakes, lizards, and insects peacefully dwell. Kids of all ages like the Wildlife Wonders Show, a live animal show performed daily, weather permitting. And if you've never been up close to an African crested porcupine or the comical road runner (they are part of the desert landscape), you will now have that opportunity. Ostriches? You bet—they found a home here, too!

If you have never been to Africa, you will get a preview at Village WaTuTu, where a traditional Kenyan village has been created with care and includes an elder's grove, petting kraal, and authentic huts. Native plants abound, and, oh, yes, look out for the animals! The botanical gardens represent 10 different ecosystems, from Madagascar to East Africa and the American Southwest to Mexico. That means if you have never seen an Arabian oryx in Dubai, you will discover one here. Check out the East African crowned crane and the Abyssinian ground hornbill and Cuvier's gazelle. Take time to visit Eagle Canyon, where large and small cats and wolves live harmoniously in nature, all in a setting that puts traditional confining zoos to shame.

Path of the **Bighorn**

Kids, be on the lookout for a posse of creatively decorated bighorn sheep wandering around the Coachella Valley. This is actually a public art project exhibiting more than one hundred painted, life-size sculptures of these legendary sheep—all placed in locations around the desert for public viewing. Celebrities (Cher, Chevy Chase, Phyllis Diller, and Stephanie Powers) decorated many of these sheep sculptures. This is one of the area's most successful continuing art projects, combining environmental awareness with some of the most lavishly decorated big horn sheep you'll ever see. You'll find these art statements displayed at the Palm Springs International Airport, the Rancho Mirage Public Library, and the Children's Discovery Museum, where kids can paint a big horn! For more details, call (760) 346-7334 or visit www .bighorninstitute.com.

Hungry? No need to dash off, because the Meerkat Café and Thorn Tree Grill have a good menu with an emphasis on sandwiches and salads and children's favorites. Shopping means the Kumbu Kumbu market for African-inspired baskets, bowls, and souvenirs. At the Palo Verde Garden Center, a retail nursery, plants, trees, and shrubs ideal for desert landscaping are displayed and organized so you can easily locate your favorites. The savvy sales team can answer your questions with more than an educated guess. Gardening classes also are scheduled. Make it a point to visit the Tennity Wildlife Hospital & Conservation Center, a 24,000-square-foot complex that has state of the art facilities capable of caring for the Living Desert's 400-plus resident animals with the latest technology. This center features an interactive experience, as visitors are able to witness live and video-taped animal-care procedures in surgery and in the treatment rooms. Vets can interact with visitors via microphones, making this an extraordinary opportunity to witness the high level of animal care here. Ask about docent-led tours visiting specific parts of the center that vary according to seasonal activities. All this is a must-see for families, we insist!

The Santa Rosa and San Jacinto Mountains National Monument Visitors Center
51–500 Hwy. 74 (3.25 miles south on Hwy. 111 at the base of the mountain); (760) 862-9984; www.blm.gov.

Plan to spend a leisurely hour at the Monument's Visitor Center, established in 2000, where you can get up close and personal with the rugged nature of the desert. Take time to explore the Ed Hastey Interpretive Garden Trail to get a better picture of the fragile ecosystem here. There are **free** hikes at 9 a.m. on Thurs and Sat year-round. The Visitor Center is open Mon to Fri from 8 a.m. to 4:30 p.m. Be sure to call for seasonal hours, special hikes, and activities in this vast 272,000-acre enclave.

McCallum Theatre
73000 Fred Waring Dr.; (760) 340-ARTS; www.mccallumtheatre.org. Call for current schedule of performances.

At this venue you'll find a stellar roster of entertainment, ranging from pop and classical to jazz, ballet, and comedy; performers from Bob Dylan and Michael Feinstein to Lily Tomlin; the Living Legends series including Englebert Humperdinck and Bernadette Peters; as well as the Blue Man Group and the Broadway Blockbuster series featuring *Young Frankenstein*. Not just for adults, this state of the art theater offers a stellar line-up from *The Nutcracker* to the Peking Acrobats, with most performances during "the season." The McCallum Theatre Institute Education and Community Outreach division has touched the lives of over 40,000 children and teachers benefitting from arts education programs and **free** performances. Parking is plentiful, and there is valet service.

Where to Eat & Stay

Grill-A-Burger. 73-091 Country Club Dr., Bristol Farms Shopping Center; (760) 346-8170. Call for seasonal hours. A burger bonanza for those with a sense of humor. Say it fast, and it sounds like "gorilla burger"! With a menu listing specialties such as the Greta

Carbo, and "burger fusion" that brings more ingredients into a burger bun than you could imagine, this popular restaurant also serves fabulous French fries that are served in a paper cone. Select from 10 sauces to dress the fries and wash it all down with a thick chocolate shake, made the old-fashioned way: Great kids menu features hot dog varietals, too! $$

Desert Springs, A JW Marriott Resort & Spa. 74855 Country Club Dr., Palm Desert; (760) 341-2211 or (800) 331-3112; www .desertspringsresort.com. Among the many lodging options available in the Palm Desert area, this one stands above the rest. As you enter this immense resort, you will be surrounded by the sounds of water flowing and birds calling. Your preferred mode of transport? Gondolas, Venetian style. While some find this a bit Disneyland-esque, people still flock here for the dramatic ambience of this mega-resort fresh from a $30 million makeover in 2007. The newly renovated 8-story atrium lobby serves as a gateway to 884 luxurious guest rooms, 36 holes of Ted Robinson championship golf, 20 multi-surface tennis courts, 17 retail shops, 5 award-winning restaurants, a 30,000-square-foot European Health Spa, fitness center and gym, and waterways entwining 9 resort swimming pools and whirlpools. This sprawling resort is home to the Kid's Klub, where kids can spend quality time pursuing their own recreational activities while Mom and Dad are on the golf course or in the spa. Designed for ages 4 to 12 (kids younger than age 4 require a babysitter, available through the concierge), the program generally operates seven days a week and features arts and crafts, putt-putt golf, boat rides, animal tours, lunch, and movie screenings. $$$$

La Quinta Resort & Club. 49499 Eisenhower Dr., La Quinta; (760) 564-4111 or (800) 598-3828; www.laquintaresort.com. Located adjacent to Rancho Mirage in the city of La Quinta, this property is a legendary hideaway, renowned since 1926 for its charm and serenity; featuring 90 holes of some of the country's best golf, including the famous Stadium Golf Course at PGA West and the picturesque Mountain Course; plus Spa La Quinta with a variety of unique indoor and outdoor treatments including open-air Celestial Showers, Sacred Stone Massage, and more. La Quinta is the longtime gold-standard ideal place for families, with something for everyone. Children will like Camp La Quinta from 9 a.m. to 3 p.m. seven days a week. Programs include nature walks, arts and crafts, and miniature golf. Evening programs are from 6 to 10 p.m. Fri and Sat only. Children 4 and older are welcome; those younger than 4 must be accompanied by a babysitter. Up to two children stay **free** in a casita with parents. Call for current pricing and schedules. $$$$

Hyatt Grand Champions Resort, Villas & Spa. 44–600 Indian Wells Lane, Indian Wells; (760) 341-1000; www.grandchampionshyatt .com. Offering your choice from 428 spacious guest rooms, with views from private balconies; 26 penthouse suites with garden, mountain, golf, or pool views; and 43 one- and two-bedroom villas with backyard, spas, and butler service that are perfect for families. This lavish resort boasts 7 swimming pools, including a 60-foot spiral water slide and a toddler-size wading pool. You'll appreciate the private cabanas complete with TV and bottled water. The Oasis Pool Bar & Roadrunner Café gets our family vote. One of the best reasons to stay here? Camp Hyatt is open 9 a.m. to 4 p.m. daily and Fri and Sat evenings from 6 to 10 p.m. for kids whose parents appreciate supervised care with an educational touch, such as tours of nearby flora and fauna. Why don't we adults head for the award-winning Agua Serena Salon, Day Spa & Medical Skin Spa? This is one complete experience. $$$$

Renaissance Esmeralda Resort and Spa. 44400 Indian Wells Lane, Indian Wells; (760)

773-4444 or (800) 228-9290; www.renaissance esmeralda.com. At the Esmeralda, there is all a family could ask for, including a "sand" beach, 3 swimming pools, lots of space to spread out, and family-friendly rates. Up to 5 guests are allowed in each spacious room. Here is the place to kick back and relax. Dad can try the links, and Mom can indulge in the stunning Spa Esmeralda. $$$$

For More Information

Palm Desert Visitor Center. 73–470 El Paseo, Suite F-7; (760) 568-1441 or (800) 873-2428; www.palm-desert.org. Definitely make this the first place to visit. This comprehensive tourism center is state of the art and first class when it comes to being eco-friendly. It is also the first Coachella Valley building to earn Leadership in Energy and Environmental Design (LEED) certification. Located in the midst of El Paseo where art galleries, shopping, and dining dominate the scene, this newly opened office stocks travel brochures, hiking maps and souvenirs. A well-informed staff stands by to help you make the most of your day in Palm Desert.

Indio

The first city in the Coachella Valley, Indio—also known as the Date Capital of the Desert—was founded in 1930 and currently has a population exceeding 84,000. Fully 95 percent of the dates grown in the United States are cultivated in and around Indio.

This is truly the "city of festivals," beginning with the National Date Festival, which was founded here more than 70 years ago. Indio looks rather plain until you drive by the fairgrounds and glimpse the exotic entrance, which comes alive each February for the National Date Festival. The multicolored plaster domes, reminiscent of a scene from Arabian Nights, are sure to make your kids wonder if they have just seen Disneyland. But there's more on this stretch of highway! Every December since 1992, the Indio International Tamale Festival has been an absolute must for those who take the art of the tamale seriously. From sweet to spicy, every type of tamale to tantalize taste buds is available over the weekend. Indio International Tamale Festival holds the Guinness World Record for the world's largest tamale—1 foot in diameter and 40 feet long. That's a lotta beans! The Food Network ranked the Indio International Tamale Festival (www.tamalefestival.net) in the top 10 "All-American Food Festivals" in the nation!

Riverside County Fair and National Date Festival

Riverside County Fairground, 46–350 Arabia St.; (800) 811-FAIR; www.datefest.org. $$.

For 10 days each February, Indio celebrates its principal crop—the tasty, versatile date. The festival is held in conjunction with the annual Riverside County Fair. The festive ambience attracts families for rides, food, games, local entertainment, and camel rides. Don't miss the Arabian Nights Musical Pageant each evening. This fair celebrated its 64th year in 2010, making it one of the oldest in California. Surely 310,394 fairgoers can't be wrong—that's how many fans made it a "date" in 2010! Competitions abound, such as a livestock auction and a fashion show for sheep and their owners.

Empire Polo Club and Equestrian Park

81–800 Ave. 51 (at Monroe); (760) 342-2762. Open Mon through Fri 9 a.m. to 5 p.m. For a polo schedule call (760) 342-2223 or visit www.empirepoloevents.org.

Indio is paradise for polo lovers. If you want to see polo in action, plan to have breakfast or lunch at the Empire Polo Club's Tack Room Tavern. This former horse shelter turned restaurant (call for seasonal hours and reservations at 760-347-9985). Off the beaten path, the setting is peaceful and very different from the weekend crowds and traffic. There is a great children's menu, too!

The park covers 175 acres of landscaped grounds, including 5 world-class polo fields, a picturesque rose garden, and the tropical Medjhool Lake (named for the delectable dates that grow on nearby Indio date farms). The Coachella Valley Music & Arts Festival calls this place home. In 2010 on the last weekend of April, Jay-Z, Muse and Gorillaz performed along with dozens of other top entertainers (www.coachella.com).

Oasis Date Gardens

59–111 Hwy. 111, Thermal; (760) 399-5665; www.oasisdategardens.com. Open 9 a.m. to 5:30 p.m. daily. $.

This is a 175-acre working date farm, where you can take a guided tour of the groves, have a picnic in a palm garden, or simply partake of the offerings at the Country Store.

The Salton Sea—**Nature's Accident**

If you're heading south from Indio, explore the 35-mile-long **Salton Sea** (760-564-4888; www.saltonsea.ca.gov), the largest body of water entirely in California and saltier than the ocean. It was formed by accident between 1905–07 when the Colorado River floodwaters filled the Salton Sink, once an ancient seabed. The sea's surface is 228 feet below sea level and is a popular area for anglers and hunters. Families should visit the Salton Sea National Wildlife Refuge and Imperial Wildlife Area (760-393-3052), where there are viewing stations for "bird's-eye" views of countless birds! Seeing the annual migrations of various birds is an experience children will find fascinating and educational, a dynamic duo. According to the US Fish and Wildlife Service, they can identify 295 species here. In the **Salton Sea State Recreation Area,** boating and saltwater fishing are the order of the day. Several campsites and nature trails are located around the "sea" shores. Call (800) 444-7274 for camping reservations and learn more details about this unusual park at www .parks.ca.gov. Opened on May 1, 2010, the Salton Sea History Museum at the historic North Shore Yacht Club honors the original architect, Albert Frey, the father of mid-century modernism. Call for seasonal hours and events at (760) 393-9222, and discover more at www.saltonseamuseum.org.

If you like dried fruits and nuts, this is the place to stock up. Look for **free** samples, too! It's a reminder of another era when many roadside businesses attracted motorists— a charming symbol of America's mid-century tourism attractions still going strong this century.

For More Information

Indio Chamber of Commerce. 82-921 Indio Blvd.; (760) 347-0676 or (800) 775-8440; www.indiochamber.org.

Chiriaco Summit

Thirty miles east of Indio and 70 miles from the Arizona state line on I-10 is a place not to be missed. Exit at Chiriaco Summit and look for the American flag. You are at what was once the entrance to Camp Young, the famous Desert Training Center. This is the site chosen by Maj. Gen. George Patton Jr. in March 1942 as a training center for desert warfare. Nearly one million American service people trained here. Patton commanded the camps for four months, departing in August 1942 to lead Operation Torch, the allied assault on German-held North Africa. The camp closed on April 30, 1944. Today, look for a fascinating museum and popular travelers' rest stop.

General Patton Memorial Museum

#2 Chiriaco Rd., Chiriaco Summit; (760) 227-3483; www.generalpattonmuseum.com. Open daily 9:30 a.m. to 4:30 p.m. $, children younger than 11 admitted free when accompanied by an adult. Military are free if in uniform.

The museum has an excellent 26-minute video, plus exhibits. Many of the artifacts were donated by service people. There are armored tanks on display, along with memorials and a small outdoor chapel. The newest addition is the West Coast Vietnam Veteran's Wall engraved with the names of service people who served during the Vietnam War (1959–1975).

Next to the General Patton Memorial Museum is the **Chiriaco Summit Southwestern Travel Center** (760-227-3227; www.chiriacosummit.com) owned by the Chiriaco family. There is a US Post Office here and a service station, as well as a Foster Freeze fast food joint. Enjoy the gift shop with antiques. Plus, there's a selection of fresh fruits, nuts, and desert dates. The General Patton Museum was established through the tireless efforts of Margit Chiriaco Rusche and the Bureau of Land Management. Margit recalls seeing the tanks from her front yard as a 5-year-old, when the Desert Training Center was in full swing. Be sure to have breakfast, lunch, or dinner at the charming coffee shop, where comfortable booths have looked out on the desert since 1933. Margit bakes the best chocolate cake, slathered with chocolate frosting and walnuts! On the menu is the DTC (Desert

Training Center) burger, made with Spam (kids, ask your grandparents about that!). There are also corn dogs with chips and many sandwiches kids will enjoy. The Traveler's Special breakfast includes two each of pancakes, eggs, and sausage patties or bacon. It's worth driving out to Chiriaco Summit for this breakfast bargain! On the weekend, enjoy the carne asada and on Wednesday don't miss Grandma Ruth's pot roast—a family recipe. Kids may find this corner of the desert an oddity but many folks of the "Greatest Generation" think of it as treasured landmark.

Joshua Tree National Park

Joshua Tree National Park

74485 National Park Dr. (park headquarters), Twentynine Palms; visitor information line: (760) 367-5500; www.nps.gov/jotr. Open year-round.

Each season adds its personality to the desert's character. There are three entrances to the park—Oasis Visitor Center, open all year 8 a.m. to 5 p.m.; Cottonwood Visitor Center, open all year 8 a.m. to 4 p.m.; and Black Rock Nature Center, open Oct through May, Sat through Thurs 8 a.m. to 4 p.m. and Fri noon to 8 p.m. There is a $15 fee per car entering the park that allows unlimited entry and exits for seven days. For $30, the Joshua Tree National Park Annual Pass admits the pass signee and accompanying passengers entering in a single, non-commercial vehicle and is valid for 12 months from the month of purchase.

Joshua Tree National Park lies 140 miles east of Los Angeles and less than an hour north of Palm Springs. You can approach it from the west via I-10 and Highway 62

Music in Joshua Tree

The California high desert is known for nurturing budding talent—such as groundbreaker Gram Parsons, folk-rock guru Donovan, and English blues legend Eric Burdon. Irish rockers U2 found inspiration here in the 1980s. The privately owned **Joshua Tree Lake Campground** located 9 miles from the park entrance is soul central for the **Joshua Tree Music Festival** in May and the **Joshua Tree Roots Music Festival** in October. On site are two performance stages featuring world music, funk, soul, jazz, and blues, plus a world market, tasty food village, and Kidzville—eco-education with Joshua Tree Tortoise Rescue, stargazing, arts and crafts, open mike, storytelling, face painting, juggling, playground, volleyball, bubbles, puppets, and nature walks and talks. Families are encouraged to camp for the entire three-day event. There are hot showers, tent sites, picnic tables, barbecue pits, a lake for fishing, and ample parking. For current information visit www.joshuatreemusic festival.com or call (877) 327-6265.

(Twentynine Palms Highway). The north entrances to the park are located at Joshua Tree Village and the city of Twentynine Palms. The south entrance at Cottonwood Spring, which lies 25 miles east of Indio, can be approached from the east or west, also via I-10. Motels, stores, restaurants, and auto services are located in the nearby towns of Yucca Valley, Joshua Tree Village, and Twentynine Palms.

Visitor centers and wayside exhibits, providing opportunities to acquaint you with park resources, are located along main roads leading into and through the park. Park rangers are here to help you have an enjoyable, safe visit. Detailed information on weather, road conditions, backcountry use, campgrounds, and regulations may be obtained at visitor centers and entrance stations. Walks, hikes, and campfire talks are conducted chiefly in the spring and fall; information is posted on campground bulletin boards, at ranger stations, and at visitor centers. Ranger-conducted activities can increase your enjoyment and understanding of the park.

There are 9 campgrounds with tables, fireplaces, and toilets. You must bring your own water and firewood. Several picnic areas for day use are available. Ask about the Junior Ranger Program; the kids will love the chance to explore and learn while having fun.

In addition to the pass information listed above, there is also an Interagency Annual Pass, which is valid for one full year from the month of purchase; this pass replaces the National Park Pass and Golden Eagle Passport. It provides access to Federal recreation sites, including National Park Service, US Fish and Wildlife, Bureau of Land Management, Bureau of Reclamation, and US Forest Service. The pass can be purchased in person at any Federal recreational fee area, including Joshua Tree National Park. You may also call (888) ASK USGS, ext. 1, or go online at http://store.usgs .gov/pass.

Even if your kids have never been to Joshua Tree National Park before, they will probably recognize the short, bristly, and oddly contorted trees that thrive here from the cover of the popular musical group U2 album *The Joshua Tree*. It was actually Mormon settlers who named the trees. They thought their thick branches, which protrude toward the sky, resembled the biblical Joshua praying.

Less than an hour's drive north of the Coachella Valley, and worth at least a half-day detour, Joshua Tree is where the southern Colorado Desert (elevation less than 3,000 feet) meets the vast expanse of the Mojave (high desert). The park covers 794,000 acres and in some places affords unobstructed views of more than 50 miles. The highlight for many kids will be scrambling about the lower portions of giant quartz-monzonite boulders and monoliths in the Mojave Desert portion of the park.

Try to schedule your visit to Joshua Tree around a sunset. The photographic opportunities here are unparalleled, especially when the shadows dance on the colossal rock formations and the cholla cacti and Joshuas seem to glow in the fading sunlight. The whole place has the feel of a rather eerie lunar landscape, a boundless place in which to take time out and wonder. It's a geographical experience no one in your family will soon forget.

High Desert Magical Journey

En route to Joshua Tree National Park, if you've exited from I-10 to Highway 62 aka Twentynine Palms Highway, you'll be on a stretch of road that takes you through some fascinating scenery and worthwhile places to stop. Just getting to Joshua Tree can be a 2- to 3-hour trip in itself, especially if you stop for lunch and visit a few museums and art galleries along the route.

The area known as the High Desert sweeps the vast region straddling San Bernardino and Riverside Counties. You know you've arrived when the temperature dips about 10 degrees from that of the stunning sun-dappled mountains of the ritzier side of I-10, that being Palm Springs. Families head for the High Desert when they want to explore a portion of the 800,000-acre Joshua Tree National Park and environs.

Along the way, you'll pass **Morongo Valley and Yucca Valley** prior to arriving at Joshua Tree. Yucca Valley lies at the gateway to the Mojave Desert's Morongo Basin.

At the Yucca Valley Community Center Complex, 57116 Twentynine Palms Highway (760-369-7212; www.yuccavalley.org), you'll find the **Hi-Desert Nature Museum** (open Tues through Sun 10 a.m. to 5 p.m.; free; www.hidesertnaturemuseum.org). This is a family-oriented facility related to the high desert's unique natural and historical environments. The museum shop has nature-themed gifts and children's science gifts. Kids can interact with resident snakes and insects or spend some time on arts and crafts.

Pioneertown (www.pioneertown.com), 4 miles outside the Yucca Valley on Pioneertown Road, was founded by Gene Autry, Roy Rogers, and Dick Curtis in 1946 and was used as a western filming location. The kids may not remember the film *Gunfight at the OK Corral*, but a few parents and grandparents might. This was filmed here along with many other stories of the Old West. This area is truly a time warp with several restaurants, saloons, horse corrals, a motel, and cabins for rent.

As you enter the town of **Twentynine Palms** along the Twentynine Palms Highway, aka Highway 62, look for the magnificent historical murals painted on the sides of 11 buildings throughout the town. They depict Indians, miners, homesteaders, and ranchers. One mural kids might find interesting is found on the south wall at 6308 Adobe Rd., "Jack Cones the Flying Constable."

Bet you never thought there was so much to see and do along the way. Like an experienced travel writer once said, "Value the journey as well as the destination."

Insider tip: A stellar attraction is **Sky's The Limit Observatory & Nature Center** on Utah Trail at the main entrance to Joshua Tree National Park (760-327-0030; www.skysthe limit29.org), the ideal destination for families who search the sky! This center is dedicated to providing hands-on learning opportunities about astronomy and environmental science. There is a telescope builder's workshop and weather station among other interactive displays that explore the magnificent Mojave Desert.

Twentynine Palms Area

Located between I-15 and I-10 on Highway 62, 57 miles east of Palm Springs and incorporated in 1987, the city of Twentynine Palms encompasses 58 square miles (larger than the city of San Francisco) and has grown from a population of 11,000 to more than 28,000 today.

Twentynine Palms is home to the Marine Corps Air Ground Combat Center. While this immense military base, rivaling the size of the state of Rhode Island, is not open to the public, it is the site on occasion of military events on the parade ground, such as the Battle Color Ceremony presented by the Marine Corps. For base info, visit www.marines.mil/unit /29palms.

Gubler Orchids

If you are fascinated by Joshua trees, you will be beguiled by the diversity of orchids at one of the nation's largest orchid farms, covering 50,000 square feet in the middle of the Mojave Desert.

It's worth the trip just to take the 45-minute tour that reveals the diversity of the orchid world. To be precise, Gubler's showcases over 5,000 orchid hybrids in a spectacular display of color. It's all waiting for you at this rather off-the-beaten-path orchid oasis in Landers, which is reached from the I-10; exit at Route 62, north to Route 247; turn east on Reche Road and north on Belfield Boulevard. Just follow the signs! Don't worry about parking; you are somewhat in the middle of nowhere—until you feast your eyes upon some of most exquisite orchids imaginable! You've come a long way to reach this orchid extravaganza; if you bring lunch you can set out a picnic, as there are indoor and outdoor picnic areas. Gubler's ships orchids throughout the world, and the establishment of their orchid paradise here in 1975 has brought hundreds of tourists to their growing grounds. Check out their gift shop for orchid postcards, calendars, shirts, and keepsakes. Gubler's is located at 2200 Belfield Blvd., Landers (760-364-2282; www.gublers.com). Call in advance to confirm your participation on the free tours Mon through Sat 10 a.m. to 3:30 p.m. Closed Sun and major holidays.

Since the 1950s, the Combat Center has grown from a few buildings, a glider runway, and about 120 Marines to more than 19,000 Marines, sailors, family members, and civilian workers, the largest and fastest-growing base in the Marine Corps.

Twentynine Palms has pristine air, beautiful natural surroundings, and a small-town lifestyle your family will enjoy visiting. Highlights include Oasis of Murals (www.oasisof murals.com) and the Old Schoolhouse Museum. The most well-known special event is the annual celebration Pioneer Days, held during the month of October, with the excitement of outhouse races, a carnival, a parade, dances, contests, chili cook-offs, and lots more fun stuff. Dig out your Stetson, your boots, and your bandana and come on along!

Where to Eat & Stay

29 Palms Inn. 73950 Inn Ave., Twentynine Palms; (760) 367-3505; www.29palmsinn .com. Founded in 1928, this is another high desert discovery. Its cozy restaurant serves lunch and dinner. Yes, you are slightly off the beaten path, but the high desert air is invigorating, and kids will find the spacious grounds perfect for exploring. Guests spending the night enjoy a complimentary continental breakfast. Brunch is served on Sun from 9 a.m. to 2 p.m. Desert cottages are roomy and ideal for a family; the decor is authentic with vintage furnishings. You may want to linger an extra day. $$$

The Moon Way Lodge. 5444 Moon Way in Wonder Valley, Twentynine Palms; (760) 835-9369; www.moonwaylodge.com. Just 10 minutes past the Joshua Tree National Park entrance on Route 62, you'll discover Wonder Valley—home to one of the most fascinating ranches anywhere. Where else would you find a museum called The Beauty Bubble, displaying beauty salon memorabilia dating to the first bobby pin and hairnet? Look around the corner from the beauty salon manned by one stylist, Jeff Hafler, and there you find an old prospector's shack transformed into a museum of vintage beauty salon memories (read: 5,000-plus artifacts), from an original baby blue Schick portable hair dryer to marvelous ads of vintage movie stars showing off their chic pageboys and "bubbles" (for those not old enough to recall, that was a mid-century hairdo). Or other

raving beauties endorsing shampoos that are a mere faded memory today (remember White Rain?). There are two lovely cottages on this 12-acre ranch adjacent to a swimming pool with 360-degree views of the Mojave Desert, making this truly a wonderful place to spend a night in the heights of the High Desert. $$–$$$

Best Western Yucca Valley Hotel & Suites. 56525 Twentynine Palms Highway (Highway 62), Yucca Valley; (760) 365-3555; www.bestwestern.com. This 95-room property has 33 suites and features a complimentary hot breakfast for the family. There are several units with kitchenettes as well. Heated outdoor pool and hot tub. Only 9 miles from Joshua Tree National Park.

Oasis of Eden Inn and Suites. 56377 Twentynine Palms Highway, Yucca Valley; (760) 365-6321; www.oasisofeden.com. If you've had a dream about spending a night in a Grecian, Roman, safari, or Oriental suite, make a reservation at the one and only Oasis of Eden Inn and Suites, where high desert hospitality means a full or studio kitchenette with adjoining rooms (perfect for a family), deluxe complimentary continental breakfast, and a marvelous heated whirlpool, surrounded by a colorful, hand-painted mural. There are 38 units total; 14 are themed. This is a one-of-a-kind hideaway with a personality. $$$

Spin and Margie's Desert Hideaway.
Joshua Tree, off Highway 62, and 10 minutes from Joshua Tree National Park; (760) 366-9124; www.deserthideaway.com. This adorable little property has a fun Southwest feel. With only 5 suites with kitchens, there is definitely a "get away from the hustle and bustle of city life" feeling here. There are videos in the rooms for the children when they are through discovering the desert for the day. $$$

For More Information

California Welcome Center–Yucca Valley. 56711 Twentynine Palms Highway (Highway 62), Yucca Valley; (760) 365-5464; www

.visitcwc.com. Located 22 miles off I-10 on Highway 62. Open Mon through Fri 9 a.m. to 5 p.m., Sat and Sun 8 a.m to 4:30 p.m. This should be your first stop along Highway 62, as there is a wealth of **free** information here to help you plan your visit to the high desert. Seen here was a copy of this book along with other souvenirs and guides that explain the attributes of the area that can be best describes as the desert's "outback." There are numerous fast food restaurants along the route taking you into Joshua Tree National Park, but as you will find from the info here, there are many idiosyncratic places tucked away along the route where history is alive and well, from locally owned restaurants to country markets and antiques shops.

Barstow Area

The western portions of the Mojave Desert, though as desolate as the lands to the east, offer a very different kind of experience than the Joshua Tree area. Barstow, a railroad crossroads and transportation center, lies halfway between L.A. and Las Vegas at the junctions of I-15 and I-40. It was named after William Barstow Strong, former president of the Atchison, Topeka and Santa Fe Railway. With a population today around 20,000, Barstow is home to Marine Corps Logistics Base Barstow and is the closest city to Fort Irwin Military Reservation. Right in the center of the Mojave, it's the traditional base from which visitors explore Mojave National Preserve, Calico Ghost Town, Rainbow Basin, and Mitchell Caverns.

Mojave National Preserve

The Mojave National Preserve is open-year round. The preserve is easily reached via I-15 or I-40 east of Barstow and west of Needles, California, and Las Vegas, Nevada. Six freeway exits provide visitor access. Road conditions vary from paved, two-lane highways to rugged four-wheel-drive roads; see a map for major routes. Maps showing all dirt roads are available at park information centers. The key is to get your family to the Kelso Depot, the primary Visitor Center (see below) for the Mojave National Preserve honoring the cultural and natural history of the surrounding desert, before your start your explorations. The Office of the Superintendent, Mojave National Preserve, is located at 222 East Main St., Suite 202, Barstow (headquarters: 760-255-8800; www.nps.gov/moja).

Many visitors to Southern California are surprised to learn how extensive the state's desert lands really are. Singing sand dunes, volcanic cinder cones, and carpets of wildflowers are all found at this 1.6 million-acre park. A visit to its canyons, mountains, and mesas will reveal long-abandoned mines, homesteads, and rock-walled military outposts. Some of the most prominent natural features in the preserve are the **Kelso Dunes,** situated in the southern section. Rising to 600 feet, the dunes are the third highest in the United States. Shifting sands on the steep side of the dunes create a unique rumbling sound that has given these mobile mounds the alias "the singing dunes." The dunes are ringed by high mountain ranges, and the overall effect is one of a great, stark beauty. Climate-wise here, expect bright clear skies, seasonally strong winds, and wide fluctuations in day-night temperatures. At low elevations, temperatures above 100 degrees F typically begin in May and can last into October.

Kelso Depot Visitor Center in the Mojave National Reserve

From I-15, exit at Baker; Kelso is 35 miles south of Baker. Or from I-40, exit on Kelbaker Road; Kelso is 22 miles north of I-40 on Kelbaker Road. (760) 252-6108; www.nps.gov/moja. Open every day except Christmas, 9 a.m. to 5 p.m. Free.

The renovated Kelso Depot is now the primary visitor center for Mojave National Preserve. Most of the former dormitory rooms contain exhibits describing various aspects of the surrounding desert, from tortoises to sand dunes to desert mining and ranching. A 12-minute film is shown in the theater. A gallery in the basement features rotating fine-art collections by local artists, focusing on the cultural history and natural splendors of Mojave. After a nearly two-decade-long hiatus, the Kelso Depot lunch room—The Beanery—is back in business, Fri through Tues, 9 a.m. to 5 p.m. What a perfect place for the family to grab a bite. You are now taking a time trip back to life in the depot in the first half of the 20th century!

Hole-in-the Wall Information Center in the Mojave National Reserve

From 1-40 exit Essex Rd. (about 49 miles east of Ludlow or 8 miles west of Fenner) continue 2 miles north of Essex Road to junction with Black Canyon Road. Bear right on Black Canyon Road and continue 10 miles to Hole-in-the-Wall. (760) 928 2572 or (760) 252-6104; www .nps.gov/moja. Free; fees for overnight camping. Check out the interpretive programs on Sat at 3 p.m. Oct through Apr and Sun at 9 a.m.

The park ranger presents talks, guided nature walks, plus an evening program suited for the entire family. There is a basic orientation and 12-minute film. Kids, start taking notes on your iPads—these natural wonders make a terrific report on the environment and ecology; your teacher will be impressed!

Providence Mountains State Recreation Area

In the northern portion of the Mojave preserve; P.O. Box 1, Essex 92332; (760) 928-2586; www.parks.ca.gov.

Some three dozen ancient volcanic cinder cones are scattered throughout the area. Bighorn sheep are often sighted near the visitor center, which is close by the limestone

Mitchell Caverns. The intrepid actor Val Kilmer found the Mitchell Caverns "a trip" in the vintage film *The Doors*. Ranger-led tours reveal the inside info on these stunning, illuminated wonders of nature. Tours are at 10 a.m., 1:30 p.m., and 3 p.m. for 90 minutes on Sat and Sun; Mon through Fri there is one tour daily at 1:30 p.m. The Mitchell Caverns are remote, yet they attract families year-round who want to explore some of the indescribable geographic wonders off the beaten path in Southern California.

Rainbow Basin and Owl Canyon

General location: 8 miles north of downtown Barstow, off Irwin Road; (760) 252-6091; www .blm.gov/ca/barstow. The canyon is open year-round and is free, although there is a fee for primitive camping sites.

You won't miss the sounds of the city one bit as you head north on Fort Irwin Road, out of Barstow, and enter the realm of Rainbow Basin, a national natural landmark, where the colors of the rainbow decorate gorge walls housing an inestimable quantity of fossilized remains that are 10 to 30 million years old.

And may the force be with you as you drive through the rock-strewn, otherworldly landscape of Owl Canyon, where the movie *Star Wars* was filmed. If your kids don't know R2D2 from C3PO, this would be the place to fill them in.

The Bureau of Land Management (BLM) field office in Barstow administers Owl Canyon. Activities to enjoy include bird-watching, camping, hiking or backpacking, picnicking, rock hounding or gold panning, scenic driving, and wildlife and wildflower viewing.

Calico Ghost Town

Located minutes off I-15, east of Barstow, 36600 Ghost Town Rd., Yermo; (760) 254-2122 or (800) TO-CALICO; www.calicotown.com. Open daily 8 a.m. to dusk (shops, playhouse, and railroad hours 9 a.m. to 5 p.m.). Closed Christmas Day. Campgrounds, cabins, and bunkhouse open 24/7. $$.

Named for the variety of colors on King Mountain that towers over the town site, this is a not-to-be-missed item on your Mojave Desert itinerary. The ghost town—the most celebrated of many once-booming settlements that pepper the Mojave—contains remnants of the flourishing mining culture of the 1880s. In the town's heyday, some 4,000 people called this dusty outpost home. Before you begin to feel too sorry for them, remember they made fortunes from silver mines that yielded $65 million worth of rich ore. One interesting nugget of information: The town was prosperous enough to keep 22 saloons in business.

In 1896 the price of silver plummeted, as did the town's fortunes. In the bat of an eyelash, Calico went from boom to bust. The town of Calico is State Historic Landmark #782, and survived in the early 1900s because of borax mining within the district. This was the last place in California that the picturesque "twenty-mule teams" were used. A stop in Calico is about as close to time travel as you'll

ever get. Some of the town's original buildings, such as Lil's Saloon, Lucy Lane's House, and the General Store, have been restored so well that western-theme movies continue to be filmed here. One third of the town is original, and the rest is reconstructed.

But Calico is more than atmospheric building facades. You can actually enter Lil's or the Top of Hill Cafe and Ice Cream Parlor for some modern-day refreshment. There are 23 shops along Main Street—the only street—a favorite being the 1880s-style candy store. You and the kids also might hop aboard a narrow-gauge train for a ride to the silver mine areas north of town. At Maggie's Mine, the very adventurous can get an inside look at the miner's workplace, the 30-mile network of tunnels and mine shafts beneath Calico, by taking a self-guided tour. Maybe you'll even spot a wedge of silver. This is one ghost town that is very much alive.

Festivals in Calico take place throughout the year. Check to see when historical reenactments are scheduled, such as President Lincoln inspecting General Grant's troops. It's better than watching a DVD.

Where to Eat

Bun Boy. 1890 West Main St., Barstow; (760) 256-8082. Open 5:30 a.m. to 10 p.m. daily. In business since 1926 and still owned/operated by the same family. One of the main attractions in Barstow itself is stopping to eat at a more-than-fast-food-but-less-than-a-restaurant kind of eatery, where all Southern Californians seem to have had a meal at some point in their lives. It's the kind of place you might imagine Jack Kerouac pulling into for a quick bite before waxing beatific about the experience. Nevertheless, families will enjoy giant-size servings of homemade peach, strawberry, and apple pie. The 20-ounce T-bone steak dinner is still $15.99! $–$$

Peggy Sue's Diner. I-15 at Ghost Town Road exit, Yermo, 8 miles east of Barstow; (760) 254-3370; www.peggysuesdiner.com. Open daily for breakfast, lunch, and dinner. Soda fountain, ice-cream parlor, pizza parlor, burgers, steaks, homemade chili and soups, old-fashioned candy, 1950s music, a 1950s-style dime store, TV and movie memorabilia, curios, and souvenir shop. Extensive children's menu. The kids will appreciate the game arcade, plus a park (dominated by a make-believe dinosaur) featuring cool lagoons and sparkling waterfalls surrounded by shady weeping willow trees. Forget fast food—this "blast to the past" is more fun and there is something for everyone. This is what American road travel was like before the monstrous freeways and monotonous chain restaurants. $$

For More Information

Barstow Area Chamber of Commerce and Visitors Bureau. 681 North 1st Ave., P.O. Box 698, Barstow, 92311; (760) 256-8617 or (888) 4-BARSTOW; www.barstowchamber .com.

California Welcome Center–Barstow. 2796 Tanger Way, Suite 106; (760) 253-4782. Located off I-15; exit Lenwood Road and follow the "traveling bear" signs to the Tanger Outlet Center. California Welcome Centers provide information on all state regions along with excellent **free** maps and brochures on special attractions. You'll find all kinds of souvenirs in Barstow's Welcome Center, from Route 66 memorabilia to coffee mugs, T-shirts, key chains, and guide books. You're also at the Tanger Outlets, which is a shopper's paradise.

Boron

Located between Barstow and Mojave, Boron was founded in 1927 when Pacific Coast Borax (now Rio Tinto Borax) discovered one of the richest deposits of borate ore here. In recent decades, Boron has served as the main runway approach for Edwards Air Force Base (the famous site of space shuttle landings and supersonic flight). During the first weekend of October, Boron celebrates its rich mining and aerospace history with the annual Twenty Mule Team Days. For more information call the Boron Chamber of Commerce at (760) 762-5810 or visit www.boronchamber.com.

Twenty Mule Team Museum

26962 Twenty Mule Team Rd.; (760) 762-5810; http://20muleteammuseum.com. Open daily 10 a.m. to 4 p.m. Kids welcome. **Free.**

If you find yourselves on Highway 58 at the junction of US 395 ("Four Corners") and think you're in the middle of nowhere, think again. Another 6 miles and you're here. Your kids may not remember the TV series *Death Valley Days* or the product Borax (it used to make our wash sparkle), but here's a good way to refresh your memory. The museum, located in a renovated house from the old Baker Mine campsite, depicts borax mining and early life in Boron. Visit the huge Saxon Aerospace Museum next door exhibiting memorabilia from nearby Edwards Air Force Base and the Mojave Airport that include an F4D airplane retired here. There's also a train station that was brought in from Kramer. A little bit of transportation history all in one place!

The Borax Visitor Center

14486 Borax Rd., off Highway 58 at the Borax Road exit; www.borax.com. Open daily from 9 a.m. to 5 p.m., excluding major holidays. Admission: motorcycles $2 and automobiles $3.

Everyone who finds his or her way to this center gets a sample of "TV rock." After watching the 17-minute video on the worldwide uses of Borax, the kids will understand why there really is a treasure in "them thar hills." And it's Borax!

Ridgecrest

While Barstow is the crossroads of the Mojave Desert as a whole, Ridgecrest—a town of some 30,000 about 70 miles to the northwest adjacent to the Naval Air Weapons Station China Lake (NAWS, or China Lake)—is the best base camp for branching out to explore the natural wonders and attractions of Mojave's northwestern portions.

Ridgecrest is the hub high desert community for visiting the natural attractions of **Mt. Whitney** and **Death Valley,** within 2 hours of the highest and the lowest points in the conterminous United States. Ridgecrest is surrounded by four mountain ranges; the Sierra Nevada on the west, the Cosos on the north, the Argus Range on the east, and the El Paso Mountains on the south.

You've seen Ridgecrest in dozens of movies, television shows, and videos. More than 500 television commercials have been filmed here since 1990. Think back to *Star Trek V*, *Flight of the Intruder*, *ET*, and *Dinosaur*, which was filmed on location at the Trona Pinnacles. Jawbone Canyon has seen the likes of *Wayne's World II*, *Desert Blue*, and *Woman Undone*. And Olancha Sand Dunes hosted *Star Trek V*. Cuddleback Dry Lake Bed was the set for scenes in the movies *Hidalgo* and *Holes*.

Head east out of Ridgecrest on Highway 178 and take in the panorama of the **Panamint Mountains,** which frame Death Valley. About 20 miles up the road, the **Trona Pinnacles** pierce the clear desert sky. The pinnacles, more than 500 in number, are composed of tufa (a porous rock formed as a deposit from springs and streams) and reach heights of 150 feet.

Maturango Museum

100 East Las Flores Ave. at China Lake Boulevard; (760) 375-6900; www.maturango.org. Open 10 a.m. to 5 p.m. daily. $.

The museum was established in 1962 to tell the story of the northern Mojave Desert. There are exhibits showcasing animals, birds, paleontology, and Native American displays. The hands-on Discovery Area appeals to children of all ages. The museum is also home to the Death Valley Tourist Center and the Northern Mojave Visitor Center.

Ridgecrest Regional Wild Horse and Burro Corrals

(760) 384-5765 or (866) 4-MUSTANGS; www.blm.gov. Open Mon through Fri 7:30 a.m. to 4 p.m. Closed federal holidays. $$.

Four miles east of Ridgecrest, off Highway 178, a right turn just as the road reaches the top side of the rise brings you to the Bureau of Land Management's Wild Horse and Burro Corrals. This is where the animals are held, fed, and prepared for adoptions locally and throughout the country. The corral facility sits on 57 acres of Navy and BLM lands. Quite a sight to see these animals!

US Naval Museum of Armament and Technology at China Lake

East end of Blandy Road in the old Officer's Club building; (760) 939-3530; www.chinalake museum.org. Open Mon through Sat 10 a.m. to 4 p.m. Guest passes allowing entrance to NAWS China Lake are available for visiting the museum. Contact the Maturango Museum to arrange them.

China Lake has been a research, development, and test site since 1943 and covers more than a million acres in Southern California's Mojave Desert. The museum's focus is on technical advances in the defense industry made at China Lake. Take a look at the refurbished FA-18 Hornet aircraft, the first of 20 prototypes manufactured for China Lake in the late 1970s. Kids can see missiles, free-fall weapons, and a variety of other intimidating weapons of war such as a Tomahawk submarine, a Shrike, and a Maverick. More benign is the Lunar Soft Landing Vehicle. Kids should find the actual Sidewinder missile to be especially awesome.

On quite a different note, the Naval Air Weapons Station (NAWS) China Lake houses the largest cache of ancient Native American rock art in North America. Little Petroglyph

Canyon, the only site open for public tours, is about 1.2 miles long, with walls 20 to 40 feet high. Elevation is about 5,000 feet. The road to the site is steep and mostly paved, with only the last 7 miles being dirt. The canyon floor is a sand and rocky wash bottom. Visitors have to negotiate over and around a variety of rocks and boulders to enter the canyon. From there, the walk is moderate.

The drive from NAWS main gate is around 90 miles round trip, so bring enough water and essentials. Reservations for this tour are mandatory, which means you must call (760) 939-1683 at least two months in advance or go to www.cnic.navy.mil/chinalake for confirmation. Identification is necessary to enter the base so check to see what documents are required. While rules and regulations are required, the result is well worth the docent-organized tour.

Where to Eat & Stay

Texas Cattle Company. 1429 North China Lake Blvd., Ridgecrest; (760) 446-6602; This family-oriented restaurant has an extended children's menu. Try the grilled cheese for sure, pardners. Serving lunch and dinner. Closed Sun. $$

The Heritage Inn & Suites. 1050 North Norma St.; (760) 446-6543 or (800) 843-0693; www.heritageinnsuites.com. The hotel offers 126 comfortable guest rooms plus 44 one-bedroom suites and features complimentary American breakfast for guests. Film crews stay here often, as do many military personnel from nearby China Lake Naval Air Weapons Center. Victoria's Restaurant on premises serves basic breakfast, lunch, and dinner daily. The 2 swimming pools, 2 whirlpools, and a fitness center/spa will make this a welcome place to wash off the desert dust! $$$

For Further Information

Ridgecrest Area Convention and Visitors Bureau. 100 West California Ave.; (760) 375-8202 or (800) 847-4830; www.visit deserts.com.

Randsburg Area

Twenty-two miles south of Ridgecrest, off US 395 where Southern California mountains meet the Sierra Nevada Range, is the home of the "living" ghost town of Randsburg (population under 100). Gold was discovered at Rand Mine near the site in 1895 and a mining camp quickly formed named Rand Camp (from the gold mining region in South Africa). While certainly not as well known as Calico Ghost Town, Randsburg shared much the same fate as its desert neighbor when the gold petered out. Today, visitors can stop for a snack, browse among antiques stores, and take a peek at the bullet slug still lodged in one of the local bars. When you turn off US 395 at the sign to Randsburg, the first building you will see is the old jail to your left. Park your car and browse among the vintage structures. This area is desolate but photogenic and has been used as a location for dozens of movies and television productions.

Desert Tortoise Natural Area

South of Randsburg, off Highways 14 and 58, near California City; (760) 384-5400; www.blm
.gov/ca. **Free.**

You've come this far, so don't miss this area just southwest of Randsburg. This
40-square-mile chunk of land has been reserved for the protection and preservation of
the largest known population of the shy desert tortoise, an endangered species. There
is an information kiosk and self-guided interpretative trails. If you want to see this desert
dweller (California's official reptile) at its most active, make your visit in April or September when there is a "TE" or "turtle emergence"! This is determined by Mother Nature,
as the tortoises leave their hibernation when the weather cools down. When they do
emerge there is a mobile interpretive center that explains their habits and relationship to
the environment. The preserve boasts a rich flora and fauna representative of the intricate Mojave Desert ecosystem. In 1980 the Bureau of Land Management, US Department
of Interior, recognized the significance of the DTNA by designating it an Area of Critical
Environmental Concern and as a Research Natural Area. For additional information, visit
www.tortoise-tracks.org.

Red Rock Canyon State Park

Red Rock Canyon State Park Headquarters. The park is 25 miles northeast of Mojave on
Highway 14, near Cantil. Go west 0.25 mile on Abbott Drive. Signage indicating the turnoff
is clearly visible on Highway 14. The park is 120 miles north of Los Angeles, via I-5 and
Highway 14. (661) 942-0662; www.parks.ca.gov. Open year-round. The visitor center is
open Fri through Sun; hours vary, so be sure to call ahead. Guided nature hikes are offered
on Sat and Sun at 9 a.m. during the spring and fall, as well as campfire programs on Sat at
7 p.m.; (661) 320-4001.

This beautiful, scenic wonder of California was established as a state park in 1968, located
where the southernmost tip of the Sierra Nevada converges with the El Paso Range. After
wet winters, the park's floral displays are amazing. Wildlife includes roadrunners, hawks,
lizards, mice, and squirrels. The colorful rock formations in the park served as landmarks
during the early 1870s for 20-mule-team freight wagons
slogging through the desert.

Just south of Red Rock Canyon State Park, stop by the
Jawbone Canyon Visitor's Center on Highway 14, site of the
annual Moose Anderson Days spring festival. For more information contact Friends of Jawbone Canyon, P.O. Box 1902,
Cantil 93519; (760) 373-1146; www.jawbone.org. Open daily.

Red Rock Canyon State Park is a favorite site for filmmakers,
and the beginning scene of *Jurassic Park* was filmed here. There is
a self-guided nature trail offering a good introduction to indigenous
plants, animals, and awe-inspiring vistas. If you'd like to see more
breathtaking desert-scapes, cross over to Highway 14, which skirts
red-, pink-, orange-, and white-colored canyons that seem to change
color as the light shifts.

Death Valley

It's awesome to imagine that 27 acres of "empty" California desert make up what we now know as Death Valley, the lowest point in the United States at 282 feet below sea level, and reportedly the hottest place on earth. The region is one of 265 areas worldwide recognized and preserved by the Man and the Biosphere organization. This one, the Mojave and Colorado Desert Biosphere Reserve, is the ideal place to share with your children the importance of environmental protection. Before you enter the dazzling desolation of Death Valley, consider making a stop in Darwin Falls, a little bit off Highway 178 before the valley. The whole family can manage the half-mile hike to the oasis of lower Darwin Falls. The upper falls aren't far behind. Your memories of green will serve you well as you head into Death Valley. Average summertime highs here are 115 degrees F, and with scarcely a tree in sight, there isn't much shade to cool off in. If you happen to come here between

Death Valley Fun Facts

(Courtesy of the National Park Service and Furnace Creek Inn & Ranch Resort.)

- The hottest recorded air temperature in Death Valley was 134 degrees F in 1913.

- The highest ground temperature recorded was 201 degrees F at Furnace Creek on July 15, 1972. The air temperature for that day was 128 degrees F. (Ground temperature on the valley floor is about 40 percent higher than the surrounding air temperature.)

- The average rainfall in Death Valley is 1.8 inches per year.

- Death Valley was named a national monument on February 11, 1933, by President Herbert Hoover.

- Death Valley became a national park on October 31, 1994, by an act of Congress.

- The average humidity in Death Valley ranges from zero to 5 percent.

- Death Valley has more than 900 species of plants, 6 types of fish, 5 amphibians, 36 reptiles, and 51 mammals native to the region.

- There are 346 species of birds that migrate through or reside in Death Valley.

- *Death Valley Days* ran as a radio show from 1930 to 1944 and as a television series from 1952 to 1968.

Junior Ranger Program

Children ages 6 and older will get the most out of visiting Death Valley National Park if they ask for the Death Valley workbook at the park's visitor center front desk. There are special credit activities on projects kids can delve into while exploring the park. Upon the completion of the listed activities, all age-appropriate kids are presented with a Valley Junior Ranger Badge, and the park staff may undertake, time permitting, a small ceremony. Check out all the details online here: www.nps.gov/learn/juniorranger.htm.

June and September, remember to take it easy and drink water frequently—dehydration is dangerous and can happen faster than you think.

But don't let the heat deter you from visiting. Or the intimidating name, for that matter. With a rich mining heritage dating from 1849 and modern tourist facilities, Death Valley can actually be a very lively place. Geological wonders have, however, always been at center stage. You can see the famous ones in a day or so, but savor the barren beauty slowly. Death Valley has more than 1,000 species of plants and more than 50 are endemic (kids, look that word up) and found nowhere else in the world—wouldn't that make an impressive report for your next science assignment?

Artist's Palette Drive is a famous byway that winds through pastel-colored hills laced with minerals. Early morning is the best time to take photographs from Zabriskie Point, which overlooks ancient lakebeds. By contrast, Golden Canyon is at its best in the afternoon. In between, you could investigate the bizarre salt formations of the Devil's Golf Course and get an elevated perspective from 5,474 feet up at Dante's View, where the Panamint Mountains and snowcapped Mt. Whitney will be visible.

Death Valley National Park

Office of the Superintendent, P.O. Box 579, Death Valley 92328; (760) 786-3200; www.nps .gov/deva. Furnace Creek Visitor Center and Borax Museum, open year-round 8 a.m. to 6 p.m. Stovepipe Wells Ranger Station, open all year, seasonal hours.

The hottest, driest, lowest place in the Western Hemisphere. Highway 190, the Badwater Road, the Scotty's Castle Road, and paved roads to Dante's View and Wildrose provide access to the major scenic viewpoints and historic points of interest within the park. More than 350 miles of unpaved and four-wheel-drive roads provide access to wilderness hiking, camping, and historical sites. All vehicles must be licensed and "street legal." Admission fees are by permit, $20 per car for seven days. Death Valley Annual Pass holder: $40 per vehicle.

Scotty's Castle

(760) 786-2392; www.nps.gov/deva. Guided, living-history tours of Scotty's Castle main house interior are conducted daily year-round. The first tour begins at 9 a.m., and the last

Hot **Tip**

Check out Death Valley National History Association (800-478 8564; www
.dvnha.org) for scheduled activities such as the Surprise Canyon Backpack
trip and other family friendly expeditions. They operate bookstores at the
Furnace Creek Visitor Center, Stovepipe Wells Ranger Station, and Scotty's
Castle Visitor Center. The Death Valley National Park home page, www.nps
.gov/deva, provides updates on roads and weather conditions.

**begins at 5 p.m. Castle grounds close at 6 p.m. Tours last approximately 50 minutes and
are given at least once every hour. Limited to 19 people per tour; the guided tour is the
only way to get inside the main house. Tour tickets are sold on a first-come, first-served
basis. $$.**

Located in the northern part of the valley in an area known as Grapevine Canyon, this
Spanish Moorish–style mansion was the creation of Walter Scott (and some of his desert
friends), who built his home in the 1920s at the cost of $200 million. The building took 10
years to complete, but you can see it inside and out in considerably less time. Save your
visit here for the second day of your Death Valley tour. Near the castle are the Ubehebe
Crater and the Sahara-scale sand dunes.

Where to Eat & Stay

Furnace Creek Resort. Highway 190, Box
1; (760) 786-2345; www.furnacecreekresort
.com. Completely inside Death Valley National
Park, this privately owned property currently
operated by Xanterra is actually one resort
with two hotels: the AAA four-diamond rated
luxurious, historic 1927 66-room **Inn at
Furnace Creek** (open only mid-October to
mid-May) and the more family-friendly 224-
room **Ranch at Furnace Creek,** circa 1933,
open year-round. Choose the ranch for you
and the kids and the inn for a couple's private
romantic getaway, based upon our experi-
ence. Wandering around the western-themed
ranch grounds, you'll feel like you've been
transported back to the 1800s but with all the
21st-century amenities: air-conditioning, TV,
telephones, a spring-fed swimming pool, ten-
nis courts, and a children's playground. Ride
a horse (except in summer season, when it's
too darn hot to trot), take a hike, or challenge

your kids to a game of horseshoes. Visit the
18-hole **Furnace Creek Golf Course,** the
world's lowest golf course at 214 feet below
sea level. Visit the general store for a quick
snack and some great gifts. Check out the
antique stagecoaches, mining tools, and the
steam locomotive at the Borax Museum. For
year-round casual, American-style dining ($$),
choose from the **Wrangler Steakhouse
and Buffet,** the **49'er Cafe,** and the Cork-
screw Saloon. It's been said about Death Valley, "You can travel greater distances but no
place will take you further away." $$$–$$$$

Stovepipe Wells Village. (760) 786-2387;
www.stovepipewells.com. Open year-round,
currently operated by Xanterra. Entirely
inside Death Valley National Park along High-
way 190 is a small way-station 24 miles north-
west of Furnace Creek against the foothills of
the Panamint Mountains. Here you'll find an
83-room basic motel (no phones in rooms,

TVs in some; all ground floor at-door parking) within steps of the swimming pool, gas station, a general store, a gift shop, a ranger station, and a restaurant/bar. Pets are allowed. There is also an RV park with full hookups. Your kids will love running around in the sand dunes surrounding the property.

Amargosa Opera House, Café and Hotel. Death Valley Junction, (760) 852-4441; www.amargosaoperahouse.com. Call for current show times, generally only Sat and Sun. Plan your trip so that you can visit this site in a ghost town on the National Register of Historic Places near the junction of Highways 127 and 190 about 30 miles from Furnace Creek and 92 miles from Las Vegas. Since 1968, performances star Marta Becket, who plays most all of the characters. Marta's murals depict gypsies, revelers, clerics, and Spanish royalty. The 14-room hotel is a rustic, historic hoot. No phones or TV mar this quirky outpost. New in 2010, the Amargosa Cafe opened for breakfast, lunch and dinner, from 7 a.m. to 8 p.m. Mon through Sat and 7 a.m. to 4 p.m. Sun as well as being open after shows for refreshments. Eccentric, yes, but charmingly unusual. Worth a stop in this desert wonderland. $$

San Diego County

What does summer vacation mean to your family? How about one with plenty of outdoor recreation—boating, hiking, biking, picnicking, swimming, golfing, baseball, surfing, or sunbathing on miles of beach? Does it include excursions to great parks full of wildlife and sea life, exciting museums with hands-on displays of fun things from outer space to automobiles, old sights with new twists, all surrounded by the Pacific Ocean, mountains, and desert and capped by a clear blue sky with mega-sunshine? The year-round answer is San Diego County, certainly one of Southern California's most popular places for an "endless summer" vacation destination, encompassing metropolitan San Diego, the coastal areas of North County including Oceanside, and to the east, the mountains and desert of the Back Country, featuring Julian and Anza-Borrego.

San Diego County's location at the extreme southwest corner of the contiguous United States helps explain not only its temperate climate (an average year-round temperature of 70 degrees) but also its friendly spirit. In this geographically varied, 4,269-square-mile region, you can head west out to sea, south into Mexico, east into forested mountains that receive more rain and snow than Seattle and deserts that are hotter and drier than Phoenix, and along 70 miles of sandy, palm-lined beaches that rival Florida. You will find country kitchens and apple farms, cosmopolitan bistros and burger joints, craft shops and giant retail malls, high-rises and bungalows, dirt roads and 10-lane freeways—inhabited by 3 million or so culturally and ethnically diverse people. Their sheer numbers make San Diego America's seventh most populous area and the Golden State's second-biggest metropolis, after Los Angeles. Get ready for some fun in the San Diego sun!

Metropolitan San Diego

Touring the greater San Diego area is best accomplished by automobile. Your choices of activities and attractions are incredibly diverse. Many families start in the Mission Bay area at SeaWorld and are entertained by the penguins, sharks, and killer whales. Or you

SAN DIEGO COUNTY

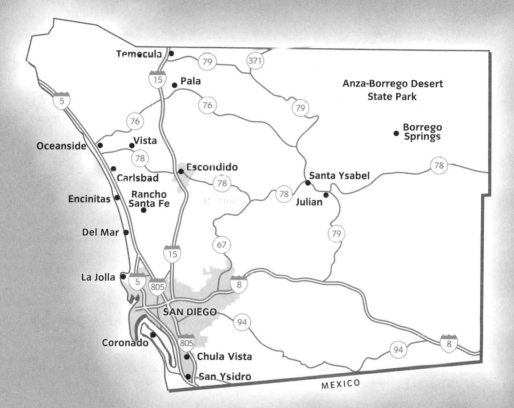

Temecula

79 371

15 Pala

76

79

Anza-Borrego Desert
State Park

Borrego
Springs

5

76

Oceanside

Vista

78

Escondido

Carlsbad

78

Santa Ysabel

78

Encinitas

Rancho
Santa Fe

78

Julian

Del Mar

15

67

79

La Jolla

5 805

8

SAN DIEGO

94

Coronado

805

Chula Vista

San Ysidro

94 8

MEXICO

might begin at the world-famous San Diego Zoo with its exotic and rare species of animals and plants. Or the San Diego Zoo Safari Park may beckon, where the animals roam free and really wild. Balboa Park's museums, art galleries, and theaters provide you with some fantastic cultural attractions. If outdoor recreation is your family's favorite, there are hundreds of beaches, parks, sailing, and fishing options. We like to begin at the beginning by visiting the Old Town State Historic Park and Presidio district, then touring the first California missions; downtown's restored Gaslamp Quarter, or Point Loma's Cabrillo National Monument, which commemorates the first European to set sight on San Diego Bay. But no matter how you divide and conquer it, you will find incredibly fun things to see, do, and taste throughout metropolitan San Diego.

Cabrillo National Monument

1800 Cabrillo Memorial Dr., Highway 209, off I-5; (619) 557-5450; www.nps.gov/cabr. Open 9 a.m. to 5:15 p.m. daily, possibly extended in summer. $$.

Cruising the Pacific Coast north of Mexico in 1542, explorer Juan Rodriguez Cabrillo first landed at Point Loma, a 400-foot-high peninsula separating San Diego Bay from the ocean. He claimed it (and everything else in sight) for Spain. Today you can marvel at the same view Cabrillo had of the southernmost tip of this narrow finger of land. On Point Loma's plateau-like surface are two military reservations, a cemetery, and informative attractions for young and old alike. You can get your bearings at the visitor center, tour the monument's small museum, and take in a **free** film or a ranger-sponsored program in the auditorium. Then let the kids climb Old Point Loma Lighthouse, with its breathtaking panorama of the city meeting the sea. This is a superb spot for winter whale-watching.

Old Town San Diego State Historic Park and Presidio Park

Located in a 6-block area bounded by Wallace, Juan, Twiggs, and Congress Streets, sandwiched between I-5 and I-8; (619) 220-5422; www.parks.ca.gov. Open daily 10 a.m. to 5 p.m. Free admission. Free guided walking tours depart the Robinson–Rose House daily at 2 p.m. All buildings are closed New Year's Day, Thanksgiving, and Christmas.

In 1769, a mere 167 years after Cabrillo arrived, Gaspar de Portolá established the first Presidio Royal (military fort) while Father Junípero Serra founded the first in a string of 21 California missions. Since both the fort and the mission were built in San Diego, they earned the city the moniker "birthplace of California." This is, of course, California-ish hyperbole, because for centuries before de Portolá or Serra, Native Americans—quite successfully, in fact—had prospered from the area's fertile lands and bountiful seas.

The fort and mission were located originally in what today is called Old Town. The cluster of adobe buildings at the base of Presidio Hill has swollen over time into a fascinating complex of historic landmarks, museums, art galleries, shops, and ethnic restaurants. These include the Black Hawk Smith & Stable, the Colorado House/Wells Fargo Museum, the Courthouse, the Johnson House, La Casa de Estudillo, the Machado-Stewart Adobe, the Mason Street School, the Plaza, the Robinson–Rose House, the San Diego Union Newspaper Museum, Seeley Stables, and the Whaley House. Our best advice is just to go, park, walk, and enjoy this family-friendly district.

Who Was **Alonzo Horton?**

For some years after California won statehood in 1850, San Diego remained a relatively quiet community with a Spanish and Mexican flavor. That changed dramatically when Alonzo E. Horton arrived in town from San Francisco in 1867. Buying up some 960 acres of waterfront land, he began the process of developing what was to become today's downtown area. **The Gaslamp Quarter,** bounded by Broadway, 4th, and 6th Streets and Harbor Drive, is the historic 16-block quarter where Horton made his first land purchase and where his legacy lives on. A 20-year restoration and cleanup campaign to return the Gaslamp Quarter to its gay 1890s splendor has paid off: The area sparkles with period streetlamps, old-time trolley stops, and, of more recent vintage, trendy restaurants, hotels, offices, artists' studios, and nightspots. For complete information, including walking tours and audiotapes, contact the Gaslamp Quarter Museum, 410 Island Ave.; (619) 233-4692; www.gaslamp quarter.org; Open Mon through Fri 10 a.m. to 2 p.m., Sat 10 a.m. to 4 p.m., and Sun noon to 4 p.m. Ask about the new Children's Historical Walking Tour and the Virtual Learning Center. Or contact the Gaslamp Quarter Association; 614 5th Ave., Suite E; (619) 233-5227; www.gaslamp.org.

Junípero Serra Museum

2727 Presidio Dr., in Presidio Park; (619) 297-3258; www.sandiegohistory.org. Open Sat and Sun, 10 a.m. to 5 p.m.; closed major holidays. $.

This museum stands above the sites of the 18th-century presidio and Father Junípero Serra's first mission in Alta, California. It's a great place to learn about San Diego's early Spanish and Mexican periods. Exhibits include artifacts from archaeological excavations at the site.

Mission Basilica San Diego de Alcala

10818 San Diego Mission Rd. (east on I-8, exit Mission Gorge Road north to Twain Avenue, then drive west to San Diego Mission Road); (619) 281-8449; www.missionsandiego.com. Open 9 a.m. to 4:45 p.m. daily except Thanksgiving and Christmas. $.

Father Serra's first mission (of the renowned chain of 21 missions throughout California), relocated east to its current location in 1774, and was burned down by Indians the following year. Rebuilt in 1781, the fully restored mission remains an active parish. Behind the chapel is a small museum containing robes, relics, and original records in Serra's own handwriting. "California's first church" is a National Historic Landmark, California Historic Landmark #242, and honored with a City of San Diego Historic Designation #113.

Westfield Horton Plaza

Between Broadway, 1st, and 4th Avenues and G Street, downtown; (800) 214-7467; www
.westfield.com/hortonplaza. Open Mon through Sat 10 a.m. to 9 p.m. and Sun 11 a.m. to 7
p.m. Hours adjusted seasonally and during holiday periods. Three hours of **free** parking
with any purchase.

Named after Alonzo Horton but opened in 1985, this 5-story, lavishly decorated and landscaped open-air mall houses more than 150 shops and restaurants, 14 movie theaters,
and 2 live performance stages. Parking is available at an adjacent garage. Kids will love the
festive atmosphere and food courts. The ARTSTIX booth at Westfield Horton Plaza near
the corner of Third and Broadway sells half-price day-of-show tickets to many local music,
dance, and theater events. Some shows also are sold in advance. Visit or call the ARTSTIX
hotline at (619) 497-5000.

Old Town Trolley Tours/Historic Tours of America

(619) 298-8687; www.historictours.com/sandiego. Every 30 minutes, daily, beginning at 9
a.m. $$$$.

Two-hour narrated tours of most of the key San Diego sites are available on propane-
powered vehicles called trolleys. You can exit and reboard anytime during the day at any
of the 10 fun stops (such as Balboa Park, Horton Plaza, Gaslamp Quarter, Seaport Village,
Embarcadero, Old Town, and Coronado) along the route. This is a wonderful way for the
entire family to become acquainted with the city without the hassles of driving and parking your own car. Also available is **San Diego SEALs Harbor Tour**'s "Boat on Wheels," a
hydra-amphibious land and sea tour that really gives you a unique perspective on the city
and waterfront action. All highly recommended.

San Diego Trolley System and the Transit Store

102 Broadway, near Horton Plaza; (619) 233-3004 or (619) 685-4900; www.sdmts.com and
www.transit.511sd.com. Runs daily 5 a.m. to 1 a.m. every 15 minutes. One-way fares start
at $2.50; day-tripper passes (unlimited use of all types of public transit) are $5 per day
(definitely recommended—take a vacation from your car!).

An electric trolley run by the Metropolitan Transit System is a superb, car-free way to
travel around San Diego. The North-South Blue Line runs from downtown San Diego to the
Mexican border at San Ysidro; the East-West Orange Line runs along the bay and includes
Seaport Village, the Gaslamp Quarter, downtown, and El Cajon. The Green Line runs from
Old Town to El Cajon and Santee as well.

Museum of Contemporary Art–San Diego

1001 Kettner Blvd. at Broadway; (619) 234-1001; www.mcasd.org. Open Thurs through
Tues 11 a.m. to 5 p.m. $; ages 25 (yes, a quarter-century old, that's right!) and under **free**
every day and **free** museum admission Thurs evenings from 5 to 7 p.m. **Free** public
tours are available every Thurs at 6 p.m. and weekends at 2 p.m.

In the spectacular 34-story America Plaza, this museum features 4 galleries on 2 levels
with permanent and changing exhibits of modern paintings, sculpture, and designs. The

San Diego **Art & Soul**

San Diego Art & Soul is an unprecedented cooperative partnership formed between the San Diego Convention and Visitors Bureau, the City of San Diego Commission for Arts and Culture, and hundreds of organizations and businesses to promote the rich cultural diversity of the area. For an updated daily list of events; links to hundreds of art, music, and cultural websites; and a **free** color brochure and discount coupons, visit www.sandiegoartandsoul .com or call (619) 533-3050.

all-glass exterior gives dramatic views of the San Diego Trolley Station, AMTRAK Depot, and the skyline. Call for current exhibitions.

USS *Midway* Museum

Navy Pier, 910 North Harbor Dr.; (619) 544-9600; www.midway.org. Open daily 10 a.m. to 5 p.m. (except Thanksgiving and Christmas Day). Last admission is at 4 p.m. $$–$$$, children younger than 6 and active-duty service people in uniform free.

The museum is located aboard the USS *Midway*, permanently docked at Navy Pier in San Diego Bay. Marvel at a floating "city at sea" and share in an odyssey that began in 1945 when the USS *Midway* was commissioned as the largest ship in the world. Audio guides are provided. New in 2010 was a family audio tour designed for families with youngsters. You'll follow the narration of Airman Sam Rodriguez on an amazing and entertaining audio tour to more than 30 locations throughout the aircraft carrier, including more than 35 exhibits and displays. You have access to the mess deck, berthing spaces, hangar deck, and flight deck. The museum includes flight simulators, a gift shop, and a cafe and is constantly adding new programs. A docent-led "Island Tour" of the superstructure above the flight deck is **free** with paid admission. You must be at least 42 inches tall to visit the Island at any time. An outstanding experience—do not miss this!

The New Children's Museum (NCM)

200 West Island Ave. on the corner of Front Street (just a block from the convention center); (619) 233-8792); www.thinkplaycreate.org. Open Mon, Tues, Fri, and Sat, 10 a.m. to 4 p.m.; Thurs 10 a.m. to 6 p.m.; and Sun 12 p.m. to 4 p.m. Closed Wed. Second Sunday of the month is free. $$.

"The Muse" reopened in May 2008 in a brand-new 50,000-square-foot, 3-story building—more than doubling previous public space. The museum has multiple galleries for hands-on experimentation, 2 meeting/birthday party rooms, a 250-seat theater, and an indoor/outdoor cafe. NCM is designed for children of all ages, from toddler to teen. Some areas and activities are age specific—like Barn Dance for toddlers and the Teen Studio for teenagers—while other parts are designed to engage children of all ages. The best time to visit is Monday morning when it is less crowded.

Maritime Museum of San Diego

1492 North Harbor Dr.; (619) 234-9153; www.sdmaritime.org. Open daily 9 a.m. to 8 p.m. (open until 9 p.m. Memorial Day to Labor Day). $$.

The museum will really get your family in a seafaring mood. You can explore three ships: the square-rigged *Star of India,* launched in 1863 and the oldest merchant vessel afloat; the ferry boat *Berkeley,* circa 1898; and the *Medea,* a steam-powered luxury yacht built in 1904.

Seaport Village

West Harbor Drive and Kettner Boulevard; (619) 235-4014; www.seaportvillage.com. Open daily 10 a.m. to 9 p.m.

Encompassing 14 acres, this village looks like a transplanted New England fishing town, complete with a carousel, lighthouse, and clock tower along with almost one hundred shops, themed eateries, and restaurants. There are 4 miles of meandering cobblestone pathways bordered by ponds, lakes, fountains, and colorful, lush landscaping and a quarter-mile-long boardwalk along the San Diego Bay. The Loof Carousel, circa 1895, is worth a whirl. You could easily spend most of the day here wandering the waterfront and enjoying a harbor cruise.

Balboa Park

Just northeast of the downtown business district; (619) 239-0512 for general information; www.balboapark.org.

In 1868 some farsighted city leaders set aside 1,200 acres of barren pueblo land for a city park. Now that land contains the world-famous San Diego Zoo and 15 museums (the largest concentration outside the Smithsonian in Washington, D.C.). The best way to see the rest of Balboa Park's attractions is on foot. Park at the Plaza de Panama lot (by Laurel Street near the Cabrillo Bridge crossing) or take the **free** tram from the Inspiration Point parking lot (the tram has 11 stops through the park). Admittance to the park grounds is **free**, but admission prices to attractions vary by institution. Memberships are also available for purchase from the museums and performing arts organizations, offering an opportunity for visitors to support these San Diego cultural treasures on an annual basis.

San Diego Zoo

In Balboa Park. From I-5 take Pershing Drive exits and follow the signs; (619) 234-3153; www.sandiegozoo.org. Opens at 9 a.m. every day; closing hours vary by season, so be sure to call ahead. $$$.

Let the zoo be your San Diego headquarters for at least two days of family adventure. The Spanish colonial buildings here were built originally along El Prado (the Promenade) for the 1915 Panama-California Exposition. Part of the exposition was a modest menagerie, which a certain Dr. Harry Wegeforth took over, expanded, and turned into what is now one of the world's rarest collections. The zoo's size is formidable: more than 4,000 animals, more than 900 species, and 100-plus magnificently landscaped acres with 6,500 exotic plants.

Passports to Balboa Park
Are a Great Value

There are so many incredible things to see and do in Balboa Park; it would probably take you a week to do it all! The **Passport to Balboa Park** discount offer is designed with that in mind. Experience up to 14 Balboa Park museums for $45 (save up to 50 percent). The Passport to Balboa is valid for seven days. Also available is the Zoo/Passport Combo for adults for only $75, a value of more than $125, and $36 for children 3 to 12, which is a value of more than $63. This combo passport includes entrance to the museums as well as one-day Deluxe San Diego Zoo Admission. New in 2010, the Stay-for-the-Day pass was only $35—choose any 5 of the 14 museums on the same day (zoo not included). Available for purchase online, at the Balboa Park Visitors Center House of Hospitality at 1549 El Prado, at participating attractions, or at the MTS Transit store downtown. *Note:* Some museums are closed Monday, and operating hours vary. Special exhibitions may be subject to an additional entrance fee. Call (619) 239-0512) for more information or www.balboapark.org/info/passport.php.

The zoo has the largest population of giant pandas in the United States and is one of only four facilities in the nation to house critically endangered giant pandas. The San Diego Zoo has had a love affair with giant pandas ever since two of the black-and-white bears came to visit in 1987. After years of red tape and tons of paperwork, the zoo and China agreed on a 12-year research loan of 2 giant pandas, Bai Yun and Shi Shi. A brand-new exhibit area was built for our panda guests, which has since been expanded and renovated and is now called the Giant Panda Research Station. Currently in residence are four giant pandas—and if you can't wait to see them in person, check out the 24/7 Panda Cam at www.sandiegozoo.org/pandacam.

Animals are "on display" outdoors year-round. Viewing is enhanced by many exhibition areas that do not have bars. Areas include Gorilla Tropics (with incredibly humanlike primates), the Tiger River section, a tropical rain habitat, the Sun Bear Forest, a Southeast Asian jungle, a Hippo Beach (with underwater viewing to see how graceful a swimmer this huge land mammal can be), and the largest koala exhibit outside of Australia. (Get ready for new stuffed teddy bear requests after this particular show!)

The Children's Zoo is user-friendly, with more chances for your kids to pet animals than you can wave a carrot at, plus an incubator for baby chicks and an animal nursery. The Skyfari tram is a great way to see the zoo by air. Our recommendation for "doing the zoo" is the Deluxe Tour, which includes admission to the big zoo, a 45-minute double-decker bus tour (marvelous view), the Children's Zoo, and a Skyfari aerial tramway ride.

Other Things to See and Do
in Balboa Park

Museums, galleries, and gardens are not the only things going on in Balboa Park for your family. The 48-passenger **Miniature Railroad** will take you and yours into a bygone era. **The Carousel** will set you spinning. **The Starlight Bowl,** where the San Diego Civic Light Opera Association presents delightful musicals, is a sure hit, so call (619) 544-7827 for current schedules. The **Spreckels Organ Pavilion** has free concerts on weekends. The pavilion houses the world's biggest outdoor pipe organ; call (619) 235-1100 for program information. The **San Diego Junior Theatre** presents year-round, family-friendly productions at the Casa del Prado Theatre (www.juniortheatre.com). The **Morley Field Sports Complex,** in the northeastern section of the park, can satisfy just about every recreational need your family can dream of (no matter how complex), with a tennis club, 2 golf courses, a swimming pool, a kiddie pool, some bocce courts, a fitness center, a playground, an archery range, a couple of baseball diamonds, assorted picnic areas, 2 recreation centers, and a zippy 18-hole Frisbee golf course.

Reuben H. Fleet Science Center

In Balboa Park, 1875 El Prado; (619) 238-1233; www.rhfleet.org. Open daily 10 a.m.; closing times vary. $$.

One of the Kath family favorite outings, this awe-inspiring facility features a planetarium, hands-on exhibits, and the incredible IMAX Dome, which features an incredible variety of new IMAX films. From birds to the Wright brothers to jets, you and the kids will thrill to the history and magical science of flight. For ages infant to 6 years, Kid City (a permanent exhibition) has conveyer belts and cranes to air chutes and grocery stores for youth to work, create, play, and learn as they experience the wonders of the everyday working world. Throughout it, tips and strategies are offered on parent-child interaction to encourage children's learning. Don't miss this. It's great for kids of all ages—we know!

San Diego Hall of Champions Sports Museum

In Balboa Park; (619) 234-2544; www.sdhoc.com. Open daily 10 a.m. to 4:30 p.m.; closed major holidays. $.

Offers a fascinating peek into local sports history via photographs, memorabilia, videotapes, and audiotapes. You can call play-by-play action for San Diego Padres' Tony Gwynn and hall-of-fame star Ted Williams in the state-of-the-art media center, follow the evolution of the surfboard, or soar with local skateboard legend Tony Hawk.

San Diego Air & Space Museum

In Balboa Park, 2001 Pan American Plaza; (619) 234-8291; www.aerospacemuseum.org. Open daily 10 a.m. until 5:30 p.m. with final entry at 5 p.m. Closed major holidays. $$.

Check out the replica of Lindbergh's *Spirit of St. Louis* and an A-12 Blackbird. The hall of fame honors heroes of aviation and space flight including an up-close and personal view of NASA's Apollo 9 Command Module.

San Diego by the Sea

The Embarcadero, located at the west end of Broadway, is the thoroughfare forming the heart of downtown San Diego's waterfront action. It's home to the Broadway Pier, with berths for cruise ships and freighters, a debarkation platform, US Customs offices, and a cool observation deck. Definitely plan on taking the kids on one of the San Diego Bay excursion cruises to view all the action around Harbor Island, Shelter Island, Point Loma, and Coronado Island. Dinner cruises and whale-watching trips also depart here. Here are some options.

- **The Original San Diego Harbor Excursions.** 1050 North Harbor Dr.; (619) 234-4111 or (800) 442-7847; www.sdhe.com. $$$. In operation since 1915. Dinner cruises also available. Scheduled departures vary seasonally. Generally they are daily between 10 a.m. and 5:30 p.m. Sights you will enjoy include the Navy fleet and the stunning Coronado Bay Bridge.

- **San Diego–Coronado Ferry.** 1050 North Harbor Dr.; (619) 234-4111 or (800) 44-CRUISE (27847). www.sdhe.com. Operates daily beginning at 9 a.m.; last trip 9 p.m. (later on Fri and Sat). $. Departs every hour on the hour from San Diego's Broadway Pier and takes you to Coronado Landing Marketplace. Reservations not necessary. This is a super way to do Coronado for the day!

- **Orion Sailing Charters.** 1380 Harbor Island Dr.; (619) 574-7504; www.orion sailing.com. $$$. Guided sailing and whale-watching cruises.

- **Hornblower Cruises and Events–San Diego.** 1066 North Harbor Dr.; (619) 686-8715; www.hornblower.com. $$$$. Reservations required for 1- or 2-hour cruises, brunch, and dinner/dancing excursions aboard these deluxe vessels.

San Diego Model Railroad Museum

In Balboa Park in the Casa de Balboa Building; (619) 696-0199; www.sdmodelrailroadm.com. Open Tues through Fri 11 a.m. to 4 p.m.; Sat and Sun 11 a.m. to 5 p.m.

Four scale-model railroad layouts detail the geography and development of the railroad industry in Southern California. Your kids will love the hands-on model railroad.

San Diego Museum of Art

In the center of Balboa Park; (619) 232-7931; www.sdmart.org. Open Tues to Sat 10 a.m. to 5 p.m., Sun 12 p.m. to 5 p.m.; closed major holidays. $$.

The lovely facility has a permanent collection of Italian Renaissance works, Spanish baroque Old Masters, and American, Asian, and Native American art and culture.

San Diego Museum of Photographic Art

1649 El Prado, in Balboa Park; (619) 239-5262; www.mopa.org. Open daily 10 a.m. to 5 p.m. Closed major holidays and for special events. Call first. $$.

Devoted exclusively to the photographic arts. Year-round changing exhibitions display everything from fine-art photography to images from around the world.

San Diego Museum of Man

In Balboa Park, the group of buildings around the California Quadrangle; 1350 El Prado; (619) 239-2001; www.museumofman.org. Open daily 10 a.m. to 4:30 p.m.; closed major holidays. $$.

These multifaceted exhibit halls explore the origins of humankind and feature the cultures of American Indians, ancient Egypt, Mexico, and Latin America. Special features on folk art, textiles, and early man. Laura's kid kin affectionately call this the "Mummy Museum."

San Diego Natural History Museum

East end of Balboa Park; (619) 232-3821; www.sdnhm.org. Open daily 10 a.m. to 5 p.m. Hours subject to change. Be sure to call first. Closed on Thanksgiving and Christmas Day. hours may be extended seasonally.

Houses both permanent and changing exhibits and displays detailing the plants, animals, and geology of San Diego County as well as Baja California. Be sure to call for current displays.

Timken Museum of Art

1500 El Prado, in Balboa Park; (619) 239-5548; www.timkenmuseum.org. Open Tues through Sat 10 a.m. to 4:30 p.m. and Sun 1:30 to 4:30 p.m.; closed Mon and major holidays. Always free admission and tours.

This charming gallery contains Old Masters, 18th- and 19th-century American paintings, and Russian icons.

Diversity Dining

From ethnic takeout to historic hangouts to oceanfront glimmer, San Diego chefs use the region's freshest ingredients to create hearty and intriguing dishes. The county's estimated 6,400 restaurants offer everything from new taste sensations to traditional favorites and are attracting some of the nation's top culinary talents. You can sample the tastes of Thailand one evening and Mexico the next, and snack on such local favorites as fish tacos and smoothies in between. Best bet? Ask your hotel's front desk for nearby favorite dining spots or contact the San Diego Convention and Visitors Bureau (www .sandiego.org) for its list of restaurant members (more than 300 choices). Just a couple of our spots to consider: **Corvette Diner** in Hillcrest district near Balboa Park for meatloaf sandwiches and milk shakes (619-542-1476); the **Filippi's Pizza Grotto** downtown in Little Italy (family owned since 1950; 619-232-5094; numerous locations throughout the metro area); **Phil's BBQ** in Point Loma (619-226-6333); and **Old Town Mexican Café** for the fresh tortillas and combo plates (619-297-4330).

Botanical and Floral Gardens, Botanical Building

In Balboa Park; (619) 235-1100; www.balboapark.org. Gardens are open year-round. Building is open 10 a.m. to 4 p.m. daily except Thurs and some holidays. Free.

Revitalize yourself and give the kids some fresh air by heading into Balboa Park's magnificent display of botanical wonders. Included are more than 7,600 trees, 67 kinds of palms, and 2,200 rosebushes, plus desert cacti, lilies, ferns, orchids, bamboo, and other oxygen-rich flora. Tour the building (an old Santa Fe railroad station) for explanations of what you've just encountered.

Qualcomm Stadium

9449 Friars Rd., in Mission Valley; (619) 641-3100; www.sandiego.gov/qualcomm. Home to the National Football League's San Diego Chargers (619-280-2121 for schedules; www .chargers.com) and the San Diego State University Aztecs (619-283-SDSU; www.goaztecs .cstv.com).

This venue was the site of the Super Bowl in 1998 and 2003, and it hosts many other events and concerts during the year, including Poinsettia Bowl and Pacific Life Holiday Bowl. It is owned by the city of San Diego and has a football spectator seating capacity of 70,561.

PETCO Park

100 Park Blvd., located downtown, within walking distance to hotels, shopping, and the waterfront; (619) 795-5000 or (888) MY-PADRES; www.padres.com.

The 46,000-seat facility has spacious concourses, garden terraces, and state-of-the-art services and amenities with some of the best sight-lines in baseball. Behind-the-scenes guided tours are available Apr to Sept depending on event schedules and times for a nominal fee. For more details visit http://sandiego.padres.mlb.com, call the Tour Hotline at (619) 795-5011, or e-mail tours@padres.com.

Mission Bay Park

2688 East Mission Bay Dr., just minutes west from Mission Valley; (619) 276-8200 (visitor center); www.sandiego.gov. Open 9 a.m. to dusk daily. **Free.**

The park is on a former mud flat transformed into a 4,600-acre aquatic playground by creative dredging, filling, and landscaping. You can easily worship outdoor recreation at its finest here: swimming, power boating, fishing, sailing, volleyball, softball, horseshoes, bicycling, roller-skating, kite flying, Frisbee tossing, and jogging—framed by 27 miles of beaches on Mission Bay and 17 miles of Pacific Ocean frontage. Spread throughout Mission Bay are great resort hotels and campgrounds. The *Bahia Belle* is an old-time stern-wheeler that plies the bay between the Bahia and Catamaran Hotels most evenings during the summer and weekends in the winter. More info: www.bahia hotel.com.

SeaWorld San Diego

1720 South Shores Rd., on Mission Bay; (619) 226-3901 or (800) SEA-WORLD; www.seaworld .com/sandiego. Open daily 10 a.m., earlier in the summer; closing hours change daily and seasonally. Be sure to call for current times. Parking is $12 per car. $$$$.

For kids, this is probably the number one reason to visit San Diego. Opened in 1964, this celebrated 189-acre marine amusement park features trained killer whales, ponderous sea lions, playful otters, and lovable dolphins. You can take in 5 different shows and more than 20 educational exhibits, including the Penguin and Shark Encounters, containing the world's largest collection of these species. Don't miss Journey to Atlantis, a wet and wild thrill ride with a 60-foot plunge into a lake. In 2010, SeaWorld's Dolphin Stadium was completely renovated and reopened in May for the park's new Blue Horizons, a spectacular show combining up to 16 energetic dolphins and 2 pilot whales, with 50 rock doves, soaring exotic birds, and two dozen trainers, amazing aerialists, divers, and bungee performers. Truly spectacular spectacle! There's also Caribbean Realm, just south of Dolphin Stadium, which includes the Calypso Bay Smokehouse restaurant and Pineapple Pete's Island Eats plus 2 retail stores—Splish Splash, a children's water gear and clothing store, and Caribbean Breeze gifts.

How about Forbidden Reef, an underwater cave with eels and bat rays, and the not-to-be-missed whale and dolphin Petting Pool? Of course, you've got to see Baby Shamu, only the sixth killer whale to be born in a zoo, in a fantastic performance alongside other killer whales (www.shamu.com). Spring 2006 welcomed the debut of Believe, a brand-new Shamu whale show in a greatly expanded and enhanced performance pool. You and the kids will scream with laughter at the crazy antics of Clyde and Seamore, the infamous sea lion duo. Try out the family adventure land, Shamu's Happy Harbor, where you get to crawl, climb, jump, and definitely get wet in a dozen or so play areas. The 2-acre Sesame Street Bay of Play themed interactive area has 3 kid-friendly rides: Elmo's Flying Fish, Abby's Sea Star Spin, and Oscar's Rocking Eel, along with the musical production *Big Bird's Beach Party* at Pets Playhouse stadium, and the movie *Sesame Street Presents Lights, Camera, Imagination!* in 4-D starring Elmo, Bert and Ernie, Cookie Monster, and Big Bird at the park's Mission Bay Theater.

And to satisfy all your hunger urges, check out the new All-Day-Dining Deal—where you pay once and can eat at various restaurants throughout the park opening to closing. In 2010, the fees were adult $29.99 plus tax; child (ages 3 to 9) $14.99 plus tax. Certain restrictions apply, but we found this to be a handy option and stress reducer! Try the Shipwreck Reef Cafe: it will handle any castaway's appetite (the best dining among 20 or so food options).

SeaWorld **Special Programs**

For some unforgettable experiences, check out these special programs. You can share a meal with an orca family in Dine with Shamu—a scrumptious all-you-can-eat buffet with SeaWorld's biggest star. You will eat at a reserved table alongside the killer-whale habitat in an area restricted to trainers and animal-care specialists. Buffet breakfast or dinner includes a special just-for-kids menu.

For an amazing hour, take a public behind-the-scenes tour that brings you to areas you will not find on the SeaWorld map. Many of the tours are interactive, and each is a unique aquatic adventure. Offered daily, this 1-hour tour gives you a glimpse at animal care, training, and rehabilitation. Group size is limited to 25 plus the educator/guide, so you really get the "insider's view."

The Public Animal Spotlight Tour is a 2-hour interactive tour with a chance to touch and feed bottlenose dolphins, feed moray eels and sea turtles, and touch sharks. This tour is offered Wed through Sun year-round for an additional fee that is well worth the time and money. Private tours can also be arranged as well as Trainer for a Day, sleepovers, and group day-camper programs. All are highly recommended as wonderful ways to enhance your family's up-close nature experience.

Hotel Circle Drive and Mission Valley

Mission Valley is a suburban area of metro San Diego that is bisected by I-8 (east-west) and I-805 (north-south). In this district, Fashion Valley Center (www.simon.com) and Mission Valley Center (http://westfield.com/mission valley) are mega-malls each with more than 200 stores, restaurants and theaters that can provide you and your family with plenty of dining and entertainment options. They are conveniently located next to a big concentration of accommodations at Hotel Circle (www.hotelcircle.net), where you will find an abundant selection of family friendly properties, such as the Doubletree Club Hotel (1515 Hotel Circle South, 619-291-8790; http://doubletree1.hilton .com); Residence Inn San Diego Mission Valley, 1865 Hotel Circle South, 619-881-3600, www.residenceinnsd.com,) and Comfort Inn & Suites (2201 Hotel Circle South, 619-881-6800; www.comfortinnhotelcircle.com).

Belmont Park/Giant Dipper

3146 Mission Blvd., Mission Bay; (619) 491-2988; www.giantdipper.com. Open every day generally at 11 a.m., but hours vary with the season. Call for current schedule. Free admission to amusement park, but you pay as you go for your choice of rides and games.

Fun, fun, and more fun. Take a ride on the Giant Dipper, a completely restored and rowdy 2,600-foot-long wooden roller coaster, first put into service in 1925 (current cost is $5). Then take another dip in the Plunge, the world's largest indoor swimming pool. Pirate's Cove is an indoor playground designed for children ages 2 to 12, accompanied by parents. The arcades and Virtual Reality Zone will send everyone for another loop.

Where to Stay

Omni Hotel San Diego. 675 L St.; (619) 231-6664; www.omnihotels.com. This 32-story luxury hotel with 511 rooms and suites is connected via sky bridge to the fab PETCO Park, home of Major League Baseball's San Diego Padres. With an excellent location in the heart of the historic Gaslamp Quarter and across the street from the convention center, the hotel is a superb headquarters for enjoying the city's top sites and attractions, only minutes away. The San Diego Trolley stops in front and the train station is 6 blocks away, so staying car-free is an option, too. (Moreover, the hotel is only 8 minutes or 4 miles from San Diego International Airport.)

All accommodations have a choice of views of San Diego Bay, PETCO Park, or the city; they are very attractively furnished with outstanding 21st-century amenities (and windows that open, unique for a high-rise, so you can catch the fresh ocean breezes). For dining, the hotel offers McCormick & Schmick's Seafood Restaurant, which serves 40 varieties of fresh seafood, pastas, and salads in a casually elegant atmosphere; open for breakfast, lunch, and dinner. Morsel's espresso bar and gift shop has an assortment of delicious desserts and treats. The Terrace Grill offers great barbecue and poolside beverage service with a view of the bay. Be sure to ask about ballpark packages and other family discount specials—you will score a lodging home run for sure at this property. $$$$

Sommerset Suites Hotel. 606 West Washington St. (just west of Highway 163, near Balboa Park and San Diego Zoo); (619) 692-5200 or (800) 962-9665; www.sommerset suites.com. There are 80 one-bedroom suites with fully equipped kitchens. Complimentary continental breakfast and evening refreshments. Outdoor pool, spa, barbecue area. Very family-friendly environment; call for special rates and packages. $$$

Town & Country Resort Hotel. 500 Hotel Circle North, in Mission Valley; (619) 291-7131 or (800) 77-ATLAS; www.towncountry.com. This 32-acre resort has 1,000 comfortable rooms and suites of every motif and configuration to suit your family's particular needs. There are 4 swimming pools and whirlpools, 9 restaurants and lounges, an 18-hole golf course, tennis courts, and a shopping village. Bella Tosca Day Spa, Salon and Fitness Center

is a luxurious 14,000-square-foot Mediterranean style facility that we adults enjoy. The trolley on property to get you to and fro will be popular with the kids! Best of all, kids stay **free** and there are innumerable package plans that include tickets to nearby SeaWorld and the zoo. A venerable choice for your San Diego lodging headquarters. $$$

For More Information

San Diego Convention and Visitors Bureau. 401 B St., Suite 1400; (619) 232-3101; www.sandiego.org.

San Diego International Visitor Information Center. 1040⅓ West Broadway, on the Embarcadero, corner of Harbor Drive and West Broadway; (619) 236-1212. Open 8:30 a.m. to 5 p.m. Mon through Sat year-round. In the summer, open on Sun from 11 a.m. to 5 p.m. Experienced, multilingual staff members are super helpful to all visitors, especially foreign travelers.

Chula Vista

Located in the southern tip of San Diego County, just 7 miles from downtown San Diego and 7 miles from the Mexican border, the city of Chula Vista ("beautiful view"), with a population of more than 220,000, offers an interesting variety of visitor attractions. The city was incorporated in 1911 and will be celebrating its centennial in 2011 with a variety of events, including popular annual festivities such as the Lemon Festival, Starlight Parade, and Chula Vista Rose Festival.

ARCO/US Olympic Training Center

Eight miles east of I-805 at Telegraph Canyon Road and Wuente Road, 2800 Olympic Parkway; (619) 656-1500; www.teamusa.org. A guided tour is available each Sat at 11 a.m. on a walk-in basis. Tour times are subject to change; call (619) 482-6222 for additional information. Guests can also visit Tues through Sun from 9 a.m. to 4 p.m. to walk the mile-long Conrad N. Hilton Olympic Path where the training venues can be viewed. Holidays excluded, varies seasonally.

Opened in 1995, this is the nation's first warm-weather, year-round, multisport Olympic training complex, which complements the US Olympic Committee's other training centers at Colorado Springs, Colorado, and Lake Placid, New York. The 150-acre training site includes a 50-lane archery range and support building; a 6-bay boathouse and a 2,000-meter course for canoeing, kayaking, and rowing; a cycling course and support building; a synthetic surface field hockey pitch and support building; 4 regulation grass fields and support buildings for soccer; a 4-court complex and support building for tennis; a 400-meter track and support building; and a separate, dedicated 5-acre throwing area for field events. In the Copley Visitors Center, a short film captures the dedication and emotion involved with the Olympic movement.

Knott's Soak City—San Diego

2052 Entertainment Center (next to the Amphitheater); (619) 661-7373; www.knotts.com. Open daily Memorial through Labor Day; Sat and Sun only during May, Sept, and Oct. Hours of operation vary; be sure to call ahead on your preferred day to splash. $$$$.

Comprised of 32 waterlogged acres packed with 22 of the most intense water rides imaginable and appointed with a 1950s San Diego surf theme. Body slides, tube slides, wave pools, beaches, and a kiddie play zone will supply your youth with a water wonderland filled with surprises. Food and snacks available on the premises.

Cricket Wireless Amphitheatre (formerly Coors Amphitheatre)

2050 Entertainment Circle, (619) 671-3600; www.livenation.com.

The area's first major outdoor concert facility designed specifically for music with reserved seating for 10,000 and additional seating for 10,000 on an attractively landscaped lawn. The 2010 season saw performances from Jonas Brothers and Green Day to Brad Paisley. Check schedule for current concerts.

Chula Vista Nature Center

1000 Gunpowder Point Dr.; (619) 409-5900; www.chulavistanaturecenter.org. Open 10 a.m. to 5 p.m. every day except Thanksgiving and Christmas. Free for children under age 4. $$.

This nature center has international recognition for some of its breeding programs, endangered species rescues, and educational programs and plays host to the annual Bird Festival every winter. It sits on the 316-acre Sweetwater Marsh National Wildlife Refuge and is not a natural history museum—rather a thriving place for exhibits like Raptor Row and Eagle Mesa. Owls, pelicans, gnatcatchers, and eagles are just a few of the residents. Very interactive displays and habitats your kids will not squawk at!

For More Information

Chula Vista Convention and Visitors Bureau. 233 4th Ave., 91910; (619) 426-2882. Open Mon through Fri 9 a.m. to 5 p.m.

Visitor Information Center. 750 E St., at the Bayfront Trolley Station off I-5; (619) 425-4444; www.chulavistaconvis.com. The friendly and knowledgeable staff is available to assist you at the visitor center seven days a week. *Se habla español.*

Coronado

Coronado (translated as Crown City) lies between San Diego Bay and the Pacific. Coronado Beach is recognized annually by the Travel Channel as one of the best family beaches in North America. A vast expanse of white sand greets families toting umbrellas, sand toys, beach towels, and picnic coolers for an all-day stay. Recreational activities abound with paddleball, sandcastle building, kite flying, and volleyball. Many people call Coronado an "island," but it is actually a peninsula connected to the mainland on the south by a long, narrow sandbar, the Silver Strand, that boasts a year-round population of 24,000. You will want to enter this picturesque city by way of the dramatic San Diego–Coronado Bay Bridge. This 2-mile expanse of graceful splendor dates from 1969. The Ferry Landing Marketplace has plenty of shopping and dining options to handle your family's needs if you come over by ferry (another pretty option, especially if you just plan on spending the day). We recommend you spend at least one night (there's a choice of 17 hotels, including 3 world-class resorts), and over 70 restaurants. High end boutiques, art galleries, day spas, yacht marinas, a stunning 18-hole golf course, and endless recreational opportunities complete the resort lifestyle yet with some real Midwestern feel to it! Its 1-mile-long main street, Orange Avenue, is still populated with mom-and-pop shops and patriotic parades. No surprise, since the US military has been a presence in Coronado since 1913 when the Army first came here. A decade later the Navy established Naval Air Station North Island which today occupies the entire north half of Coronado and is home to three aircraft carriers; plus at the southern end of town is the Naval Amphibious Base (home of the Navy SEALs). "The Enchanted Isle," as it's sometimes called, is worth your family's while. We love coming here and have for many years.

Bikes & Beyond

1201 1st St. at the Coronado Ferry Landing; (619) 435-7180; http://hollandsbicycles.com. Rates vary; call for current hours and schedules.

Your family's source for rental bicycles, skates, and surreys in Coronado. A super way to explore Crown City. Another source is Bikes & Beyond's sibling, Holland's Bicycles, at 977 Orange Ave. (619-435-3153).

Where to Stay

Hotel Del Coronado. 1500 Orange Ave.; (619) 435-6611 or (800) 468-3533; www .hoteldel.com. "The Del," as the hotel is known here, has attracted the rich and famous, including 13 US presidents, since its opening in 1888. The turrets, tall cupolas, hand-carved wooden pillars, and Victorian filigrees of this stunning, magnificently restored 691-room National Historic Landmark resort have served as the backdrop for many movies and films. It was the largest structure outside New York City to be electrically lighted, and the installation was supervised by Thomas Edison himself!

Today the Del offers a wide variety of accommodations to suit any family's taste and pays close attention to the needs of children and teens. Kidtopia Camp & Crafts Program, for ages 4 to 12 features bright and fun colors, underwater murals, and separate beach-themed rooms for crafts, stage performances, and playtime. There's also a fun climbing unit, a crazy funhouse mirror, and high-tech entertainment stations with computers, movie-time media, and a Dance Dance Revolution game. Kidtopia offers 3-hour camps and 1-hour programs with ocean-themed crafts and activities in the summer season and holidays. For reservations, please e-mail recreation@hoteldel .com or call (619) 522-8815. Please note that Kidtopia programs are subject to cancellation based on enrollment numbers. There is also a Vibz Teen Lounge for teens age 13 to 17.

Food and beverage options abound and children's menus flourish. Choose from the formal main dining room, 2 restaurants, and a 24-hour deli. The Del's beach provides great swimming and sunbathing, plus rental boats, windsurfers, and paddleboats. Just watch out for some of the smaller, original rooms, and you'll be in grand shape at this venerable place. $$$$

Loews Coronado Bay Resort. 4000 Coronado Bay Rd.; (619) 424-4000 or (800) 815-6397; www.loewshotels.com. Located on a private, 15-acre peninsula named Crown Island, surrounded by water and astonishing views of the downtown San Diego skyline and marina. There are 5 guest-room towers featuring 438 very deluxe guest rooms with minibars and fax machines. There are 3 outdoor pools, whirlpools, and decks; 5 tennis courts; an exercise club; and a private 80-slip marina with rentals galore—sailboats, paddleboats, Wave Runners, Jet Skis, and beach equipment.

Most important for your family is the award-winning Kids Club, offering supervised educational and entertaining options for ages 4 to 12 provided by fully licensed caregivers. Offered seven days a week, activities change daily and include nature walks, sand-castle building, face painting, arts and crafts, and G-rated video screenings. Full-day, half-day and evening programs are available. Families with more than one child get to send the second child at half price. Call for current rates. In 2010, it was named one of the 10 Best Beach Vacations in the US & Caribbean by *Parents* magazine.

Kids also enjoy the game room with pinball, video, and Ping-Pong. Also ask about the "Teen Education Package" for teens age 13 to 17.This program is a real winner. We think your family will enjoy this resort enormously. Be sure to call for special holiday programs and value packages that combine SeaWorld and other attractions' tickets, too. A very helpful staff is ready and waiting for your family. Like the slogan says, "Loews Loves Kids," and it shows! $$$$

For More Information

Coronado Visitors Center. 1100 Orange Ave.; (619) 437-8788 or (800) 622-8300; www .coronadovisitorcenter.com. Open Mon to Fri 9 a.m. to 5 p.m. and Sat and Sun 10 a.m. to 5 p.m.

La Jolla

Reversing direction from Coronado and heading up the coast along Pacific Coast Highway 1 from Mission Bay and Pacific Beach will lead you directly into the tony suburb of La Jolla (say la-ho-ya; it's Spanish for "the jewel"). This truly precious area is home of the University of California–San Diego (UCSD) and the distinguished Salk Institute for Biomedical Research. There is also some fabulous real estate along the beaches, coves, and caves, and trendy shopping and dining along downtown's Prospect Avenue, the Rodeo Drive of San Diego.

Birch Aquarium at Scripps Institution of Oceanography

2300 Expedition Way, off La Jolla Village Drive, on the campus of UCSD, overlooking La Jolla and the Pacific; (858) 534-3474; www.aquarium.ucsd.edu. Open daily 9 a.m. to 5 p.m. except Thanksgiving and Christmas. $$.

These facilities are among the most prestigious world leaders in research and instruction. Inside the aquarium you can see more than 3,000 fish in 30 tanks, including a 2-story, 70,000-gallon kelp forest with species from the waters of the West Coast, Mexico's Sea of Cortez, and the South Pacific. There is also a human-made interpretive tide pool. The innovative and interactive museum introduces the world's largest oceanographic exhibition, Exploring the Blue Planet. The bookshop has educational souvenirs and books for all

Go San Diego Card

There is so much to see and do in greater San Diego, you and your family may start feeling overwhelmed and wonder how to afford all the great attractions. Not to worry! Check out the **Go San Diego Card**—for one low price, you can get unlimited sightseeing with **free** general admission to more than 50 area attractions; save more at shops and restaurants, plus get **free** gifts at certain places; and, to make it really simple, a full-color pocket guidebook to the city, with which you can plan your itinerary. Visit the attractions at your own pace, without the hassle of buying separate tickets and paying separate admission fees. Here's how easy it is: First, purchase the Go San Diego Card in one-, two-, three-, five-, or seven-day increments. It is valid for that day and the number of consecutive calendar days that you have purchased. Second, go to a participating attraction, restaurant, or shop. Third, present your Go San Diego Card at the ticket office/desk, and you'll be granted general admission or get the stated discount. The card becomes active the first time you use it.

You can buy a Go San Diego Card directly on the website, www.gosan diegocard.com, or if you're in San Diego, at a variety of outlets—most conveniently at the International Visitor's Information Center, 1040⅓ West Broadway, at Harbor Drive (619-236-1212). This is an outstanding value and a highly recommended way for you and your family to save considerable time and money in greater San Diego. (A card is now available for Los Angeles as well. Be sure to surf the website for all details and save!)

ages on the science of the seas. This attraction strikes an educational counterpoint to the frenetic action of SeaWorld.

Museum of Contemporary Art, La Jolla

700 Prospect St.; (858) 454-3541; www.mcasd.org. Open 11 a.m. to 5 p.m. daily except Wed. Hours change seasonally. Ages 25 and under free year-round; plus Free museum admission from 5 to 7 p.m. on the third Thursday of the month. $$.

Children can enjoy the outdoor sculpture garden and food court. Everyone will view outstanding examples of minimalist, conceptual, and California art in a beautiful setting.

For More Information

La Jolla Visitor Center. 7966 Herschel Ave., Suite A; (619) 236-1212; www.lajollaby thesea.com.

North County— Coastal Communities

Just north of La Jolla along the ocean, be sure to take the drive up Pacific Coast Highway for a relaxing trip through some classic Southern California beach communities, inhabiting what the locals call North County San Diego. The charming seaside hamlets of **Solana Beach, Cardiff-by-the-Sea, Encinitas, Del Mar,** and **Leucadia** have miles of sandy beaches with rocky coves, cliffs above, and lots of friendly folks waiting to welcome you at the small shops, restaurants, and inns in these charming enclaves.

Torrey Pines State Beach Natural Reserve

12500 North Torrey Pines Rd., San Diego; (858) 755-2063; www.torreypine.org. Open daily 9 a.m. to dusk. $.

This 2,000-acre beach/reserve stretches between La Jolla and Del Mar. Enjoy one of just two places in the world where the Torrey pine tree grows (the other is Santa Rosa Island, near Santa Barbara). A visitor center has interpretive displays, and there are 8 miles of great hiking and nature trails. The beach below is a favorite for swimmers; the cliffs above are a popular take-off spot for hang gliders. Guided nature walks are offered on weekends and holidays.

Del Mar Fairgrounds & Race Track/San Diego County Fair

2260 Jimmy Durante Blvd., Del Mar; (858) 755-1141; www.sdfair.com. $$.

This is where "the turf meets the surf" with two attractions. The San Diego County Fair runs here mid-June to early July. Then thoroughbreds are off and running July through

Sept. The combined facility is a gorgeous, 350-acre historic site overlooking the Pacific. More than a hundred events are held here each year. Call for this year's schedule. At the Del Mar Thoroughbred Club (858-755-1141 or 858-793-5533; www.dmtc.com), races are held July through Sept, dark Tues. Ages 17 and younger are **free** but must be accompanied by a parent. Camp Del Mar (www.campdelmar.com) is open every race day for children ages 5 through 12 for supervised recreational activities while parents are enjoying their day at the club. What a deal!

San Diego Botanic Garden
(formerly Quail Botanical Gardens)

230 Quail Gardens Dr., just east of I-5, Encinitas; (760) 436-3036; www.sdbgarden.org. Open daily 9 a.m. to 5 p.m.; closed major holidays. $$.

The gardens contain one of the world's most diverse plant collections, including California natives, exotic tropicals, palms, and bamboo. This site was formerly owned by avid plant collector and naturalist Ruth Baird Larabee, who donated her 30-acre estate to the public in 1957. The gardens are open for self-guided tours as well as a super chance to see the resident quails in a natural bird refuge. When it opened to the public in 2003, the Seeds of Wonder became the West Coast's first interactive children's garden. It includes living topiaries and a grassy "rolling hill"—grass stains complimentary—as well as an exotic Baby Dinosaur Forest and sculpture and interactive nature-play areas. In June 2009, Hamilton Children's Garden opened, the largest interactive children's garden on the West Coast. It's kid tested and approved by the Kath family, since it's good clean fun that can get kind of dirty if you're repotting plants! The garden has myriad special events and exhibitions. For example, in 2010, there was the Butterfly Bed and Breakfast, an enclosure for caterpillars to eat, rest, and transform into butterflies—all the stages of butterfly metamorphosis.

For More Information

San Diego Coastal Chamber of Commerce. 1104 Camino del Mar; (858) 755-4844; www.sandiegocoastalchamber.com

Encinitas Chamber of Commerce and Visitors Center. 859 2nd St.; entrance on the corner of H and 2nd; (760) 753-6041 or (800) 953-6041; www.encinitaschamber.com.

Rancho Santa Fe

If you've had it with hype and just want to reeee-laaaax, the postcard-perfect Spanish colonial–style village of Rancho Santa Fe is known for its quiet, peaceful setting. Go 6 miles inland, amid magnificently fragrant eucalyptus trees. They were planted by the Santa Fe Railroad in hopes they would make great railroad ties—but the wood was too soft even to hold a spike! Today these trees provide a magnificent backdrop for the family-welcoming upscale village.

Hot-Air **Ballooning**

North County is famous for its hot-air balloon rides. Several companies offer sunrise and sunset flights that feature scenic views of the coastline, rolling hills, and reservoir-dotted valleys. Most companies fly year-round, weather permitting. Rides depart early in the morning or just before dusk and last about an hour. All pilots are FAA certified. Package and family plans are offered. Not advised for children age 8 or younger. Companies offering rides include **Skysurfer Balloon Company** (858-481-6800), **California Dreamin' Balloon Adventures** (800-373-3359), and **Sky's the Limit** (760-602-5060). Call for current prices and schedules.

Where to Eat & Stay

Inn at Rancho Santa Fe. 5951 Linea Del Cielo; (858) 756-1131 or (800) THE-INN-1; www.theinnatrsf.com. This is a classic family-owned and family-friendly inn. On the 22 manicured acres there are 23 cottages with 89 individually styled accommodations, including many family suites—all set against a magnificent backdrop of eucalyptus trees and lush gardens. The entire clan can enjoy tennis, croquet on the front lawn, or a swim in the heated outdoor pool. The spa and the gym have your basic workout gear, and you can dine in for breakfast, lunch, or dinner at Inn Fusion dining room, helmed by international award-winning executive chef John Beriker who creates the East meets West cuisine, featuring the finest and freshest local ingredients. $$$$

Carlsbad

The picturesque beach community of Carlsbad (named for the famous Karlsbad spa in Europe) is home to many coves and the Batiquitos Lagoon, as well as golf resorts, bistros, inns, and antiques emporiums. LEGOLAND California, a must-do family experience, opened here in 1999 and put this city on the family fun map forever more.

LEGOLAND California (ages 2 to 12 recommended)

1 Legoland Dr. (just off I-5; exit Cannon Road or Palomar Airport Road and follow signs); (760) 918-LEGO or (877) LEGOLAND; www.legoland.com. Open daily; hours vary seasonally; call for times and special package pricing. $$$$.

Since opening in 1999 to well-deserved and continued acclaim (Best Children's Park in the World award, *Amusement Today* magazine; one of the best theme parks in the world, Forbes.com), this 128-acre theme park features more than 50 interactive attractions and rides that are "kid powered," where kids push, pull, steer, pedal, squirt, climb, or build their way through myriad activities. In 2008 the park welcomed Sea Life LEGOLAND California, a 2-story, 36,000-square-foot aquarium featuring play zones, fun facts, quiz trails, and marine exhibits designed to educate children about life under the sea. In March 2008 a forgotten city, Land of Adventures, debuted with four new rides and attractions, including Lost Kingdom Adventure, the park's first dark ride; Beetle Bouncers; Pharaoh's Revenge play area filled with catapulting foam balls; and Cargo Ace. In 2007 Miniland welcomed Miniland Las Vegas, built out of more than two million bricks. Pirate Shores, the park's largest expansion, opened in 2006 with four water-based attractions: Splash Battle, Treasure Falls, Swabbies Deck, and the Soak-N-Sail giant play structures. Other activities and attractions to enjoy include Block of Fame (a gallery of famous busts made of LEGOs), Coastersaurus (a Jurassic-themed roller coaster), Dig Those Dinos (an interactive archaeological site), Fun Town Fire Academy (families can test their teamwork), LEGO TECHNIC Coaster, BIONICLE Blaster, Captain Cranky's Challenge, and Knights' Tournament. Be sure to schedule a day to really enjoy LEGOLAND at your youngsters' pace.

LEGOLAND Water Park Debuts

The LEGOLAND Water Park celebrated its grand opening on May 28, 2010 with a big splash! It is located at the north end of LEGOLAND California adjacent to Fun Town. The centerpiece is a 45-foot-tall tower designed to immerse children in the creative world of LEGO. Four main water slides originate with this tower: Orange Rush, a family tube slide where up to four people can ride together down a 312-foot-long curving track on an 11-foot in diameter half pipe; Twin Chasers, 2 side-by-side enclosed red tube slides that stretch nearly 130 feet and pour into a wading area below; and Splash Out, an open body slide that invites you to slide 240 feet and "splash out" into the water below. Other activities include Build-A-Raft River; DUPLO Splash Safari, a water play area designed especially for toddlers; Joker Soaker, a fun interactive platform in the wade pool where kids can aim water cannons at each other; and the Imagination Station, interactive, educational, and imaginative fun where kids can build bridges, dams, and cities out of DUPLO bricks and test them against the flow of water. When you get hungry or thirsty, the Beach Front Grill is a quick service restaurant specializing in gourmet burritos, wraps, and salads. Admission price for the Water Park is a $12 upgrade from the standard LEGOLAND California ticket or you can purchase Park Hopper tickets and Resort Hopper tickets.

Did You **Know?**

There are more than 15,000 LEGO models in the park created from more than 35 million LEGO bricks. These models range from a Brontosaurus named Bronte (made of more than 2 million LEGO bricks) to a tiny rabbit in a magician's hat in Miniland Las Vegas made of just four LEGO bricks. There are 22 LEGO models throughout LEGOLAND Water Park. Five of them are jumbo LEGO friends who stand 6 feet tall and weigh about 250 pounds.

Biplane Rides and Aerial Dogfights/Barnstorming Adventures, Ltd.

6743 Montia Court; (760) 438-7680 or (800) SKY-LOOP; www.barnstorming.com. Open year-round during daylight hours. Call for prevailing winds, schedules, and fees. $$$$

Open-air flights in vintage cockpit biplanes and mock aerial combat in military-style aircraft could make for an unforgettable family adventure. All pilots are FAA certified, and safety comes first, followed by fun! Since 1994, this family-owned business based at Palomar Airport has been committed to preserving and sharing aviation history. Named one of the 101 Top Things to Do by the Travel Channel. Tell "Tailspin Tom" and "Cash Register Kate" we sent you.

Flower Fields at Carlsbad Ranch

East of I-5 at Palomar Airport Road and Paseo del Norte; (760) 431-0352; www.theflower fields.com. Open Mar through May generally, during daylight hours. $$

The only commercial ranunculus (buttercup) field in the world that is open to the public. Wear comfortable walking shoes as you and the kids traipse through more than 50 acres of gently sloping hillside covered with a floral rainbow.

Where to Eat

Tip Top Meats & Deli. 6118 Paseo Del Norte, just off I-5 at Palomar Airport Road; (760) 438-2620. www.tiptopmeats.com. Open daily 6 a.m. to 8 p.m. Don't be fooled by the name—this local favorite offers the best value meals for miles around. A full breakfast starts at $4.98 (1 egg, home-fried potatoes, toast, and ham, bacon, or sausage); burgers are $3.49; dinners start at $7.98 (prime rib roast, potatoes, cabbage, sauerkraut, soup or salad, and roll is only $9.98). Just enter through the market and proceed to the deli area, where you'll place your order. Pick a seat in the dining room and wait for your number to be called—and dig in to a tip-top meal! Say hi to owner "Big John" Haedrich for us. $

Where to Stay

Grand Pacific Palisades Resort & Hotel. 5805 Armada Dr. (exit Palomar Airport Road east from I-5); (760) 827-3200; www.grand pacificpalisades.com. Across the street from LEGOLAND, overlooking the Carlsbad Flower Fields and the Pacific Ocean, this should be your family's headquarters for affordable fun in North County. You can leave your car in the hotel parking lot and walk across the street to the side entrance to LEGOLAND, the new Water Park, and Sea Life Aquarium. Return during the day for naps and lunch breaks—an ideal way to plan your stay. The contemporary Mediterranean architecture of the hotel encloses 90 spacious hotel rooms and 161 fully equipped vacation villas with full kitchens. A full-service restaurant, room service, 2 inviting outdoor heated pools and whirlpools, concierge services, a social activity director, a game room, and a fitness center—all staffed with friendly, helpful people—make this a grand place! $$$

For More Information

Carlsbad Convention and Visitors Bureau. 400 Carlsbad Village Dr.; (760) 434-6093 or (800) 227-5722; www.visitcarlsbad .com.

Oceanside

Bustling Oceanside, at the mouth of the San Luis Rey Valley, is home base to the US Marine Corps' Camp Pendleton (approximately 125,000 acres—the largest of all USMC amphibious training bases—www.pendleton.usmc.mil) and the ever-popular Municipal Pier—California's longest, which planks in at a whopping 1,942 feet. Check out the great fishing, seafood restaurants, and ice-cream shop located on this wooden wonder.

California Surf Museum

312 Pier View Way; (760) 721 6876; www.surfmuseum.org. Open daily from noon to 4 p.m. (unless the surf is awesome!). Call for special events and seasonal operating hours. **Free** admission; donations appreciated, dudes.

Everything you wanted to know about surfing—for the novice to learn and for the experienced to enjoy. A real kicked-back gem since 1986 (since early 2009 located in a renovated drug store building now only 3 blocks from the beach).

Helgren's Sportfishing Center

315 Harbor Dr. South; (760) 722-2133; www.helgrensportfishing.com. Open year-round; call for times and fees. $$$$.

Take your choice of charter fishing vessels—half-day, full-day, and overnight trip options— as well as whale-watching cruises between Dec and Feb. This is the best place for all your ocean-going boating/fishing needs.

Mission San Luis Rey

4050 Mission Ave., 4 miles east of town on Highway 76; (760) 757-3651; www.sanluisrey .org. Open Mon through Sat 10 a.m. to 4:30 p.m. and Sun noon to 4:30 p.m. $.

This "king of the missions" is number 18 in the famous chain of 21 California churches begun by Franciscan Father Junípero Serra. It's also the largest and has wooden double-dome construction. The museum houses exhibits relating to the colorful history of the area and includes artifacts from Native American, Spanish Mission, Mexican

Secularization, and American Military periods. Picnicking facilities are available on the attractive grounds.

Where to Eat

101 Cafe. 631 South Coast Highway; (619) 722-5220; www.101cafe.net. Open daily from 6:30 a.m. to midnight. Established in 1928, this family diner serves up traditional American-style home-cooked meals. The hamburgers are the best, and the milk shakes a dream. Bountiful kids menu for the 10-and-under crowd. There are historic photos all over the walls. Old-fashioned cash only (but an ATM is available on-site). $

Where to Stay

Oceanside Marina Suites. 2008 Harbor Dr. North; (760) 722-1561 or (800) 252-2033; www.omihotel.com. Secluded at the tip of Oceanside's bustling harbor, the inn offers 64 one- and two-bedroom units with kitchens. Wonderful water views; many units have fireplaces and balconies. A pool, spa, and barbecue area are other highlights. This perfect family waterfront stopover is close to many North County attractions. $$

For More Information

California Welcome Center–Oceanside. 928 North Coast Highway; (760) 721-1101; www.visitoceanside.org or www.visitcwc .com/oceanside.

Escondido & Vicinity

Inland from the Pacific, the north-south I-5 and I-15 run several miles apart, embracing gently rolling hillsides, forests, and streams that will make you pinch yourself and wonder, "Are we still in California?" In the center of it all is the city of Escondido. Other scenic communities scattered through inland North County include Fallbrook, San Marcos, Poway, Rancho Bernardo, La Costa, Vista, and Valley Center.

Escondido History Center

321 North Broadway in Grape Day Park, Escondido; (760) 743-8207; www.escondidohistory .org. Open Tues through Sat 1 to 4 p.m. Free.

Includes a Victorian house, Indian *metate* (grinding stones), a circa-1888 Santa Fe Railroad depot, Wagonworks Shop, and the Bandy Blacksmith Shop.

California Center for the Arts, Escondido

340 North Escondido Blvd., Escondido; (760) 839-4138 or (800) 988-4253; www.artcenter .org. Call for current programs, schedules, and fees. $; children 11 and under free.

This center, located on a twelve-acre campus, has an art museum, a 1,500-seat concert hall, and art education programs for young people in a world-class facility. Also here is the Escondido Children's Museum (760-233-7755; www.escondidochildrensmuseum .org). Open Tues through Sat 10 a.m. to 4 p.m.; Sun 12 noon to 4 p.m.; closed Mon. The

4,500-square-foot space houses Wildlife Tree House, Bubble Tower, and River in the Garden exhibits.

Iceoplex

555 North Tulip, Escondido; (760) 489-5550; www.iceoplexescondido.com. Open daily at 8:30 a.m.; closing times vary. $$.

This is a massive facility that boasts 2 Olympic-size ice-skating rinks, a fitness center, a spa, an Olympic lap pool, a Jacuzzi, a sauna, and a training room. You can chill out here after all your fun in the sun!

San Diego Zoo Safari Park
(formerly Wild Animal Park)

15500 San Pasqual Valley Rd., located 5 miles east of I-15 on Highway 78, just outside Escondido; (760) 747-8702 or (760) 234-6541; www.sandiegozoo.org/park. Open daily beginning at 9 a.m. Closing times vary by season. $$$$.

On 2,100 acres of prime sanctuary land, and without a doubt the showpiece of North County, the park was designed originally as a breeding facility for the San Diego Zoo (its sister facility). You and your family will want to spend a full day here to see more than 3,000 wild animals roaming freely in settings that resemble their native habitats. The Journey into Africa Tour, aboard an open-air tram inspired by the legendary safari trains of Africa, brings you eye-level with white rhinoceros, Cape buffalo, Roosevelt's gazelles, and African crowned cranes. The African Express runs on eco-friendly biodiesel as it traverses the perimeter of the park's three expansive African field enclosures: Lion Camp, Heart of Africa, and Nairobi Village.

You will see large herds of antelopes, gazelles, deer, rhinos, and exotic sheep and goats. Flocks of flamingos, pelicans, cranes, geese, ducks, herons, ostriches, vultures, and storks live in the big enclosures as well. Even the single-species exhibits—herds of African and Asian elephants, families of gorillas and chimpanzees—are large and natural, such as a 1-acre lion habitat. There is also DINOS, a life-size robotic dinosaur display, and the bird show Frequent Flyers.

The 17-acre Nairobi Village holds most of the visitor facilities, including restaurants, gift shops, and picnic areas. Plan to attend the wild animal show and elephant demonstrations held here. And make some new friends in the petting kraal.

The Kilimanjaro Hiking Trail is a 1.75-mile walking safari where you can see rhinos, tigers, elephants, cheetahs, and giraffes up close and personal. Special Photo Caravan Safari Tours take you right into the middle of the habitats in a large, open-air truck for an additional fee. We cannot recommend this activity highly enough. The chance to pet a rhino or feed a giraffe as it bends over your head is a thrill of a lifetime. Other special experience options include the Cheetah Run Safari, Sleepovers (for kids and adults, too), VIP Tours, Cats & Carnivores Tour, Savanna Safari, and the Vets Center Tour. We really were impressed and amazed here. Do not miss this! (Note that the park's name was changed from the previous Wild Animal Park in 2010.)

Kit Carson Park/Queen Califia's Magical Circle

3333 Bear Valley Pkwy., Escondido; (760) 839-4691; www.queencalifia.org or www.ci.escondido.ca.us/events/califia. Open from sunrise to sunset daily. Free.

The park was named after Christopher "Kit" Carson, the famous scout who guided Capt. John C. Fremont over the Sierra Nevada during an exploration expedition. This large regional day-use park features 100 developed acres and 185 undeveloped acres, beautiful walking/hiking trails, ball fields, lighted tennis courts, soccer fields, 3,000-seat outdoor amphitheater, 3 ponds, tot lot/playground, shaded picnic areas with tables and barbecues, Sports Center complex with pro shop, 20,000-square-foot skate park, 2 full-size roller hockey arenas, and 1 full-size and 1 mini soccer arena.

Opened in 2003, Queen Califia's Magical Circle in the Iris Sankey Arboretum is the only American sculpture garden created by the renowned French-American artist Niki de Saint Phalle. The garden's outside diameter measures 120 feet and is encircled by an undulating wall across which slither large, playful serpents decorated in colorfully patterned mosaics. The Snake Wall has one entrance into the garden—a mazelike passageway whose walls and floor are also decorated in bold patterns of black, white, and mirrored tiles. The garden takes its name from the legendary black Amazon queen, Califia, who was believed to rule a terrestrial island paradise of gold and riches. Be sure to include a visit to this amazing, unique structure to indulge your family's magical senses.

The Wave Waterpark

161 Recreation Dr. off Broadway, Vista, 7 miles inland on Highway 78; (760) 940-WAVE; www.thewavewaterpark.com. Open May through Sept; call for daily schedule, always subject to change. $$$.

The state-of-the-art wave maker is called Flow Rider, and your family can body surf all day long and never have to wait for that perfect wave—because they're all perfect! Four wild water slides, an underwater playground, an Olympic-size pool, and a picnic area make this inland water spot a great experience. It's a great value, too.

San Pasqual Battlefield State Historic Park and Museum

15808 San Pasqual Valley Rd., Escondido; (760) 737-2201; www.parks.ca.gov. Open Fri through Sun 10 a.m. to 5 p.m. Free.

The museum honors those who participated in the 1846 San Pasqual Battle during the Mexican-American War. See videos and exhibits regarding that historic time.

Antique Gas and Steam Engine Museum

2040 North Santa Fe Ave., Vista; (760) 941-1791 or (800) 5-TRACTOR; www.agsem.com. Open daily from 10 a.m. to 4 p.m. $; children 5 and under free.

Weekend threshing bees in June and October are really fun! Our kids were impressed with the blacksmith. Catch a bit of history at the museum. There are 40 acres of turn-of-the-last-century farming equipment, all maintained in working order. Kids can see actual corn, wheat, and oat crops harvested from the field and into the kitchen—what a concept!

Where to Eat

Bates Nut Farm. 15954 Woods Valley Rd., 3 miles east of Valley Center; (760) 749-3333; www.batesnutfarm.biz. Open daily 9 a.m. to 5 p.m. This is a family favorite because of its **free** petting zoo, shady picnic grounds, fresh produce, and terrifically tasty array of fruits, nuts, and candy. There are arts and crafts fairs each Apr and Nov; pumpkins predominate in Oct, and fir trees in Dec. $

Where to Stay

Welk Resort, Museum, and Dinner Theatre. 8860 Lawrence Welk Dr., 7 miles north of Escondido off I-15; (760) 749-3000 or (800) 932-9355; www.welksandiego.com. This 1,000-acre hideaway has 146 one- and two-bedroom suites (all with kitchenettes or full kitchens), on-site golf course, tennis, 5 swimming pools, spa, Canyon Grille Restaurant, and Boulder Springs Water Park & Club House. Museum (**free** admission) opens daily at 10 a.m.; closing times vary. Dinner-theater performances offer musical variety for the whole family. Call for times, programs, and ticket prices. Not just for Grandma and Grandpa, with their memories of the legendary band leader, it's a great place for that multigenerational reunion. (But the suites are on 3 floors with no elevators, so if you don't want the extra steps, be sure to ask for the ground floor!) $$$$

For More Information

San Diego North Convention and Visitors Bureau—Visitor Center. 360 North Escondido Blvd., Escondido; (760) 745-4741 or (800) 848-3336; www.sandiegonorth.com.

Temecula Valley

The town of Temecula was founded in 1882 and served as an important stop on the Butterfield Stagecoach Route between San Bernardino and San Diego. The name Temecula means "sun shining through the sea mist," in Luiseno tribal lore. Today it is a fast-growing community nestled between San Diego and Riverside Counties with some award-winning vineyards, more than a dozen wineries, horse ranches, seven golf courses, harvest festivals, and antiques shops.

Old Town Temecula

Front Street between Moreno Road and Third Street. Open daily, hours vary. Old Town Visitor Center is located at 28464 Old Town Front St.; www.oldtowntemecula.com.

Get a walking-tour map and visit the Welty Building, jail, First National Bank, and G. Machado's store. Many of these historic buildings are antiques malls now, sure to delight shoppers. But there's no predicting how long they will grab your kids' attention (before they start acting like the proverbial bull in a china shop). Probably a half hour will do it.

Mission San Antonio de Pala Asistencia

Pala Mission Rd., north of Highway 76, Pala; (760) 742-1600. Open Tues through Sun 10 a.m. to 3 p.m. $.

A branch of the Mission San Luis Rey, it was built in 1816 as part of an inland chain of missions that provided assistance to the main ones. The chapel, gardens, and mineral room have all been restored. Very quaint, with a still-active parish.

Where to Eat & Stay

Pala Mesa Resort. 2001 Old Hwy. 395, off I-15, Fallbrook; (760) 728-5881 or (800) 722-4700; www.palamesa.com. This impressive enclave on 270 acres is ideal for families, with its 133 connecting rooms, views of rolling hills, 18-hole golf course, and irresistible family-size swimming pool. You'll find plenty of outdoor recreation, including horseshoes, croquet, volleyball, tennis, badminton, a whirlpool, and a spa. AquaTerra restaurant is open 6 a.m. to 2 p.m. and 5:30 to 10 p.m. and has a nice golf-course view. The early California decor will make you appreciate the reasonably priced children's menu even more. $$$$

Temecula Creek Inn. 44501 Rainbow Canyon Rd., Temecula; (909) 694-1000 or (800) 962-7335; www.temeculacreek inn.com. Opened in 1969 and beautifully enhanced in 2008, with 130 deluxe rooms and suites overlooking lush grounds that feature Native American art. Golf is king and queen here, with 27 holes (rated four stars by *Golf Digest*); plus tennis, swimming pools, fitness studio, and Temet Grill. Excellent packages for families. $$$$

Warner Springs Ranch. 31652 Hwy. 79, Box 10, Warner Springs; (760) 782-4200; www.warnersprings.com. With 25,000 acres nestled in the foothills of Palomar Mountain, Warner Springs Ranch offers plenty of room to roam. Stay in one of the 240 cozy bungalows (most with fireplaces); no phones or TVs. Miles of scenic walking, horseback riding, and hiking trails. Three pools (one is heated with hot spring water), 18-hole championship golf course, basic health spa, plus a private airport and glider school. High marks for the equestrian program, which is very kid-friendly (kids 8 and older on trail rides; ages 6 and older for riding lessons in the arena; pony rides/animal-care sessions for really young children). The ranch offers a variety of stuff designed specifically for kids: arts and crafts, nature walks, movie nights, a game room, and more. There are no streetlights, so bring a flashlight here! Outstanding activities schedule means your kids will never say they're bored! $$$$

For More Information

Temecula Valley Convention & Visitors Bureau. 26790 Ynez Court, Temecula; (951) 676-5090 or (866) 676-5090; www.temecula cvb.com

The Mountains (Back Country)

Don't miss the eastern portion of San Diego County, affectionately known by locals as the Back Country. Bisected by three main roads—Highways 76, 78, and 79—the Back Country offers mountain peaks rising more than 6,000 feet, dazzling foliage in fall, snowfalls in winter (and sometimes even in April!), and desert flora year-round. This land of contrasts has fabulous hiking, biking, camping, and fishing options for your active times and plenty of bucolic beauty for your off-tour hours.

Palomar Mountain Observatory and State Park

From Oceanside, off Highway 76 (about 11 miles inland on County Road S6); (760) 742-2119; www.astro.caltech.edu/palomarnew. Open daily 9 a.m. to 4 p.m. Free. Self-guided tours.

For a grand perspective, ascend Mount Palomar (elevation 6,140 feet) to the observatory. Inside this striking white-domed structure, you'll find one of the world's largest scientific instruments—the 200-inch Hale Telescope. You and the kids can watch its inner workings and see a video at the museum nearby describing all the functions of this scientific wonder. Along with the observatory, enjoy the completely uncrowded state park (760-742-3462 for general information or www.parks.ca.gov), with wildlife, fishing, camping, and hiking trails. Coniferous forests cover much of the 1,862 acres, in contrast to the dry lowlands surrounding the mountain.

For More Information

San Diego East Visitors Bureau and the California Welcome Center–Alpine. Located in the Viejas Outlet Shopping Center, 5005 Willows Rd., Suite 208 and Suite H110, Alpine; (619) 445 0180 or (800) 463-0668; www.visitsandiegoeast.com. California Welcome Center's hours are 10 a.m. to 5 p.m. Mon through Fri and 11 a.m. to 4 p.m. Sun at Suite H110.

Julian & Vicinity

For a piece of living history, continue toward the interior of North County along Highway 78, and you'll arrive at Julian. In the hills only 60 miles inland from Oceanside, Julian lies in the heart of the Cleveland National Forest. Beautiful downtown Julian looks much as it did more than a century ago. It was founded in 1870 by settler Drew Bailey and his cousin Mike Julian, hence the name. A gold strike yielding nearly $5 million made the town of Julian famous back in the 1870s. When the gold rush ended, apples became the cash crop of choice. Now Julian is famous for hillside acres of apple orchards (Julian is known as Southern California's apple capital) and beautiful fields of spring wildflowers. The 2-block-long Main Street and surrounding area has everything you'll want within easy walking distance. Yes, you are still in Southern California—just an early-1900s version!

Eagle Mining Company

North end of C Street, downtown; (760) 765-0036. Open daily 10 a.m. to 3 p.m., weather permitting. $$.

Seeing Julian in Slow Motion

Our favorite way to see Julian is by way of **Country Carriages** (Pickup location is at the corner of Washington and Main Streets; 760-765-1471), located right downtown on Main Street. To get your bearings on the area, begin with a ride on a horse-drawn carriage, all hitched up and ready to go. A 30-minute clop-clop trip around town costs $30 per couple with 2 children—worth it for the history lesson alone. After your buggy ride, stay in the old-fashioned mood with an ice-cream treat at **Ye Olde Soda Fountain/ Miner's Diner** (760-765-3753) at the Julian Drug Store. Kids of all ages love the chance to sit on the old-fashioned stools and see how such classics as an egg cream or black cow are made by hand (and you can grab breakfast and lunch here, too).

Guided tours through this old gold mine will show you how those shiny, precious flakes were extracted from Mother Earth. A fascinating journey into the mountainside for the entire family.

Cuyamaca Rancho State Park

15027 Hwy. 79, 15 miles south of Julian; (760) 765-0755; www.parks.ca.gov and www .cuyamaca.us. Open daily year-round. $$.

Comprised of 26,000 acres of beautiful terrain include pine, oak, and cedar trees; meadows; lakes; streams; and the Green Valley waterfall. Explore via 100 miles of trails for mountain biking, hiking, and horseback riding. You can see more than a hundred species of birds in the area, or perhaps even a mule deer or coyote. Lake Cuyamaca, operated by the Helix Water District, is 2 miles north of Paso Picacho campground and offers boating and fishing. Interpretive programs are offered during the summer season. The park has a visitor center, gift shop, and a museum depicting the gold rush days at the Stonewall Mine during its 1886–91 peak. We love just going for a simple picnic.

Mission Santa Ysabel Asistencia

23013 Hwy. 79, Santa Ysabel; (760) 765-0810. Open daily 7 a.m. to dusk. Free.

You can take a self-guided tour of this charming satellite mission built in 1818. There is also an Indian burial ground and museum. It's a pleasant stopover on your way to Julian.

Where to Eat

Dudley's Bakery and Snack Bar. on Highway 78 in downtown Santa Ysabel; (760) 765-0488; www.dudleysbakery.com. Open Mon 9 a.m. to 1 p.m., Thurs to Sun 9 a.m. to 5 p.m. Closed on Tues and Wed. Hours can vary seasonally. Here you will find an incredible selection of 17 famous breads, plus cookies, pies, and yummy pastries since 1963. This is a great place to have breakfast or lunch with your family and pick up treats for later. Don't miss this place. It's usually pretty busy, a testament to the goodness!! $

The Julian Grille. 2224 Main St.; (760) 765-0173. Housed in a homey cottage, the restaurant serves lunch daily and dinner Tues through Sat. The menu features steaks, pasta, and seafood your family will savor. $$

Where to Stay

Pine Hills Lodge. 2960 La Posada Way, Julian; (760) 765-1100; www.pinehillslodge

.com. A variety of rustic and very nicely refurbished accommodations are offered in 16 lodge and cabin units at reasonable rates. Brunch is served every Sunday on the 5 Cedars Deck from 9 a.m. to 2 p.m.; only $14.95 for adults, $10.95 for children 10 and under. It's a simple place for your backcountry family retreat. $$

For More Information

Julian Chamber of Commerce. 2129 Main St.; (760) 765-1857; www.julianca.com.

Borrego Springs

This peaceful resort community is located inside the Anza-Borrego Desert State Park and has a wide variety of camping, dining, golf, and recreation options. The community hosts a Grapefruit Festival in April. The Borrego Days Festival in October includes a parade and an arts and crafts fair to welcome back snowbirds for the warm winter season. We think the absolutely most beautiful time to visit the area is during the spring, when desert wildflowers are in magnificent bloom.

Anza-Borrego Desert State Park

Approximately 2 hours east of downtown San Diego, just west of County Road S22 and surrounding the quaint town of Borrego Springs. The visitor center is located at 200 Palm Canyon Dr.; (760) 767-4205 for general information or (760) 767-4684 for recorded wildflower information; www.parks.ca.gov. Open daily Oct through May 9 a.m. to 5 p.m.; rest of year open sporadically—call for current schedule. Camping fees vary, and reservations are strongly suggested. $.

This is the biggest state park in California, with 600,000 acres of wildly rugged mountains (highest elevation 6,000 feet) and desert (elevation 40 feet), along with flora, fauna, and fossils dating back 540 million years. You will see mesquite, yucca, and smoke trees; cacti; and thousands of native plants and flowers, as well as the chance to see roadrunner, golden eagles, kit foxes, mule deer, and bighorn sheep as well as iguanas, chuckwallas, and the red diamond rattlesnake.

Start your visit at the magnificent 7,000-square-foot visitor center, built into the hillside, with exhibits, maps, natural history books, a 20-minute video presentation, and volunteers who are eager to help your family plan your desert experience. There are nature walks, campfire programs, fossil programs, and guided hikes to choose from. The park is geared for off-road travel and exploration. The most dramatic and popular attraction is the spring wildflowers. Our favorite hikes include the Borrego Palm Canyon Nature Trail, a gentle 3-mile round-trip, as well as the Pygmy Trail, a 1-mile round-trip that leads to 50 short palm trees. Among the park's many other points of interest: the Box Canyon Historical Monument, Coyote Canyon, the Culp Valley Overlook, the Elephant Tree Discovery Trail, the Mason Valley Cactus Garden, and the Vallecita Stagecoach Station.

For More Information

Borrego Springs Chamber of Commerce and Visitors Bureau. 786 Palm Canyon Dr., P.O. Box 420, Borrego Springs 92004; (760) 767-5555 or (800) 559-5524; www.borregospringschamber.com.

Annual Events

Note: Contact information can change from year to year. Your best bet is to call tourism offices for the cities or areas listed to determine the most current and detailed information. Keep in mind that dates are always subject to change, too.

The Central Coast

The Central Coast covers a lot of wonderful territory, but your Southern California family fun has only just begun! These events are subject to change without notice. Please call ahead.

JANUARY

Winter Bird Festival—Morro Bay
(805) 772-4467 or (800) 231-0592

Guided tours of estuary and surrounding areas; plentiful bird-watching. **Free.**

International Film Festival—Santa Barbara
(805) 963-0023

Premieres and screenings of independent US and international films; gala opening, celebrity awards, panels, and seminars by film professionals. Admission fees vary.

FEBRUARY

Whale Celebration—Ventura
(805) 644-0169

Celebrate the annual gray whale migration with music and entertainment, environmental booths, and touch tanks in Ventura Harbor Village. **Free.**

Celebration of the Whales—Oxnard
(805) 385-7545 or (800) 269-6273

Weekend celebration highlights gray whale migration; full-day trips, arts and crafts, and photo exhibit. **Free.**

MARCH

Free Museum Day—Santa Ynez Valley
(800) 742-2843

All eight museums in the area offer **free** admission on the first Sat of March each year.

Taste of Solvang—Solvang
(805) 688-6144 or (800) 458-6765

This annual food and wine festival features a dessert reception showcase, walking smorgasbord, wine tasting room walking tour, a BYO Picnic in the Park and live entertainment. Fees vary.

APRIL

I Madonnari Italian Street Painting Festival—San Luis Obispo
(805) 781-2777

Event features sidewalk and street pastel creations. **Free.**

Children's Day in the Plaza—San Luis Obispo
(805) 781-2777

More than 40 booths featuring spin art, water toys, face painting, and a petting zoo; singers, dancers, clowns, and jugglers. **Free.**

Presidio Day—Santa Barbara
(805) 966-1279

Celebration of early California arts, crafts, and music at historic 1782 Presidio Park. **Free.**

MAY

Garden Festival—San Luis Obispo
(805) 781-2777

Floral displays and sale at judges' show with speakers, exhibits, demonstrations, children's activities, music, and commercial and gardening booths. **Free.**

California Strawberry Festival—Oxnard
(805) 385-7578

Strawberry foods, contests, music, and arts and crafts.

I Madonnari Street Painting Festival—Santa Barbara
(805) 569-3873

More than 200 local artists and children create chalk paintings in front of the Old Mission; Italian market and entertainment. **Free.**

JUNE

Summer Solstice Celebration—Santa Barbara
(805) 965-3396

See complete description in Central Coast chapter. **Free.**

Seafest—Ventura
(805) 644-0169

Celebrate the beginning of summer with entertainment booths, environmental instruction, a chowder cook-off, and a children's harbor land and show.

Elks Rodeo and Parade—Santa Maria
(805) 922-6006

Calf roping, bull riding, bronco riding, steer wrestling, and barrel racing.

JULY

Check local city listings for Independence Day parades and fireworks and festivals.

Santa Barbara County Fair—Santa Maria
(805) 925-8824

Country fair includes carnival, produce, livestock, and western music.

AUGUST

California Mid-State Fair—Paso Robles
(805) 239-0655 or (800) 909-FAIR

The Central Coast fair includes five stages of entertainment featuring top names daily, PRCA rodeo, Destruction Derby, animal exhibits, arts and crafts, a working farm, wine tasting, pig races, and nightly dancing. Admission fees vary.

Annual Salsa Festival—Oxnard
(805) 483-4542

Salsa-making contest, 5K run, arts and crafts, dancing, music, and a carnival for children. **Free.**

Old Spanish Days (Fiesta)—Santa Barbara
(805) 962-8101

See complete description in Central Coast chapter. **Free.**

Ventura County Fair—Ventura
(805) 648-3376 or (800) 333-2989

Traditional county fair features top-name entertainment, exhibits, livestock, motor sports, rodeo, food, and fireworks. Admission fees vary.

SEPTEMBER

Taste of the Town—Santa Barbara
(805) 892-5556

More than 80 local restaurants and wineries provide tastes of their best fare in the beautiful Riviera Research Park overlooking the city. Always held the first Sunday after Labor Day as a benefit for the local branch of the Arthritis Foundation. Ticket prices vary.

Simi Valley Days—Simi Valley
(805) 581-4280

Fair features a carnival, hoedown, barn dance, horse show, parade, 5K and 10K runs, food, and entertainment. Admission fees vary.

Danish Days—Solvang
(805) 688-6636 or (800) 468-6765

Annual celebration of Solvang's rich Danish heritage features Danish folk dancing, music, food, parade, and entertainment. **Free.**

Aloha Beach Festival—Ventura.
(805) 200-8674

Three stages of entertainment, food, a surfing contest, and beach volleyball. **Free.**

Los Alamos Old Days—Los Alamos
(805) 344-1717

Founded in 1876, this three-day weekend celebrates the town's western heritage with entertainment, barbeques, dances, peddler's mart, classic car show, and Sunday morning parade. **Free.**

Book Fair—West Hollywood
(323) 848-6515

Founded by the City of West Hollywood as a means of encouraging reading, writing, and literacy and to heighten the community's awareness of books. More than 300 authors, 100 exhibitors, and 25,000 guests attend the event.

OCTOBER

California Avocado Festival—Carpinteria
(805) 684-0038

Annual avocado celebration includes food, arts and crafts, music, and a flower show. **Free.**

Lemon Festival—Goleta
(805) 967-4618

Family event featuring a lemon pie–eating contest, food, arts and crafts show, children's activities, farmers' market, and entertainment. **Free.**

NOVEMBER

Holiday Walk and Light the Downtown—Paso Robles
(805) 238-4103

Lighted trees, candlelight caroling, farmers' market, and Santa and Mrs. Claus. **Free.**

DECEMBER

Julefest—Solvang
(805) 688-6144

Month long Danish Village celebration features thousands of twinkling lights, carolers around town, tree lighting ceremony, parade, Santa Lucia Pageant and Nativity Pageant, open houses, and concerts. **Free.**

Holiday Boat Parade of Lights—Santa Barbara
(805) 897-1962

Colorful parade of decorated lighted boats on Santa Barbara waterfront plus **free** festival on Stearns Wharf.

Holiday Parade—San Luis Obispo
(805) 541-0286

Holiday celebration includes floats, marching bands, youth organizations, and Santa Claus. **Free.**

Ventura Harbor Parade of Lights—Ventura
(805) 644-0169 or (800) 333-2989

Colorful parade of decorated lighted boats on Ventura Harbor. **Free.**

Holiday Boat Parade of Lights—Oxnard
(805) 389-9495 or (800) 269-6273

Lighted boat parade in the Channel Islands Harbor, holiday activities, and entertainment. **Free.**

Greater Los Angeles

The following list of Greater Los Angeles–area events is subject to change without notice. Please always call ahead to verify.

JANUARY

Tournament of Roses Parade—Pasadena
(626) 449-4100

World-class parade of flowers features music and fantasy. The annual Rose Bowl collegiate football game follows.

Dr. Martin Luther King Jr. Day Parade and Festival—Long Beach
(562) 570-6816

Parade, entertainment, and celebrations. **Free.**

Martin Luther King Jr. Celebration—Santa Monica
(310) 434-4209

Interfaith celebrations with music, dramatic readings, and inspirational messages. **Free.**

FEBRUARY

Golden Dragon Parade—Los Angeles
(213) 617-0396

Chinese New Year parade. Colorful floats, multicultural performances, arts and crafts. **Free.**

APRIL

Los Angeles Times Festival of Books—Los Angeles
(213) 237-5000; www.latimes.com

More than 800 exhibitors and 600 authors, speakers, and celebrity presentations, plus a giant children's area, all take over the UCLA campus for the weekend. For the love of reading, don't miss this! **Free.**

Toyota Grand Prix—Long Beach
(562) 436-3645 or (800) 4LB-STAY

International field of world-class drivers and high-performance racecars negotiate the tight turns of the city in heated wheel-to-wheel competition.

Pasadena Spring Art Show—Pasadena
(626) 795-9311

Fine arts and crafts, children's amusement area, international food court. **Free.**

MAY

Cinco de Mayo—Los Angeles
(213) 485-6855

Celebrate Mexico's 1862 victory over French forces in Pueblo, Mexico, with popular and traditional music, cultural presentations, dancing, and ethnic cuisine. **Free.**

Old Pasadena Summer Fest—Pasadena
(626) 797-6803

Festival includes Taste of Pasadena, arts and crafts, children's activities, jazz festival, and entertainment. **Free.**

JUNE

International Film Festival—Burbank.
(818) 438-4736; www.burbankfilmfestival.org

Capturing its home city's rich history and movie-making magic by promoting fresh pieces of cinematic art by from up-and-coming filmmakers from around the world.

Theater and Arts Festival—North Hollywood
(818) 508-5115 or (818) 508-5156

More than 15 theaters host 2 days of live theater and entertainment, arts and crafts, food booths, and a children's court. **Free.**

JULY

Check local city listings for Independence Day parades and fireworks and festivals.

Celebration on the Colorado Street Bridge—Pasadena
(626) 441-6333

Festival features bands, local restaurants, classic autos and motorcycles, art exhibits, and performance groups.

Art Festival—Malibu
(310) 456-9025

Live music, food fair, orchid display and sale, pancake breakfast, and more than 200 artists on hand with exhibits. **Free.**

San Fernando Fiesta—San Fernando
(818) 898-1200

San Fernando's largest family event, including food, games, carnival rides, top-name Latin entertainment, and a consumer trade show. **Free.**

Lotus Festival—Los Angeles
(213) 485-8745

Experience a variety of Asian cultures, entertainment, art exhibits, ethnic cuisine, and children's activities.

AUGUST

Catalina Ski Race—Long Beach
(714) 994-4572

World's largest water-ski race involving 110 boats pulling skiers from Long Beach's Belmont Pier to Catalina.

Taste of San Pedro—San Pedro
(310) 832-7272

San Pedro restaurants present their signature entrees. Arts and crafts and a vintage car show are other highlights.

African Marketplace and Cultural Faire—Los Angeles
(323) 734-1164

More than 2,000 performing artists, 300 vendors and exhibitors, 15 cultural and ethnic festivals, 7 stages of live performers, an international food court, and a children's village.

SEPTEMBER

Catalina Festival of the Arts—Avalon
(310) 510-2700

Exhibits include mixed media, photography, crafts, and sculpture. **Free.**

Los Angeles County Fair—Pomona
(909) 623-3111

California's sensational county fair you can't miss! It takes at least a full day to visit the flower and garden exposition, midway, and various entertainments. Kids can participate in educational activities.

OCTOBER

Catalina Jazz Festival—Avalon
(818) 347-5299; www.jazztrax.com

Contemporary-jazz musicians and instrumentalists perform in the renowned Catalina Casino ballroom.

Scandinavian Festival—Santa Monica
(626) 795-9311

Daylong smorgasbord celebrates the riches of Denmark, Finland, Iceland, Norway, and Sweden with food, music, imports, costumes, arts, crafts, and a raffle.

Oktoberfest—Pasadena
(626) 795-9311

Music, dancing, German food, games, and a pumpkin patch. **Free.**

Sabor de Mexico Lindo Festival—Huntington Park
(323) 585-1155; www.hpchamber1.com

Cultural celebration that pays tribute to the heritage of Mexico through music, dancing, food, displays, and arts and crafts. The festival brings together more than 125 food, arts and crafts, and commercial exhibitors, plus concerts, live entertainment, 2 amusement and carnival areas, and a petting zoo. Three days and nights. **Free.**

NOVEMBER

Doo Dah Parade—Pasadena
(626) 795-9311

Eccentric parade features unique performing groups and artist teams; includes wacky costumes and cars. **Free.**

DECEMBER

Main Street Merchants Holiday Festival—Santa Monica
(310) 395-3648

Sand sledding, face painting, and loads of holiday festivities kids will enjoy. **Free.**

Christmas Parade—Whittier
(562) 696-2662

Hailing the holiday season with marching bands, drill teams, floats, and antique and classic cars and an appearance by Old Saint Nick. **Free.**

Holiday Open House—Avalon
(310) 510-2414

Each year the Catalina Island Museum hosts open house at the Inn at Mount Ada, formerly the Wrigley Mansion. The mansion is exquisitely decorated for Christmas. The event culminates with a raffle of an all-expense-paid stay at the inn to benefit the Catalina Island Museum. **Free.**

The Hollywood Christmas Parade
(323) 469-2337

This festive parade features celebrities, marching bands, classic cars, and, last but not least, Santa Claus!

The Glory of Christmas at the Crystal Cathedral—Garden Grove
(714) 544-5697

A blending of Christmas carols, live animals, flying angels, and special effects brings the nativity to life in this highly orchestrated stage show.

Orange County

The following list of Orange County events is subject to change without notice. Please call ahead to confirm.

FEBRUARY

Festival of Whales—Dana Point
(800) 290-DANA

This is one of Southern California's largest seafaring celebrations attracting over 100,000 visitors each year. Highlights include an opening day parade, Whale of a Block Party, art exhibits, classic car exhibits, paddling events, sand sculpting, concerts, environmental activities, educational opportunities, and of course, whale watching excursions. **Free.**

MARCH

Swallows Day—San Juan Capistrano
(949) 248-2048

This fiesta celebrates the annual return of the swallows to Capistrano, featuring pageantry, entertainment, and food.

APRIL

Glory of Easter—Garden Grove
(714) 971-4069

This annual Easter play features special events, live animals, and a cast of more than 200 in the dramatic presentation of the last seven days of Christ on earth.

MAY

Strawberry Festival—Garden Grove
(714) 638-0981

Festival features strawberry dishes (including strawberry shortcake, pie, and tarts), entertainment, beauty contests, arts, crafts, and rides. **Free.**

JULY

Check local city listings for Independence Day parades and fireworks and festivals.

Sawdust Art Festival—Laguna Beach
(949) 494-3030

Laguna Beach becomes a magical village created by artists. The two-month (July and Aug) festival includes handcrafted treasures, entertainment, jugglers, and storytellers, and jazz, country, rock, and contemporary musicians. Become an artist yourself by attending one of the many hands-on workshops.

Festival of Arts and Pageant of the Masters—Laguna Beach
(949) 494-1145 or (800) 487-3378

Colorful exhibit of fine, strictly original creations by 160 South Coast artists; includes the world-famous Pageant of the Masters "living pictures" performances.

Orange County Fair—Costa Mesa
(949) 708-1543

This rural fair in an urban setting offers livestock, a carnival, a rodeo, commercial wares, themed attractions, and fiber arts.

AUGUST

US Open of Surfing—Huntington Beach
(714) 366-4584

Watch the best surfers in the world compete for a large sum. **Free.**

SEPTEMBER

Taste of Newport Beach—Newport Beach
(949) 729-4400

Savor the cuisine of more than 30 Newport Beach restaurants; entertainment.

OCTOBER

Oktoberfest—Huntington Beach
(714) 895-8020

Old-world village features German food, drink, and oompah bands. **Free.**

NOVEMBER

Sawdust Art Festival Winter Fantasy—Laguna Beach
(949) 494-3030

Unique holiday arts and crafts festival features 150 artists and craftspeople from around the country, with artist demonstrations, hands-on workshops, children's art activities, continuous entertainment, Santa Claus, and a snow playground. Continues through December.

DECEMBER

Glory of Christmas—Garden Grove
(949) 544-5679

Live nativity scene includes animals, flying angels, holiday music, and pageantry.

Christmas Boat Parade—Newport Beach
(949) 729-4400, (949) 729-4417, or (800) 94-COAST

More than 200 illuminated and decorated boats cruise the harbor. **Free.**

Christmas at the Mission—San Juan Capistrano
(949) 248-2048

Holiday celebration includes music, entertainment, and refreshments. **Free.**

The Inland Empire & Beyond

The following list of events in the Inland Empire is subject to change. Please always call ahead.

FEBRUARY

Whiskey Flat Days—Kernville
(760) 376-2629 or (800) 350-7393

Parade, carnival, rodeo, gunfighters, various contests, frog jumping, arts and crafts, a petting zoo, and much to eat. **Free.**

MARCH

Redlands Bicycle Classic—Redlands
(909) 798-0865

Thousands of cyclists from around the world compete. **Free.**

Winterfest—Mammoth Lakes
(760) 934-6643 or (800) 367-6572

Winter celebration with cross-country ski races, snowmobile competition, and fun rides for the kids.

APRIL–MAY

Ramona Pageant—Hemet
(909) 658-3111 or (800) 645-4465

Unique outdoor pageant portrays the lives of the Southern California mission-period Indians and Hispanics. Play adapted from Helen Hunt Jackson's 1884 novel *Ramona*.

Indian Powwow—Kernville
(760) 376-2696 or (800) 350-7393

A celebration of American heritage, dancers, drumming, Native American foods, arts and crafts. **Free.**

Orange Blossom Festival—Riverside
(951) 715-3400

This citrus celebration takes place in downtown Riverside. Besides three entertainment stages, citrus cooking demonstrations, and arts and crafts booths, the festival has a children's grove and a living-history village.

MAY

May Trout Classic—Big Bear Lake
(909) 585-6260 or (800) 4-BIG-BEAR

Since 1983, the Fishing Association of Big Bear Lake has sponsored this event which provides major funds for fish plants; artificial habitat structures; conservation projects and monthly tournaments for designated species. All ages welcome, prizes and fun are no fish story!

Spring Aire Arts and Crafts Faire—Big Bear Lake
(909) 585-3000

Show features hundreds of handcrafted items. Vendors, raffles, and loads of antiques.

JUNE

Huck Finn's Jubilee—Victorville
(760) 245-2226

River celebration and campout relives the life and times of Huckleberry Finn. Raft building, parade, big-top circus, hot-air balloon rides, music, crafts, and more. **Free.**

JULY

Check local city listings for Independence Day parades and fireworks and festivals.

All Nations Powwow—Big Bear
(909) 584-9394 or (800) BIG-BEAR

American Indians from across the United States participate in traditional dancing and crafts.

Jazz Jubilee—Mammoth Lakes
(760) 934-2478

World-class jazz bands perform outdoors.

Sierra Summer Festival—Mammoth Lakes
(760) 934-3342 or (800) 367-6572

Music festival spotlights master's classes, plus chamber, pop, and folk music.

AUGUST

Labor Day Arts and Crafts Festival—Mammoth Lakes
(760) 873-7242

More than 70 arts and crafts booths in an outdoor setting, along with entertainment, kids' activities, and lots of food.

SEPTEMBER

Apple Harvest—Oak Glen
(909) 797-6833

Southern California's top apple-growing region is the site for this event, with apple picking, a candy factory, hayrides, arts and crafts on display, an art show, and (yum!) barbecues. **Free.**

Eastern Sierra Tri-County Fair and Wild West Rodeo—Bishop
(760) 873-3588

Old-fashioned country-fair fun, with exhibits, a carnival, pig races, pony rides, a petting zoo, horse shows, and a PRCA rodeo.

Fall Festival Arts and Crafts—Big Bear Lake
(909) 585-3000

The Big Bear Lake Convention Center hosts various arts, crafts, games and musical concerts.

Kern County Fair—Bakersfield
(805) 833-4900

Family entertainment par excellence, a livestock show, a carnival, agricultural and floricultural exhibits, plus an auction.

OCTOBER

Calico Days Festival—Calico
(760) 254-2122 or (800) TO-CALICO

Go back in time to Calico's glory years with a Wild West parade, a gunfight, stunts, burro races, rock pulling, and games circa the 1880s.

Desert Empire Fair—Ridgecrest
(760) 375-8000

Five-day event with 4-H competition, arts and crafts, entertainment, a rodeo, a demolition derby, and a livestock auction.

Oktoberfest—Big Bear Lake
(909) 866-4607

Music, singing, dancing, contests, arts and crafts, food, and games in a mountain setting. *Wunderbar!*

Wild West Daze Rodeo—Kernville
(760) 378-3157

Wild horse races, bull riding, saddle broncoing, bareback riding, steer decorating, barrel racing, and mutton busting.

NOVEMBER

Gem and Mineral Society Show—Ridgecrest
(760) 377-5192

Dozens of gem and mineral exhibits, plus field trips. Educational.

Harvest Fair—San Bernardino
(909) 384-5426

Re-creation of an 1881 Old West town, with a country/bluegrass show, crafts, and a unique car show.

DECEMBER

Children's Christmas Parade—Victorville
(760) 245-6506

More than 150 holiday-theme floats, bands, novelty vehicles, and marching by equestrian units. **Free.**

Christmas Parade—Lone Pine
(760) 876-4444

Old-fashioned Christmas parade with (you guessed it) Santa Claus.

Festival of Lights—Riverside
(909) 683-7100 or (909) 683-2670

Holiday lighting of the historic Mission Inn and surrounding downtown locations. Entertainment and specialty booths. **Free.**

Torchlight Parade—Big Bear Lake
(800) 4-BIG-BEAR or (909) 866-6190

Snow Summit hosts this spectacular sight of skiers and snowboarders gliding down the mountain holding torch lights on New Year's Eve.

The Deserts

The following list of events is subject to change without notice. Please always call ahead to verify.

JANUARY

Palm Springs International Film Festival—Palm Springs
(760) 322-2930

More than 200 international films with a special awards gala honoring industry greats.

FEBRUARY

Riverside County Fair and National Date Festival—Indio
(760) 863-8247 or (800) 811-FAIR

The festival features exhibits of dates and produce; fine arts; floriculture; gems and minerals; a livestock show; and pig, camel, and ostrich races. See more in Deserts chapter.

MARCH

La Quinta Arts Festival—La Quinta
(760) 564-1244

Takes place at Center for the Arts (south of Highway 111). Stunning art creations from more than 270 juried artists. Families will enjoy the Children's Art Garden; with activities for ages 7 through 12 (must be accompanied by an adult). It all takes place 30 minutes from downtown Palm Springs in a dramatic desert setting at the base of the Santa Rosa Mountains, as it has annually since 1982. Live entertainment and tastes of Coachella Valley's great restaurants.

APRIL

Joshua Tree National Park Festival—Twentynine Palms
(760) 367-5522

Painting, sculpture, photography, ceramics, and jewelry are some of the media included. Sponsored by the Joshua Tree National Park Association, a nonprofit organization that provides support and assistance to the Park's interpretive, educational and scientific programs. **Free.**

MAY

Grubstake Days—Yucca Valley
(760) 365-6323

Parade, carnival events, dancing, demolition derby, games, food, hometown crafts booths, children's activities, PRCA rodeo; takes place Memorial Day weekend. **Free.**

SEPTEMBER

Rodeo Stampede—Barstow
(760) 252-3093

Featured events are bareback riding, steer wrestling, tie-down roping, saddle bronc riding, bull poker, barrel racing, bull riding and children join in the time honored rodeo tradition of mutton bustin', where contestants try to ride a runaway sheep for as long as possible. This is an official PRCA sanctioned event. October

Mardi Gras Parade—Barstow
(760) 256-8657

Halloween parade includes floats, bands, horses, clowns, costumed children, plus contingents from the military, fire, and sheriff's departments.

DECEMBER

Festival of Lights Parade—Palm Springs
(760) 778-8415 or (800) 927-7256

Illuminated bands, floats, and automobiles make this one of the area's top holiday events.

Tamale Festival—Indio

Discover the rich heritage of the tamale-- a traditional Latin American dish made of masa (corn), which is steamed or boiled in a leaf wrapper and filled with meats, cheese, vegetables, chilies and more. See also listing in Deserts chapter. Info: (760) 391-4175. **Free.**

San Diego County

The following list of events is subject to change without notice. Please call in advance to confirm dates and times.

MARCH

Shamrock Festival—San Diego
(619) 233-4692

St. Patrick's Day block party in San Diego's Gaslamp District with live music, Irish entertainment, food, and face painting. **Free.**

APRIL

Santa Fe Market—San Diego
(619) 299-6055

Festival of southwest American Indian arts and crafts, including guest artists and cultural demonstrations. **Free.**

Encinitas Street Fair—Encinitas
(760) 943-1950

More than 300 vendors, children's rides, face painting, clowns, arts and crafts. **Free.**

MAY

Fiesta Cinco de Mayo—San Diego
(619) 299-6055

Mexican celebration in Old Town includes nonstop entertainment and food booths. **Free.**

Carlsbad Village Faire—Carlsbad
(760) 434-8887

One-day street fair features 800 booths; arts, crafts, antiques, international foods, and live entertainment.

JULY

Check local city listings for Independence Day parades and fireworks and festivals.

San Diego County Fair—Del Mar
(858) 792-4262

Annual county fair featuring world-class entertainment, rides, exhibits, livestock, and food.

AUGUST

Latin American Festival—San Diego
(619) 299-6055

Latin American crafts, artists, demonstrations, entertainment, and food booths. **Free.**

SEPTEMBER

Fall Fiesta—Old Town San Diego
(619) 220-5422

Celebrating the Hispanic heritage of Alta California with foods, crafts, music, and dance. **Free.**

Harbor Days—Oceanside
(760) 721-1101

Celebrate a festival of crafts and events at the beautiful Oceanside Marina and Harbor. **Free.**

OCTOBER

Oktoberfest—Carlsbad
(760) 434-6093 or (800) 227-5722

Patriotic, traditional German music; children's games and lots of German food.

NOVEMBER

Community Tree Lighting—Julian
(760) 765-1857

Old-fashioned Christmas tree lighting, costumed carolers, living nativity pageant, and horse-drawn carriage rides. **Free.**

Festival of Lights—San Diego
(619) 299-6055

Celebration includes dances from around the world and dramatic nativity-scene lighting. **Free.**

DECEMBER

Holiday of Lights—Del Mar
(858) 755-7161

Holiday light display featuring more than 200 themed entries, including Santa's elves, Twelve Days of Christmas, and a magical forest. **Free.**

Holiday in the Park—San Diego
(619) 220-5422

Candlelight tours of museums and historic homes featuring period decorations and entertainment.

Mission Christmas Faire—Oceanside
(760) 721-1101

More than 200 booths, amusement rides for children, and entertainment. **Free.**

Harbor Parade of Lights—Oceanside
(760) 721-1101

Lighted boat parade through the Oceanside harbor. **Free.**

Index

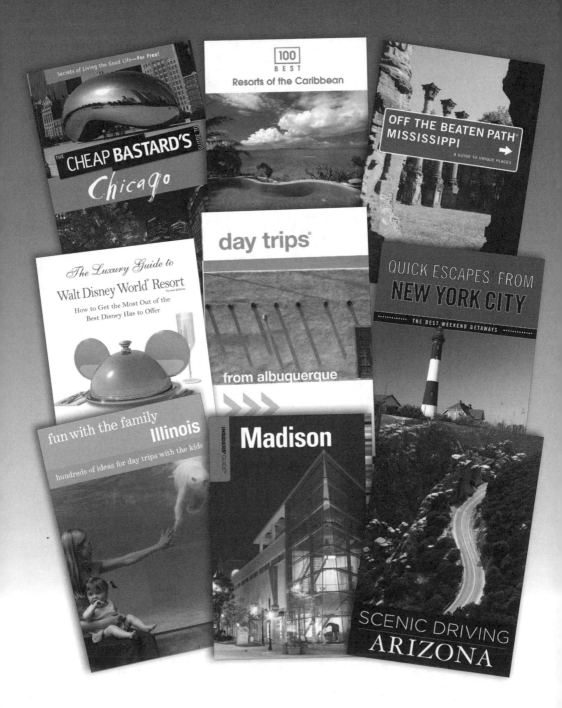